A MILITARY TRANSFORMED?

Wolverhampton Military Studies

www.helion.co.uk/wolverhamptonmilitarystudies

Submissions

The publishers would be pleased to receive submissions for this series. Please contact us via email (info@helion.co.uk), or in writing to Helion & Company Limited, 26 Willow Road, Solihull, West Midlands, B91 1UE.

Titles

A Military Transformed?

Adaptation and Innovation in the British Military, 1792-1945

Wolverhampton Military Studies No. 3

Edited by Michael LoCicero, Ross Mahoney & Stuart Mitchell

Helion & Company Limited

Helion & Company Limited
26 Willow Road
Solihull
West Midlands
B91 1UE
England
Tel. 0121 705 3393
Fax 0121 711 4075
Email: info@helion.co.uk
Website: www.helion.co.uk
Twitter: @helionbooks
Visit our blog http://blog.helion.co.uk/

Published by Helion & Company 2014

Designed and typeset by Bookcraft Ltd, Stroud, Gloucestershire
Cover designed by Paul Hewitt, Battlefield Design (www.battlefield-design.co.uk)
Printed by Berforts Ltd, Eynsham, Oxfordshire

ISBN: 978 1 909384 46 0

British Library Cataloguing-in-Publication Data.
A catalogue record for this book is available from the British Library.

For details of other military history titles published by Helion & Company
Limited contact the above address, or visit our website: http://www.helion.co.uk.

We always welcome receiving book proposals from prospective authors.

Contents

List of Contributors

Neal Dando obtained his BA in History and Heritage in 2002 from Plymouth University after working in business for fifteen years. His recently completed PhD thesis seeks to provide some fresh insights into the Western Desert campaign of 1940-1943, and will be published by Helion in 2014. This study re-appraises archival material to consider the impact of terrain on operations from the strategic to the tactical level and has a secondary theme about how terrain influenced doctrine for a considerable period. His main focus of research continues into British methods of fighting primarily in the Twentieth Century. He has worked as an Associate Lecturer at Plymouth University and now teaches in Devon.

Andrew Duncan did his undergraduate degree and his MLitt, both in Modern History, at the University of St Andrews. His MLitt dissertation, on the British Army's medical services, formed the basis of his chapter in this volume. He is now at the University of Birmingham where, under the supervision of Dr Jonathan Boff, he is researching military education of British regular army officers in the years leading up to 1914.

Richard Dunley is a Contemporary Records Specialist at The National Archives, Kew. He has recently completed a PhD at Kings College, London looking at the development of mine warfare in the pre-First World War Royal Navy with a particular focus on its relationship with strategy and organisational culture.

Matthew Ford is a Lecturer in International Relations at the University of Sussex. With a particular interest in technology and organisational change, Matthew has published in a number of journals including the *Journal of Strategic Studies*, *Small Wars and Insurgencies*, *War in History*, *Studies in Conflict and Terrorism* and *Parameters*, the journal of the US Army War College. Matthew is a former West Point Fellow and winner of the Society for Military History's Russell F. Weigley Graduate Award.

Aimée Fox-Godden is a PhD candidate at the Centre for War Studies, University of Birmingham. Her PhD thesis examines instances of formal and informal learning within the British army during the First World War. She has been a Haig Scholar for the Douglas Haig Fellowship, a Summer Vacation Scholarship student at the Australian War Memorial, and HM The Queen Mother Great War Scholarship student at the Royal British Legion and the *Historial de la Grande Guerre*.

Martin Gibson was awarded a PhD by the University of Glasgow in early 2012 for his thesis on 'British Strategy and Oil, 1914-1923.' He had previously completed an MLitt in War Studies at the same university. Before that, he worked for over 20 years as an investment analyst for a major asset management company, latterly specialising in the global oil industry. He studied Economics at undergraduate level at the University of Edinburgh.

Peter Grant is Senior Fellow in Grantmaking, Philanthropy and Social Investment at Cass Business School, City University. London. His latest book is *Philanthropy and Voluntary Action in the First World War* and his other publications include titles on cricket, voluntary sector history and management. He is a former Chair of the Voluntary Action History Society and a trustee of the DHL and Amy Winehouse Foundations.

Richard Hammond completed his PhD at the University of Exeter in 2011, researching the British anti-shipping campaign in the Mediterranean, 1940-44. He has published in the *Journal of Strategic Studies* and the RAF *Air Power Review*. In 2010, he was elected an Associate of the Higher Education Academy and awarded the 'Effective Researcher Award for Excellence' by the University of Exeter. He has held teaching posts at the Universities of Exeter and Wolverhampton and currently works as a Lecturer in Strategic Studies for the University of Portsmouth, based at RAF Cranwell.

Spencer Jones is a Research Fellow at the University of Wolverhampton. His research focuses on battle tactics of the Anglo-Boer War and the First World War. His publications include *From Boer War to World War: Tactical Reform of the British Army 1902 - 1914* (2012), *Stemming the Tide: Officers and Leadership in the British Expeditionary Force 1914* (2013) and *The Great Retreat of 1914: From Mons to the Marne* (2014).

Simon Justice is an independent scholar. He completed an MA in British First World War Studies in 2009 and has written on the role of the British Army's Cavalry Corps on the Western Front. His most recent publication was, 'Behind the Lines: Sir Douglas Haig and the Cavalry Corps, September – October 1918' in Gary Sheffield and Peter Gray (eds.), *Changing War: The British Army, The Hundred Days Campaign and the Birth of the Royal Air Force, 1918* (2013).

Andrew Limm is a third-year Doctoral student in History at the University of Birmingham. His thesis examines the conduct and performance of the British Army in the French Revolutionary and Napoleonic Wars, with special reference to the campaigns and amphibious expeditions mounted by the British to the Low Countries in the years 1793 to 1814. Andrew holds a BA in War Studies from the University of Birmingham and is a two-time winner of the annual General Sir Mike Jackson Prize for the best performance in War Studies.

Michael LoCicero is an independent scholar specializing in First World War military operations. He earned his PhD under the combined aegis of Dr John Bourne and Professor Gary Sheffield at the University of Birmingham in 2011. Previously employed as a contracted researcher by the National Archives and the Soldiers of Oxfordshire Trust, he is currently engaged in a wide-ranging number of academic and editorial activities including student advisement for the University of Birmingham's respected MA programme, a visiting lectureship at the University of Wolverhampton and editorial work on behalf of Helion. His past and pending publications include a chapter on Brigadier-General Edward Bulfin in Spencer Jones (ed) *Stemming the Tide: Officers and Leadership in the British Expeditionary Force 1914* (2013) and the forthcoming *A Moonlight Massacre: The Night Operation on the Passchendaele Ridge, 2 December 1917* (2014).

Ross Mahoney is the Royal Air Force Museum's resident Aviation Historian and has just completed his PhD at the University of Birmingham on the subject of, 'The Forgotten Career of Air Chief Marshal Sir Trafford Leigh-Mallory, 1892-1939: A Social and Cultural History of Leadership Development in the Inter-War Royal Air Force'. He is a specialist in air power history, leadership and command, military culture and professional military education. In 2011, he was a West Point Fellow in Military History at the United States Military Academy.

Sarah McCook is a PhD candidate in the Department of History, Durham University. Her PhD thesis examines the adaptability of the British Army in the Second World War through communications and despatch riders. She has been a William Ivy Hair Award, Marjorie Prentice Award, and Joseph F. Steelman Award recipient at Georgia College & State University. She has also been the Graduate Assistant and Editorial Administrator for *Georgia Historical Quarterly* and *Educational Review*, respectively.

Stuart Mitchell is Senior Lecturer in War Studies at the Royal Military Academy Sandhurst where he specialises in learning, transformation and leadership in the British Army during the First World War. He is also a member of the Centre for War Studies at the University of Birmingham, British Commission for Military History, Western Front Association and the Institute for Historical Research.

James Pugh holds a BA (Hons) in Contemporary Military and International History (Salford), an MA in International History (Wales), and a PhD in Modern History (Birmingham). He currently works for Library Services at the University of the West of England and is a Visiting Lecturer with the University of Birmingham. He specialises in air power studies and the history of the First and Second World Wars. His thesis explored the conceptual origins of the control of the air in Britain between 1911 and 1918. He has also written on air power leadership and doctrine.

Peter Randall is PhD student in Strategic Studies at the University of Reading. His thesis is a comparison of the formulation, dissemination and application of doctrine in the British and German armies between 1933 and 1945. He holds a BA in War, Peace and International Relations, and an MA in International Security Studies, both from the University of Reading.

The Wolverhampton Military Studies Series
Series Editor's Preface

As series editor, it is my great pleasure to introduce the *Wolverhampton Military Studies Series* to you. Our intention is that in this series of books you will find military history that is new and innovative, and academically rigorous with a strong basis in fact and in analytical research, but also is the kind of military history that is for all readers, whatever their particular interests, or their level of interest in the subject. To paraphrase an old aphorism: a military history book is not less important just because it is popular, and it is not more scholarly just because it is dull. With every one of our publications we want to bring you the kind of military history that you will want to read simply because it is a good and well-written book, as well as bringing new light, new perspectives, and new factual evidence to its subject.

In devising the *Wolverhampton Military Studies Series*, we gave much thought to the series title: this is a *military* series. We take the view that history is everything except the things that have not happened yet, and even then a good book about the military aspects of the future would find its way into this series. We are not bound to any particular time period or cut-off date. Writing military history often divides quite sharply into eras, from the modern through the early modern to the mediaeval and ancient; and into regions or continents, with a division between western military history and the military history of other countries and cultures being particularly marked. Inevitably, we have had to start somewhere, and the first books of the series deal with British military topics and events of the twentieth century and later nineteenth century. But this series is open to any book that challenges received and accepted ideas about any aspect of military history, and does so in a way that encourages its readers to enjoy the discovery.

In the same way, this series is not limited to being about wars, or about grand strategy, or wider defence matters, or the sociology of armed forces as institutions, or civilian society and culture at war. None of these are specifically excluded, and in some cases they play an important part in the books that comprise our series. But there are already many books in existence, some of them of the highest scholarly standards, which cater to these particular approaches. The main theme of the *Wolverhampton Military Studies Series* is the military aspects of wars, the preparation for wars or their prevention, and their aftermath. This includes some books whose main theme is the technical details of how armed forces have worked, some books on wars and battles, and some books that re-examine the evidence about the existing stories, to show in a different light what everyone thought they already knew and understood.

As series editor, together with my fellow editorial board members, and our publisher Duncan Rogers of Helion, I have found that we have known immediately and almost by instinct the kind of books that fit within this series. They are very much the kind of well-written and challenging books that my students at the University of Wolverhampton would want to read. They are books which enhance knowledge, and offer new perspectives. Also, they are books for anyone with an interest in military history and events, from expert scholars to occasional readers. One of the great benefits of the study of military history is that it includes a large and often committed section of the wider population, who want to read the best military history that they can find; our aim for this series is to provide it.

Stephen Badsey
University of Wolverhampton

Foreword

Innovation and transformation in military organisations are fashionable and important topics. While 'Innovation and stagnation have been important themes since the earliest writings on warfare'[1], recent developments have propelled transformation up the agenda of practitioners and academics alike. The impact of emerging, IT-based technologies produced the 'Revolution in Military Affairs' debate of the 1990s. This was, of course, fuelled by the US-led Coalition's use of technologies, including cruise missiles, AWACs, attack helicopters and J-STARS during the 1991 First Gulf War. The extent to which the Gulf War was genuinely revolutionary is questionable. Much of the Coalition's approach to warfighting was a blend of the new and the old. This was neatly encapsulated by advanced SLCMs being fire from a battleship, a platform that had seen service during the Korean War, 40 years earlier. A respectable case can be made that in 1991 new technology was added to conservative methods mostly to do old things better rather than to do genuinely new things. More than twenty years on, however, it is obvious that some aspects of the Gulf War pointed toward future developments.

The Gulf War coincided with the end of the Cold War, leading to wholesale downsizing of militaries and a rash of counter-insurgency-style operations. Grappling with the new challenges posed by operations in the Balkans and elsewhere, armies, navies and air forces were forced to restructure, doctrinally, mentally and culturally as well as physically. Operations in Iraq and Afghanistan presented further challenges. In particular, the British army has come in for withering criticism and has gone in for a prolonged period of soul-searching accompanied by some fairly radical organisational change.[2] Having spent twenty years as an applied historian working for the British armed forces, I am a firm believer that historical study can give important insights into current concerns. Certainly the fine scholarship in this collection should be read by

1   Adam Grissom, 'The Future of Military Innovation Studies', *Journal of Strategic Studies*, 29 (5) (2006), p.905.
2   For a sample of the literature, from very different perspectives, see Frank Ledwidge, *Losing Small Wars: British Military Failure in Iraq and Afghanistan* (New Haven & London: Yale UP, 2011) and Brigadier Ben Barry, 'Stabilisation Operations in Iraq', *British Army Review*, 160 (2014) pp.12-29.

those involved with military transformation. The big themes that emerge, such as the difficulties inherent in effecting substantial change in organisational culture, would no doubt resonate with practitioners.

Reading the chapters in this book has given me much food for thought. They represent an important contribution to the historical debate about how and why militaries change, the extent of change, and the role of the key individual. The latter two points strike me as critical, and are prompted by reading four chapters in particular. Andrew Limm's chapter on the early nineteenth century British army depicts an organisation which certainly changed over time, but which cannot be said to have 'transformed'. Peter Randall's chapter on the post Napoleonic, pre-Crimea army likewise presents a force which was resistant to far-reaching change. The Duke of Wellington features in both chapters. From 1808 to 1815 he was a remarkable commander and leader who took an imperfect, only partially reformed army and turned it into a formidable instrument of war. After 1815, Wellington was a stumbling block to reform. By comparison two chapters on the Royal Navy by Richard Dunley and Martin Gibson and offer both positive and negative responses to innovation in the late nineteenth and early twentieth centuries. Of course the RN was responsible for one of the most far reaching examples of innovation in history, the move to the Dreadnought class battleship, thus rendering existing capital ships obsolete. A comparative study of the army and navy's attitudes to innovation across the long nineteenth century is a research topic begging to be done.

This is an extremely interesting and intellectually stimulating volume, and the editors and authors alike, both mostly early-career scholars, deserved much credit. I will certainly be engaging with some of their arguments in my own work. *A Military Transformed?* deserves the widest possible readership.

Gary Sheffield
Professor of War Studies
University of Wolverhampton
2 June 2014

Acknowledgements

As is appropriate with any edited collection, the editors would like to start by thanking the contributors for their contributions and forbearance with this project. This book is the outgrowth of a successful symposium on the subject of transformation in the British military that was held at the University of Birmingham in April 2011. The editors would like to thank all the presenters and delegates for making the event a success. The symposium would not have happened without the support of staff in the Centres for First and Second World War Studies (now the Centre for War Studies) at the University of Birmingham and we would like to thank Professor Gary Sheffield, Air Commodore (ret'd) Dr Peter Gray, Dr Steffan Prauser, Dr Pierre Pursiegle and Dr Michael Snape for their support. We would also like to thank Professor Sheffield for kindly providing the foreword to this book. Additionally, thanks must go to Professor John Buckley who kindly delivered the symposium's keynote address. We would also like to thank the College of Arts and Law Graduate School at the University of Birmingham for financially supporting the symposium in the form a grant from the Roberts Training Fund.

The editors and contributors would also like to thank various friends and colleagues for their support in the production of this volume, Dr John Bourne, Professor W.H. Bragg, Dr Jonathan Boff, Andrew Choong, Sebastian Cox, Julia Dawson, Professor Jo Fox, Dr Christina Goulter, Dr Victoria Henshaw, Dr Jonathan Krause, Professor Andrew Lambert, Professor William Philpott, Professor Peter Simkins, John Mason Sneddon, Professor Richard Overy, Air Commodore Dr Neville Parton, Dr Duncan Redford, and Dr Daniel Whittingham. The contributors are grateful to the staffs of the various archives consulted in the course of their research. Dr Richard Hammond is grateful to the Head of the Air Historical Branch for permission to quote from the papers of Marshal of the Royal Air Force Viscount Portal. We would also like to thank Duncan Rogers of Helion and Professor Stephen Badsey, the series editor, for their patience and support in the production of this book. Finally, the editors and contributors would like to thank their families for their constant support throughout this project.

Michael LoCicero, *Helion & Company*
Ross Mahoney, *Royal Air Force Museum*
Stuart Mitchell, *Royal Military Academy Sandhurst*

Introduction

Michael LoCicero and Stuart Mitchell

The British military is one that prides itself on tradition. From the diverse regimental honours and histories of the British army to the hallowed names of Royal Navy vessels like HMS *Invincible, Warspite*, and *Victory*. Even the youngest service, the Royal Air Force founded on 1 April 1918, has Cranwell, the Supermarine Spitfire and Marshal of the Royal Air Force Viscount Trenchard as pillars of its collective identity. It would be simple to see these cultural touchstones as evidence of a conservative force resistant to change and rooted in its past glories. However, these traditions bely a history of adaptation and innovation that has seen the three services transform themselves in light of shifting strategic, technological and political realities of the time.

This volume charts these changes using the starting point of the Revolutionary and Napoleonic Wars and concluding with the closure of the Second World War. During this time a new independent arm, the Royal Air Force, was created; the age of sail gave way to the age of coal and oil driven vessels; and the nation fielded its first mass army able to defeat the main enemy in the main theatre of operations. The evolution of Britain's armed forces was not a smooth and even process as budgetary oversight, organisational structure, inter-service competition and a lack of external stimulus could inhibit innovation.

From the mid-nineteenth century both the British army and Royal Navy showed considerable capacity to overcome the problems that had previously hamstrung efforts to transform the forces. With the dawning of the twentieth century the British army consciously evaluated its own performance in colonial campaigns such as the Second South African War (1899-1902) and employed civilian expertise to improve its own administrative functions. Concurrently the Royal Navy was undergoing its own profound transformation as oil increasingly became the preferred fuel for vessel propulsion while the future armaments and ships that carried them were hotly debated. The Military and Naval Wings of the Royal Flying Corps, operating under the aegis of the army and Royal Navy respectively until they were formally divided in 1914, tackled diverse technological, tactical and doctrinal problems associated with early air power. The experiences of the two World Wars raised further operational dilemmas for the services. Yet with varying success they were able to surmount problems of staff work, communications, reorganising forces in the field and co-ordinating combined arms operations to make significant contributions to the final defeat of their enemies.

It is the purpose of this book to chart how such innovation and transformation occurred and was managed within the three services. In doing so it contributes towards both the burgeoning field of organisational transformation and innovation, while making a significant contribution to existing debates within the operational military histories of the British army, Royal Navy and Royal Air Force. The roots of modern military organisation, tactics and methods can be found in the developments that took place in European forces since the Napoleonic Wars. By looking as far back as 1792 the success or otherwise of Britain's military can be seen within the broad context and wider conclusions reached. The trouble of co-ordinating amphibious operations during the Napoleonic War and the supposed stagnation of the British army following that conflict stand as low points in the military's overall development. However, as later chapters show they are certainly not indicative of an overall trend towards peacetime inertia. By casting the chronological net wide it is possible to draw out some of the broader themes and trends.

Defining Transformation, Adaptation and Innovation

The term 'transformation', as applied to armed forces, was first coined in the US and popularised by the expansive literature exploring the concept of revolutions in military affairs (RMAs) during the 1990s and early 2000s.[1] It was used to describe the realignment of the American military from the large land forces required by the rivalry with the Soviet Union towards a more flexible 'modular' military capable of reacting rapidly to the changing security challenges that the post-Cold War world required. This usage hearkens back to Martin van Creveld's *Transformation of War*, which sought to explain the likely changes in the character of future combat. Although focused on the ways wars would be fought and not strictly on armed forces it envisioned a similar fundamental shift in conduct that authors focusing on RMAs or national forces predicted.[2] Irrespective of context the term has been widely used to indicate profound organisational change that redefines either the form or function of the institution undergoing the process. Arthur K. Cebrowski, a former US Vice Admiral and key figure in the development of both military transformation and so-called network-centric warfare, expanded upon this idea of major change by stressing that there was no clearly defined end-point to transformation; rather it was

---

1   Theo Farrell, 'The Dynamics of British Military Transformation', *International Affairs*, Vol. 84, No. 4 (2008) pp.777-778; Ian Roxborough, 'From Revolution to Transformation – The State of the Field', *Joint Forces Quarterly*, Vol. 32 (Autumn, 2002) pp.68-78; Paul K. Davis, 'Military Transformation? Which Transformation, And What Lies Ahead? in Stephen J. Cimbala (ed.), *The George W. Bush Defense Program Policy Strategy and War* (Washington DC: Potomac Books, 2010) pp.11-12.

2   Martin van Creveld, *Transformation of War* (Oxford: Maxwell Macmillan, 1991); 'The Transformation of War Revisited', *Small Wars and Insurgencies* Vol.13, No.2 (2008).

an ongoing process.[3] Military effectiveness, efficiency and the political goals were the key factors that promoted and shaped transformation.[4]

Transformation then, is a useful term to indicate the scale and significance of the British military's development. Nonetheless, as Robert T. Foley, Stuart Griffin and Helen McCartney have noted, it is military innovation by another name.[5] The literature for this has been given considerable attention by social scientists, and increasingly historians, over the last three decades. Barry Posen and Stephen Rosen offered competing top-down interpretations of the causes of military innovation. Posen argued that change was brought about by civilians championing the causes of 'military mavericks'.[6] This was challenged by Rosen, who considered change to come about internally through innovators who realigned the opinions and roles of subordinates.[7] The gradual change within the organisation would then be solidified as these juniors propagated the thinking which brought about change. Theo Farrell has more recently brought together a number of historiographical explanations for change within the armed forces and observed that they can be split into internal and external factors. Military culture and civil-military relations shape the internal catalysts for change while international threats and emulation of other militaries are powerful external factors.[8] A number of authors have pointed out these explanations are all essentially top-down.[9] In response to this a semantic divide has been erected. Innovation has come to describe the large-scale institutional process of change instigated, or accepted at the highest levels, while adaptation covers the adjustment of tactics, techniques or technologies to bring about operational improvement.[10] Although originating from the necessity of reintroducing operational experience into the discussion of transformation and change, care must be taken not to infer that innovation is the sole preserve of generals and statesmen and adaptation the realm of the sailor, soldier or pilot. Between 1792 and 1945 the British military never spoke of operational or systemic

---

3   James Blaker, 'Arthur K. Cebrowski A Retrospective', *Naval War College Review* Vol. 59, No. 2 (2006) p.142.

4   *Ibid.*, pp.142-143.

5   Robert T. Foley, Stuart Griffin and Helen McCartney, '"Transformation in Contact': Learning the Lessons of Modern War', *International Affairs*, Vol. 87, No. 2 (2011) p.253.

6   Barry R. Posen, *The Sources of Military Doctrine: France, Britain and Germany Between the World Wars* (Ithaca, NY: Cornell University Press, 1984).

7   Stephen P. Rosen, *Winning the Next War: Innovation and the Modern Military* (Ithaca, NY: Cornell University Press, 1991); see also Rosen, 'New Ways of War: Understanding Military Innovation' *International Security*, Vol. 13, No. 1 (1988).

8   Farrell, 'Military Transformation', pp.782-783; see also Theo Farrell and Terry Terriff (eds.), *The Sources of Military Change: Culture, Politics and Technology* (Boulder, CO: L. Rienner, 2002).

9   Foley, Griffin and McCartney, '"Transformation in Contact", p.254; Farrell, 'Military Transformation', p.783; see also Theo Farrell, 'Improving in War: Military Adaptation and the British in Helmand Province, Afghanistan, 2006-2009', *The Journal of Strategic Studies* Vol.33, No. 4 (2010) pp.568-569.

10   Farrell, 'Improving in War', p.569.

improvement in such a clearly delineated manner. This volume demonstrates that those at the top of the organisation influenced the process of adaptation in theatre, and correspondingly the success of such measures promoted greater institutional effects. Both adaptation and innovation are useful concepts for understanding the origins and scale of change that occurred, but the link between top-down and bottom-up change must be broken lest it overshadow the interconnectedness of the two concepts throughout this period.

Theo Farrell's definitions have offered the clearest outline of what the two concepts entail and as such have been largely followed in this volume. Innovation is 'major change that is *institutionalised* in new doctrine, a new organisational structure and/ or new technology.'[11] Adaptation accounts for change which stops short of bringing about wide-scale organisational reform.[12] The breadth and lasting impact of change plays an important role in dictating how subsequent historians and social scientists have thought about it. Farrell's definition of innovation includes structural reform within an organisation, yet as Neal Dando has demonstrated in his chapter, tactical deficiencies within certain theatres prompted new ways of conceiving of operational structure. This belies any easy definition of innovation or adaptation; force composition could be radically altered in-theatre which might contribute to wider debates within the organisation. It is important to recognise the limits of the terminology and it is easy to get lost down the rabbit hole of semantics when classifying certain developments as adaptive or innovative. The lack of contemporary usage and interconnectedness between the two labels mean these terms should be conceived of more as guides to the origins of transformation as opposed to firm classifications.

The Shape of British Military Transformation

British military transformation was neither consistent nor did it owe its origins simply to great reformers or generals. Past campaigns, national politics and individual influence all affected the shape the constituent services took. The contributors to this volume have drawn on a diverse historiography and significant original archival research to offer some important insights into critical aspects of the British military's transformation during the industrial age. However, this is not the first book to cast a wide gaze upon the British forces. Hew Strachan has written widely on the British army during the 19th and 20th Centuries as well as analysing the relationship between the political and military spheres. The role of Staff College's relationship to the Victorian Army has been probed by Brian Bond while Saul David has written an account of Britain's wars during the nineteenth century.[13] It is not just the British

---

11   *Ibid.*, p.569.
12   *Ibid.*, p.570.
13   Hew Strachan, *From Waterloo to Balaclava: Tactics, Technology, and the British Army 1815-1854* (Cambridge: Cambridge University Press, 1985); *The First World War: Volume One:*

army that has received significant attention. Andrew Lambert has written extensively on Britain's naval warfare, grand strategy during the nineteenth century and thoroughly assessed its most important naval leaders, while scholars such as Andrew Gordon and Marcus Faulkner have provided in-depth analyses of naval warfare in the twentieth century.[14] Despite the relative youth of the service the Royal Air Force and preceding air services have received no shortage of scholarly treatments. Historians such as John Buckley have explored aerial warfare in the twentieth century while Richard Overy has provided, within the context of a broader analysis, a thorough account of the Royal Air Force's role in the strategic air offensive against Germany. Similarly, Peter Gray has offered a thought provoking analysis of the Royal Air Force's role in the strategic air offensive against Germany through the lens of leadership and decision-making processes.[15] Despite this wealth of material no volume has brought these significant historiographies together to enable an assessment of the development of the military as a whole. The transformation of the British military was not conducted by each branch in isolation and by bringing together scholars of each of these organisations a broad picture of institutional change can be formed.

The Revolutionary and Napoleonic Wars posed significant operational challenges globally for the British and campaign failures have often been overlooked in favour of the eye-catching victories of Wellington and Nelson. As Andrew Limm has demonstrated this has papered over the deficiencies that existed within the British forces when it came to certain methods of war. With Napoleon defeated by the Seventh Coalition the British armed forces faced a new set of problems ranging from economic retrenchment to competition from new organisations such as the Metropolitan Police Force. Peter Randall has explored the significant challenges the British army faced in the wake of the Napoleonic war and offered some important context to the growing debate on the stagnation of the organisation after the first 'Great War' on the Continent. An army cannot function if its men are sick or injured and Andrew

To Arms (Oxford: Oxford University Press, 2001); The Politics of the British Army (Oxford: Oxford University Press, 1997); Brian Bond, The Victorian Army and the Staff College 1854-1914 (London: Eyre Methuen, 1972); Saul David, Victoria's Wars: The Rise of Empire (London: Penguin, 2006).

14   Andrew Lambert, War at Sea in the Age of Sail (London: Cassell, 2000); The Challenge: America, Britain and the War of 1812 (London: Faber, 2012); The Crimean War: British Grand Strategy 1853-56 (Manchester: Manchester University Press, 1990); Admirals (London: Faber, 2009); Andrew Gordon, The Rules of the Game: Jutland and British Naval Command (London: John Murray, 1996); Marcus Faulkner, 'Naval Warfare 1919-1945: An Operational History of the Volatile War at Sea' in The Journal of Strategic Studies Vol.34, No.2 (2011); War at Sea: A Naval Atlas 1939-1945 (Barnsley: Seaforth Publishing, 2012).

15   John Buckley, Air Power in the Age of Total War (London: UCL Press, 1998); Richard Overy, The Bombing War: Europe 1939-1945 (London: Allen Lane, 2013); The Air War 1939-1945 (Washington D.C.: Potomac Books, 2nd ed. 2005), Peter Gray, The Leadership, Direction and Legitimacy of the RAF Bomber Offensive from Inception to 1945 (London: Continuum, 2012).

Duncan's broad assessment of the British medical services between the Crimean War and the outbreak of the First World War offers an important addition to a branch of the army that is too often overlooked. The Victorian Navy's need for a viable torpedo delivery system and the consequent difficulties of development and institutionalisation are ably examined by Richard Dunley.

Heated internal debate over what kind of infantry assault tactics the British Army would adopt occurred during the period leading up to the First World War. This often contentious exchange of ideas is explored by Spencer Jones within the context of contemporary weapons technology development and survivability on the battlefield. The almost unknown application of Edwardian business administration methodology as taught in an innovative series of courses sponsored by the War Office over a seven-year period from 1907 to 1914 is examined by Peter Grant. Technical innovation through a process of observation and experiment was the carefully considered approach adopted by the Royal Navy during the controversial process of conversion from coal to oil. The final outcome, as Martin Gibson demonstrates, was a relatively secure technological edge by the summer of 1914.

Adoption of new technologies can result in a dichotomy of application and thought between rival services. The realities and consequences of the doctrinal divide between the Military and Naval Wings of the fledgling Royal Flying Corps in the period 1912-14 are adeptly reconsidered by James Pugh. The supposed inefficiency of the staff during the First World War is challenged by Aimée Fox-Godden in a chapter on the meritocratic transformation of the often overlooked brigade command level. The largely disruptive impact of the British Expeditionary Force's reorganisation of component infantry divisions from twelve battalions to nine in early 1918 resulted in organizational dislocation on the eve of the great German offensives. Nevertheless, as Simon Justice convincingly argues, these largely unpopular reductions were subsequently adapted under the most unpromising operational and tactical circumstances. The revaluation of advances in First World War communications technology within a broader (1914-40) historical context is analysed by Sarah McCook.

Neal Dando chronicles the inherent tactical strengths and weaknesses of celebrated Colonel 'Jock' Campbell's innovative mixed armoured columns during the Western Desert campaign. Organisational learning and resultant adaption provide the central theme of Ross Mahoney's study of the learning process and the Royal Air Force's response to the disastrous Dieppe Raid. The subject of air power themed innovation is continued in Richard Hammond's study of the establishment of effective Royal Navy-Royal Air Force cooperation in the Mediterranean theatre during the Second World War. The future of military transformation and Great Britain's armed forces is summed up in a compelling epilogue by Matthew Ford. It is hoped, despite the often disparate case study themes found in this volume, that the reader will recognise how important subsidiary aspects and detailed analysis of fit within the larger historical framework of transformation and innovation.

1

The British Army 1795 to 1815
An Army Transformed?

Andrew Limm

The main paradigm of the historiography of the British Army of the French Revolutionary and Napoleonic Wars is that, after defeat in the Low Countries in 1793 to 1795, the Army was transformed by a series of reforms introduced by the new Commander-in-Chief, His Royal Highness Frederick Duke of York. Proponents of this paradigm argue that these reforms enabled the Army to rapidly improve its performance so as to achieve victories against the French in Egypt, the Mediterranean, the Iberian Peninsula and finally at Waterloo.[1] This chapter explores why the narrative of improvement is deceptive. It took a long time for the reforms to be embedded effectively enough for the British to achieve success and it was only achieved in certain circumstances, usually when the Duke of Wellington was in command. Furthermore, the reforms did not address the fundamental reason for Britain's repeatedly poor military performances. There was no mechanism that allowed the armed forces to study and learn effectively from past mistakes. Unlike Prussia in 1806, there was no cognitive response to the challenges of war.[2] Consequently, despite the reforms, the British continued to make the same mistakes. These were: poor strategic planning

---

1   His Royal Highness Frederick Duke of York served as Commander-in-Chief of the Army in two separate periods, the first in 1795 to 1809 and the second from 1811 to 1827. Some of the many adherents of the 'Transformation Thesis' include: Richard Glover, *Peninsular Preparation, The Reform of the British Army, 1795-1809* (Cambridge: Cambridge University Press, 1963); John Peaty, 'Architect of Victory: The Reforms of the Duke of York' Presented at the International Commission for Military History Annual Congress, Madrid 26 August 2005 (British Commission for Military History: 2005), pp.31-39; David Gates, 'The Transformation of the British Army 1783-1815' in David Chandler and Ian Beckett (eds.), *The Oxford History of the British Army* (Oxford: Oxford University Press, 1994), pp.132-160.
2   For a study of Prussia's cognitive response to defeat in 1806 see Peter Paret, *The Cognitive Challenge of War: Prussia 1806* (Princeton: Princeton University Press, 2009).

by politicians; delays caused by the inefficient decision making process of the various political and military boards; dysfunctional Anglo-Allied relations; reliance on unreliable intelligence reports; the inability to undertake effective operational planning, outlining what British troops were to do once an expedition was launched and the lack of emphasis on the education and training of officers for command above the regimental level.

This chapter briefly explores these issues and concludes by comparing two British expeditions to the Low Countries in 1799 and 1809. Defeat in the Low Countries had been the catalyst for the reforms, but the expeditions to the Helder and the Scheldt demonstrate clearly that even here the underlying weaknesses were not being addressed. Furthermore, the Army continued to suffer defeats in other areas of the world.

The Main Reforms and their Impact

The main reforms introduced by the Duke of York sought to improve the training of the Infantry, Cavalry and Light Infantry, alter the rules governing the purchase of commissions to the officer corps and establish the training of junior officers. The reforms made the Army more administratively efficient and provided a basis for improving the training of officers and men at the regimental level. However, they did not prepare the Army for the large-scale character of warfare in Europe nor for planning and conducting combined operations. In contrast, the Prussian Army, when faced with the need to reform in the wake of the Seven Years' War, had made use of massed manoeuvres so perform better in large scale operations in future war.[3]

The British Army rarely drilled its men in large formations in peacetime and did not embed skills necessary to conduct large-scale operations. The reasons for this were varied. One was beyond the Army's control, in that since rule of Cromwell's Major Generals[4] the British public had opposed measures to gather the army together in peacetime, for fear of the return of military dictatorship. Another was that until 1795, the Army lacked dedicated barracks, with soldiers spread thinly across the country.[5] Nevertheless, the main reason why the British did not form peacetime training camps on the Prussian model was that the high command did not grasp the urgent need to create them. It was not until the opening of hostilities in 1793 between Britain and France that an attempt was made to train several regiments of infantry and cavalry

3   Claus Telp, *The Evolution of Operational Art, 1740-1813: From Frederick the Great to Napoleon* (London: Frank Cass, 2005) p.20. Christopher Duffy, *The Army of Frederick the Great* (London: David & Charles, 1974), p.37.

4   For more on the subject of British publics aversion to standing armies see Hannah Smith, 'Politics, Patriotism, and Gender: The Standing Army Debate on the English Stage, circa 1689—1720' *Journal of British Studies*, Vol. 50, No. 1 (JANUARY 2011), pp. 48-75.

5   J.A Houlding, *Fit for Service: The Training of the British Army, 1715-1795* (Oxford: Clarendon Press, 1981), pp.21-36.

together, but this was already wartime and the plan had to be shelved.[6] One of the only instances in which a sizeable force of troops was gathered occurred in 1800, when some 32,000 men were assembled near Bagshot Heath.[7] However, the purpose of this gathering was ceremonial, rather than for training purposes.[8] The only occasion during the period in which a British General sought to train the Army for a specific operation was in 1801 when Sir Ralph Abercromby prepared his troops for beach-landings before the successful Egyptian campaign.[9] However, the British did not seek to learn from this. As Houlding notes, most British regiments, 'Went to war with little or no experience of manoeuvring in brigade, let alone in the lines and columns adopted on campaign by the army as a whole…most were obliged to learn their business on the spot.'[10]

This 'on the spot' approach was far from successful. British generals and senior regimental officers often struggled to adapt to command at higher levels on campaign. The lack of experience of large-scale manoeuvres in the Army, coupled with the focus on regimental responsibilities in preparing officers for their careers, meant that there was nothing to encourage officers to undertake practical training in the use of large formations. This also resulted in a similar lack of training for British staff officers. As a result, many British generals and their chosen aides, found themselves out of their depth when placed in a senior command position. Moreover, the majority of the generals who populated the higher levels of the Army List in the years 1795 to 1809 had had little or no experience of European warfare in their careers. Instead, the vast majority had developed their skills on garrison duty and in the relatively small-scale operations mounted by the Army in India, the West Indies and the Americas during the Seven-Years War and the American War of Independence. It was not until late in the Napoleonic Wars that a new generation of generals emerged to lead the Army, but even then, many proved unable to adapt to the rigours of senior generalship.[11]

Sir Arthur Wellesley, later Duke of Wellington, was an educated soldier. Before purchasing a commission in the regular Army, the usual first step taken by the wealthy gentleman wishing to rise to the higher levels of the officer corps, Wellesley was instead sent by his family to the French city of Angers in 1786 to enrol in the

---

6   Martha Watson, 'The Duke of York and the Campaigns of the British Army in the Low Countries 1793-1795', (MA Thesis, University of Warwick, 2006), p.44.
7   Bruce Collins, *War and Empire: The Expansion of Britain 1790-1830* (Harlow: Pearson Longman, 2010), p.408.
8   *Ibid.*
9   Piers Mackesy, *British Victory in Egypt: The End of Napoleon's Conquest* (London: Tauris Parke, 2010 [1995]), pp.38-49.
10   Houlding, *Fit for Service*, p.348.
11   For a study of the career path of Wellington's senior officers in the Peninsula see, Robert Burnham and Ron McGuigan, *The British Army against Napoleon: Facts, Lists and Trivia 1805-1815* (Barnsley: Frontline Books, 2010); T.A Heathcote, *Wellington's Peninsular War Generals and their Battles: A Biographical and Historical Dictionary* (Barnsley: Pen & Sword, 2010).

French Royal Academy of Equitation.[12] Part military school, specialising as the name suggests in the training of cavalrymen, and part gentlemen's finishing school, the Royal Academy of Equitation, was one of many such institutions to be found across France and the rest of Europe for the education of future gentlemen officers.[13] The first military school set up in France had opened in 1679 at Douai, specialising in the training of officers of the Ordnance, whilst the French also had experimented with the training of young infantry officers.[14] Over the next century and a half, a network of military schools opened across the continent.[15] During the French Revolutionary Wars [1792-1802], the French Army fielded no less than 255 generals and admirals who had had the benefit of military schooling.[16] Of Napoleon's Marshals, eight had attended a military academy including Davout, Grouchy, Kellermann, Marmont, Macdonald, Perignon, Poniatowski and Serurier.[17]

Unlike Wellington, however, the majority of British officers had no experience of formal military education. Book learning was simply not on the agenda.[18] This British aversion to the development of new military thinking is best illustrated by the overwhelming disparity in the number of works of military theory produced by Europeans, as opposed to the limited number of works written by British military thinkers. Celebrated European thinkers of the age included the Frenchmen Pierre Joseph de Bourcet and Jacques Antoine Hippolyte Comte de Guibert and the German intellectual duo of Gebhard von Scharnhorst and Fredrick von Bülow.[19] By contrast, the only famous British-born military theorist of the period was Henry Lloyd, whose

12   Elizabeth Longford, *Wellington: The Years of the Sword* (London: World Books, 1971), p.21.
13   Keith John Bartlett, 'The Development of the British Army during the wars with France 1793-1815', (PhD Thesis, Durham University, 2006), p.152.
14   John A. Lynn, *Giant of the Grand Siècle: The French Army, 1610-1715* (Cambridge: Cambridge University Press, 1997), pp.270-273.
15   Christopher Duffy, *The Army of Maria Theresa: The Armed Forces of Imperial Austria, 1740-1780* (London: David & Charles, 1977), pp.28-30; Christopher Duffy, *Russia's Military Way to the West: Origins and Nature of Russian Military Power 1700-1800* (London: Routledge & Kegan Paul, 1981), pp.142-145; John L.H Keep, *Soldiers of the Tsar: Army and Society in Russia 1462-1874* (Oxford: Clarendon Press, 1985), pp.242-243; Telp, *The Evolution of Operational* Art, p.20; Duffy, *The Army of Frederick the Great*, pp.37-39.
16   Paddy Griffith, *The Art of War of Revolutionary France 1789-1802* (London: Greenhill, 1998), p.127.
17   David G. Chandler (ed.) *Napoleon's Marshals* (London: Weidenfeld & Nicholson, 1987), p.7 (General Introduction).
18   Gary Sheffield, 'Review of Anthony Clayton, *The British Officer: Leading the Army from 1660 to the Present*', *The American Historical Review*, 111 (5) (2006), p.1593; John P.Kiszely, 'The Relevance of History to the Military Profession: A British View' in Williamson Murray and Richard Hart Sinnreich (eds.), *The Past as Prologue: The Importance of Military History to the Military Profession* (Cambridge: Cambridge University Press, 2006), p.24.
19   Azar Gat, *The Origins of Military Thought, From the Enlightenment to Clausewitz* (Oxford: Clarendon, 1989); Paret, *The Cognitive Challenge of War*, pp.79-81; R.R Palmer, 'Frederick the Great, Guibert, Bulow: From Dynastic to National War' in Peter Paret (ed.), *Makers of Modern Strategy: From Machiavelli to the Nuclear Age* (Oxford: Clarendon, 1986), pp.91-

work studied the developments in warfare during the Seven Years' War. Lloyd, however, was relatively unknown in Britain and was, in essence, a European soldier, who had spent much of his career in the service of the French and Austrian armies.[20] What all of the European military thinkers had in common was a shared devotion to the study of war as an academic activity and the recognition of the importance of the study of history in educating future officers and political leaders in the art of war. Central to this activity was a belief in the importance of learning from the past. This approach was not replicated in Britain.

An education in the art of war for officers of the line in the Army before the reforms of the Duke of York was almost non-existent. The only form of education open to junior officers was for members of the Royal Artillery and Engineers, who were educated at the Royal Military Academy at Woolwich, established in 1741.[21] The development of a Royal Military College (RMC) by the Duke of York, with the help of Lieutenant-Colonel Gaspard Le Marchant in 1799-1802, was long overdue. Before being granted its Royal title in 1801, Le Marchant and the Duke of York had established a Military College for entrants to the regular army in 1799. The College was eventually split into two departments, with a senior department based at High Wycombe, while a junior counterpart for the training of potential staff officers was opened at Great Marlow.[22] Although several graduates of the RMC performed well on Wellington's staff in the Peninsular War,[23] the young age of the entrants, meant that for much of the period the Army was unable to reap the benefits of the reforms to education.

Additionally, there existed no process for the high command to monitor the Army's administration and finance. This was partially resolved with the creation of the Commissioners of Military Enquiry in 1806. From 1806 to 1815, eighteen commissions were established; each designed to review a specific department of the Army. However, these reports did not specifically seek to analyse the reasons for military failure, but were chiefly concerned with how each army department was structured and financed. The commissioners did not try to assess whether the Duke of York's reforms had resulted in an improvement in the performance of the Army on campaign. This clearly indicates the continued lack of awareness amongst the Army's high command of the need to think constructively about how reforms affected performance. Only with irregular Public Inquiries following large-scale military disasters, such as the Inquiry into the Expedition to the Scheldt in 1810, was there any semblance of an

119; Spenser Wilkinson, *The French Army before Napoleon* (Oxford: Clarendon, 1915), pp.33-67.
20   Gat, *The Origins of Military Thought*, pp.67-68.
21   Jeremy Black, *European Warfare 1660-1815* (New Haven & London: Yale University Press, 1994), p.237.
22   Hugh Thomas, *The Story of Sandhurst*, (London: Hutchinson, 1961), pp.33-34.
23   S.P.G Ward, *Wellington's Headquarters, A Study of the Administrative Problems in the Peninsula 1809-1814* (London: Oxford University Press, 1957), p.25.

attempt to analyse and evaluate the reasons for defeats.[24] Even here, however, lessons were not identified, and nothing was learnt.

This was also true of the Army's role in amphibious operations. The British had cultivated extensive experience in amphibious warfare during the American War of Independence.[25] The lack of a culture of learning in the British officer corps in the aftermath of the conflict, however, meant that this amphibious expertise was not codified. The diminishing prestige of the Army because of the defeats suffered in America in 1776-1783, and again in Europe, in 1793-95 and elsewhere resulted in a breakdown in Army-Royal Navy (RN) relations. Joint approaches to generating new ideas about how best to operate together on campaigns were practically non-existent and past mistakes were not evaluated. Army and naval commanders did not seek to meet to develop shared knowledge or skills. In addition, the fact that the RN possessed its own elite amphibious force, in the form of the Royal Marines, was perhaps another reason why naval officers did not see it necessary to develop an amphibious methodology with the Army.[26]

As a result, success in major Army-RN combined expeditions was often left to chance. What made matters worse, was that in actual operations, even if the Army successfully disembarked, effective operational planning as to what should happen next was poor. Throughout the period, the repeated failure of the Army to gather accurate intelligence about the geography of the area in question, strength of the enemy and the willingness of the local populace to support them, regularly undermined British operations ashore. Detailed operational plans outlining how the Army sought to achieve their strategic objectives were also routinely lacking. The two case studies that follow demonstrate these shortcomings in detail and provide evidence of the ineffectiveness of the Duke of York's reforms.

The Expedition to the Helder, 1799

The first major European campaign fought by the Army after the reforms had been introduced was in Holland in 1799.[27] The architect of the expedition was the Foreign-Secretary, Lord William Grenville, who sought to wrest the Low Countries from

---

24 For list of the subjects covered in the reports see: Parliamentary Papers (PP), House of Commons, General index to the reports of the commissioners of military enquiry: 1806-1812. Ordered by the House of Commons to be printed, 23 February 1816.

25 David Syrett, 'The Methodology of British Amphibious Operations during the Seven Years and American Wars' *The Mariner's* Mirror, 58 (3) (1972), pp.269-280.

26 Britt Zerbe, '"That most useful body of men": The Operational Doctrine and Identity of the British Marine Corps, 1755-1802', (PhD Thesis, University of Exeter, 2010).

27 Piers Mackesy, *Statesmen at War, The Strategy of Overthrow 1798-1799* (London: Longman, 1974), *passim.*

French influence and in so doing, 'liberate' the Dutch.[28] Grenville was confident of a quick victory, believing the Dutch to be ripe for counter-revolution against the French. Grenville also placed great faith in a series of intelligence reports, which claimed that the French Army in Holland was extremely weak.[29] Eager to launch an expedition as quickly as possible, Grenville failed to scrutinise the provenance of the reports. This was a grave mistake since the reports were far from accurate.[30] Blind to the dangers, Grenville accelerated the preparations and delegated the preparing of the army to the Secretary of State for War and the Colonies, Sir Henry Dundas.

Dundas faced a difficult task. Short of manpower, the British had negotiated for a Russian contingent to support them in Holland.[31] Even more troops were needed, however, since the Army had lost thousands of troops to disease in the fever-ridden West Indies.[32] Desperate for extra manpower, Dundas passed an Act to enable Militiamen to transfer to a number of regular infantry regiments.[33] This process, alongside the procurement of shipping, took precious time. The British realised that they needed to land an advance guard in Holland, so as to free up transports for the newly drafted militiamen and, more important, to ship the Russians from the Baltic to the Dutch coast.

What was lacking in this process, however, was the development of a clear operational plan, detailing where and how the initial British contingent was to land and secure a beachhead, and, additionally, what the Anglo-Russian Army was actually to do once all the troops were landed. Responsibility for this planning process rested with the army and naval commanders. Major-General Sir Ralph Abercromby commanded the first contingent of British troops.[34] Viscount Duncan, and his subordinate, Rear-

---

28   The British Library (BL), Add MSS 72703L, Letter from Baron Grenville, as Foreign Secretary, to William Pitt the Younger, Cleveland Row, 1 August 1799; John M. Sherwig, 'Lord Grenville's plan for a concert of Europe, 1797-99', *Journal of Modern History*, 34 (3) (1962), p.292.

29   BL, Add MSS 40101, Lord Grenville to Sir Henry Dundas, 30 July 1799, Melville Papers. Vol. II (ff. 95); Letters of William Wyndham Grenville, Baron Grenville, Secretary of State for Foreign Affairs, to Henry Dundas, 1798-1801, pp.25-29.

30   Mackesy, *Statesmen at War* , p.191.

31   Anon, *British Minor Expeditions, 1746 to 1814: Compiled* in the Intelligence Branch of the Quartermaster-General's Department, (London, 1884) p.32; John A. Lukas, 'Russian Armies in Western Europe: 1799, 1814, 1917', *American Slavic and East European Review*, 13 (3) (1954), p.332; A.B. Piechowiak, 'The Anglo-Russian Expedition to Holland in 1799', *The Slavonic and East European Review*, 41 (96) (1962), p.184.

32   Michael Duffy, *Soldiers, Sugar and Seapower: The British Expeditions to the West Indies and the War against Revolutionary France* (Oxford: Clarendon Press, 1987), pp.328-333.

33   Sir John Fortescue, *A History of the British Army Vol. IV, Part II*, 1789-1801 (London: Macmillan, 1906), pp.641-642.

34   The National Archives (TNA), WO 1/180, Projected arrangement of the troops ordered for service under the command of Lieutenant-General Sir Ralph Abercromby, June 1799 Commanders Dispatches, Helder Expedition, p.5; TNA, WO 1/179 Deputy Adjutant-General Sir J. Hope, State of the troops under the command of Lieut-General Sir Ralph

Admiral Andrew Mitchell, commanded the naval force.[35] Eager to get on with the expedition before the good summer weather turned stormy, Abercromby and Mitchell (Duncan was taken ill) ignored the need to procure accurate intelligence about the Dutch coast and the state of the enemy. Instead, they appear to have simply taken the decision to set sail as quickly as possible disregarding, until the last minute, the location of the point at which Abercromby's force would land.[36]

The ensuing landing was a complete shambles. Neither Mitchell nor Abercromby had thought it necessary to discuss beforehand the method by which the flat-bottomed rowing boats would be organised, or how the different British battalions would stay in order as they were rowed to the shore.[37] The British stormed ashore in a chaotic mass, units and officers jumbled together. Contrary to what the ministers had said, the Dutch forces, supported by French troops, fought hard for every inch of ground. The only success achieved was by the fleet, which cornered and forced the surrender of the Batavian fleet under Admiral Storij.[38] This distracted Mitchell who spent much of the rest of the campaign out of contact with the shore, much to the army's frustration.[39]

The second phase of the campaign was marked by further frustration. In the absence of an operational plan, or a clear objective, Abercromby waited for reinforcements.[40] It was several weeks before they arrived, in the form of the Allied Commander-in-Chief, the Duke of York, and two Russian contingents, under General Ivan Hermann. The Duke of York chose to commence an immediate advance in the hope of seizing Alkmaar. Instead of meeting with his subordinates in order to create a practical operational plan, the Duke of York simply split the army into columns and ordered an advance.[41] Lacking a detailed plan, the Russian force advanced too early and got bogged down along the coastal road in the vicinity of the village of Bergen, whilst the

Abercromby 31 July 1799; TNA, WO 1/179 Hope to Dundas, Return of the Troops under the command of Sir Ralph Abercromby, 4 Aug 1799.

35   David Davies, 'Adam Viscount Duncan, 1731-1804' in Peter Le Fevre and Richard Harding (eds.), *British Admirals of the Napoleonic Wars: The Contemporaries of Nelson* (London: Chatham Publishing, 2005), p.63.

36   TNA, WO 1/179, Sir Ralph Abercromby to Sir Henry Dundas, HMS *Isis*, 14 August 1799 Commanders Dispatches Helder expedition.

37   G.D Walsh, *A Narrative of the Expedition to Holland in the autumn of the year 1799: Illustrated with a map of north Holland and Seven Views* (London: G.G and J. Robinson, Pater-Noster, S. Hanson, 1800), pp.27-28.

38   James Lord Dunfermline, *Lieutenant-General Sir Ralph Abercromby 1793-1801: A Memoirs by his son* (Uckfield: The Naval & Military Press in association with the National Army Museum, 2009 [1861]), p.172.

39   TNA, WO 1/179, Abercromby to Dundas, The Helder, 4 September 1799.

40   Mackesy, *Statesmen at War*, p.206.

41   TNA, WO 1/180, H.R.H Duke of York to Henry Dundas, 19 September 1799, pp.125-130.

newly drafted and inexperienced ex-Militiamen in the British centre, were engaged in a bloody battle of attrition in the muddy hinterland.[42]

Before the battle commenced the Duke of York had sent Abercromby, with nearly 13,000 British veterans, on a flanking march, some thirteen miles away to the allied left.[43] Lacking maps and having no means of communicating with the Duke of York, Abercromby spent the day of the battle in isolation, unsure whether to march to the sound of the guns or to stay where he was.[44] The Duke of York's decision to dispatch Abercromby left the Allied forces too weak to push for victory. Defeat of the Russians at Bergen dissipated the momentum of the Allied Army. The British unjustly heaped much of the blame for the fiasco on the Russians.[45] Unsavoury Anglo-Russian relations quickly undermined the campaign altogether. The Duke of York had suffered yet another defeat in the Low Countries.

Further unsuccessful expeditions against Napoleon followed the brief respite offered by the Peace of Amiens in 1802-1803. In 1805, Britain could not defend her interests in Hanover. In 1806-7, the twin-expeditions to South America culminated in the surrender of a Army under the incompetent General Whitelocke to the Spanish.[46] In 1808, the expedition to Sweden had to be aborted. Whilst Sir John Moore's Iberian campaign of 1809 was only saved because of a desperate battle for the survival of Moore's army at Corunna. There were a select number of British successes in this period, but apart from the attack on Copenhagen in 1807, the majority were only small- scale successes. One such minor victory was won in Italy in 1806, when a small Army under General Stuart, defeated a French force at the battle of Maida.[47] British historians over-inflate the significance of these victories, especially Maida, as they have been eager to point to the battle as a mark of the transformation of the Army. Given the catalogue of failures cited above, more realistically, Maida should be viewed as an isolated victory, rather than a mark of transformation. Granted the British attack on Copenhagen in 1807 may well have been, 'Britain's most ruthlessly brilliant coup of the entire war' but once again, the experience of Copenhagen was

42   TNA, WO 1/180, Herbert Taylor ADC to the Commander-in-Chief H.R.H Duke of York, Report of the proceedings of the Right column of Russians under the command of Lieut-General Hermann in the attack of the 19 Sept 1799, Head Quarters Schaagen Brug, 20 September 1799, pp.169-183; TNA, WO 1/180, Major-General Coote to Lieutenant-General Sir James Pulteney, 20 September 1799, pp.156.

43   TNA, WO 1/180 His Royal Highness Frederick Duke of York to Henry Dundas, 19 September 1799, pp.125-130. William Surtees, *Twenty-Five Years in the Rifle Brigade* (London: T Cadall, 1833), pp.10-13.

44   Lieutenant-General Sir Henry Bunbury, *Narratives of some passages in the Great War with France: From 1799 to 1810* (London: Richard Bentley, 1854), p.50.

45   Piechowiak 'The Anglo-Russian Expedition to Holland', p.190.

46   Jeremy Black, *Britain as a Military Power 1688-1815* (London: UCL Press, 1999), pp.250-251

47   Brent Nosworthy, *Battle Tactics of Napoleon and his Enemies* (London: Constable, 1995), pp.146-149.

not analysed effectively to inform future operations.[48] Thus, the confidence that the British gained from Copenhagen proved to be unrealistic and, as the defeats in 1808 and 1809 were to show, continued lack of sound strategic and operational planning were to prove disastrous.

The Expedition to the Scheldt, 1809

British failure to conduct accurate planning and learn from past mistakes, reached its nadir in the case of the British expedition to the Scheldt in 1809.[49] The expedition, the largest mounted by Britain during the period, was the brainchild of the Secretary of State for War and the Colonies, Viscount Lord Castlereagh. Castlereagh was eager to launch another major expedition to the Low Countries in order to destroy the French naval base at Antwerp, and provide support for the Austrians, who sought a resumption of hostilities with France.[50] Castlereagh initially sought advice from some military officers, who agreed that the expedition would be difficult, but not impossible. However, the advice given by the men at the Horse Guards was not based on close analysis of past mistakes; rather it was a consideration of the likely logistical issues that might have to be addressed if such a campaign took place. None of the participants sought to create a study of how previous British expeditions had been conducted in the region, nor did any of the advisors try to assess how the British forces would seek to improve on the recent failings of the army that had been forced to evacuate from Corunna earlier in the year.[51]

All agreed, however, that swiftness of action was needed if the British were to make the most of remaining summer campaigning weather, and to divert French troops from the Austrian front in order to aid the Habsburg war effort.[52] Despite these intentions, delays in the procurement of adequate shipping, combined with the time needed

---

48   John Bew, *Castlereagh: Enlightenment, War and Tyranny* (London: Quercus, 2011), pp.249-252.

49   The expedition is also known as the Walcheren expedition. Gordon C. Bond, *The Grand Expedition, The British Invasion of Holland in 1809* (Athens: University of Georgia Press, 1979); Martin R. Howard, *Walcheren 1809: The Scandalous Destruction of a British Army* (Barnsley: Pen & Sword, 2012). Dutch histories of the expedition include T van Gent, *De Engelese invasive van Walcheren in 1809* (Amsterdam: 2001) and V Enthoven (ed.), *Een Haven Te Ver. De Britse expeditie naar de Schelde van 1809* (Nijmegen, 2009).

50   James Allen Vann, 'Habsburg Policy and the Austrian War of 1809', *Central European History*, 7 (4) (1974), p.291.

51   *Correspondence, Despatches, And other papers of Viscount Castlreagh, Second Marquess of Londonderry.* Edited by his brother, Charles William Vane, Marquess of Londonderry, *Second Series, Military and Miscellaneous*, Vol.VI (London: William Shorberl, 1851), pp.270-271. Castlereagh received memorandums from Sir David Dundas, Lieutenant-Colonel Willoughby Gordon, the Adjutant-General Sir William Calvert, the Quartermaster-General Sir Robert Brownrigg and General Alexander Hope.

52   Bond, *The Grand Expedition*, pp.13-16.

to ready the army for active service so soon after the retreat from Corunna, meant that the British took months to ready their forces. The delays proved crucial. Even before British forces sailed for the Dutch coast, news had reached London that the Austrian Army had been soundly defeated at the Battle of Wagram.[53] With the Austrian war effort in jeopardy and weather conditions worsening, Castlereagh opted to continue with the expedition and hurried the final preparations.

Castlereagh's choice for the command of the army was Lieutenant-General John Pitt, 2nd Earl of Chatham, whilst the Admiral selected to command the fleet was Admiral Sir Richard Strachan. Both men were senior officers in their respective services, but neither had extensive experience of amphibious operations. With the commanders chosen, the expedition was ready to depart, but yet again there was little detailed planning about how the army was to land and coordinate its operations with the RN, nor about how it was to make its way to Antwerp. For instance, when questioned about the planning process at the Scheldt Inquiry in 1810 Chatham stated that, 'No plan in detail was ever concerted for the attack on Antwerp: it must have depended entirely on circumstances after we had landed on the continent.'[54] If this was not bad enough, the British also neglected to procure accurate intelligence about the Dutch coast and the state of the French Army in the area. It was 1799 all over again.

The British expedition to the Scheldt sailed on 28 July 1809.[55] The first task that Strachan was eager to undertake was the clearance of the French from the northern shore of the island of Cadsand, whose gun-batteries guarded the entrance to the western channel of the River Scheldt.[56] The rest of the Fleet would anchor off the south west of Walcheren, in preparation for landing the main force close to Flushing. A small force was also to land to the north of Walcheren. The men overseeing the landing on Cadsand were Lieutenant-General the Marquis of Huntly and Captain Owen.[57] Despite knowing their tasks, there was no plan in place detailing exactly

53 Fortescue, *A History of the British Army, Vol. VI*, p.55. For more on the battle of Wagram see John H. Gill, *Thunder on the Danube: Napoleon's Defeat of the Habsburgs, Vol. III: Wagram and Znaim* (London: Frontline Books, 2014)
54 PP, House of Commons, Lieutenant-General The Right Hon. Earl Chatham to the Right Hon, Sir John Anstruther, Bart, 22 February 1810 Minutes of evidence taken before the Committee of the whole House, appointed to consider of the policy and conduct of the late expedition to the Scheldt, p.183. Hereafter referenced as 'Scheldt Inquiry.'
55 TNA, WO 133/16, Lieutenant-General the Earl of Chatham, 28 July 1809. Journal of the Proceedings of the Army under the command of Lieutenant-General the Earl of Chatham, p.1.
56 National Maritime Museum (NMM), M.S. 52/061, COO/2/B.1, Admiral Sir Richard Strachan to Captain Owen of His Majesty's Ship Clyde, 21 July 1809, Admiral Sir Edward Campbell Rich Owen, collection of papers relative to the Walcheren Expedition, 10 July – 3 August 1809, pp.1-6.
57 When summoned to sit in the House of Lords in 1807 Huntly temporarily assumed the title of Baron Gordon of Huntley, a minor peerage in the county of Gloucestershire, which had formerly been held by his late father. Athough Huntly continued to hold his orginal title, and eventually abandoned the name 'Huntley,' he was wrongly referred to as

where and when their forces were to land on the island. Nor had the British seen it necessary to provide Huntley and Owen with a map of Cadsand. Huntley's instructions from Chatham were vague, and did not inform the general of what his troops might expect to encounter once they had landed. Huntley was ordered to land around 2,000 men in one wave; the other details were to be decided on the spot.[58] Off Cadsand, however, the situation was confused, with Owen possessing only enough boats for 700 men to be landed at any one time.[59] Inclement July weather forced Huntley and Owen to postpone the landings. With precious time being lost and unsure of what to do, Huntley was forced to board a brig and seek clarification from Chatham in person. Thick sea mist, however, prevented Huntley from finding Chatham, with the Marquis forced to return to his station off Cadsand.[60]

In the meantime, the British were forced to change the location of their main landings, from near Flushing, to the far north of Walcheren, following the appearance of French warships at Flushing.[61] In making this decision, Chatham and Strachan surrendered the strategic initiative and inadvertently altered the dynamics of the entire expedition. From this point, the Army would now need to conquer the whole of Walcheren before reaching Flushing. What Castlereagh had envisaged as a lighting strike against Antwerp had turned into a battle of attrition, to oust the French from Walcheren, and the surrounding islands, before the British could advance further. The movement of all available boats to the north of Walcheren also deprived Owen of the means to land Huntley's troops. The bad weather also played its part in keeping Huntley's troops stranded aboard ship. As July turned to August, Strachan finally stopped the Cadsand operation.[62]

The absence of a British force on Cadsand enabled the French to reinforce the garrison on Walcheren. This had a knock-on effect, in that with Flushing reinforced, the British were forced to besiege Flushing before being able to move closer to Antwerp. The British had not planned to conduct a siege so early in the campaign and were forced to wait nearly two weeks on Walcheren while a siege-train was hastily assembled and the guns dragged across the muddy roads to Flushing.[63] The French, in the meantime, were able to inundate some of the surrounding fields, a move which flooded the British trenches and added to the miserable state of the

as the 'Marquis of Huntley' in the minutes of the Scheldt Inquiry. In order to avoid any further confusion I have chosen to ignore Huntly's temporary title and have referred to the general throughout by his more prestigious title: the Marquis of Huntly.

58   PP, Scheldt Inquiry, Instructions from Quartermaster General Sir Robert Brownrigg to Lieutenant-General the Right Hon. The Marquis of Huntly, Ramsgate 25 July 1809, pp.143-144.
59   PP, Scheldt Inquiry, Captain Owen to the Committee, p.74.
60   PP, Scheldt Inquiry, Huntly to the Committee, p.145.
61   NMM, COO/2/B.1, Admiral Sir Richard Strachan to Captain Owen of His Majesty's Ship Clyde, 26 July 1809.
62   NMM, COO/2/B.1: Strachan to Rear-Admiral Lord Gardner, 3 August 1809.
63   Fortescue, A History of the British Army, Vol.VII, pp.75-76.

roads.[64] Inter-service relations were also deteriorating. Chatham was frustrated with Strachan's sluggishness to cut the link between Cadsand and Flushing; the general had asked Strachan to blockade Flushing on 28 July, but the Admiral only acquiesced to the request on 11 August.[65] Frustration at the slow pace of the siege spread further discontent, a particularly outspoken critic of the senior Royal Engineer commanders came from Royal Engineer Captain William Pasley, who, in a letter dated 9 August 1809, noted that the senior engineers were not up to the task in hand:

> We were offered the whole Army to act under us. The Staff Corps everything at our disposal…but what could we do with a parcel of old men or rather old women at our head, with fellows without Souls to direct the operations of Armies. With fellows old in years, poor in spirit, beardless in military experience, destitute of knowledge, not merely block heads but block bodies…Gen. Brownrigg says that the Engineers are not fit to be employed in war.[66]

As the British waited, discontent was not the only thing to spread in the British camp as deadly form of malarial fever quickly developed amongst the British troops. 'Walcheren fever', as it came to be termed, quickly laid the army low and forced the British to cease active operations in the Scheldt.[67] Such was the scale and virulence of the epidemic, that as late as February 1810, long after the expedition had returned to Britain, some 11,513 officers and men were still suffering from fever, while a total of 3,960 officers and men, some 10% of the expeditionary force, died from the disease. By contrast, the total number of British deaths sustained in combat was just 106.[68]

Although the British could not have prepared for the sheer number of cases, nor possessed the medical knowledge to prevent the disease from spreading, the British should have had a much greater medical presence on the island given that British

64   Colonel William Fyers, R.E, 'Journal of the Siege of Flushing in the year 1809 by a detachment of the Army commanded by the Earl of Chatham. Under the Immediate orders of Lieutenant-General Sir Eyre Coote, K.B' edited by Major Evan W.H Fyers, *Journal of the Society for Army Historical Research*, 13 (1934), p.157; Christopher Hibbert (ed.), *A Soldier of the Seventy-First: The Journal of a Soldier of the Highland Light Infantry 1806-1815* (Leo Cooper: London, 1976), p.43.
65   TNA, WO 133/16, Chatham, 28 July 1809: Journal of the Proceedings of the Army, p.13; TNA, ADM 1/3987, Sir Richard Strachan, 12 August 1809: A Precise of all the papers in the Admiralty office which have any relation to the Expedition to the Scheldt from the first intelligence to the enemy's forces collecting at Antwerp, down to the final evacuation of Flushing, p.40.
66   A.D. Harvey, 'Captain Pasley at Walcheren, August 1809', *Journal of the Society for Army Historical Research*, 49 (277) (1991), pp.17-18.
67   Howard, *Walcheren 1809*, p.145, Martin Howard, 'Walcheren 1809: A Medical Catastrophe'. *The British Medical Journal*, 319 (7225) (1999), p.1643; National Army Museum (NAM), 1979-12-21-1: Diary of an unidentified Soldier of 38th (1st Staffordshire) Regiment of Foot, p.10.
68   Burnham and McGuigan, *The British Army against Napoleon*, p.229.

forces had had similar experiences in the Low Countries. In 1793, for instance, British troops under Sir Charles Grey had been plagued by sickness whilst in garrison at Ostend, during the siege of Dunkirk.[69] The main reasons why the Medical Services failed to meet the challenges of the disease were twofold. Firstly, the medical services were chronically understrength, owing to the attrition suffered over the course of the previous fourteen years of war. Chatham's army of 40,000 officers and men was supposed to have been served by some ninety-six medical personnel, including thirty-seven surgeons and sixty hospital mates. The actual number of serving medical personnel was much smaller, with Chatham's army having barely thirty-three surgeons and an equal number of hospital mates.[70] The shortfall in medical staff meant that there simply were not enough surgeons for the number of troops involved. For example, Huntley's Division had barely one surgeon and one hospital mate to care for nearly 6,000 officers and men.[71] Secondly, and most importantly, in a bid to keep the objectives of the expedition a secret for as long as possible, Castlereagh did not inform the Army Medical Board of the expedition's destination until barely before the British forces sailed for the Scheldt. Lacking any idea of where the troops would be campaigning, the Medical Board had taken the pragmatic decision to equip the medical staff attached to Chatham's army with a mixture of medical supplies and medicines, to cover every conceivable illness. Although this was eminently sensible, it meant that key remedies, like quinine-rich Peruvian bark, which would be necessary to treat diseases prelevent in the swamps of the Low Countries, were in short supply. Although greater quantities of supplies were dispatched to the Scheldt once the Medical Board finally knew the destination of the expedition, Walcheren fever had already begun to spread rapidly. In this context, it is little wonder that the British forces succumbed so quickly to the epidemic on the island. Several battalions in the Army were plagued with the disease for the rest of the war, with heavy rain and extreme heat often triggering renewed bouts. Wellington famously complained in 1811 that his 'Walcheren battalions' were a major liability.[72]

The expedition to the Scheldt was an unmitigated disaster for the Army and the British government led by the Duke of Portland. Following political pressure from the Press and Opposition Whigs, a Public Inquiry into the expedition was swiftly

69   TNA, WO 1/167, General Sir Charles Grey to Sir Henry Dundas, Ostend, 7 November 1793 War Department In Letters and Papers French Wars- Flanders Campaign Sep-Dec 1793, pp.575-578.
70   T.H McGuffie, 'The Walcheren Expedition and the Walcheren Fever' *The English Historical Review*, 62 (243) (1947), p.194.
71   NAM, 1968-07-261-1, Distribution of the Medical Staff taken from Misc. Notes and Journals of General Sir Frederick William Trench, 'Diary of the Walcheren Expedition, 1809' General Orders-Landing-Reserve-John Hope. Orders for Officers of Quartermaster-General's Department. Reserve to which I was attached as Assistant Quartermaster-General, Aug 1-Sept 1, p.5.
72   Christopher D. Hall, *British Strategy in the Napoleonic War, 1803-1815* (Manchester: Manchester University Press, 1992), p.178.

established, but despite providing an excellent opportunity for the military to assess what went wrong and enable them to identify lessons to be learnt, both Chatham and Strachan, simply sought to discredit each other, instead of trying to assess what could be done better in future.[73] Despite the scale of the defeat suffered, the British squandered the opportunity for learning which presented itself in the form of the Scheldt Inquiry and chose instead to conduct a witch-hunt. The British failure to recognise the need to learn from the Walcheren experience ensured that the same mistakes would be made all over again in the years to come, particularly in the Crimea.

Summary

As these case studies illustrate the Army of the Napoleonic period often struggled to deal with the changing character of conflict in this era. At times the army found it difficult to communicate and learn lessons from the operations it undertook. Recognition of this makes the victories achieved by the troops under Wellington appear all the more remarkable, in that instead of marking a general qualitative increase in military performance, they should instead be viewed as atypical of the generally poor performance of the army in this period. Even so, veterans of the Peninsular War struggled to emulate the success they achieved in Spain and Portugal when deployed elsewhere and under less competent commanders. At the Battle of New Orleans in 1815, a ramshackle American Army all but destroyed a force of Peninsular War veterans due to poor planning and incompetent generalship.[74] Similarly, Wellington himself was not immune to failure, as the bungled Burgos campaign in 1812 and the reverse at Quatres Bras in 1815, demonstrate. Thus, the reforms of the Duke of York changed, but did not transform the Army in this period.

73 Howard, *Walcheren* 1809, p. 203, Bew, *Castlereagh*, p. 272. See also David R. Fisher, 'The Scheldt divisions, 1810' http://www.historyofparliamentonline.org/periods/hanoverians/scheldt-divisions-1810.
74 Phillip J. Haythornthwaite, *The Armies of Wellington* (London: Brockhampton, 1998), pp.260-261.

2

'Forsaking the good cause'?
The Changes and Obstacles in Reforming the British Army, 1815-1854

Peter Randall

The French Revolutionary and Napoleonic Wars lasted 23 years, and were waged on a truly global scale, from the Iberian Peninsula to the Deccan; from the Nile to the Moskva. Until the First World War stripped it of its title, the conflict was often referred to as the 'Great War' in Great Britain. The period is regarded, as having not only changed how armies conducted war, but also the character of war itself and it is not unusual to find the wars listed among 'Revolutions in Military Affairs' (RMA).[1] The title of this chapter is taken from Lieutenant-Colonel John Mitchell's exhortation in the preface to *Thoughts on Tactics and Military Organization* that officers who had encouraged him to write the work did not, 'forsake the good cause' of reforming the institutions of the British Army in the years after these wars.[2] Mitchell was an advocate of tactical and organisational reform within the Army during the 1820s and 1830s and Strachan has described him as, 'Clausewitz's outstanding [British] pupil.'[3]

1 Franklin L. Ford, 'The Revolutionary-Napoleonic Era: How Much of a Watershed?', *The American Historical Review*, 69 (1) (1963), p.23; Williamson Murray, 'Thinking About Revolutions in Military Affairs', *Joint Force Quarterly* (1997), p.70; Colin S. Gray, *War, Peace and International Relations: An Introduction to Strategic History* (Abingdon: Routledge, 2007), p.55; Andrew N. Liaropoulos, 'Revolutions in Warfare: Theoretical Paradigms and Historical Evidence – The Napoleonic and First World War Revolutions in Military Affairs', *Journal of Military History*, 70 (2) (2006), pp.363-384.
2 Lieutenant-Colonel J. Mitchell, *Thoughts on Tactics and Military Organization: Together with an enquiry into the power and position of Russia* (London: Longman, Orme, Brown, Green, and Longmans, 1838), p.ix.
3 Hew Strachan, *From Waterloo to Balaclava: Tactics, Technology, and the British Army, 1815-1854* (Cambridge: Cambridge University Press, 1985), p.8; Christopher Bassford, *Clausewitz in English: The Reception of Clausewitz in Britain and America, 1815-1945* (Oxford, Oxford University Press, 1994), p.39-41.

Given that the wars were so wide-ranging, and that they had so much importance attached to them, it is hardly surprising that they provoked a period of change
in many militaries throughout Europe. Armies sought to imitate and emulate both
the successes of Napoleon and those who defeated him. A key example of this was
the spread of both the corps system and of general staffs in the period. There was
also a period of theoretical introspection, as military philosophers such as Carl von
Clausewitz and Baron Antoine Henri de Jomini grappled with the implications of the
Napoleonic paradigm and attempted to codify its central tenets in order for it to be
replicated in future wars.[4]

Received wisdom holds that Great Britain was an exception to this process of
modernisation. This thesis is supposedly supported by British experiences in the
Crimea, in which disunited leadership, poor medical conditions and an outdated army,
as well as a previously unprecedented level of war reporting, combined to produce a
narrative of a horrific war, with the troops suffering unnecessary losses. There is some
truth to be found in such analysis. Many of the commanders of the Crimean War had
been dusted off after being placed in storage after Waterloo; while the Minié Rifle had
largely replaced the Land Pattern Musket (popularly known as 'Brown Bess'), there
were still units that disembarked British ships in the Crimea shouldering muskets
designed before the Battle of Waterloo.[5] Nevertheless, these changes do not signify an
Army greatly affected by years of war against the French. Whereas Prussia and other
European states had, or were in the process of, overhauling their entire armed forces
in response to the experiences of the wars of the French Revolution and Napoleon,
the Army was remarkably unchanged. This was as a result of major obstacles that
prevented effective change being made in the Army, these principally being the dukes
of York and Wellington, and the Horse Guards, while Britain's empire made reform
undesirable, and the Royal Navy (RN) made it unnecessary.

The Army was not some curious case, set in a vacuum unaffected by the Napoleonic
Wars. Firstly, there were changes because of the Napoleonic Wars, though military
historians often overlook these. These changes must be recognised in order for there
to be a true picture of the period, rather than have it misrepresented. Additionally,
conservative reaction to the Napoleonic Wars and the resistance to making large-scale
change are in themselves exemplary of the wider influence of the Napoleonic Wars in
Great Britain. Many of the changes result from the unprecedented size of the Army

4   Carl von Clausewitz, *On War*, translated and edited by Michael Howard and Peter Paret
    (Princeton, NJ: Princeton University Press, 1976, 1984); Antoine-Henri Jomini, *The Art of
    War*, translated by Captain G. H. Mendell and Lieutenant W. P. Craighill (Philadelphia,
    PA: J. B. Lippincott & Co., 1862). For overviews see: Beatrice Heuser, *Reading Clausewitz*
    (London: Pimlico, 2002) and John Shy, 'Jomini' in Peter Paret (ed.), *Makers of Modern
    Strategy from Machiavelli to the Nuclear Age* (Princeton, NJ: Princeton University Press,
    1986), pp.143-185.
5   Lieutenant George Shuldham Peard, *Narrative of a Campaign in the* Crimea (London,
    1855), p.146.

that had been necessary to conduct the Napoleonic Wars, and the subsequent reduction thereof, with increased colonial commitments stretching the Army. The half-pay system saw the Army become choked with officers for which they did not have the need, this having a detrimental effect on command of the Army. The reduction did allow for the creation of modern police forces, and an increase in military publication. The Napoleonic Wars caused an unprecedented engagement with military theory in Britain, and prompted some changes in drill.

Reducing the Size of the Napoleonic British Army

The immediate legacy of the Napoleonic Wars that demanded attention was the size and cost of the armed forces that had been necessary to defeat Napoleon's armies. In 1815, the Army stood at around 200,000 men, though only a proportion of these had ever been available to the Duke of Wellington. For the occupation of France, at first anticipated to be five years long, but in the end only taking place for three, the Army reduced to 150,000 men. By 1821, the Army numbered 100,000 men. With these reductions, there was a corresponding reduction in the armed forces themselves; thirty-five infantry and eight cavalry regiments were disbanded.[6] In order to support the size of the Army of the Napoleonic Wars it had been necessary to increase spending on the military. Despite the introduction of the unpopular income tax, national debt stood at £792,000,000, or 250% of national income. An obvious target for making a reduction in spending was the armed forces. In 1815 public expenditure on the military amounted to over £43,000,000; this was reduced to £10,000,000 by 1820 before decreasing again to £8,000,000.

The size of and spending on the Army reduced, though there was not a corresponding reduction in Great Britain's colonial commitments; indeed, these had increased because of the Napoleonic Wars, with the addition of territories in Africa, the Mediterranean and Caribbean Seas, and the Indian Ocean. As a result, Great Britain's reduced forces were stretched thinly across the globe, in order to police, and expand, her colonial possessions. With the size of the Army reduced and colonial possessions demanding ever more of the armed forces' attention, it could not be expected to be called upon in times of crisis on the continent of Europe. While some within Britain called for France to be humiliated and lose her war-making abilities with the Secretary of State for Foreign Affairs, Robert Stewart, Viscount Castlereagh, feared that Great Britain's colonial commitment would prevent her from sending troops to Europe and that Austria and Prussia alone were insufficient to oppose potential domination of the continent by Russia.[7] As a result, France was needed in

---

6   Adam Clayton, *The British Officer: Leading the Army from 1660 to the present* (Harlow: Pearson Education, 2006), p.74.

7   Sir Archibald Alison, *Lives of Lord Castlereagh and Charles Stewart and the Second and Third Marquesses of Londonderry*, Volume II (London: William Blackwood and Sons, 1861),

order to balance Russia for Great Britain, and Castlereagh made efforts to ensure that France was not treated too harshly, in order that it might become a 'useful, rather than a dangerous member of the European system.'[8] As Bew pointed out in his biography of Castelereagh, 'an overly emasculated France, which benefited Britain's newfound allies and fair-weather friends, was not in Britain's national interests.'[9]

Despite military budgets slashed by post-war governments, following the Battle of Waterloo a greater proportion of expenditure within the Army was dedicated to those on half-pay. The half-pay system was partly in place as a generous recognition of services rendered, but also in order to provide a pool of officers with military experience, available to be called up and take command at a time of need. This was fine in principle, but in Britain's case left a surfeit of officers, for which there could not have been any use, continuing to draw a salary from the military at the expense of the rest of the establishment. In 1818, 600 generals were on full- or half-pay, and thirty years later there were still more generals than there were regiments for them to command.[10] In addition to the financial burden they placed on the Army, when recalled to active duty, officers who had been on half-pay were unaware of developments made in their time away from active service, and often in poor health.[11] Given that the Army was continually operating to defend and expand the empire between 1815 and 1854, officers on full pay were able to receive first-hand experience of warfare, further negating the requirement for a pool of experienced officers on half-pay. Had the Army reduced the number of officers on half-pay in line with the rest of the army, then the officer pool, though smaller, may have been younger and better experienced.

Policing

Having large numbers of servicemen on half-pay or pensions did have some benefits, if not for the Army, but for society at large, as it allowed the creation of a police force. Previously law and order in Great Britain and Ireland had in part been one of the responsibilities of the Army, which had at times proven unpopular with those policed. This provoked riots against the perceived brutality of the Army as well as adding to its burden. The duty was also deeply unpopular with the Army itself. In 1768 the Secretary at War, William Wildman Shute Barrington, Viscount Barrington, wrote to the Secretary of State for the Northern Department, Thomas Thynne, Viscount

pp.497-498.
8   *Ibid*, p.631.
9   John Bew, *Castlereagh: From Enlightenment to Tyranny* (London: Quercus, 2011), p.358.
10   N. Gash, 'After Waterloo: British Society and the Legacy of the Napoleonic Wars', *Transactions of the Royal Historical Society*, Fifth Series, 28 (1978), pp.147-148.
11   Hew Strachan, *Wellington's Legacy: The Reform of the British Army, 1830-54* (Manchester: Manchester University Press, 1984), p.114.

Weymouth, complaining that the Army was 'continually wanted for a most *odious* service, which nothing but necessity can justify.'[12]

In the nineteenth century, police forces emerged to carry out the task of law and order in part because of the difficulties facing the existing organs that included the Army and local militias. Sir Robert Peel, who was instrumental in the founding of the first modern police force in Great Britain when he introduced the Metropolitan Police Act in 1829, formed the Irish Constabulary (later the Royal Irish Constabulary) in 1814. In the Metropolitan Police of London, ex-servicemen formed a large proportion of both the officers and ordinary ranks. The first Commissioner of Police of the Metropolis (the head of the Metropolitan Police), Lieutenant-Colonel Sir Charles Rowan, was a veteran of the Peninsular Campaign and Waterloo. The majority of his subordinates were non-commissioned officers of the Napoleonic Wars: thirteen of the seventeen superintendents had been Sergeant Majors in the Army before joining the Metropolitan Police.[13] This preference for Army officers to staff the upper echelons of the newly formed police forces was significant as it demonstrates the key role that these figures were to have in the formation of the modern police force, this made possible by the large numbers of ex-servicemen available because of the ending of the Napoleonic Wars.[14]

Military Publications and Institutions

One consequence of so many men passing through the ranks of the Army in the Napoleonic Wars was that a great proportion of the public developed knowledge of, and interest in, military affairs. This increase led to the circulation of dedicated military publications to which current or ex-servicemen contributed. The first of these publications was the *Naval and Military Magazine*, first published in 1827, later becoming the *United Service Journal and Naval and Military Magazine* in 1829. In the prefatory address of the first issue of the *United Service Journal,* the editor stated that:

> Within its pages, communications on every branch of knowledge connected with the Naval and Military Services shall, as occasions occur, find *careful* and *impartial* admission, - they shall serve as far as our zealous ministries may avail, to chronicle the achievements, record the services, and embody the suggestions of men whose examples are illustrious, and of those who emulated such models.[15]

---

12 William Wildman Shute Barrington to Thomas Thynne, 18th April 1768, in Charles M. Clode (ed.), *The Military Forces of the Crown: Their Administration and Government,* Volume 2 (London: John Murray, 1869), p.628.
13 Captain W. White: *The Police* Spy (London: W. Strange, 1838), p.34.
14 N. Gash, 'After Waterloo', pp.149.
15 *The United Service Journal and Naval and Military Magazine,* Part I (1829), p.1.

In a similar vein were the weekly publications *The United Service Gazette and Naval and Military Chronicle* and *The Naval and Military Gazette and Weekly Chronicle of the United Service*, both first published in 1833. There were also frequent publications on military topics in wider-ranging publications, such as *Blackwood's Magazine* and the *Edinburgh Review*. Never before in Great Britain had such dedicated military publications existed, providing forums for the discussion of military matters. The weekly publications had estimated sales of 1,300 per week, however, they probably had a far wider readership, as regimental and garrison messes held many of these subscriptions.[16] These works make odd reading, containing works of poetry, humorous anecdotes from service, and even works of satirical fiction reminiscent of *Gulliver's Travels*, however, the importance, influence and novelty of these publications should not be underestimated.[17] While the Army of the period is characterised by conservatism and opposition to change, these publications were a soapbox from which contributors could advertise and lobby for reforms to the Army. In 1838, a contributor lobbied for promotion examinations in the Army, eventually adopted in 1849.[18] The publications were also influential in provoking reforms in military sanitation.[19] Many reforms adopted after the Crimean War were expressed in the above publications prior to 1854. That such publications were necessary in order to provoke reforms can be illustrated by Colonel Firebrace's statement that, 'any reform that is required must be produced by 'pressure without', and that if left to the discretion of those who are supposed to have the power, it will be produced *sine die*.'[20]

A further institution set up for the study of military science, and a success of the military publications, was the Naval and Military Library and Museum, presently known as the Royal United Services Institute for Defence and Security Studies, or RUSI.[21] The formation of such an institution was first proposed in an item of correspondence to the editor of the *United Service Journal*, published in the February of

16   Albert Tucker, 'Military' in J. Don Vann and Rosemary T. Van Arsdel (eds.), *Victorian Periodicals and Victorian Society* (Toronto: University of Toronto Press, 1994), p.67.

17   Pardoe, 'The Young Soldier's Farewell', *The United Service Journal and Naval and Military Magazine*, Part I (1833), p.23; 'Glorious Uncertainty of War', *The United Service Journal and Naval and Military Magazine*, Part II (1830), p.90; Thomas Jones, 'Some Account of the Country and Naval Force of the Ohwhyisitsosians', *The United Service Journal and Naval and Military Magazine*, Part III (1838), pp.504-510.

18   'Suggestions on the advantages of accustoming Soldiers to the Duties of a Ship, and on the due qualification of Officers', *The United Service Journal and Naval and Military Magazine*, Part III (1838), pp.111-114.

19   Walter F. Willcox, 'The Development of Military Sanitary Statistics', *Publications of the American Statistical Association*, 16 (121) (1918), pp.908-909.

20   Colonel Firebrace, 'On the Errors and Faults in our Military System', *Colburn's United Service Magazine and Naval and Military Journal*, Part II (1843), p.199.

21   Damian P. O'Connor, *Between Peace and War: British Defence and the Royal United Service Institute, 1831-2010* (London: Royal United Services Institute for Defence and Security Studies, 2011), *passim*.

1829, written by an enigmatic 'Old Egyptian Campaigner' who has been identified as one Captain W.H. Smyth.[22] The letter called for the creation of:

> ...a Museum, to be formed, conducted, and maintained, solely by the military, medical, and civil branches of the Royal Navy, the King's Army, the Hon. East India Company's services and their connexions: to be called the *United Service Museum*.[23]

Established in order to 'give a tone of science to the character of both services', this proposal met with instant approval.[24] In the next edition of the *United Service Journal*, a correspondent wrote in support of the Old Egyptian Campaigner's proposal.[25] The similarly enigmatically named 'Artillero' published a further letter in the June edition of the United Service Journal on this subject. He offered the payment of a subscription toward the creation of such a museum, this letter prompting an editorial response that, 'a plan for forming a Committee and for promoting the ultimate objects of the proposed Museum, is in a state of forwardness' with an announcement to be made shortly.[26] Future issues of the journal brought further offers of aid, both personal and financial, as well as a full-length article, which fronted the August edition.[27] On 16th December 1829, a meeting was held in order to, 'concert the necessary measures for founding such an institution.'[28] At this meeting, a Provisional Committee, headed by Major-General Sir Howard Douglas, was formed, and the process of creating the museum was subsequently begun.[29] Douglas was a noted author of a number of works of military science, including *A Treatise on Naval Gunnery*, which had become the principal work on naval gunnery.[30] The Provisional Committee also included Captain

---

22   An Old Egyptian Campaigner, 'United Service Museum', *The United Service Journal and Naval and Military Magazine*, Part I (1829), p.239; O'Connor, *Between Peace and War*, p.3.
23   *Ibid.*
24   *Ibid.*
25   H.P., 'United Service Museum', *The United Service Journal and Naval and Military Magazine*, Part I (1829), pp.366-367.
26   'Artillero', 'United Service Museum', *The United Service Journal and Naval and Military Magazine*, Part I (1829), p.759.
27   'The United Service Museum', *The United Service Journal and Naval and Military Magazine*, Part II (1829), pp.129-143; H.P.: 'United Service Museum', p.107; Lieutenant Chas. Brand, R.N., 'United Service Museum', *The United Service Journal and Naval and Military Magazine*, Part II (1829), pp.238-239; W.H. Smyth: 'United Service Museum', *The United Service Journal and Naval and Military Magazine*, Part II (1829), p.625; Lieutenant Charles Hopkins, R.N.: 'United Service Museum', *The United Service Journal and Naval and Military Magazine*, Part II (1829), p.753.
28   'Naval and Military Library and Museum', *The United Service Journal and Naval and Military Magazine*, Part II (1831), pp.411-412.
29   *Ibid*, p.412.
30   Christopher J. Valin, *Fortune's Favorite: Sir Charles Douglas and the Breaking of the Line* (Tucson, AZ: Fireship Press, 2009), p.86; Colonel Sir Howard Douglas: *A Treatise on*

Francis Beaufort, inventor of the Beaufort wind force scale. On 25th June 1831, the Provisional Committee called a meeting at which the Naval and Military Library and Museum was founded, with the Duke of Wellington being made vice patron, King George IV having previously assented to give his patronage to the museum.[31] An announcement of the institution's formation was made in the June edition of the *United Service Journal*, with its aims stated as being, 'to foster the desire of useful information, and to facilitate its acquisition.'[32] While the organisation did not meet its lofty goal for membership (aiming for 100 per cent of junior officers to become members), by its second decade of existence the United Service Institution (as it had been renamed in 1839) boasted over 4,000 members, and provided a forum for a regular series of lectures and papers.[33]

While the creation of magazines and institutions was unprecedented within the British military community, their true effect was felt most keenly after the Crimean War, when reforms were debated. While it is plausible that individual members of these institutions, or readers of these magazines, were motivated to adopt changes because of articles, papers or lectures, it took the occurrence of the Crimean War for these magazines and institutions to influence changes in the structure and operation of the Army.

Military Theory

Great Britain is charged with having not adequately engaged with military theory after the Napoleonic Wars, but this is not a fair assessment. There was a wide reading and debate concerning Jomini's *Treatise of Grand Military Operations* and, to a lesser extent, Clausewitz's *On War* in Great Britain during the period. Additionally, a native body of theoreticians existed who attempted to examine military theory in the light of the experience of the Napoleonic Wars. This demonstrates that there was a genuine effort to engage with contemporary military theory within Britain. Influenced by the Revolutionary and Napoleonic Wars, Jomini studied military theory in light of his experience. In comparison to his reception on the continent, Great Britain appears to have been remarkably slow to take notice of Jomini's theories. The first review of his 1805 work *Treatise of Grand Military Operations* appeared in 1821, when an extraordinarily thorough review appeared in the *Edinburgh Review* by Sir William Napier.[34] Napier glowingly referred to the work as, 'unquestionably one of the most profound,

Naval Gunnery (London: John Murray, 1820).

31   'Naval and Military Library and Museum', *The United Service Journal and Naval and Military Magazine*, Part II (1831), pp.411-416.

32   'Formation of a Naval and Military Museum', *The United Service Journal and Naval and Military Magazine*, Part II (1831), p.225.

33   Shelford Bidwell, 'A History of the Royal United Services Institute', *The RUSI Journal*, 136 (2) (1991), pp.69-72; O'Connor, *Between Peace and War*, pp.1-20.

34   Sir William Napier, 'Traité des grandes operations militaires', *The Edinburgh Review*, XXXV (1821), pp.377-409.

original, and interesting, that has appeared in our day; and, were we to be strictly dealt with, we would know not how we could excuse ourselves in having not introduced it sooner to the knowledge of our countrymen.'[35] Nonetheless, once dedicated military publications were established, Jomini's theories were an oft-debated feature of these publications and in its first year of circulation, *The United Service Journal* featured such articles as 'Remarks on a Part of Jomini's Theory'.[36] This paper was far less complimentary of Jomini's theories than Napier had been. It was critical as the unidentified author did not feel that Jomini's theories stood up to the test of history, for example, the writer took umbrage with the claim that having the line two-deep with bayonets fixed was only suitable for taking the defensive, contrasting this with the experiences of the battles of Maida and Waterloo.[37] Jomini was widely read, more so, it seems, in the original French than in English. The first English translation of Jomini's *Traité des grandes operations militaries* by J.A. Gilbert struggled to sell.[38] Gilbert stated in the preface that, 'The Treatise upon great Military Operations by the Baron de Jomini is too well known to men of military science in general, and too highly appreciated by them, to render necessary any eulogy of his work on my part'.[39] This suggests that a large number of his intended readership were already acquainted with Jomini's work.

The other author widely credited as having best approached the issue of military theory in the light of the French Revolutionary and Napoleonic Wars is Clausewitz, whose seminal work *On War* remains the foremost work of military theory.[40] Much as with his reception on the continent in the nineteenth century, Clausewitz lived in the shadow of Jomini, his works being less read and less well received by those who read it. In Britain there was little scope for *On War* to be read by as wide an audience as there was for Jomini's works, as French was widely understood by the learned classes while German was spoken by very few. Additionally, an English translation did not exist until 1873.[41] John Mitchell, in his work *Thoughts on Tactics*, commented that *On War* was, 'a very able, though lengthy, and often obscure book'.[42] The Duke of Wellington was aware of *On War*, having had it recommended to him by Charles Jenkinson, Earl of Liverpool, in 1840. In his letter, Jenkinson commented that Clausewitz' work was, 'of exceeding interest'.[43] While Liverpool, who was able to read the original German,

35   *Ibid*, p.377.
36   'Remarks on a Part of Jomini's Theory', *The United Service Journal and Naval and Military Magazine*, Part II (1829), pp.415-419.
37   *Ibid*, p.419.
38   Strachan, *From Waterloo to Balaclava*, p.2.
39   J.A. Gilbert, *An Exposition of the First Principles of Grand Military Combinations and Movements, compiled from The Treatise upon Great Military Operations by the Baron de Jomni* (London: T. Egerton, Military Library, 1825), p.iii.
40   Peter Paret, 'Clausewitz' in Paret (ed.), *Makers of Modern Strategy*, pp.186-216.
41   Heuser, *Reading Clausewitz*, p.16.
42   Mitchell, *Thoughts on Tactics and Military Organization*, p.7.
43   University of Southampton, Special Collections, 2/71/28, Personal Papers of the First Duke of Wellington, Letter from the Earl of Liverpool to the Duke of Wellington, 10

did furnish Wellington with a translation of a section of Clausewitz's study of the Waterloo campaign, he sadly omitted any military theory for which Clausewitz is famous, and instead focused primarily on Grouchy's operations at Waterloo. Nevertheless, Wellington still made a detailed response to Claueswitz's account, countering perceived criticisms of how he conducted the Battle of Waterloo.[44] This memorandum is of interest because it demonstrates both an oft-overlooked connection between Wellington and Clausewitz but is also one of the very few examples where the former personally responded to a history of the Waterloo campaign.[45] The other significant example of this is his interaction with Captain William Siborne and his model of the Battle of Waterloo commissioned by RUSI in 1830.[46]

In addition to these foreign authors, there existed a home-grown body of authors of military theory. Among them were Sir William Napier, whose multi-volume work *History of the War in the Peninsula* rested on the theoretical framework of Jomini, and John Mitchell, who took his theoretical lead from Berenhorst's *Reflections on the Art of War*, but was also influenced by Clausewitz in formulating his *Thoughts on Tactics and Military Organization*. Finally, there was Edward Yates, who also presented his own interpretation of Jomini's theories in his *Elementary Treatise on Strategy*. All were, in some manner, influential with Napier's *History* often held up as an exemplary work of military theory. Napier would go on to be a major influence on the great sea power theorist Alfred Thayer Mahan, who claimed as a result of the work he was in a 'new world of thought…[and]…appreciative…of the military sequences of cause and effect.'[47] Additionally, Napier was an influence on the next generation of British military theorists, with his son-in-law, Lieutenant Sir Patrick MacDougall having explicitly stated in the preface to *The Theory of War* that he drew his first chapters from Clausewitz, Jomini, and the British authors Napier and Yates.[48] Mitchell was critical of the organization of the Army, and Leonhard Schmitz has suggested that the reforms made after the Crimean War had their roots in Mitchell's arguments.[49]

September 1840.

44   Duke of Wellington, 'Memorandum on the Battle of Waterloo' in Arthur Richard Wellesley (ed.), *Supplementary Despatches, Correspondence, and Memoranda of Field Marshal Arthur, Duke of Wellington* (London: John Murray, 1863), pp.513-531.

45   Bassford, *Clausewitz in English*, p.41.

46   O'Connor, *Between Peace and War*, pp.9-10; Peter Hofschröer, *Wellington's Smallest Victory: The Duke, the Model Maker and the Secret of Waterloo* (London: Faber and Faber, 2004), *passim*.

47   Robert Seager II, *Alfred Thayer Mahan: The Man and His Letters* (Annapolis, MD: Naval Institute Press, 1977), p.135.

48   Lieutenant-Colonel P.L. MacDougall, *The Theory of War: Illustrated by Numerous Examples from Military History*, Third Edition (London: Green, Longman and Roberts, 1862), p.ix.

49   Leonhard Schmitz, 'A Memoir of the Author' in Major-General John Mitchell, *Biographies of Eminent Soldiers of the Last Four Centuries* (London: William Blackwood and Sons, 1865), p.xvi.

Changes in Drill and Tactics

At the beginning of the Napoleonic Wars, the official drill manual of the Army was Colonel David Dundas' *Principles of Military Movements*. During the wars, however, regiments found it expedient to adjust the Dundas' regulations; while the changes made were necessary for the war, they also introduced a lack of uniformity. As a result, in 1824 Major General Sir Henry Torrens, Adjutant-General to the Forces, was charged by the Commander-in-Chief with the task of compiling these changes into a new drill manual, *Field Exercise and Evolutions of the Army*. In the introduction to the text, Torrens noted the influence of the wars in the evolution of drill within the Army, and the disunity caused thereby:

> Improvements, however, have been suggested by practical experience, during the late eventful war; which though important and essential in the abstract, were partially adopted, without adherence to any general or fixed principle of formation: The result was a practice at once desultory, and disunited; and the advantages to be derived from these improvements, were liable to become nugatory by the revival of that discordant variety of system, with its consequent evils, which had called forth the labours of Sir David Dundas; and to the remedy of which the science and accuracy of that eminent Officer had been so successfully applied.[50]

The changes are minor: more instruction is given on the stances 'at ease' and 'attention'; more facings are described; speeds of marches are reduced (slow march, for example, is reduced from 80 steps a minute in Dundas' original manual to 75 steps a minute in Torrens' revision);[51] more attention is paid to drill with arms. The greatest change was in the increasing and diminishing the front of an open column, with the front being increased and diminished on the reverse flank, whereas Dundas had recommended the pivot-flank. The latter is the flank wheeled upon, while the former is the flank opposite to this one. To diminish or increase the front is to make the front of a battalion closer or further apart depending on conditions.[52] What is missing from Torrens' manual are the examples of the practice of drill found the practical reports from the Seven Years War that Dundas' manual provides. Despite informed by the experiences of the Napoleonic Wars, no such examples appear in Torrens' manual and the work is poorer for it.

Even with the changes, there was disunity. An article in an 1829 edition of the *United Service Journal and Naval and Military Magazine* outlined how:

---

50 Major General Sir Henry Torrens, *Field Exercise and Evolutions of the Army* (London: William Clowes, 1824), p.v.

51 Torrens, *Field Exercise and Evolutions of the Army*, p.17, 42.

52 William Duane, *A Military Dictionary* (Philadelphia, PA: William Duane, 1810); Brevet-Major James Pattoun Sparks, 'Observations upon Infantry Drill' *Colburn's United Service Magazine and Naval and Military Journal*, Part I (1846), p.100.

...the cavalry soldier is obliged, when mounted, to conform to the instructions laid down by Sir D. Dundas...when dismounted, he is desired to follow those recently established by Sir H. Torrens...and as these two systems are different, it will be easily imagined what difficulty and embarrassment is experienced.[53]

Additionally, Torrens' drill, which required officers to learn light infantry drill, was unpopular with disciplinarians who preferred the rigid control afforded to them in heavy infantry drill, this contributing to further Napoleonic War era officers entering the half-pay list.[54] Further to this, many who had served under Dundas' system of drill did not see the need for there to be changes made, arguing that, 'we fought and conquered the most warlike nations of Europe (not to mention those of Asia) under the system of old Dundas'.[55] This opposition to change resulted from the victory of the Napoleonic Wars and was endemic within the Army at the time.

Britain was not, however, the only country to make poorly reasoned conclusions from the Napoleonic Wars. The French, owing to their defeat by Great Britain, actually looked to emulate the Army going forward in the post-Napoleonic era. A French Colonel averred that the French Army would benefit from adopting Torrens' amended drill manual *Field Exercise*.[56] The infantry square, used to great effect by the Army, for example, at the battles of Waterloo and Fuentes de Oñoro, took on mythical qualities, being viewed as almost unbreakable. For example, in Antoine Fortuné de Brack's 1831 work *Cavalry Outpost Duties* the advice given is to instead encircle the square and yell 'Prisoner' at the enemy.[57] In his work *Thoughts on Tactics*, Mitchell stated that, 'All the military nations of the Continent follow, it will be said, the same system of tactics we are here condemning'.[58] It is clear that in Great Britain, and abroad as well, the victory at the Battle of Waterloo served to promote the existing practices of the Army, and obscure any suggestion major reforms be made.

Obstacles to Change

An obstacle to reform of the structure and operation of the Army was Prince Frederick, the Duke of York. During the Napoleonic Wars, the Duke of York's service in the Army was lauded by Parliament; in 1905, Sir John Fortescue praised the duke for the

---

53   'Cavalry' *The United Service Journal and Naval and Military Magazine*, Part II (1829), p.190.
54   Scott Hughes Myerly, *British Military Spectacle: From the Napoleonic Wars Through the Crimea* (Cambridge, MA: Harvard University Press, 1996), p.83.
55   Centurio Peninsularis, 'Grievances of a Veteran' *The United Service Journal and Naval and Military Magazine*, Part III (1833), p.537.
56   *Ibid*, p.16.
57   Antoine Fortuné de Brack, *Cavalry Outpost Duties* (Auzielle: LRT Editions, 2008), p.164.
58   Lieutenant-Colonel John Mitchell, *Thoughts on Tactics* (London: Longman, Orme, Browne, Green, and Longmans, 1838), p.vi.

reforms he made during the Peninsula War, and claimed that the duke 'did more for the Army than any one man has done for it in the whole of its history.'[59] Following the Napoleonic Wars, however, the duke became obstinate in his opposition to reform, seeing it as unnecessary. Writing after the Duke of York had died, Stocqueler stated:

> If His Royal Highness [the Duke of York] had lived in a time of 'progress,' as it is called, he would, we dare say, have done much more for the solider than he really did accomplish, with the best desires in the world.[60]

In particular, Stocqueler thought that the Duke of York should have done more to reform the kit of the infantry, particularly Brown Bess, which was heavy, inaccurate and prone to misfiring, its only advantages being its large calibre, allowing troops to use musket balls of other European armies, and its length, making it more effective with bayonet attached.

Also influential in preventing reform was the apparatus with which the Duke of York had surrounded himself and that carried on in his spirit after his death in 1827 – the Horse Guards. Whereas the War Ministry was the parliamentary control of the Army, Horse Guards existed to exercise the control of the Crown. Therefore, any attempt at reform was seen as an attempt to undermine the Crown.[61] Since its creation in 1798, the Horse Guards had increasing amounts of control over promotions and commissions, yet was still reliant on Parliament for funding. With Parliament resentful of the Horse Guards' control over the Army, withholding funds was a way of managing Horse Guards. Even if there had been a particular inclination within Horse Guards to carry out reform, the Parliamentary control made any such reform near impossible.

The final figure in preventing reform is the Duke of Wellington. The Peninsula War assured his fame and the Battle of Waterloo elevated him to near legend.[62] As a result, Wellington was able to exercise considerable influence over the political landscape after the Napoleonic War, right up until (and even beyond) his death in 1852. At various times, he was Prime Minister, Home Secretary, Foreign Secretary, Commander-in-Chief (twice), and Master-General of the Ordnance. That the Army remained quite so much unchanged owes much to the influence of Wellington and his acolytes at the Horse Guards. With such influence, Wellington could have been a great reformer, reshaping the Army from top to bottom. Yet he saw no need for

---

59   John William Fortescue, *The British Army, 1783-1802: Four Lectures delivered at the Staff College and Cavalry School* (London: Macmillan, 1905), p.109.

60   J. H. Stocqueler, *The British Soldier: An Anecdotal History of the British Army. From its Earliest Formation to the Present Time* (London: William S. Orr and Co., 1857), p.163.

61   Richard L. Blanco, 'Reform and Wellington's Post Waterloo Army, 1815-1854', *Military Affairs*, 29 (3) (1965), pp.124-125.

62   Huw Davies, *Wellington's Wars: The Making of a Military Genius* (New Haven, CT: Yale University Press, 2012), pp.248-249.

reform, much as how when he became Master-General of the Ordnance he wrote to Lord Mulgrave and told him that, 'I should wish to leave everything as it is.'[63] Additionally, he not only failed promote reform himself, but obstructed attempts by others to make reforms. For example, his opposition effectively killed off the reform of the ordnance in 1837 and 1849.[64]

While it is clear that forces existed to obstruct reform in the Army, the role of the empire was a key factor that made it undesirable to carry out Napoleon- or Prussian-style reforms. Unlike in Prussia or France, the primary purpose of the Army was not to fight and win wars in continental Europe; instead, the Army existed to fight in Africa and Asia in pursuit of Britain's colonial goals. In Europe, Napoleon was able to achieve his RMA thanks to the agricultural revolution that had taken place, and the network of roads that existed. Operating in Africa and Asia required the Army to be able to cover difficult terrain with little scope for foraging.[65] As a result, even if there had been the inclination to carry out wholesale changes to the structure and operation of the army along the lines of those made in Prussia, it would have hampered the ability of the Army to carry out their colonial commitments.

The Senior Service

Though the Army existed to defend and expand the British Empire, to an island nation with a far-flung empire such as Great Britain, the RN was the most important service in the nineteenth century: for maintaining the empire; for defending the British Isles; and for meddling with the continental balance of power. An article in *Blackwood's Magazine* in 1825 demonstrated the RN's importance in maintaining the empire when it stated that:

> To retain our Colonies, we must retain our naval supremacy. The Navy is the link which connects the scattered members of the Empire together as a whole. If we ever lose our supremacy on the ocean, the Empire will be torn limb from limb; the trunk may be left us, but the members which are so essential for its due nourishment will be lost for ever.[66]

While the Army was necessary to maintain and expand the colonies, their role would have been impossible to carry out were it not for the RN. The RN also proved a more

---

63   Duke of Wellington to Lord Mulgrave, 1819, in Arthur Richard Wellesley (ed.), *Despatches, Correspondence, and Memoranda of Field Marshall Arthur Duke of Wellington, K. G.*, Volume I (London: John Murray, 1867), p.20.

64   Michael Partridge, 'Wellington and the Defence of the Realm, 1819-52' in Norman Gash (ed.), *Wellington: Studies in the Military and Political Career of the First Duke of Wellington* (Manchester, Manchester University Press, 1990), p.241.

65   Strachan: *From Waterloo to Balaclava*, p.2.

66   'The Late Session of Parliament', *Blackwood's Edinburgh Magazine*, XVIII (1825), p.222.

adept way for the governments of the day to interfere in European affairs or promote a moral or ideological cause. In the years between the Battle of Waterloo and the Crimean War, Great Britain used her navy to suppress the slave trade, to intervene on the side of Greece in the Greek War of Independence, and to combat piracy in Asia.[67] In addition to its usefulness, because of the lack of control Parliament was able to exercise over the Army, the RN became the favoured service.[68] Land defences were only updated in the 1860s when a series of war scares and developments in steam power caused Parliament to fear invasion.

Conclusion

The Army of the post-Napoleonic period represents something of quandary for historians examining military innovation. While demonstrable changes did arise because of the Napoleonic Wars, these largely affected society, rather than the Army itself. The establishment of modern police forces, and the expansion on military publications only had secondary impacts upon the Army - that is lessening their domestic commitments and increased consumption and production of works of military theory – they did not produce large-scale changes in the structure or operation of the Army. However, key obstacles, such as the dukes of York and Wellington, in conjunction with the Horse Guards, prevented major change. As a result, the army that arrived in the Crimea was largely the same as that which had contested the Battle of Waterloo nearly forty years previously, itself a relic of the Seven Years' War. Though the Army was ultimately successful in its conduct of the Crimean War, this victory was achieved in such a manner that led to criticisms being made, many of which had been voiced in the ante bellum, and might have been avoided had changes been made earlier.

---

67   Bernard Edwards, *Royal Navy Versus the Slave Traders: Enforcing Abolition at Sea, 1808-1898* (Barnsley: Pen and Sword, 2007); Nicholas C. Christy, *Greco-British Relations During the Greek War of Independence* (Medford, MA: Tufts College, 1951); Hunt Janin, *The India-China Opium Trade in the Nineteenth Century* (Jefferson, NC: McFarland & Company, 1999), pp.131-150.
68   Blanco, 'Reform and Wellington's Post Waterloo Army, 1815-1854', p.125.

3

Resistance and Reform
Transformation in the British Army Medical Services 1854-1914

Andrew Duncan

The medical services of the British Army made a series of considerable innovations between 1856 and 1914. While these advances led to improvements in the army's health, the situation did not transform until cultural changes in the rest of the army made it possible for medical and organisational innovations to take full effect. The literature on transformation covers various aspects of change: doctrinal development, strategic or operational goals, and the creation of new combat arms, but gives less consideration to organisational change or to a force's supporting arms.[1] This chapter seeks to bring organisational innovation in a supporting arm into the wider debate on transformation. It explores the medical situation during the Crimean War and the Indian Mutiny; it then sets out the most significant reforms and medical advances of the era and their impact on army health. The developments leading to the creation of the Royal Army Medical Corps (RAMC) will be charted, as they embody some of the key improvements in organisation and capability within the medical services. The performance of the RAMC in the Boer War raises difficult questions about why the army, with a far more professional and capable medical service, suffered from many of the same problems it faced in the Crimea. In terms of how the medics coped, the contrast between the Boer War and the First World War is stark. But the RAMC had completed its organisational and medical innovations by 1899. It saw no further significant change between the two wars. The main change between 1899 and 1914 was in the culture of the rest of the army. This development, which brought the army's mind-set into line with the capabilities of the RAMC, transformed the army's ability to keep its men healthy in wartime.

---

1   Theo Farrell and Terry Terriff, 'The Sources of Military Change', in Theo Farrell and Terry Terriff (eds.), *The Sources of Military Change: Culture, Politics, Technology* (Boulder, CO:, Lynne Rienner, 2002), pp.4-7.

The British Army in the 1850s: Crimea and the Indian Mutiny

The army's medical organisation suffered numerous problems during the Crimean War. Each regiment had its own surgeon, but beyond that, a Director-General, four Inspectors-General, 11 deputy inspectors, and 163 officer-surgeons constituted the entire medical department, and they were spread worldwide in numerous garrisons. Medical officers could not purchase a commission, but they were selected by nomination rather than by objective criteria, and the conditions of entry were not particularly rigorous.[2] In 1854, one of the requirements for entrants to the medical service was familiarity with *Cullen's Nosology*, published in 1769.[3] Medical officers received no specialised training for military practice; they simply studied in civilian medical schools and then joined the army. While their education was up-to-date when they joined, there was no provision for further study or time to learn new skills; therefore, medical officers were unable to maintain their professional skill set in light of new discoveries and practices.[4] During the 1850s, the debate about whether contagion or miasma (micro-organisms or bad air) caused disease was still ongoing, which made it more difficult to arrange concerted efforts to cure or prevent illness.[5] Worse, medical officers had no power to advise their commanding officer about health or sanitary needs, let alone compel necessary action.[6] The low status of medical officers was highlighted by their unique 'relative ranks' outside of the hierarchy of every other officer of all other corps, with titles like 'surgeon-major' or 'brevet surgeon Lieutenant Colonel'.[7] Under such conditions, units lost more men to disease than to enemy action, and sometimes were nearly destroyed by illness—during the China War of 1839-42, fully half the force lost their lives to infections.[8] Soldiers wounded in battle had poor prospects. Surgery was rudimentary. Amputation was the most common operation; it risked immediate haemorrhage and shock, and likely infection and gangrene later, but it was the only option for a heavily damaged limb, especially a seriously fractured bone. Some wounds, like those to the abdomen, were virtually untreatable and tended to be rapidly and painfully fatal.[9]

2   Peter Lovegrove, *"Not Least in the Crusade:" A Short History of the Royal Army Medical Corps* (Aldershot: Gale and Polden, 1952), p.9-12.

3   John Shepherd, *The Crimean Doctors: A History of the British Medical Services in the Crimean War* (2 volumes; Liverpool: Liverpool University Press, 1991), Vol. 1, p.53.

4   Anne Summers, *Angels and Citizens: British Women as Military Nurses 1854-1914* (Newbury: Threshold, 2000 [1988]), p.18.

5   Shepherd, *Crimean Doctors*, Vol. 1, p.53.

6   Lovegrove, *"Not Least in the Crusade"*, p.12.

7   Dr J.S.G. Blair, *In Arduis Fidelis: Centenary History of the Royal Army Medical Corps* (Edinburgh: Scottish Academic Press, 1998), pp.xxiii.

8   Lieutenant General Sir Neil Cantlie, *A History of the Army Medical Department*, 2 volumes (Edinburgh: Churchill Livingstone, 1974), Vol. 1. p.480.

9   Richard Holmes, *Sahib: The British Soldier in India 1750-1914* (London: Harper Collins, 2006 [2005]), pp.403-404.

This was the state of the Army Medical Department during the Crimean War, so it is not surprising that while the army lost 2,755 men killed, with a further 1,847 dying of wounds (from 18,283 total wounded), it had 144,390 sick, of whom 17,225 died.[10] The first year of the war was the worst. By the end of 1854, Britain had more than 10,000 men ill in hospital, and while there were still 20,000 troops available in December, by mid-January 1855 the number had fallen to only 13,000.[11] Of the 25,000 men initially dispatched to the Crimea, only 7,000 were still alive at the end of the year.[12] Deaths in hospital outnumbered deaths in battle by about four to one.[13]

The Indian Mutiny followed hard on the heels of the Crimean War, and illness was again widespread. Lieutenant George Elers described a hospital in Seringapatum where 'all the private soldiers were lying on the bare ground, some in the agonies of death. The heat and the smells were dreadful... few who breathed this pestiferous air ever came out alive.'[14] The British force which laid siege to Delhi at one point mustered 9,866 men, with a further 2,972 in hospital sick—a quarter of the force made ineffective by disease.[15] During the Mutiny, British losses to disease outnumbered those to enemy action by roughly ten to one. Regiments regularly lost more men to heatstroke than to the enemy.[16]

Internal Causes of Reform: The Experiences of Crimea

Reform began before the Crimean War ended. Both medical and combat officers recognised that inadequate clothing, bare feet, lack of fuel and shelter, and wet sleeping conditions in winter-time would produce high rates of illness, and gradually the army improved conditions in the front lines by fixing supply problems and providing adequate food, fuel and shelter; the first winter had seen dire logistical failures.[17] Frederick Robinson, assistant surgeon with the Scots Fusilier Guards, recorded in his diary on 22 January 1855 that he could not do his job properly for 'want of medicines, and almost every necessary comfort.'[18] The blame for this falls on the Commissariat and Ordnance Departments; the former was part of the Treasury

10   Fielding Hudson Garrison, *Notes on the History of Military Medicine* (New York: Hildesheim, 1970 [1922]), p.172.
11   Winfried Baumgart, *The Crimean War 1853-1856* (London: Arnold, 1999), pp.140-143.
12   Julie Finucane, 'Civilian Legacies of Military Nursing', *Health and History*, 6 (2) (2004), p.97.
13   Lovegrove, *"Not Least in the Crusade"*, p.10: Baumgart, *The Crimean War*, p.143.
14   Holmes, *Sahib*, p.407.
15   Donald Featherstone, *Victorian Colonial Warfare: India from the conquest of Sind to the Indian Mutiny* (London: Cassell, 1992), p.117.
16   Cantlie, *Army Medical Department*, Vol. 2, p.371.
17   Shepherd, *Crimean Doctors*, Vol. 1, pp.289-292, 300-304.
18   Frederick Robinson, *Diary of the Crimean War* (London: Richard Bentley, 1856), p.248.

and thus entirely outside army control, and both were hampered by bureaucracy and largely or wholly staffed by civilians.[19]

Other problems, however, were more directly medical in nature. Camps were poorly placed, so soldiers lived in crowded and insanitary conditions. Even basic precautions were neglected; Frederick Robinson noted that 'the most prominent objects... visible everywhere in riding, are the carcasses of dead horses; and (but for the somewhat greater care taken with their remains) those of dead men.'[20] The hospital at Scutari was drastically overcrowded, and men slept in unheated wards that swarmed with vermin. The diet was poor, and lack of facilities meant that amputations were carried out in the wards in full view of other patients.[21] While hospital mortality rates only once reached the dismal peak of 60%, rates of 40% or 50% were not uncommon in 1854. Efforts were made to fix these deficiencies, and by 1856 British troops were much better fed and housed, and hospitals were drastically improved. In the final six months of the war, 25,392 men were admitted to regimental hospitals, and 460 of them died, a mortality rate of 1.8%. The army absorbed at least some of these lessons and applied them elsewhere. The second round of the China Wars, in 1858-60, saw 14,000 men landed in China. They were well fed, properly clothed, and care was taken over sanitary matters. Two hospital ships were provided, and the mortality rate was just over 3% per annum.[22] By that point, the medical services were changing in response to governmental inquiries as well as in reaction to operational realities.

Investigations into the army's medical provision began in 1856 and uncovered substantial failures; the Royal Commission on the Sanitary State of the Army saw evidence demonstrating that even in peacetime the army had twice the mortality rate of a comparable civilian population.[23] Such findings prompted numerous reforms. A statistical branch was created, and the army soon was able to draw on statistical work far ahead of anything else in Europe. New hospitals were built at Netley and Woolwich. Higher standards were required from medical applicants and selection began to be by competitive examination.[24] The Army Medical School opened in 1860 to provide specialist teaching in hygiene, tropical diseases, and military surgery to medical officers before they joined their units.[25] Medical officers gained the power to advise commanding officers on the health of troops, but not the authority to enforce needed reforms.[26] Pay and promotion prospects remained poor, and 'relative rank'

19   John Sweetman, *War and Administration: The Significance of the Crimean War for the British Army* (Edinburgh: Scottish Academic Press, 1984), pp.41, 54.
20   Robinson, *Diary of the Crimean War*, p.249.
21   Lovegrove, *"Not Least in the Crusade"*, p.10.
22   Statistics compiled from Shepherd, *Crimean Doctors*, Vol. 1, pp.572-604.
23   *Ibid*, pp.594-595.
24   Lovegrove, *"Not Least in the Crusade"*, pp.12-17; Cantlie, *Army Medical Department*, Vol. 2, p.202.
25   Shepherd, *The Crimean Doctors*, Vol. 2, pp.596-597.
26   Lovegrove, *"Not Least in the Crusade"*, p.12.

continued, albeit with the authority of the corresponding regular rank for the first time.[27] The Medical Staff Corps, of orderlies and stretcher-bearers, did gain regular military rank, but it was separate from the Medical Department, and had only non-commissioned officers.[28] Regimental surgeons and hospitals survived, needlessly compartmentalising medical resources. The reforms could have gone further but important organisational and administrative change had still taken place.

The Army Medical School at Netley, which opened only in 1860, was conducting excellent teaching and research by the 1870s. A series of pioneering surgeons held the Chair of Surgery. Sir David Bruce, who discovered the cause of 'Malta' fever and then introduced measures that virtually ended its incidence amongst the British Malta garrison, created the bacteriology course, which was the first ever held in a British medical school.[29] The School rapidly gained an international reputation; not only did officers from Germany, Russia, and the United States come to study there, but those countries soon established similar institutions of their own.[30] The value of the School's research, and the international reputation it had won, was amply demonstrated on the death of Edmund Parks, Professor of Hygiene from 1860-1876, when Field-Marshal von Moltke said that 'every regiment in Europe ought to parade on the day of his funeral and lower their standards in honour of one of the greatest friends a soldier ever had.'[31] British academia extended their recognition to the School as well. Edinburgh University recognised the hygiene course as qualifying for a Diploma of Sanitary Science, and the University of Cambridge recognised the practical hygiene course as being valid for a Diploma of Public Health.[32] Despite the School's evident value, the government considered closing it in 1876. With Medical Officers enlisting for only ten years in Cardwell's reformed short-service army, the government felt that four months of training was too large a portion of the total service. The Medical Department managed to keep the School, in part by emphasising that it taught subjects like tropical medicine and the physiology of food and drink which were available nowhere else. More cunningly, they compared the Medical School to the Army School of Engineering, which cost £20,000 annually and produced fewer graduates than the Medical School which cost merely £6,271 each year.[33] Thanks to the School, new Medical Officers who joined their units in the 1870s were better trained

27   Cantlie, *Army Medical Department,* Vol. 2, pp.202-204.
28   Lovegrove, *"Not Least in the Crusade",* p.15.
29   Lovegrove, *"Not Least in the Crusade",* p.14; Roy Porter, *The Greatest Benefit to Mankind: A Medical History of Humanity from Antiquity to the Present* (London: Harper Collins, 1999 [1997]) p.444.
30   Cantlie, *Army Medical Department,* Vol. 2, p.225.
31   Lovegrove, *"Not Least in the Crusade",* p.14. It should be noted that the provenance of this remark is disputed: Cantlie attributes the quotation to Baron Munday of the University of Vienna. Cantile, *Army Medical Department,* Vol. 2, p.226.
32   Cantlie, *Army Medical Department,* Vol. 2, pp.225-226.
33   *Ibid,* p.225.

than their predecessors, and they remained competent and up-to-date because they were given periodic leave to refresh their skills. Fifteen years after the Crimean War, significant organisational and professional innovation had occurred. The remainder of the century brought a body of medical advances that greatly increased the ability of doctors to prevent and treat illness and the ability of surgeons to safely and humanely operate on wounded men.

External Influences on Reform: The Prussians, New Tools and New Techniques

Not long after the Crimean investigations ended, the Franco-Prussian War provided another impetus to reform. The army, answering a French appeal for medical help, sent Red Cross ambulances staffed by men on leave from the army to help the wounded while observing the effects of modern warfare.[34] Every army in Europe took note of Prussian methods, organisation, and the General Staff, but the medical lessons of the war were also noteworthy.[35] Prussian troops had been vaccinated against smallpox and suffered only 4,835 cases and 278 fatalities (5.7% mortality) from a total force of 1,113,700 men. French troops taken prisoner had not been vaccinated, and from a far smaller number of men, suffered 14,178 cases of smallpox, with 1,963 deaths (13.8% mortality). Prussian losses to other illnesses were also low.[36] In contrast, the French provided further salutary warnings about poor medical practice. They had not adopted Lister's antiseptic practice (discussed below), and of 13,000 amputations they had 10,000 fatalities from gangrene or fever.[37] It was against this backdrop of impressive—and worrying—military prowess that Edward Cardwell, Secretary for War 1868-74, pushed through a series of army reforms.

Within the larger changes in the army, the Medical Department pushed for reforms they had desired since 1856 and completely restructured the army's medical organisation. In 1873, all regimental hospitals, save those of the Guards and the Household Cavalry, were replaced by garrison hospitals equipped with chemistry labs, libraries, museums and expert instruction, a great improvement on what had typically been available before. Each battalion would now have a Medical Officer, dedicated stretcher-bearers, and access to a network of field and base hospitals for use on larger campaigns. Crucially, because Medical Officers were on the strength of the Medical Department and no longer attached permanently to a regiment, they could take leave

---

34   Bertrand Taithe, 'The Red Cross Flag in the Franco-Prussian War: Civilians, Humanitarians And War in the "Modern Age"' in Roger Cooter, Mark Harrison and Steve Sturdy (eds.), *War, Medicine and Modernity* (Stroud: Sutton, 1998), p.30.
35   Michael Howard, *War in European History* (Oxford: Oxford University Press, 1976), pp.100-101; Geoffrey Wawro, *The Franco-Prussian War: The German Conquest of France in 1870-1871* (Cambridge: Cambridge University Press, 2003), p.47.
36   Fielding Hudson Garrison, *Notes on the History of Military Medicine* (Washington DC: Association of Military Surgeons, 1922), pp.178-179.
37   Porter, *The Greatest Benefit to Mankind*, p.372.

periodically to update or improve their skills.[38] This completed most of the reforms that the Medical Department had advocated since the 1850s.

While anaesthetics had been discovered in the 1830s, allowing surgeons to operate precisely, rather than quickly to minimise the patient's agony, this did not materially alter a patient's odds of survival.[39] In 1867, Joseph Lister published 'On the Antiseptic Principle in the Practice of Surgery,' arguing that infection was caused by particles in the air entering wounds during surgery. He used carbolic acid to prevent infection and slashed his post-operative mortality rate from 45.7% to 15%.[40] Not only did antiseptic surgery play a role in the growing acceptance of germ theory, which was widely discounted before 1870, but, in combination with anaesthesia, it made surgery far more humane and considerably more effective by increasing both the number and complexity of operations that could be undertaken.[41] Surgery went from a brutal and dangerous last resort to an effective treatment.

Significant advances in bacterial research soon followed developments in surgery. Robert Koch discovered the tuberculosis bacillus in 1882, and isolated the organism that causes cholera in 1884.[42] His pupils isolated the organisms that cause typhoid, pneumonia, meningitis, plague, whooping cough, and a whole host of other infectious agents.[43] The isolation and study of these bacilli led, sometimes very rapidly, to methods of prevention and treatment; the plague bacillus was identified in 1894, an inoculation developed in 1896, and more than a million people were successfully inoculated during an outbreak in Punjab in 1901-2.[44] Between roughly 1880 and 1900, many of the most lethal infections were identified and studied, and the resulting vaccinations and treatments meant that Medical Officers, now able to keep abreast of rapid developments, were better placed to maintain the health of the army than ever before. By the end of the nineteenth century, the medical services had undergone marked organisational and scientific change. They were notably more effective than during the 1850s, as the army's mortality figures show.

Troops on home service died at a rate of 17.9 per 1000 each year in 1837-46, a rate which fell to 8.56 per 1000 in 1859-61. For the army as a whole, including the troops in less healthy overseas garrisons, the mortality rate fell from 32.9 per 1000 in 1839-53 to 9.03 per 1000 in 1889-98.[45] Accumulating organisational reform, specialist training, and advances in medical understanding underpinned results that were a credit

38 Lovegrove, *"Not Least in the Crusade"*, pp.16-17.
39 Porter, *The Greatest Benefit to Mankind*, p.370.
40 *Ibid*, pp.371-372.
41 J.N. Hays, *The Burdens of Disease: Epidemics and Human Response in Western History* (New Brunswick: Rutgers University Press, 1998), p.232.
42 Mark Harrison, *Disease and the Modern World: 1500 to the Present Day* (Cambridge: Polity, 2004), p.125.
43 Porter, *The Greatest Benefit to Mankind*, pp.436-437.
44 Harrison, *Disease and the Modern World*, p.132.
45 Cantlie, *Army Medical Department*, Vol. 2, p.210, 370.

to the Medical Department. However, this success was not unalloyed. Far fewer men were dying of disease, but more and more men were lost to non-fatal illness, particularly venereal disease (VD). In the late 1850s, VD cases were 25% to 33% of all army hospital admissions, and in some places, the infection rate reached 503 per 1000 annually.[46] Legislation introduced medical measures, but these were repealed in 1883 after a morality campaign.[47] The rules did reduce VD rates initially, but rates rebounded even before repeal.[48] Between 1854 and 1914, VD rates were largely independent of medical measures; cultural and organisational matters outside of medical control seemed to be the main influence on infection rates. The new short-service enlistment meant more young men in the army, and the proportion of married soldiers fell from 30% in the 1850s to 4% by 1894.[49] VD cases in Britain were a manageable, if not acceptable, 203 per 1000 in the 1890s, but cases in India climbed from 180 per 1000 in 1871, to 361 per 1000 in 1877, and then to a peak of 522.3 per 1000 in 1895.[50] Indian legislation established licensed brothels with regular medical inspections, but infection rates continued climbing. In 1886, the quartermaster general told commanding officers to ensure that the women in such establishments were sufficiently attractive to discourage use of unlicensed brothels. Lieutenant-Colonel Frederick Parry, 2nd battalion Cheshire regiment, immediately requisitioned 'extra attractive women' from the cantonment magistrate, because he felt the six women of the regimental brothel to be insufficient for his 400 men. Growing moral objections produced stringent brothel regulations, and stern warnings for soldiers about the risks they ran.[51] However, the problem remained so severe that during the Tirah Campaign of 1897-8, more men (1,065) were admitted to hospital for VD than for gunshot wounds (948).[52]

In October 1897, all brothels were ordered to be closed.[53] However, there is some evidence that at least a few brothels continued to exist with regimental connivance, despite the official ban. Colonel H.E. Shortt refers, in his unpublished memoir, to an illicit brothel that was nevertheless inspected weekly at least as late as 1910. Facilities offering free treatment to the poor were opened, and medical officers were given the authority to expel anyone who refused treatment. VD became the only infection for which a soldier had his pay stopped during treatment.[54] This set it apart from other

---

46   *Ibid*, pp.372-375.
47   Porter, *The Greatest Benefit to Mankind*, p.421: Garrison, *Notes on the History of Military Medicine*, p.184.
48   Cantlie, *Army Medical Department*, Vol. 2, p.375.
49   *Ibid*, p.378.
50   Holmes, *Sahib*, p.483: Cantlie, *A History of the Army Medical Department* Vol. 2. p.378.
51   Holmes, *Sahib*, p.481.
52   Cantlie, *Army Medical Department*, Vol. 2, p.380.
53   Imperial War Museum (IWM), Personal Papers of Colonel H.E. Shortt, 11385, *In the Days of the Raj, and after, Doctor, Soldier, Scientist, Shikari*, Unpublished Manuscript, pp.17-18.
54   Lutz D. H. Sauerteig, 'Sex, Medicine and Morality during the First World War' in Cooter, Harrison and Sturdy (eds.), *War, Medicine and Modernity*, p.174.

infections, but also, via the accompanying stoppage of family allowances, provided *de facto* notification to a soldier's wife or dependants that he was infected. The army allowed more soldiers' wives to travel to India with their husbands. Commanding officers kept their men busy, and impressed on them the dangers of prostitutes. In 1898, VD rates fell to 362.9 per 1000.[55] By 1909, VD rates in India had fallen to just 67 per 1000.[56] The rise and fall of VD rates took place largely independently of the Medical Department's actions. It was able to treat sufferers, but while inspecting and excluding prostitutes probably reduced infection rates, it was army-wide changes in attitudes and behaviour which made the major difference. Neither the efforts, nor the methods or abilities, of the medics changed over this period; the dramatic improvement in VD rates between 1898 and 1909 had more to do with the army's efforts to avoid potential illness and infection through changes in behaviour than it did with the actions of Medical Officers.

South Africa: Partial Progress and British Army Culture

The Second Boer War served to drive this lesson home, showing starkly the limitations of what even a well-prepared medical branch could do without wholehearted assistance and understanding from the rest of the army. The reforms of the nineteenth century had culminated with a Royal Warrant, of 23rd June 1898, ordering the creation of the RAMC.[57] Long-standing complaints about relative rank and disunited medical services were resolved. Medical Officers now held normal ranks; the only exception was Surgeon General, to address fears among combat officers that a Medical Officer might attempt to command a battle if he ranked as a General.[58] The Army Medical Department and the Army Hospital Corps were integrated; the medical services were at last a unified and rational whole. Although the women of the Army Nursing Service (ANS) remained organisationally separate, the ANS was tiny, with only 72 personnel in 1898, and tended to be ignored by both the army and the RAMC.[59] The Corps first saw action in the Sudan during 1898, earning Kitchener's praise for 'unremitting energy, untiring zeal and devotion to their duty.'[60] It seemed that the army and the new RAMC were fully reformed and ready for a major war, but the shortcomings of both would be revealed during the Boer War.

The men of the RAMC were, by 1899, better prepared than ever before. Their instruction prior to joining their units included sixteen lectures on military surgery and six on 'lunacy' (psychiatry), instruction on a wide variety of tropical diseases, fungal infections and parasites, and a great deal of hygiene training, with particular

55   Cantlie, *Army Medical Department*, Vol. 2, p.380.
56   Holmes, *Sahib*, p.484.
57   Lovegrove, *"Not Least in the Crusade"*, p.21.
58   Blair, *In Arduis Fidelis*, pp.xviii-xix.
59   Lovegrove, *"Not Least in the Crusade"*, p.21; Summers, *Angels and Citizens*, pp.72, 129.
60   Lovegrove, *"Not Least in the Crusade"*, p.25.

emphasis on water filtration in the field and the proper placement of camps, field kitchens and latrines.[61] Hospitals were very well equipped, and even the semi-mobile general hospitals which travelled with campaigning armies boasted x-ray machines, electric lighting, incinerators, and disinfecting sheds for the fever wards.[62] The mortality rate of wounded men during the Boer War stood at 8.7%, roughly half that of earlier wars.[63] Yet the war was anything but a triumph for the RAMC. Typhoid became epidemic, and in the camp at Bloemfontein, the death rate exceeded ten men a day.[64] Over the course of the war, the Corps treated 22,000 men for wounds, injuries or accidents, but more than twenty times that number were admitted to hospital for illness. More than 74,000 admissions had either typhoid or dysentery, both entirely preventable conditions.[65] Typhoid alone produced 57,684 cases, of which 8,022 proved to be fatal.[66] Enemy action caused the deaths of 8,000 British soldiers, but disease killed 14,000 men.[67] The disparity between the combat fatalities and disease fatalities was certainly narrower than in earlier campaigns, but the fact remained that a single preventable disease—typhoid—had killed more British soldiers than had the enemy. Condemnation of the army and of the doctors appeared in the press. A particularly lurid letter, written by the MP W. Burdett-Coutts, appeared in *The Times* in May 1900, describing hundreds of typhoid cases, ill-fed and improperly cared for, lying on the bare ground, with only three doctors among 350 patients.[68] It could have been the Crimean War all over again, and just as happened then, investigations took place into conditions and standards of care.

The initial force dispatched in October 1899 numbered 51,958, which required 2,168 RAMC men, including 254 Medical Officers, as support. Unfortunately, in October 1899, the establishment strength of the Corps was only 2,106, and when the reserves were mobilised, it could call on a mere 2,866 men, exclusive of Medical Officers. In other words, once the first force was sent to Africa, there was virtually nobody left in Britain to run the base hospitals, or to provide support to any reinforcements that might need to be sent. On 7 October, four days before war was declared, British newspapers carried an advert seeking 'a limited number of civilian medical practitioners for temporary service with the troops in the United Kingdom.'[69] The most serious shortage was of surgeons, and two experienced London surgeons were contracted as consultants for £5,000 a year. The medical services had no chance of

61 Blair, *In Arduis Fidelis*, pp.16-18.
62 *Ibid*. pp.39-40.
63 *Ibid*. p.74.
64 Thomas Pakenham, *The Boer War* (London: Weidenfeld and Nicolson, 1979), p.382.
65 Lovegrove, *"Not Least in the Crusade"*, p.26.
66 Blair, *In Arduis Fidelis*, p.90.
67 Sir William Osler, *Bacilli and Bullets: An Address to the Officers and Men in the Camps at Churn* (London: Oxford University Press, 1914), p.4.
68 Blair, *In Arduis Fidelis*, pp.47-48.
69 *Ibid*. p.11.

keeping up with the requirements of the war; the army doubled, then tripled in size, then militia regiments were embodied, and eventually 557,653 men were mobilised.[70] More than 700 civilian surgeons served at the front, and more worked in military hospitals in Britain. The unprecedented growth of the army left the RAMC in an impossible position. Only the large-scale service of civilian practitioners enabled the troops in South Africa to take the field at all. In such circumstances, the medical services did all that could have been hoped, and indeed this is the conclusion that most of the contemporary observers reached. Sir Ian Hamilton praised the Corps. Kitchener felt that the medical arrangements had been efficient, and praised the treatment of the sick and wounded as 'in every way admirable.'[71] Indeed, the failures of sanitation and hygiene were deemed not to be the responsibility of the RAMC, but rather the fault of a lack of awareness among soldiers and combat officers. Surgeon General Jameson testified before the Elgin Commission that 'if sanitation had been understood, not alone by our own [RAMC] officers, but by the rank and file and the military officers… I think it would have saved thousands of lives.'[72] The reforms that were made after the Boer War were aimed just as much at the rest of the army as at the medical services, and indeed the RAMC largely continued or expanded upon earlier measures.

After the Boer War: Bringing Change to the Rest of the British Army

A Hospitals Commission travelled to South Africa while the war was still on and its report in January 1901 cleared the RAMC of any blame, criticising a 'deplorable want of foresight by the War Office' as being primarily responsible for the problems apparent in troop health.[73] A Royal Commission in 1903 arrived at the same conclusion. It criticised the failure to inoculate troops, and the lack of bacteriological services available in the field. The medical services were censured for failures of hygiene, but the blame largely fell elsewhere.

Much of the trouble in South Africa was caused by shortages of medical personnel, due in part to a British Medical Association campaign.[74] Following the Egyptian War of 1882, military budget cuts fell disproportionately on the medical services, with losses of up to half of the personnel and bed-spaces.[75] The number of Medical Officers was cut from 943 to 891, despite the strenuous protests of the Director-General

---

70   Statistics drawn from, *Ibid.* p.11-20; Lovegrove, *"Not Least in the Crusade"*, p.27.

71   Lovegrove, *"Not Least in the Crusade"*, p.29.

72   *Report of His Majesty's Commissioners Appointed to Inquire into the Military Preparations and Other Matters Connected with the War in South Africa*, (London: H.M.S.O., 1903), p.106. (henceforth called *Elgin Commission*).

73   As quoted in Blair, *In Arduis Fidelis*, p.51.

74   Ernest Muirhead Little, *History of the British Medical Association 1832-1932* (London: British Medical Association, 1932) pp.152-154.

75   Blair, *In Arduis Fidelis*, p.4.

because reduced numbers meant staff could not be given leave to update their skills.[76] In protest, virtually every British medical school stopped putting forward candidates for the medical services, which so restricted the supply of doctors to the army that 'there were no examinations held at all for some time, as there was nobody to sit them.'[77] The War Office eventually conceded, but not before twelve years of boycott had left the army with too few Medical Officers even for peacetime needs.[78] The medical schools once again sent candidates to the exams for places in the army medical services, however, the level of pay on offer meant that the best and brightest doctors all opted to enter civilian practice. The creation of the RAMC in 1898, with the attendant improvements in pay and conditions, was too late to make good the deficiencies in numbers and quality before the Boer War. The scale of the military effort that Britain made in South Africa compounded all of this. The RAMC may have acquitted itself tolerably well in challenging circumstances, but further reforms followed once the war in South Africa ended.

The Medical School at Netley was moved to London in 1907, where it became the Royal Army Medical College. For those who passed the rigorous exams (six hours daily for five days in the case of the Indian Medical Service) the College gave three-month courses with financial prizes to encourage good results.[79] The move to London was intended to further raise professional standards and develop the clinical and scientific work of the Corps. For similar reasons, publication of a monthly *Journal of the Royal Army Medical Corps* began in 1903. Equally firm and energetic steps were taken with regard to sanitation.

A School of Sanitation opened at Aldershot in 1906 to train non-medical officers and men to form the nucleus of sanitary detachments in their units. Courses on sanitation were given at Staff College, at Sandhurst, and at Woolwich; lectures on the subject were given within regiments, and sanitation appeared in the syllabus of all officer examinations.[80] These exams required practical knowledge and focused on sanitary matters on active service. For example, the Senior Class of gentlemen cadets at Woolwich sat a Sanitation Exam in December 1909 that asked them to identify the most dangerous infectious diseases on campaign, and required them to explain how enteric fever spread and the precautions to prevent it doing so.[81] All combat officers were given a *Manual of Elementary Military Hygiene*, which, in 97 pages, laid out the dangers of military life and the precautions to be taken.[82] There

76   Cantlie, *A History of the Army Medical Department,* Vol. 2. p.355.
77   *Elgin Commission,* p.104.
78   Lovegrove, *"Not Least in the Crusade",* p.19.
79   IWM, Shortt Papers, 11385, *In the Days of the Raj,* pp.7-8.
80   Lovegrove, *"Not Least in the Crusade",* pp.30-31.
81   Royal Military Academy Sandhurst, WO 314, Woolwich Exam Papers, Examination Papers 1909.
82   War Office of Great Britain, *Manual of Elementary Military Hygiene 1912,* (London: H.M.S.O., 1914[1912]).

were even specifically medical manoeuvres held on Salisbury Plain in 1910.[83] Colonel Leishman was one of several men carrying out cutting-edge research; he developed a typhoid inoculation which became available from 1907.[84] While the medical branch continued to innovate, Lord Haldane, the Secretary of State for War 1906-1912, was reforming the rest of the Army. He created the Territorial Army, the Officer Training Corps, and the General Staff.[85] The first two were of immediate practical importance for the medical services, because both constituted a reserve of trained medical personnel available for mobilisation that had not been there before.[86] This filled a need amply demonstrated by the Boer War. The General Staff, a long-overdue development for the army, would engage in long-term military planning to ensure that the chaos which had characterised the war would not recur.

While the developments specific to the RAMC built on what had been done in the nineteenth century and served to further develop the training and expertise of Medical Officers, it was those measures which spread sanitary practices and an awareness of their importance through the rest of the army that proved the crucial difference. In the decade before 1914, the RAMC changed little beyond the expansion of the available reserves; the great bulk of organisational and medical innovation between 1854 and 1914 had already taken place. The wide gap between the conditions soldiers faced in South Africa and those they faced on the Western Front was due to changes in attitude in the army as a whole, rather than anything particular to the medical services. This begs the question why such a change could not have taken place prior to 1899.

Many of the post-Boer-War changes affected the army as a whole, and brought about a cultural shift in the way that the army viewed disease and responded to the professional recommendations of the RAMC. The Medical Department had been insisting on the establishment of something like the RAMC for decades, but it was only when the British Medical Association lent its full weight to the campaign, and attracted attention in the press, that the War Office submitted.[87] The Duke of Cambridge, Commander-in-Chief from 1856 to 1895, did his best to obstruct reforms; it was largely his influence that prevented the creation of a General Staff until after the Boer War.[88] He was certainly not the only senior officer to take a dim view of progress. Just before the Boer War, General Wolseley, generally a forward-thinking and reforming officer, described Sanitary Officers as the most useless men in the army, and advised

83   Blair, *In Arduis Fidelis*, p.104.
84   *Ibid*, pp.110-111.
85   On Haldane's reforms, see: Edward Speirs, *Haldane: An Army Reformer* (Edinburgh: Edinburgh University Press, 1980).
86   Blair, *In Arduis Fidelis*, p.114.
87   Little, *History of the BMA*, pp.154-156; See, for example: *The Times*, Tuesday, May 16, 1893; p.11; Issue 33952; col E, 'The Army Medical Service. Deputation To Mr. Campbell-Bannerman.' See also: *The Times*, Friday, Apr 02, 1897; pg. 7; Issue 35167; col F, 'The Army Medical Service.'
88   R.C.K. Ensor, *England 1870-1914* (London: Clarendon Press, 1936), p.16.

any commander who had such an 'encumbrance' on his staff to leave him behind.[89] A disregard for the advice and expertise of Medical Officers was apparent on campaign despite the army having reformed its peacetime practices, and the way that officers thought about war appears to have been the cause.

Combat officers were well aware of the dangers of disease and poor medical care; they risked death by disease or wounds just as their men did. Cholera killed General Anson, the Commander-in-Chief of India in 1857, and killed Major General Sir Henry Barnard, commander of the Delhi Force.[90] Officers knew the risks they faced, and they often were well aware of how the risks might be mitigated. After Tel-el-Kebir in 1882, some of Nevil Macready's men drank from a canal contaminated with dead men and horses and 'every kind of filth' despite strict orders to the contrary, and he knew that this introduced 'the seeds of future disease' to the battalion.[91] The fact that disease could strike anyone, of whatever social class, was one of the reasons for civilian sanitary reform, but the same facts did not bring about corresponding interest in military reform among officers. Part of the reason may be that the army, under strict discipline, did not cause the same fear of social upheaval from below which governments felt could occur if disease was left unchecked in the civilian population.[92] However, it seems more likely that disease, which throughout history had killed more soldiers than had battle, was accepted as one of the risks of military life, comparable with the risk to life and limb in combat.

Officers certainly demonstrated willingness, indeed eagerness, to face risk on and off the battlefield. Officers hunted dangerous game, like man-eating tigers or rhino, as a pastime.[93] At least one officer hunted lions on horseback with a spear for sport—his Colonel forbid it as overly risky, but not before saying, 'My God! I should like to have been there!'[94] Officers were often very keen to see combat, taking every possible chance to get to where fighting was taking place. Frank Maxwell delivered a message to his Colonel and three companies up a hill on the North West Frontier in April 1895. He climbed up and realised that they were 'under showers of bullets.' He delivered his message, then 'finding myself there, I jolly well stayed there, and a most exciting time we had.'[95] It was not unknown for officers still recovering from a serious battle wound to apply to at once depart on a new campaign.[96] Seeing action was felt to improve

---

89   Lovegrove, *"Not Least in the Crusade"*, p.24.
90   Holmes, *Sahib*, p.473.
91   Nevil Macready, *Annals of An Active Life* (London: Hutchinson & Co., n.d.), Vol. 1. p.48.
92   Porter, *The Greatest Benefit to Mankind*, p.405.
93   Charlotte Maxwell, *Frank Maxwell Brigadier-General, VC, CSI, DSO: A Memoir and Some Letters Edited by his Wife* (London: John Murray, 1921), pp.130-131; Richard Meinertzhagen, *Kenya Diary (1902-1906)* (London: Eland Books, 1983 [1957]), pp.58, 70-71.
94   *Ibid*, pp.96-97.
95   Maxwell, *Frank Maxwell*, p.27.
96   Tom Bridges, *Alarms and Excursions: Reminiscences of a Soldier* (London: Longmans Green and Co, 1938), p.50-52.

promotion prospects, but it was also the central facet of military life. Facing risk to life and limb bravely and without qualms was an essential part of being an officer, and a strong sense of duty drove men to face danger regardless of risk to themselves. Richard Meinertzhagen walked unarmed towards two deserters who were both armed with rifles: 'Fox shouted to me that if I came on I would get shot, but from a pure sense of duty I had to go on, though I was petrified with fear.'[97] Examples of officers' efforts to get into action, and their disregard for their personal safety once in action, could be multiplied almost endlessly. Keegan identifies a fatalistic streak in the mind-set of British officers, and it seems that some of this fatalism carried over into their attitudes towards disease.[98] Even when improvements in sanitation and medical care had made peacetime soldiering far safer in the 1890s than it had been in the 1850s and officers were well aware of the necessary precautions and the risks of neglecting them, disease was still widespread on campaign, as the statistics of the Boer War show.

There is some indication that officers on active service felt that their overriding responsibility was to prosecute the campaign, and that sanitation was of secondary importance; Wolseley's advice about leaving Sanitary Officers behind when going campaigning does not appear to have been an isolated sentiment. Meinertzhagen, on campaign in Africa, was very annoyed by an order to send a patrol to the depot for soap. He wrote:

> I have no intention of doing so. Either we are on active service or we are not… Cleanliness is a most important part of discipline in peacetime, but I decline to make my men turn out here… as they would on parade in Nairobi. The idea is too absurd.[99]

The intersection of officers' dutiful disregard of personal risks and the historically constant threat of illness on campaign created a fatalistic attitude towards disease in wartime. This changed between 1902 and 1914, but it required the widespread education of the officer corps, via the measures already discussed, to successfully crown the advances made by the medical services since 1856 with a cultural change in the rest of the army. Including sanitation in the curriculum for officer cadets and in promotional exams altered the mind-set of combat officers, who began to view disease as something other than the norm on campaign. In 1914, it was possible for a Medical Officer to address troops and speak of bacilli as 'the more important enemy' and clearly separate the 'legitimate and honourable deaths [of those who died] from wounds' from those who 'perish miserably' because of sanitary neglect.[100] This idea, that becoming

97   Richard Meinertzhagen, *Army Diary 1899-1926* (London: Oliver and Boyd, 1960) p.33.
98   John Keegan, *The Face of Battle* (London: Cape, 1976), p.190; Featherstone, *Victorian Colonial Warfare*, p.115.
99   Meinertzhagen, *Kenya Diary*, p.282.
100 Osler, *Bacilli and Bullets*, p.3.

a casualty outside of battle was dishonourable, was an interesting—and significant—extension of the notion of being honourably wounded in battle. This was reflected in the way that officers behaved during the war. Having seen Major General Thompson Capper court danger at the Battle of Loos, George Barrow wrote that:

> it may be the duty of an officer, staff or not staff, to invite death where example calls for it; it is equally his duty not to put himself rashly in the way of it, for when dead he is no longer capable of being any service to his country.[101]

Officers were no less willing to risk their lives for their country, but they no longer considered it acceptable to risk unnecessary death from disease, and this cultural change helped to crown the efforts of the RAMC with the wholehearted cooperation of the rest of the army.

The importance the army placed on maintaining good health reflected the changing status of Medical Officers. An officer who served in Field Marshal Haig's headquarters during the First World War wrote that 'the successful medical results won in this war were largely due to the fact that—contrary to the system of other wars—the doctor had a real influence and power at G.H.Q. In his own department he was supreme.'[102] Prevention of illness, and treatment of the sick and wounded, had so far improved by 1914 that the First World War reversed prevailing trends in which far more men had succumbed to disease than to enemy action, and between 1914 and 1918 the army lost ten men to the effects of wounds for every man it lost to disease.[103] The army and the RAMC had succeeded in bringing onto the battlefield the improvements in hygiene and sanitation already evident in peacetime.

Conclusion

Florence Nightingale, who got the government's attention by calculating that the immediate post-Crimean reforms saved the Treasury £285,000 annually through lower mortality rates, had mooted efficiency in military medicine.[104] Peacetime improvements in the army's health were well established by 1899, but these improvements carried over into wartime only once the whole army recognised both the possibility and necessity of doing so. The events in South Africa, along with a growing recognition that a war in Europe would likely see the army committed as the main instrument of British strategy, added an edge of importance to the newly instituted

---

101 Sir George de S. Barrow, *The Fire of Life* (London, Hutchinson and Co., n.d.), p.123.
102 "G.S.O.", *G. H. Q. (Montreuil-sur-Mer)* (London: Philip Allan & Co., 1920), pp.96-7.
103 Geoffrey Noon, 'The Treatment of Casualties in the Great War' in Paddy Griffith (ed.), *British Fighting Methods in the Great War* (London: Frank Cass, 1998 [1996]), pp.87-88.
104 Cantlie, *Army Medical Department*, Vol. 2, p.210.

army-wide sanitary education. By 1914, the army sought military efficiency through good health in wartime just as eagerly as in peacetime.

Between 1856 and 1914, several periods of reform dramatically altered the organisation and status of the army's medical services. These reforms, allied to significant developments in medical knowledge, technique, and tools, had made medics vastly more capable of sustaining the health of troops and providing effective treatment for sick or wounded men. However, as this chapter has demonstrated, the full impact of these developments was not felt until 1914, although the organisational and medical innovations were essentially complete by 1899. Peacetime soldiering, it is true, had become far safer by 1899, but despite this, the burden of disease for troops on campaign in South Africa had more in common with the Crimean experience than with that of the First World War. The RAMC was both able and willing, but, as with the fight against VD, it could do only so much if the rest of the army were not informed and eager participants in preventative measures. In 1899, the culture of the army and its attitudes to disease had not yet adjusted to the realities of medical innovation. It was only after widespread education directed at the entire army that the full impact of medical innovation was felt. The suddenness of this change, after the gradual, if steady, improvement in medical ability, meant that only 12 years separated two wars in which the ratio of losses to disease and to enemy action was reversed. It was fortunate for Britain that this change took place when it did.

4

'The Most Resistless and Revolutionary Weapon of Naval Warfare that has Ever Been Introduced'
The Royal Navy and the Whitehead Torpedo 1870-1890

Richard Dunley

In June 1871, the Royal Navy (RN) purchased the rights to build the Whitehead loco-motive torpedo, following a comprehensive series of trials.[1] The RN had immediately recognised the potential of this weapon, with the Director of Naval Ordnance (DNO) writing that, 'the invention is one of the *very highest importance* to any maritime power' (emphasis in original).[2] This view was supported by the committee formed to look into the subject, and would remain the general belief of naval officers throughout the 1870s and 1880s.[3]

Having decided to adopt the Whitehead torpedo and invested a considerable sum of money in the rights to the weapon, the issue facing the RN was a simple one. How best to deploy the radical new weapon to further the organisation's strategic aims? The Whitehead, like its ancestor the spar torpedo, seemed ideally suited for use from a small, fast craft. Indeed both weapons were originally envisaged as being operated in coastal waters principally against blockading squadrons. This was where the problem lay. The mid-Victorian RN was, in contrast to its rivals, an ocean fleet. It was designed to control the world's seas and if necessary take the fight to an enemy's coastline. Throughout the second half of the nineteenth century Britain was indisputably the supreme maritime power. This meant that the RN had very different requirements to those of its rivals. Small vessels designed for coastal operations against blockading

---

1   The National Archives (TNA), ADM 116/135; TNA, ADM 116/146, Agreement of the British Government with Messrs Luppis and Whitehead, 11 June 1871.
2   TNA, ADM 116/135, Cooper-Key Memo, 5 November 1868.
3   Murray F. Sueter, *The Evolution of the Submarine Boat, Mine and Torpedo From the Sixteenth Century to the Present Time* (Portsmouth, J Griffin & Co, 1907), p.297; Alan Cowpe, *Underwater Weapons and the Royal Navy: 1869-1918* (PhD Thesis, University of London, 1980), p.16.

fleets had no place in the RN. If this radical new weapon were to transform the organisation and fulfil its obvious potential it would have to find a role within the established strategic outlook, without this it would remain little more than a novelty. Historians of technology have long acknowledged the difficulties of institutionalising dissonant innovations.[4] Despite a strong material focus navalists, and military historians in general, have been slow to notice the literature coming out of this field relating to how complex organisations addressed questions of technological change where it did not fit within the current strategic paradigm.[5] This, however, was exactly the problem facing the RN in the early 1870s.

Coastal Assault and the Admiralty Torpedo Committee

Arthur Hood, the new DNO, took the first step in this process as early as 1869, when he submitted his views on an initial trial. He wrote that, 'small steamers or even steam launches specially fitted to carry one or two tubes...to fire the torpedo...could probably be employed at night in smooth water against vessels at anchor.'[6] With its supremacy at sea effectively unchallenged, the RN invested considerable time and money in plans to destroy its rival fleets inside their fortified bases.[7] Hood immediately saw the potential of the torpedo in furthering such a policy. The result was the development of the RN's first torpedo craft, *Vesuvius*. She was a small vessel designed around the principles of 'noiselessness and comparative invisibility' with the aim of using stealth to break into an enemy's harbour at night.[8] As such, *Vesuvius* had a very low profile, and special engines designed to burn coke rather than coal; the little smoke produced was exhausted underwater. Her armament consisted of a single submerged torpedo tube forward. It appears that *Vesuvius* was never trialled in her design role, instead becoming an experimental platform attached to the torpedo school, *Vernon*.[9] As a delivery system, *Vesuvius* enabled the Whitehead torpedo to fit into the RN's broader strategic outlook in the period, a vital step in the establishment of any revolutionary new technology.

4   Edward W. Constant II, *The Origins of the Turbojet Revolution* (Baltimore: The John Hopkins University Press, 1980); Thomas P. Hughes, 'Technological Momentum' in Merritt Roe Smith & Leo Marx (eds.), *Does Technology Drive History: The Dilemma of Technological Determinism* (Cambridge Mass.: The MIT Press, 1994).

5   One obvious exception to this is William M. MacBride, *Technological Change and the United States Navy 1865-1945* (Baltimore: John Hopkins University Press, 2000).

6   TNA, ADM 116/135, Hood Memo, 1 October 1869.

7   John F. Beeler *British Naval Policy in the Gladstone – Disraeli Era 1866 – 1880* (Stanford, Stanford University Press, 1997), p.211-5.

8   TNA, ADM 1/6348, Barnaby Memorandum, 26 September 1874.

9   The Royal Navy Torpedo Schools were named after the hulks in which they were based; see, E.N. Poland, *The Torpedomen: HMS Vernon's story 1872-1986* (Privately Published, 1993), p.9-26.

Vesuvius represented an important start in the process of developing the Whitehead torpedo within the structures of the RN, but she had limited capabilities. Her low speed and poor seaworthiness prevented her from being used for anything other than her specific design role. For the torpedo to have a transformative effect on the RN it had to be brought into the heart of the organisation, namely the ocean-going fleet. In 1872 John Fisher, a young officer who had made his name as an underwater weapons expert, wrote a paper to the Admiralty demanding that a full committee be set up to look into all questions relating to submarine weapons. One of the main issues in Fisher's mind was, 'the place which Whitehead's locomotive torpedoes are to occupy in future wars and the kind of vessel to be fitted with them'. He expressed his own views with characteristic clarity, stating that, 'high speed and great capabilities of manoeuvring seem to be the qualities required in Whitehead vessels intended for ocean service.'[10] Arthur Hood, by contrast, made the point that the Whitehead could deployed from the steam launches fitted to major warships and seemed quite content with the design of *Vesuvius*, then on order. Nonetheless, as Fisher suggested, the Admiralty formed a Torpedo Committee to look at the subject in the round.[11] In their preliminary report in October 1873, the Committee raised the issue of deploying Whitehead torpedoes from ocean-going ironclads. Such vessels, they argued, could be equipped with 'fittings on the broadside for projecting the torpedo at right angles to the keel. Vessels so armed could either take their place in the line of battle, or act independently.'[12] With this in mind the Committee began experimenting on submerged broadside torpedo tubes using the hulk *Actaeon*, which had recently been attached to the *Vernon* as a test bed. The results were broadly positive, although the conditions were, in truth, far from realistic.

An Ocean-going Torpedo Vessel?

One of the fundamental problems facing the RN in this period was the uncertain state of naval tactics. Technological change had revolutionised naval *matériel* in the space of two decades. Steam freed ships from the vagaries of the wind, whilst extraordinary progress in armour and guns raised serious issues regarding how to fight. Thrown into this mix was the resurgence of the ram as a potential weapon, after its successful use at the Battle of Lissa. As a result, differing views proliferated as to the conduct of future naval battles and this naturally fed through into ship design.[13] The pace

---

10   TNA, ADM 1/6273, Naval Torpedo Warfare, 14 November 1872.
11   *Ibid.*, Hood Memo, 26 February 1873.
12   The National Maritime Museum (NMM), PHI/109/2, Preliminary Report of the Admiralty Torpedo Committee, 15 October 1873.
13   Gerard H. U. Noel, *The Gun, Ram and Torpedo: Manoeuvres and Tactics of a Naval Battle in the Present Day* (Portsmouth, J. Griffin & Co, 1874); Matthew Allen, 'The Deployment of Untried Technology: British Naval Tactics in the Ironclad Era', *War In History*, 15 (3) (2008), pp.269-293.

of technological change, which meant that ships were frequently superseded before being commissioned, then compounded the problem. This left little room for effective evaluation of technology and its incorporation into a tactical system.

One aspect of this on-going debate was the question as to whether an ocean-going torpedo vessel was a suitable solution to the technical and tactical circumstances of the period. The former Controller, Robert Spencer Robinson used his considerable influence to repeatedly and publicly press for such a ship.[14] The first official step in this direction appears to have come from the Chief Naval Architect, Nathaniel Barnaby. He wrote that, 'the time appears to have come when a ship should be built not for harbour work, but for service at sea'. The characteristics he saw as essential were speed, manoeuvrability and enough armour to resist any 'light and rapidly worked guns'. The design Barnaby proposed was revolutionary; a cigar shaped hull with a very low freeboard supported a light superstructure with rudders fore and aft providing manoeuvrability, while armament consisted of a submerged torpedo tube in the bow.[15] The DNO, Henry Boys, agreed with Barnaby that the time had come for an ocean-going torpedo vessel to be built, however he was concerned about the radical nature of the design. Boys also raised questions about the armament. The first torpedoes were very limited weapons with a short range and a top speed of between nine and 12 knots. The desirability of having a vessel capable of between 17 and 20 knots firing a torpedo from the bow, which would travel much slower, and was therefore liable to being overrun, was obviously questionable. Boys also placed great faith in the submerged broadside ejection proposed by the Admiralty Torpedo Committee, writing that 'no torpedo vessel should be constructed without this arrangement'. He therefore suggested that the issue should be postponed until the results of the Committee's trials had been established.[16]

At this point and for reasons that remain unclear Barnaby reversed his position and claimed that the Navy did not need specialist torpedo craft, and instead argued that torpedoes should be issued to the faster vessels within the fleet. Intriguingly he specifically stated that the matter should not be put before the Board of Admiralty, and instead should be dealt with by the Controller, DNO and himself. The issue of ship design was, in the light of the *Captain* disaster, a highly politically charged matter. The question of the most suitable designs had been the subject of considerable controversy even before the Navy's newest ship capsized and sank, killing nearly 500 men including the son of the First Lord of the Admiralty. Although the precise reasons are unclear it is obvious that the question of the application of the Whitehead torpedo was caught up in this politics.[17]

14   Parliamentary Papers, Letter of Admiral Sir Spencer Robinson to The First Lord of the Admiralty on the Report of Committee on Designs of Ships of War, 1872.
15   TNA, ADM 1/6348, Barnaby Memo, 26 September 1874.
16   *Ibid.*, Boys Minute, 8 October 1874.
17   TNA, ADM 1/6348, Barnaby Minute, 19 November 1874, Barnaby Memo, 9 December 1874.

Barnaby's decision left the whole question of the deployment of torpedoes within the RN in a state of confusion. More than three years after the decision to purchase the weapon there was no clear policy on how and where to deploy the torpedo to further the RN's strategic ends. As a result, the Admiralty formed a Special Torpedo Committee in early 1875 to look into the matter.[18] This was a high-powered committee led by the influential Second Naval Lord, Geoffrey Phipps-Hornby, and containing Boys, Barnaby, Thomas Brandreth, the Captain of the gunnery training school, and Morgan Singer, President of the Admiralty Torpedo Committee. The selection of Phipps-Hornby to chair the committee was important as he was widely viewed as the leading authority on naval tactics, something that left him well placed to pass judgment on what was a very thorny subject. The Committee concluded that submerged broadside firing was the only effective solution and recommended additional trials take place using the coastal assault ship *Glatton*. Crucially the report concluded that 'they therefore do not think it will be necessary at present to build any special ship for torpedo warfare at sea'. They did, however, suggest that a fast launch should be developed which could carry two torpedoes, following up on earlier ideas of deploying the weapon from ships' boats.[19]

The report of the Committee was clearly intended to set the agenda for the development of the Whitehead torpedo and its delivery systems for the foreseeable future, however its conclusions were undermined by a technical development within months of being written. By the summer of 1875, Robert Whitehead had perfected a new design of torpedo capable of 20 knots for 600 yards or 16 knots for over 800 yards. Initially the Admiralty response was to ignore this development and look to the Royal Laboratory, who were manufacturing British torpedoes, to match this performance. John Fisher, the very vocal Captain of *Vernon* was not satisfied. He wrote to Phipps-Hornby that the RN was lagging behind its continental rivals, who had ordered new torpedoes from Whitehead.[20] He went on to reopen the question of how best to use torpedoes in ocean warfare, arguing that the increased speed of the weapon produced a range of new possibilities, particularly relating to bow discharge, as the risk of the torpedo being overrun was much reduced. Fisher considered that 'the best mode of applying the Whitehead will be above water and ahead in line with the keel' and rejected submerged discharge altogether as costly and unnecessary.[21] Despite reaching entirely different conclusions as to the best delivery system and implicitly tactics to be used with the torpedo it is important to emphasise that, in common with his colleagues, Fisher's faith in the weapon itself remained as strong as ever. He confidently asserted to Phipps-Hornby that the torpedo 'is undoubtedly for ocean warfare

18   *Ibid.*, Milne Minute, January 1875.
19   *Ibid.*, Report of the Special Torpedo Committee, 9 March 1875.
20   NMM, PHI/121/4, Fisher to Phipps Hornby, 9 December 1875; Memorandum Respecting the Whitehead Torpedo, 11 January 1876.
21   *Ibid.*, Fisher to Phipps Hornby, 10 February 1876.

the most deadly and resistless weapon yet conceived'.[22] That an officer as knowledgeable and influential as Fisher could come to an entirely different set of conclusions regarding the deployment of torpedoes to that of the recent committee gives a good indication of how challenging it was to institutionalise this radical new technology, especially when it was developing so fast.

To Sea at Last

Fisher's pressure to adopt the new torpedo eventually paid off and in August 1876 a meeting was arranged between Whitehead, Phipps Hornby and the Controller, Houston Stewart.[23] As a result of this meeting, and following the report of yet another committee, it was decided to purchase Whitehead's new design.[24] This still left the question of how best to deploy the torpedo from ocean-going vessels resolutely unresolved. The necessity of adopting the new faster torpedoes was not the only subject that Fisher aired with the Second Naval Lord. He forcefully explained that the policy of waiting for the development of broadside-submerged tubes meant that the RN had a large stock of torpedoes, but only one vessel, *Vesuvius*, capable of firing them. This had the additional effect of severely limiting the opportunities for education and training with torpedoes within the fleet.[25] The questions surrounding underwater discharge remained unresolved, and it was not suitable to fit into existing ships. What was required was a system for launching torpedoes from the current ships within the fleet. The solution came from the Admiralty Torpedo Committee in the form of torpedo carriages. These somewhat resembled the gun carriages used at the time for heavy artillery, were relatively mobile and used compressed air to fire the torpedo, either from the deck or through an above water port cut into the armour.[26] These carriages were far from ideal, being rather rudimentary affairs with little scope for proper aiming due to considerable and inconsistent deflection and difficulties in depth taking. They did, however, have those essential Victorian virtues of being simple to operate and cheap. From 1876 onwards this system was gradually introduced into the fleet, initially in the unarmoured cruisers *Shah*, *Boadicea* and *Bacchante*, and then in the active ironclads.[27] It was using one of these carriages that the *Shah* fired the first torpedo in anger at the rebel Peruvian ironclad *Huascar* in 1877.

With the added impetus given by the Russian war scare of 1878, the installation of torpedo fittings in the larger ships of the major fleets of the RN was completed very rapidly. This was a crucial step in the development and application of the technology.

22   *Ibid.*, Fisher to Phipps Hornby, 9 December 1875.
23   TNA, ADM 116/164, Hall to Stewart, 19 August 1876.
24   *Ibid.*, Report of Fiume Committee, 20 November 1876.
25   NMM, PHI/121/4, Fisher to Hornby 14 February 1876.
26   TNA, ADM 116/163, Carriage for Whitehead Torpedo, 23 March 1876.
27   TNA, ADM 12/985, Cut 59.8, "Shah, Boadicea and Bacchante as to be prepared to use Whitehead torpedoes", 3 April 1876.

Clearly, the physical placing of the weapons system aboard ships on active duty was a major advance, and one without which practical application such as that by the *Shah* would have been impossible. In many ways, however, it is the less obvious results of this development that had the greatest impact on the process of institutionalisation. In order to use and maintain torpedoes within the fleet a large number of officers and men had to be specially trained. In addition to this *Vernon* introduced the Long Course of instruction designed to produce specialist torpedo lieutenants.[28] The sudden expansion of *Vernon* greatly increased the relative importance of the torpedo establishment and the influence of those running it on naval policy. Even more importantly, the creation of torpedo lieutenants meant that a small but growing group of officers tied their careers to this technology, forming a powerful interest group going forward. This was assisted by a perception at the time that the technical branches offered the best routes to promotion, which meant that *Vernon* was capable of attracting some of the most promising young officers. The results of this combination can be seen in the number of Long Course graduates who would come to occupy crucial positions in the late Victorian and Edwardian RN. In the shorter term the installation of torpedoes and the regular practice with them in the fleet meant that the weapon came to be viewed as more than a mere novelty. Indeed, this perception of value was perhaps the most important outcome of the decision. The realistic effectiveness of these early torpedo arrangements is a matter of some debate; however, it is obvious that there were still serious flaws in both the weapon and its delivery system. Crucially, however, the commitment of time and money necessary to adopt the weapon all but ensured that the RN would persevere with this radical new technology.

The Torpedo Flotilla

The deployment of torpedoes on the existing ships within the fleet did little to solve the on-going questions of how best to fit the torpedo within the strategic and tactical structures of the RN. One obvious policy was to copy the ideas being developed overseas. The mid 1870s saw a sudden interest from a number of European governments in small fast launches for torpedo work. Leading the way in the development of such craft was the firm Thornycroft & Co, based in Chiswick, London. As early as 1873, the RN had accepted a tender from the firm to construct a boat designed for use with Whitehead torpedoes.[29] In the ongoing debate over the torpedo and its application this order was, however, cancelled. Despite this, Thornycroft continued to lobby the Admiralty to purchase one of their launches. The Special Torpedo Committee specifically rejected this idea, the implication being that the vessel would be too small for

---

28   E. N. Poland, *The Torpedomen: HMS Vernon's story 1872-1986* (Privately Published, 1993), Appendix A.
29   TNA, ADM 12/985, Cut 59.8, Lightening Special Torpedo Vessel, Dated 12 Dec 1873.

ocean work and yet too large to be carried aboard ship.[30] Within months this decision had been reversed and an order was placed for the RN's first torpedo boat, *Lightning*.[31] She was 84 feet long, capable of 18 knots and carried two torpedoes.[32] Following successful trials the RN ordered a further eleven almost identical First Class torpedo boats, and twelve smaller, Second Class torpedo boats designed to be carried aboard ironclads.[33]

From a purely technical perspective the decision to construct what was rapidly named the torpedo flotilla seems an obvious one. The suitability of small fast craft for delivering torpedoes of all descriptions was well known; however serious questions remained as to the role of these vessels within the RN. The First Class torpedo boats were too small to operate in any kind of a seaway and certainly could not be expected to travel long distances independently. Furthermore whilst they were capable of high speeds in perfect conditions their small size and fragile construction meant that this advantage was rapidly lost even in moderate seas. As a design they were well adapted to operate out of protected harbours and in coastal waters, unfortunately the RN had little demand for such a craft.[34] It was fully expected that the ironclad fleet would be more than capable of defending the coasts of Britain and its Empire against all challenges. There was no obvious role for the First Class torpedo boats.

The Second Class boats offer a more interesting response to the challenges presented by the torpedo. They were of course, smaller, slower and even less seaworthy than their First Class cousins, however because they could be carried aboard the larger ironclads they represented a far more flexible solution. In this period it was expected that the RN would establish a forward base close to an enemy's port, from where a blockade could be mounted and offensive operations planned. In such a scenario these small handy craft could be deployed to advantage. The value the Navy placed on having a number of torpedo boats deployable around the globe was revealed during the 1878 war scare with Russia. As tensions rose the Admiralty purchased an almost complete merchantman and converted her into a specialist torpedo depôt ship, *Hecla*. She was designed to carry six Second Class torpedo boats and supply all of the mining and torpedo equipment required by the fleet.[35] In the confined waters of the Baltic these vessels could have been potentially very useful to a British fleet operating against the

30   TNA, ADM 1/6348, Report of the Special Torpedo Committee, 9 March 1875.
31   TNA, ADM 12/985, Cut 59.8, Singer Report on Proposed Torpedo Boat, 13 September 1875.
32   John Donaldson, 'The Thornycroft Torpedo-Vessels; Their Construction, Armament, &c., and the Results of Certain Experiments That Have Been Made with Them', *The Journal of the Royal United Services Institution*, Vol. 21, No. 91 (1877), pp.611-632.
33   TNA, ADM 12/1004, Cut 59.1, Lightening Trial, 26 May 1877; TNA ADM 12/1004, Cut 59.8, Thornycroft Order, 12 September 1877.
34   Norman Friedman, *British Destroyers: From the Earliest Days to the Second World War* (Barnsley, Seaforth Publishing, 2008), p.24.
35   TNA, ADM 7/875, W. H. Smith Memo, 30 March; G. Wellesley Memo, 14 May; W. Arthur Report, 1 August; W. H. Stewart Minute, 8 August 1878.

Russians. In the end the crisis was settled through diplomatic means and so there was no opportunity to fully evaluate this novel weapons system. It is though, worth noting that the Admiralty considered the vessel sufficiently important to order Rear-Admiral Henry Boys and Captain Morgan Singer, two officers intimately connected with torpedo matters, to conduct full trials with her. Singer reported that the behaviour of the torpedo boats was 'on the whole very favourable'.[36] The flexibility offered by the Second Class torpedo boats whether deployed from the ironclads or a specialist vessel such as *Hecla* represented one of the most innovative solutions to the challenges presented by technological and tactical change. The true potential of such a system is very difficult to ascertain, but it is easy to understand why the Navy was interested in the concept, especially considering any conflict would likely be fought in the relatively calm waters of the Baltic or Mediterranean. As a result by the early 1880s the RN had acquired a considerable number of torpedo boats, both First and Second Class. Regular service, however, fully exposed the failings of these craft. They were simply not robust enough for the type of work expected of them, suffering from both structural and engine problems.[37] Whilst the strategic idea behind Second Class torpedo boats was promising the technology was simply not advanced enough to turn this into a reality; torpedo boats did not represent the answer to the challenge of applying the torpedo to the strategic aims of the RN.

Submerged Broadside Discharge

Considering the difficulties experienced by the RN in finding an effective means of deploying the torpedo, it is unsurprising that a strong focus remained on submerged broadside discharge, this being the one system that seemed to have almost universal support. The expectation that naval battles would take the form of either an uncontrolled melee or a broadside duel between two lines of ironclads at close range meant that this was seen as the ideal delivery system. The reasons for this are obvious; the submerged discharge promised superior accuracy and depth taking together with the intangible benefit of a permanent structure than the rather more extempore torpedo carriages. Placing the torpedo tubes below the waterline provided protection for them in any engagement, something considered particularly important due to the potential danger of enemy fire detonating torpedoes. The expectation that a Captain would attempt to ram any vessel in front of him ensured that the small arc of fire of submerged tubes was not seen as a major defect. The decision to fit submerged tubes to the coastal assault ship *Glatton* for further trials followed the success of the trials in *Actaeon* and the report of the Special Torpedo Committee. The main problem with this system of torpedo discharge was that the water passing the hull struck

---

36   TNA, ADM 1/6443, Singer to Boys, 6 December 1878.
37   TNA, ADM 189/4, Report on Experimental Trials and Exercises with First and Second Class Torpedo Boats at Portland, 4 August 1884.

the torpedo as it was ejected from the ship, twisting it whilst still partially in the tube and damaging the tail. This problem was obviously exacerbated with increasing speed. The solution developed by the Admiralty Torpedo Committee was a folding shield placed just forward of the mouth of the tube to deflect the water away from the torpedo until it had cleared the hull.[38] The trials held aboard *Glatton* in 1876 appear to have been a qualified success, showing enough progress for the Admiralty to start looking to incorporate the technology into the new ship designs.[39]

The first opportunity came with the controversial battleship *Inflexible*. The ship was originally designed and laid down in the early 1870s. Her construction was delayed and at times stopped by frequent changes in specification, and an ongoing dispute between her designer Barnaby and his predecessor Edward Reed over her stability, which resulted in a Parliamentary investigation.[40] *Inflexible* was initially designed before any provision for deploying Whiteheads from ironclads was made, however, due to the delays it was decided in late 1877 to fit her with submerged broadside tubes. The detailed reasoning behind this move appears to have been lost, however it is clear that it was not supported by Barnaby. He was far from convinced by the whole argument of ironclads using torpedoes, believing that they would expose themselves to return fire in the process. He minuted, 'I cannot persuade myself that she should ever use such weapons with such risks, when attendant vessels of equal speed and greater maneuvering power could use them for her, and the loss of which vessels would not be comparable with hers'.[41] Despite Barnaby's strong views the Admiralty pressed forward with the move and chose to install a new design of underwater tube attached to a ball and socket joint that allowed for a limited degree of training fore or aft.

The decision to fit submerged torpedo tubes to *Inflexible* represented one school of thought within the on-going debate over fleet tactics and ship design. Some officers argued that it was best to incorporate all three major weapons systems, ram, torpedo and artillery in one ship, such as *Inflexible*.[42] Others as we have seen from Barnaby's minute quoted above, preferred the idea of ironclads that focused on gunnery, supported by smaller vessels designed to exploit the ram and the torpedo. This, in part, fed into the argument made very publicly by the old Admiral, George Sartorius,

---

38   TNA, ADM 116/158, "The Projection of the Whitehead Torpedo from the Broadside", 8 November 1875.

39   TNA, ADM 12/1004, Cut 59.8, *Glatton* Submerged Torpedo Discharge, Report dated 23 May 1876.

40   John Beeler, *Birth of the Battleship: British Capital Ship Design 1870-1881* (London, Chatham Publishing, 2001), chap.7.

41   NMM, Ships Cover 75, Barnaby Minute, 1 January 1878, Appendix II Underwater Torpedoes in the Inflexible, Remarks by Sir Cooper Key and the Director of Naval Construction upon the Necessity of Providing Small Sea-Going Torpedo Vessels.

42   For example, see, NMM, Ships Cover 78, Wellesley Minute, 8 March 1876, Sketch Design for Torpedo Ram.

that what the RN really required were armoured rams with no other weapons at all. It is in many ways indicative of the trouble that the RN had in coming to terms with the technological revolution going on around it, that at the same time as equipping the *Inflexible* with torpedoes it was also looking once again at the issue of a torpedo craft for ocean service. This led to the reviving of Barnaby's original concept for a high-speed vessel, based around a semi-submerged hull. Development of a new design incorporating a ram bow, with a submerged torpedo tube through the centre emerged due to the growing influence of Sartorius and his ideas.[43] This also included two broadside torpedo tubes on either beam.[44] The principles behind the design, however, remained the same. It relied on speed to close rapidly with an enemy, and avoid the slow firing heavy guns before deploying torpedoes, or potentially ramming tactics. By placing the majority of the hull underwater limited armour was needed to protect against quick-firing guns. Despite this, the increased size of the vessel, driven by the recent changes forced the adoption of more powerful and novel machinery.[45] Vacillation over the design meant that the *Polyphemus* as she was called was not laid down until 1878 and difficulties in construction resulted in her not being commissioned until 1881.

The extended building times for both *Inflexible* and *Polyphemus* had a serious impact on RN policy regarding torpedoes. Without the vessels in commission to act as test beds for the technology and for the tactical principles which they enshrined, there continued to be no real ground for informed decision making. This, however, did not dampen the RN's interest in, or enthusiasm for the torpedo. The extent of ongoing debate over torpedoes and their place within RN strategy was revealed in 1880 by the extraordinary response of the Admiralty to a report from John Fisher. Fisher was at this time Flag-Captain aboard *Northampton* on the North American Station and, most likely, with the intention of reminding the Admiralty of his talents, he put forward a series of radical proposals on ship design and the torpedo. He argued that the torpedo should be the preeminent weapon in naval combat and ideally should be fired from a submerged bow tube. He went on to suggest that all masts and rigging should be removed from ironclads to enable them to carry a number of Second Class torpedo boats. Unfortunately, no copy of Fisher's report appears to have survived, and we can only piece together his arguments because the Admiralty took the unusual step of requesting the responses of a large number of senior officers on active service, down to and including the rank of Commander.[46] This is truly remarkable as it suggests a serious lack of confidence within the Admiralty as to their ability to deal with the issues at hand. It is fair to say that the officers questioned were in no better position to provide any comprehensive answers, responses ranged from complete concurrence

43   *Ibid.*, Barnaby to Houston Stewart, 8 January 1876.
44   *Ibid.*, Barnaby to Houston Stewart, 16 June 1877.
45   Beeler, *Birth of the Battleship*, p.83-5.
46   TNA, ADM 1/6629, Part 2, Responses to Fisher's Report on Torpedo Experiments.

with Fisher's remarks, to their outright rejection, whilst some simply admitted that they did not know. Compounded by the continuing lack of practical knowledge concerning the torpedo, this reaction from some of the most senior officers in the RN demonstrated how challenging it was to rationalize the extraordinary changes in technology, many of which were still far from fully mature.[47]

It is not clear how this exercise helped the Senior Naval Lord, Astley Cooper-Key in his decision-making, however, it is indicative of the regard the Admiralty had for John Fisher and importance of torpedo issues that, on commissioning *Inflexible*, he was appointed as her first Captain. Throughout this period, Fisher exploited his strong personal relationships with both Phipps-Hornby and Cooper-Key to drive policy on Whiteheads in directions he favoured. This is an excellent example of how patronage systems and informal relationships were a crucial part of how the Victorian Navy operated. 1881 also saw the commissioning of the *Polyphemus* and these vessels represented the culmination of a decade long struggle to adapt the torpedo for ocean-going naval service. Unfortunately they did not prove the unconditional success hoped for. The submerged broadside discharge, on which so much had been staked, did not work efficiently. At low speeds the torpedoes could be fired properly, however as the speed of the vessels increased the flow of water passed the hull twisted the torpedo in the tube damaging it. The only solution to this problem was to increase the impulse given to the torpedo through compressed air; invariably this also had the side effect of damaging both the torpedo and the tube.[48] This failure presented a major problem for the RN. The submerged broadside discharge had been the one constant theme running through British torpedo policy for the past decade, and it had been found wanting. Unfortunately, at this very time the requirement for such a system was becoming ever more pressing. The development of larger quick-firing guns rendered the deployment of torpedoes above the waterline in an ironclad very dangerous.[49] For this reason, the Senior Naval Lord formed a committee to solve the problems related to submerged discharge.[50] This naturally left the entire question of how to utilize torpedoes in limbo. More than a decade after the RN had decided to adopt the weapon it still lacked a clear means of applying it in its primary strategic environment.

The failure of the RN to come up with a solution to the problem of deploying the torpedo was a major concern for the Admiralty. In 1880, prior to the completion of the *Polyphemus*, the Senior Naval Lord, Astley Cooper Key wrote of the necessity of providing more torpedo vessels for work with the fleet. The *Polyphemus* had proved to be very expensive to construct, and due to her radical design and lack of guns, was

47   *Ibid.*, Précis of Remarks and Observations of the DNO, 9 December 1881.
48   TNA, ADM 116/224, *Inflexible*: Whitehead Torpedo Practice, 22 March 1882; TNA, ADM 189/4, Remarks by Commander Wilmot, 1 October 1883, on Captain Beaumont's Report on German Mines and Torpedoes.
49   TNA, ADM 116/290, Report by the Submerged Torpedo Discharge Committee, 18 February 1887.
50   TNA, ADM 116/224, Cooper Key Minute, 28 February 1883.

not suitable for peacetime cruising work on foreign stations. As a result Cooper-Key recommended the construction of a class of torpedo-cruisers, with submerged broadside tubes which could be deployed abroad and brought back for fleet work in the event of war.[51] This proposal ran into opposition, mainly from Nathaniel Barnaby, who favoured constructing a simplified *Polyphemus*.[52] In the end, Cooper-Key got his way and in the 1882-3 Estimates provision was made for the construction of a vessel, to be called *Mersey*, based on the design of the cruiser *Leander*.[53] Very quickly, this plan began to unravel. In May 1882, Barnaby noted that 'since it was decided to build this vessel doubts have been raised as to the possibility of obtaining satisfactory results from an underwater broadside discharge.'[54] On-going issues concerning how to deploy torpedoes led to the decision to equip the vessels with a heavy gun armament in addition to two submerged tubes, initially for trial purposes.[55] In November 1882, a rather dejected sounding Cooper-Key wrote that 'I am compelled to allow that our knowledge of the best mode of using locomotive torpedoes from fast vessels is yet incomplete.'[56]

Despite the recurring failures the question of how to deploy torpedoes in a fleet context continued to pre-occupy Cooper-Key and following the revelation that the French were building a number of small torpedo cruisers the question was reopened. In March 1883, the Senior Naval Lord noted in a minute that he was 'deeply impressed with the necessity of providing considerable numbers of small fast sea-going torpedo vessels to accompany squadrons in time of war'.[57] The continuing failure to resolve the issues surrounding submerged broadside discharge meant that it was decided to return to above water discharge, together with a submerged tube in the bows. The resulting *Scout* class torpedo cruisers were barely a third of the size of the *Mersey* class they followed, and much more closely matched the brief repeatedly laid out by torpedo officers.[58] Two ships of this class were constructed in private yards, quickly followed by eight vessels of the slightly modified *Archer* class. This design dropped two of the four broadside tubes and the bow tube, these being replaced by a much stronger gun armament.[59]

51   P.H. Colomb, *Memoirs of Admiral The Right Honble Sir Astley Cooper Key* (London: Methuen & Co, 1898), pp.435-6.
52   NMM, Ships Cover 75, Barnaby Memo, 2 January 1882, Remarks by Sir Cooper Key and the Director of Naval Construction upon the Necessity of Providing Small Sea-Going Torpedo Vessels.
53   NMM, Ships Cover 95, Barnaby Memo, 8 January 1883.
54   *Ibid.,* Barnaby to Controller, 13 May 1882.
55   *Ibid.*, Underwater Torpedo Tubes, n.d., 1886.
56   *Ibid.*, Sea-Going Protected Torpedo Ship: Remarks by Sir A Cooper-Key, 10 November 1882.
57   NMM, Ships Covers 97, Cooper-Key Memo, 21 March 1883.
58   *Ibid.*, Wilmot Minute, 27 July 1883.
59   NMM, Ships Cover 113, New Scout, 2 December 1884; N. A. M. Rodger, 'The First Light Cruisers', *Mariners Mirror*, 65 (3) (1979), pp.217, 222-6.

These vessels did not prove the success that Cooper-Key envisaged. They were rather slow for the task intended and proved poor sea-boats. On a more fundamental level, it was far from clear that they were really equipped to undertake torpedo work with the fleet. The location of the torpedo tubes above water left them very vulnerable considering that the vessels would have to close to within 500 yards of an enemy ironclad to launch a successful attack. This problem was greatly exacerbated by the development of heavier quick-firing guns. The entire ocean torpedo vessel concept was based around a perceived weakness in the armament of contemporary ironclads, namely that their heavy artillery was too slow to load and fire, whilst the quick-firing ordnance lacked stopping power. The 1880s saw the development of rapid firing artillery more than capable of destroying lightly armoured craft such *Polyphemus* and her successors. Such ordnance also threatened the deployment of torpedoes from ironclads themselves. As one officer commented on a report of the Submerged Discharge Committee, 'the modern rapid gunfire renders above water discharge of but little value', this served to focus further attention on the work of the committee.[60] Unfortunately, it was not until 1889 that an effective solution emerged and new style tubes were fitted in the battleships *Sans Pareil* and *Trafalgar* then under construction.[61] In truth, however, the first era of torpedo development had, by this stage, passed. Quick-firing guns had rendered attacks by unarmoured vessels highly dangerous, whilst new breech-loading artillery saw gunnery ranges being pushed well past the limits of the torpedoes of the period. The torpedo had lost its relevance in a battlefield once again dominated by the gun. It would take the development of a range of new technologies such as heater motors and gyroscopes within the torpedo itself, and the destroyer and submarine in terms of delivery systems, for the torpedo to once again threaten to transform the RN.

Conclusion

The RN in the mid-Victorian era was arguably the most complex military organisation in the world with a history of developing and exploiting technological change to further its strategic ends. From its very inception, the torpedo represented a radical break with the traditional conception of naval warfare. Torpedoes, as a dissonant technology, appeared to preface a transformation in the way the RN exerted power at sea. The challenge facing the RN was how to develop the weapon and crucially its delivery system in such a way as to facilitate its full incorporation within the organisation's strategies and goals. Despite devoting large amounts of time and money to the subject, it is very apparent that the RN broadly failed to turn the torpedo from an exciting experiment into a war-winning weapon in the twenty years following its adoption. This was not due to a lack of resources or unwillingness on the part of the Admiralty to embrace change. The problem was a deeper one.

---

60   TNA, ADM 116/290, Willies Memo, 19 February 1887.
61   TNA, ADM 189/9, Introductory Remarks; Submerged Discharge.

In order to exploit the latent potential within the technology the RN needed to develop a delivery system capable of deploying the torpedo to advantage in a global, or at least a European setting and working in conjunction with the existing technological systems, namely the ironclad fleet. The battlefleet both physically and culturally embodied the dominant strategic paradigm of this period and to become fully institutionalised the torpedo needed to be assimilated within this. A variety of problems, in most part of a technological nature, prevented this from taking place in the period up until 1890. The RN's failure to exploit the torpedo in the latter part of the nineteenth century despite consistent efforts in this direction gives a clear indication of how difficult it is to develop and institutionalise a new technology.

5

The Thin Khaki Line
The Evolution of Infantry Attack Formations in the British Army 1899-1914

Spencer Jones

The rapid development of weapon technology from the mid-nineteenth century onwards posed a number of serious tactical problems for European armies. The range, accuracy, rate of fire and stopping power of infantry weapons increased dramatically, and these developments were matched by similar improvements to artillery and the introduction of machine guns. Yet, as the firepower of modern weaponry increased, the survivability of the infantry who would have to face it declined proportionately. The thorny problem of how to close with the enemy without suffering annihilating casualties taxed the minds of military thinkers across the continent.

However, for the British Army of the nineteenth century, such problems were more theoretical than practical. The Army had not fought a European opponent since the Crimean War (1854-1856) and its primary duty in this period was the security of the Empire. The main business of the Army was fighting so-called 'small wars' on imperial frontiers. The opposition encountered in such conflicts rarely possessed modern firearms; more often they were armed with melee weapons and antiquated guns. Finding little to fear from enemy firepower, the Army retained a robust belief in the value of traditional, close order tactics. These formations served the Army well in a multitude of colonial conflicts, where it was found that a well-ordered bayonet charge was enough to rout all but the most resolute or fanatical opposition.[1]

Yet the Army was not ignorant of developments on the continent and had seen the effectiveness of its own firepower against colonial foes.[2] These strands of thought had prompted discussion throughout the 1890s over the appropriate tactics to adopt

---

1   C.E. Callwell, *Small Wars* (London, H.M.S.O., 1906), p.376.
2   Frederick Maurice, 'Omdurman', *Nineteenth Century*, Vol. XLIV (1898), p.1054.

against enemy fire.[3] Such thinking was put to the acid test in the Anglo-Boer War (1899-1902). In South Africa, the British Army was forced to confront an enemy almost uniformly armed with modern, magazine loading rifles and even possessing small quantities of the latest artillery. The problems posed by fighting such an opponent necessitated an overhaul in Army's infantry tactics. Although such changes were ultimately successful in defeating the Boers, they prompted a vociferous debate on the applicability of such tactics to future warfare.

The debate was long and complex.[4] This chapter will focus upon a single element in these new tactics; namely, the change of formation to emphasise widely extended lines. Although apparently narrow in focus, the debate over infantry extension was one that vexed officers throughout the pre-First World War period. Its ramifications were considerable. Linked to the question of infantry formations, its change affected many other aspects of the debate over infantry tactics such as the conduct of the firefight, the role of junior officers and non-commissioned officers, and the nature of artillery support. Thus, by examining the debate over formations, light will be indirectly shed on the wider issues of Army tactical reform in this period.

Tactics on the Eve of the Anglo-Boer War

Prior to the Anglo-Boer War, the Army had a mixed attitude to crossing the fire swept zone. Forced to draw upon historical examples, the Army's key problem in developing a response was lack of battlefield experience. In common with most European armies, the British looked towards the Franco-Prussian War (1870-71) for inspiration. German assault formations in this conflict had consisted of three lines; a firing line in skirmish order; followed by a support line in close formation; with a third reserve line in close formation some distance behind. In theory, the firing line was to pin the enemy, begin the firefight, and then be carried forward in the assault as the support line advanced through their position.[5] The reserve line was in place to lend additional strength to a stalled attack, or to quickly consolidate a captured position to resist counterattacks.

However, in practice the support line suffered severely from misaimed fire directed against the firing line. Stung by fire to which they could not reply these supporting troops showed a propensity to push into the firing line prematurely. Unfortunately, this often resulted in confusion, premature assaults and severe casualties for the

---

3   Howard Bailes, 'Patterns of Thought in the Late Victorian Army', *Journal of Strategic Studies*, 4 (1) (1981), pp.29-45.

4   For a fuller discussion, see: Spencer Jones, *From Boer War to World War: Tactical Reform of the British Army 1902-1914* (Norman, University of Oklahoma Press, 2012).

5   For a description of how the British interpreted German infantry tactics, see: Anon, *The Official Records of the Guards' Brigade in South Africa* (London, J.J. Keliher, 1904), pp.13-15; for deeper discussion and criticism see, G.F.R. Henderson, *The Science of War* (London, Longmans, Green & Co., 1905), pp.143-148.

German attackers. As the war, continued, British observers noticed a tendency for the Germans to abandon the division between firing line and supports, and instead combine the two into a single large group of skirmishers, with the reserve line ready to push the assault home.[6] Such 'skirmisher swarms' were only loosely extended so as to allow officers to retain close control; as a result, although they possessed weight in the assault, they frequently suffered heavy casualties from enemy fire.[7]

Drawing inspiration from the German experience, the Army adopted a similar approach. This consisted of a 'firing line' that was subdivided into skirmishers and supports, and a close formation 'reserve line' that would carry the attack forward into the final assault. The skirmishers were not expected to be widely extended; as Colonel Francis Clery noted in his famous *Minor Tactics*, 'The maximum extent of front … should mainly depend on the degree of supervision and control afforded to the officer immediately in command'.[8] Clery suggested extending to a minimum of one and a half yards per man would allow individual soldiers room to use their rifle whilst allowing the officer to retain control of the advancing lines.[9] When to assume extended formation was left to the discretion of the local officers. The *Infantry Drill Book 1896* suggested assuming extended order approximately half a mile from the enemy position, and did not anticipate that attackers would experience serious fire at ranges above 1500 yards.[10]

However, it is difficult to gauge the extent to which such concepts received acceptance in the Army. Individual colonels often had considerable independence when it came to the training of their battalions, and there is evidence to suggest that for reasons of time, space or personal preference, many preferred to focus upon formations more suitable for the drill ground than the battlefield. For example, Field Marshal Sir Evelyn Wood remembered that some officers stationed in Britain 'delighted in practicing complicated movements in lines of columns' with results that were often 'ludicrous' and certainly of no use in war. Nevertheless, success in such manoeuvres was prized and they were practiced as often as three times a week.[11] Leo Amery claimed that exercises at Aldershot in the late 1890s often featured densely packed attacking lines, with an average of three men per yard being common.[12] Prior to the Anglo-Boer War, even the forward thinking theorist Colonel G.F.R. Henderson was a proponent of close order. He rejected the concept of 'great clouds of skirmishers' and argued, 'close order was now, as heretofore, the backbone of the attack, extended order no

6   *Ibid*, p.131.
7   *Ibid*, pp.143-148.
8   Francis Clery, *Minor Tactics*, (London, Keegan Paul, 1888), p.130.
9   *Ibid*.
10   War Office, *Infantry Drill Book 1896* (London, HMSO, 1896), p.55.
11   Evelyn Wood, *From Midshipman to Field Marshal* (London, Methuen, 1906), pp.236-237.
12   Leo Amery (ed.), *The Times History of the War in South Africa* (7 vols. London, Sampson Low, Marston and Company, 1902 - 1910), Vol. 2, p.184.

more than an essential accessory.'[13] He noted with satisfaction 'Close and extended order combined are officially taught as the form for infantry; close order whenever it is possible, extended order only when it is unavoidable.'[14] How such attitudes translated into training was described by a junior officer stationed with a British regiment in India, who noted that his battalion assault training in July 1899 consisted of the attacking line being separated into 'tight little bunches of about twenty men each' advancing in a line to within 200 yards of the enemy position. The officer recorded his opinion of the training in his diary: 'I could not believe it was serious practice for modern warfare. We should all have been wiped out.'[15] These backward attitudes were mercilessly lampooned in the 1904 parody work *Tactics and Military Training*, where the fictitious, blimpish author 'Major-General D'Ordel' proclaims his firm belief in the value of cramming fifteen men per yard into the firing line![16]

In the late 1890s, there was a challenge to the close order orthodoxy in the form of the Tirah campaign. This military operation took place on the notorious North West Frontier of India (the modern Pakistan-Afghanistan border) against the local Afridi tribesmen. Unlike most colonial opposition, the Afridi were armed with a quantity of modern rifles and proved themselves to be skilful skirmishers. Fighting such opposition in the rugged, mountainous terrain caused a tactical reappraisal amongst the British force and prompted a considerable degree of introspection.[17] However, before this process could produce any lasting reforms, the Anglo-Boer War absorbed the full attention of the Army.

The Experience of Combat, 1899 - 1902

The South African conflict was made unique by the nature of the opposition. In contrast to the majority of colonial foes, the Boers had a long-standing and well-deserved reputation as skilful marksmen.[18] The rifle possessed a degree of symbolism within Afrikaner society, being seen as both a means and a metaphor for self-reliance and independence. As Major-General Sir Frederick Maurice noted in the British *Official History of the War in South Africa*, 'A rifle had at all times an irresistible fasci-

---

13   Henderson, *Science of* War, pp.152-153.

14   *Ibid*, p.153.

15   Richard Meinertzhagen, *Army Diary 1899-1926* (Edinburgh, Oliver & Boyd 1960), pp.15-16.

16   "George D'Ordel" [Mark Sykes & Edmund Sandars], *Tactics and Military Training* (London, Bickers and Son, 1904), p.27.

17   Major-General Sir W.F. Gatacre, 'A Few Notes on the Characteristics of Hill-Fighting in India', *Journal of the Royal United Services Institution*, 43 (1899), pp.1066-1076.

18   For a detailed discussion of Boer marksmanship in the conflict, see: Spencer Jones, 'The Shooting of the Boers was Extraordinary: British Views of Boer Marksmanship in the Anglo-Boer War 1899-1902' in Karen Jones, Giacomo Macola and David Welch (eds.), *Guns and Identities: A Cultural History of Firearms in the Age of Empire* (Aldershot: Ashgate, 2013), pp.251-266.

nation for a Boer.'[19] Although the vast majority of the military forces available to the Boer republics consisted of untrained militia, this cultural affinity for firearms went some way towards offsetting the lack of formal training. Perhaps more importantly, the steadily deteriorating relations between Britain and the Boer republics in the 1890s had prompted the Afrikaner governments to import large numbers of Mauser rifles for distribution to the volunteer commandos. These rifles were formidable weapons that benefited from magazine loading and smokeless powder. Thus, although lacking formal training, the standard of Boer marksmanship and the quality of their weaponry made them a uniquely dangerous opponent. Devising successful tactics that would allow advances to take place across the largely barren South African terrain into the teeth of Boer firepower was to prove a major problem for the Army.

The difficulties were exacerbated by the lack of tactical options open to the British in the opening months of the conflict. Shortage of cavalry in the early part of the war deprived the British of mobility and meant that the infantry were forced into making frontal attacks against Boer positions. Unfortunately, frontal attacks against modern weapons were a difficult undertaking. An officer of the 60th Rifles recorded his experiences at the Battle of Talana Hill, 20th October 1899:

> I don't suppose I am ever likely to go through a more awful fire than broke out from the Boer line as we dashed forward. The ground in front of me was literally rising in dust from the bullets, and the din echoing between the hill and the wood below and among the rocks from the incessant fire of the Mausers seemed to blend with every other sound into a long drawn-out hideous roar. Half way over the terrace I looked round over my shoulder, and I confess I was rather horrified at what I saw...the whole ground we had already covered was strewn with bodies[20]

Confronted by such fierce defensive fire, the Army adapted quickly. With the notable exception of the notoriously incompetent Major-General Fitzroy Hart, who would launch a bungled close order attack at the Battle of Colenso (15 December 1899), the majority of the Army immediately adopted extended order tactics.[21] Writing after the war, G.F.R. Henderson commented on this rapid adaptation:

> The truth is, however, that our ordinary formations, previous to the war, were almost identically the same as those of other armies; but that our officers, thanks to the experience of the Tirah campaign, and to a very general instinct in favour

19   Frederick Maurice (ed.), *History of the War in South Africa 1899 – 1902* (4 Vols. London, Hurst and Blackett Ltd., 1906), Vol. 1, p.80.
20   Quoted in Amery, *Times History*, Vol. 2, p.164.
21   B.F.S. Baden-Powell, *War in Practice: Some Tactical and Other Lessons of the Campaign in South Africa, 1899-1902*, (London, Isbister & Company, 1903), p.52.

of less rigid methods, recognised, before even a shot was fired, that what they had practised in peace was utterly unsuited to the Mauser swept battlefield.[22]

However, the scale of extension advised by pre-war regulations – between one and a half and three yards per man – was soon found to be inadequate. At the Battle of Enslin (25 November 1899) the 245 officers and men of the Naval Brigade formed for the attack extended to four paces per man.[23] However, inexperience meant that the unit naturally began to converge together as they advanced, and as they approached the Boer position they came under withering fire from the front and the left flank.[24] The Brigade was mauled by this fusillade and the formation suffered 44% casualties, including virtually all its officers and NCOs.[25] British commander Lord Methuen attributed these casualties to the overly dense formation, a view echoed by post war writers such as Leo Amery and Captain H.M. Johnstone.[26] Both Amery and Johnstone noted the contrast between the Naval Brigade's bloody repulse and the more successful advance of the supporting Yorkshire Light Infantry. The Yorkshires, described by Amery as 'a battalion that had learned every artifice of hill-fighting in the Tirah', advanced in an extended formation of eight paces per man and suffered comparatively few casualties.[27]

Indeed, when employed skilfully, extended infantry tactics were of critical importance in allowing the British to advance. At the Battle of Elandslaagte (21 October 1899), the widely extended formation of the 1st Devons allowed them to cross a fire swept, barren plain without suffering undue casualties.[28] Amery recorded 'The Devons now came under a severe rifle fire.... [but] the fading light, the dull khaki of their uniforms, and their wide extension saved them from the slaughter that one imagined must be in store for them.'[29] The successful advance of the Devons was a key factor in the British victory at this battle and showed the value of such formations.

Extended order tactics received official sanction following the appointment of Lord Roberts to overall command of British forces in South Africa in December 1899. As well as reorganising British forces in the theatre, Lord Roberts introduced official tactical guidance in the form of a series of memorandums entitled 'Notes for Guidance in South African Warfare.' For the infantry, these notes suggested the abandonment

22   Henderson, *Science of War*, p.372.
23   Amery, *Times History*, Vol. 2, p.337.
24   *Ibid.* p.338; H.M. Johnstone, *A History of Tactics* (London, Hugh Rees, 1906), p.176.
25   Amery, *Times History*, Vol. 2, p.337-338.
26   The National Archives (Hereafter TNA), WO 108/237, South Africa Despatches, Lord Methuen's Despatch, 26 November 1899.
27   Amery, *Times History*, Vol. 2, p.339 and Johnstone, *History of Tactics*, p.176
28   M.G. Jacson, *The Record of a Regiment of the Line: Being a Regimental History of the 1st Battalion Devonshire Regiment during the Boer War 1899 - 1902*, (London, Hutchinson, 1908), p.16.
29   Amery, *Times History*, p.184.

of close order formations between 1500 and 1800 yards, more than double the distance outlined in the *Infantry Drill Book 1896*. Furthermore, Lord Roberts also advised that infantry adopt an extended formation of between six and eight paces per man and make maximum use of cover.[30]

As the war continued, the scale of extension actually increased in many units. Several battalions came to favour an extended formation in the region of 10 to 20 yards, while at the Battle of Diamond Hill (11-12 June 1900), British infantry adopted an extension of 30 yards per man.[31] Furthermore, British formations soon began to modify the three-line system. As early as November 1899, it was noted that the Guards' Brigade kept only a handful of men in the reserve line, with far greater strength being placed into the firing line instead.[32] Other brigades chose to abandon the reserve line entirely, in favour of a two-line system consisting of a firing line and a supporting line, both of which would be in widely extended formation. Writing after the war, Major B.F.S. Baden-Powell noted 'The most usually adopted [formation] consisted of two simple and continuous extended lines, the rear one being perhaps 100 to 200 yards behind the front one. Such things as supports and local reserves were almost unknown.'[33]

The exchange of depth for breadth was considered a viable trade-off in South Africa. As previously noted, the support line and the reserve line were expected to be the key to launching assaults and resisting counterattacks. However, these two duties were less important due to the unique military heritage of the Boers. The Boers placed little emphasis on holding positions in the face of close assault. Instead, their preferred tactic was to deliver a passive, fire-based defence for as long as possible, and, if it were clear that the enemy could not be stopped, then they would withdraw using their mounted mobility.[34] In such circumstances, the British often found that having a greater number of troops in the firing line proved more valuable than a deep formation that carried weight in the charge.[35] These long, thin lines were difficult to pin down and were able to engage in protracted firefights against the Boers without suffering prohibitive casualties. This helped the attacking infantry to gain a lodgement near the Boer position and retain it in the face of enemy fire. Although the British infantry would often be somewhat scattered, there was no danger that the

30   TNA, WO 105/40, Lord Roberts Papers, Notes for Guidance in South African Warfare, 26 January 1900.
31   1903 [Cmd. 1789-1792] *Report of His Majesty's Commissioners Appointed to Inquire into the Military Preparations and Other Matters Connected with the War in South Africa*, 4 Vols., Vol. 2, Q13247, p.66 Q16772, p.273 (Hereafter *Elgin Commission*).
32   *The Official Records of the Guards' Brigade in South Africa* (London, J.J. Keliher, 1904), pp.16-20.
33   Baden-Powell, *War in Practice*, p.52.
34   There were of course exceptions to this rule. The Boers sustained a bloody, close range battle for control of Spion Kop for the entire day of the battle. Similarly, when denied their mobility at Paardeburg, entrenched Boers endured a protracted battle of nine days' duration.
35   *Guards' Brigade*, pp.16-17.

Boers would launch a counter charge and rout the attackers from their position.[36] Such advantages ideally suited the tactics employed by Lord Roberts, who typically used his infantry to hold the attention of the Boers while cavalry and mounted troops sought out the flanks.[37] On some occasions, achieving a lodgement could be decisive in itself. As B.F.S. Baden-Powell noted, merely the threat of assault was sometimes enough to force a retreat: '...on one occasion (a sortie from Ladysmith) the very cry of "Fix Bayonets!" caused them [the Boers] to fly in terror, even though there were, on that occasion, no bayonets to fix!'[38]

Debate and Reform, 1902-1914

In the aftermath of the war, British training and regulations enthusiastically embraced the concept of extended formation. Although training manuals were not prescriptive on the scale of extension, a 1904 memorandum issued from Aldershot Command suggested attacking infantry take up an extension of 6-20 yards per man during the advance.[39] Individual officers offered similar opinions. Colonel Charles Callwell considered that the majority of officers favoured approximately eight yards per man in the attack, while B.F.S. Baden-Powell suggested that extensions of 40 - 50 yards per man would be appropriate for holding attacks.[40] In 1904, Lieutenant-General Sir John French summed up the post-war attitude towards training and tactics when he stated, 'Personally, I believe as strongly as ever in the wide extension of Infantry in the attack... The instinct of all infantry soldiers should be to take advantage of cover, and to avoid open ground.'[41]

However, voices soon began to emerge on the dangers of drawing too much from South African experience. There were immediate concerns that developing combat doctrine from a single, albeit major, colonial war would hamstring the Army in a future conflict where conditions would inevitably differ. Major-General Sir Henry Colvile summed up the views of many of the doubters:

> it should be borne in mind that the conditions of warfare in South Africa were wholly exceptional, and it is unlikely that they will ever be reproduced. I do not think, therefore, that our tactics in South Africa, successful as they eventually

---

36 *Ibid*, p.16.
37 TNA, WO 105/40, Lord Roberts Papers, Lord Roberts's comments on "The Boer War Through German Glasses" (no pagination).
38 Baden-Powell, *War in Practice*, p.63.
39 TNA, WO 27/504, Aldershot Command Papers, 'Tactical Points' memorandum (Undated).
40 Charles Callwell, *The Tactics of Today* (London, William Blackwood & Sons, 1903), p.57; Baden-Powell, *War in Practice*, p.54.
41 TNA, WO 27/503, Aldershot Command Papers, Memorandum on Military Training, 31 January 1905.

were, have by any means solved the difficult question of how to reach the enemy's position in the face of modern smokeless magazine fire.[42]

The two factors that made the Anglo-Boer War exceptional were the terrain and the opposition. The clear atmosphere of South Africa allowed the Boers to open fire with effect at immense distances. This fire could cause casualties even at ranges of 2000 yards or more, thus necessitating the adoption of extended formations at great distances from the enemy lines.[43] Furthermore, the terrain of South Africa, although it varied from region to region, was generally characterised by a combination of rolling *veld* and dominating *kopjes*. Large-scale combat did not take place in built up urban areas or in the forest-like *bushveld*. The combination of long-range rifle fire and a depressing absence of cover meant that the British typically adopted extended formations at the outset of action, even when several miles distant from the enemy lines.[44]

These unique conditions were unlikely to occur in any country other than South Africa.[45] In particular, officers with an eye on future European entanglements noted that the presence of much thicker terrain in Europe made large extensions both impractical and difficult to manage. In South Africa, troops could usually maintain visual contact with their comrades even when widely spaced, but moving through woodland or farmland in Europe would cause men and officers to become hopelessly disconnected. Such problems emerged during the 1904 manoeuvres in Essex.[46] Here, hedgerows, trees and fences caused formations to become disorganised, and infantry were criticised for shaking out into extended formation without giving thought to using the plentiful cover. Extended lines of infantry became completely unmanageable in the dense terrain, with units becoming separated and jumbled; when they encountered the enemy they were so scattered that no real firing line could be formed.[47] Lord Methuen complained, 'I am afraid that our South African experience is still weighing upon our minds in the matter of extension of troops.... I consider that in an enclosed country, stronger and thicker shooting lines are required...'[48]

The second problem related to the opposition. As previously noted, the Boers did not hold positions to the last extremity, rarely launched counter attacks to retake lost ground, and would typically fall back if their opponents could not be stopped by

42 *Elgin Commission*, Vol.2, Q16974, p.288.
43 *Guards' Brigade*, p.18; Major William Balck, 'Lessons of the Boer War and Battle Workings of the Three Arms', *Journal of the Royal United Services Institution*, 48 (1904), pp.1273-1274.
44 *Elgin Commission*, Vol.2, Q19200, p.397.
45 Major C.E. Callwell, 'Artillery Notes from the Veld', *Proceedings of the Royal Artillery Institute*, 28 (1901-1902), pp.282-283.
46 TNA, WO 279/8, Army Manoeuvres 1904, Remarks on Operations in Close Country, pp.34-35.
47 *Ibid*, p.35.
48 *Ibid*. Extracts from Report of Senior Umpire, Blue Force [Lord Methuen], p.78.

firepower. When British charges did occur, it was noted that they were typically in the form of '...one single irregular line, or rather swarm'.[49] Such tactics had been appropriate in South Africa, but several commentators expressed concern that they would not work against a formally trained European opponent who would easily repel such a disorganised charge. Critics also worried that an overly extended British line could be swept away by a sudden counter attack, and expressed concern that the 'swarm' style charges of South Africa would be inadequate against a determined European foe.[50]

However, these debates revealed a fundamental tactical problem. Modern rifle fire was considered effective at 1400 yards. This necessitated the use of extended formation at least 800 yards from the enemy position.[51] Yet, although an extended formations allowed the attacker to close with the enemy, it did not possess enough strength to launch a direct assault once it was within charge range; indeed, there was a danger that it would be so scattered that it would be vulnerable to a swift counter charge. How to cross the fire swept zone and reach assault range, but then reform into a heavy formation that could launch an assault, was a conundrum that puzzled the Army throughout the pre-First World War era. The solution that was reached was a compromise. The firing line would advance in widely extended formation. As the firefight developed and the advance was slowed, the firing line would gradually be built up by supports advancing forward via rushes, covered by the fire from the original line. This would steadily increase the number of riflemen in the front line, contributing weight to the firefight and ultimately building such strength that a decisive charge could be launched.[52]

The practical difficulties of this approach were revealed in the Russo-Japanese War 1904-1905. Lacking mobility, the Japanese were frequently forced to launch frontal attacks against Russian defensive positions. Initially, the Japanese infantry employed a triple line system similar to that used by the Prussians in 1870. However, in the face of modern rifles, machine guns and quick firing artillery, such formations were found to be costly and ineffective, and were quickly abandoned.[53] In their place, the Japanese began to employ widely extended lines similar to those used in South Africa.[54] By the time of the Battle of Mukden (20 February-10 March 1905) Japanese infantry extension had doubled from pre-war guidelines.[55]

---

49   Callwell, *Tactics*, p.63.
50   Lieutenant-Colonel F.N. Maude, 'Continental versus South African Tactics: A Comparison and Reply to Some Critics.' *Journal of the Royal United Services Institution*, Vol. 46, No. 1 (1902), pp.318–54.
51   War Office, *Combined Training 1905* (London, HMSO, 1905), p.101.
52   Major W.D Bird, 'Infantry Fire Tactics', *Journal of the Royal United Services Institution*, Vol. 49, No. 2 (1905), p.1176.
53   General De Negrier, 'Some Lessons of the Russo-Japanese War' *Journal of the Royal United Services Institution*, Vol. 50, No. 2 (1906), p.912.
54   Ian Hamilton, *A Staff Officer's Scrap Book During the Russo-Japanese War* (London, E. Arnold, 1908), Vol. 1, p.307.
55   Major Mitake, 'The Infantry Battle Front', *Journal of the Royal United Services Institution*, 51 (1907), pp.329-330.

However, when using extended formations, the Japanese faced the problems that the British had anticipated with regard to reforming for the charge. Once within assault range, usually judged around 200-300 yards from the enemy trenches, the Japanese were forced to thicken their line. This was a slow, difficult process, often-lasting hours and sometimes spanning entire days.[56] The slow pace of the advance meant that the Japanese frequently had to entrench with each successive advance.[57] A criticism of the approach was that the slow advance cost the attackers a constant stream of casualties and gave the defenders time to prepare for the inevitable assault.[58] However, some German authors argued that the ultimate success of Japanese frontal attacks, regardless of their cost in lives, was a vindication that the British had lacked the moral strength to absorb casualties making frontal assaults in South Africa.[59]

The tactical lessons of the Russo-Japanese War offered new strands of thought for the debate on formations. There was abundant evidence that crossing the fire swept zone was now even harder than in the Anglo-Boer War, but equally the success of Japanese attacks against Russian earthworks suggested that close assault remained possible. The Russo-Japanese War also demonstrated that merely attaining a lodge-ment near the enemy firing line would not be enough to force them from their posi-tion; instead, it was necessary to drive the enemy from their trenches in an assault.

The examples of the Russo-Japanese War gave fresh ammunition to those who questioned the validity of tactics based on South African experience. The core of these concerns related to the difficult process of reforming an extended line into a strong firing line. Complaints were made that the infantry were able to advance skilfully in extended formations during training, but that there was no attempt at any stage in the attack to close up a firing line at a depth greater than 'three or four paces' per man.[60] Even proponents of extension such as Lieutenant-General Sir Ian Hamilton began to express concerns. In a 1906 article, he noted that extension was 'probably the best of the many good ideas derived from the South Africa War' but went on to caution, that even these tactics 'will not bear being turned into a fetish.'[61] In 1907, John French sounded a similar note, stating, 'I think it is well worth serious consideration whether we are not overdoing the so-called lessons of the South African War as applied to possible European war against masses of trained soldiers.'[62] By 1909, French was so

56   De Negrier, 'Some Lessons', pp.915-916.
57   Lieutenant Colonel G.M. Heath, 'Field Engineering in the Light of Modern Warfare', *Journal of the Royal United Services Institution*, 50 (1906), p.314.
58   *Ibid*, p.315.
59   Captain Ashley W. Barret, 'Lessons to be Learned by Regimental Officers from the Russo-Japanese War', *Journal of the Royal United Services Institution*, 51 (1907), pp.815-816.
60   TNA, WO 163/14, Inspector General of Forces Report for 1908, p.169 [Hereafter referred to as IGF Report].
61   Lieutenant-General Sir Ian Hamilton, 'The Training of Troops During 1906', *Journal of the Royal United Services Institution*, 50 (1906), p.1522.
62   TNA, WO 163/13, IGF Report for 1907, p.80.

frustrated with the failure to reform extended lines that he suggested an increase in close order drill work to help inculcate the importance of forming a powerful, disciplined line for the decisive attack.[63]

However, others went even further and denigrated the entire ethos of extended formations. The reaction against extension reached its peak in an article that appeared in the General Staff supported publication *Army Review* in 1912. Criticising British assault training, the author, Brigadier-General F.C. Carter, felt the flaws were due to 'The fact that the fetish of "over-extension" which, after the early disaster of the South African War, was set up as a God in the Temple of Mars, still claims some devotees among our senior officers.'[64] Urging heavy formations and frontal attacks, the article concluded:

> We must harden our hearts, as our forefathers did of old to the heavy losses that will occur…a steady advance of strong, disciplined and brave men, prepared to suffer losses, to use their bayonets with effect and to snatch victory from the jaws of death.[65]

Yet despite a number of calls for a counter reformation following the Russo-Japanese War, and the urging of officers such as Carter to follow the continental example, extension remained a key part of British infantry tactics throughout the period. Although the scale was reduced from the 20 yards per man that had been approved at Aldershot immediately after the Boer War, infantry extension in the attack remained wider in the Army than any of its European contemporaries.

There were several reasons for this development. Firstly, as alluded to by Carter, a number of senior officers retained a firm belief in the value of extension. Ian Hamilton was perhaps the most vociferous of these, writing in 1908 '…the reaction against the exaggerated extensions adopted during and immediately after the South African War has gone far enough… it is better for formations to be too open than too concentrated.'[66] Lieutenant-General Sir Charles Douglas was also a proponent of extended formations, cautioning infantry under his command in 1909, 'I cannot help thinking that we are inclined to neglect some of the lessons of the South African War which are applicable to European warfare; lessons which we learnt by bitter experience.'[67] A memo issued by Aldershot Command in 1913 during Lieutenant-General Sir Douglas

---

63   TNA, WO 163/15, IGF Report for 1909, pp.306-307.
64   Brigadier General F.C Carter, 'Our Failings in the Assault', *Army Review*, 3 (1912), p.99.
65   *Ibid*, p.104.
66   General Sir Ian Hamilton, 'Remarks by General Sir Ian Hamilton, K.C.B, D.S.O, C-in-C Southern Command, on the Training of Troops under His Command during 1908' *Journal of the Royal United Services Institution*, 52 (1908), pp.89-90.
67   TNA, WO 279/524, Remarks by Lieutenant-General Sir C.W. Douglas, Commanding in Chief, Southern Command, on the Training of the Troops in the Command During 1909, 28 October 1909.

Haig's tenure cautioned against overly dense lines, noting 'The importance of having sufficient weight of numbers well forward in the final stage of an attack does *not* mean starting operations with these men in the firing line' (emphasis in original).[68]

A second reason for the decision was the fact that the alternatives were regarded as unviable. A call to absorb casualties in mass attacks on the German or French model was not in keeping with the military or political goals of the small British Expeditionary Force. One anonymous officer summed up the problem, noting the Army was '...bound for political, financial and national reasons, to economise life, and to win our campaigns with the fewest possible casualties.'[69] Discussions at the 1911 General Staff Conference regarding the possibility of copying the methods used by the French infantry in the charge concluded that such methods were impractical and incompatible with the bulk of British regulations.[70]

These factors meant that the guidance provided by official publications continued to advise the use of extension, albeit tailored to local circumstances, with manuals stressing that it was a matter for individual commanders to decide based on the local situation.[71] This tactical freedom often resulted in individual battalions and brigades demonstrating a distinct preference for extended order tactics. This in turn could shape divisional tactics. In a 1912 inspection, it was noted that while 2nd, 3rd and 4th Divisions each had their own preferred method of attack, each division employed a broad, extended infantry line to develop the action.[72] Only 4th Division attempted to use a reserve line to carry its firing line forward in a decisive frontal attack. In a distinct echo of Boer War tactics, both 2nd and 3rd Division preferred to use extended infantry to pin the front while other troops sought to turn the enemy flank.[73]

However, although extension remained a cornerstone of infantry tactics, the problem of how to reform an extended line for decisive action remained. *Infantry Training 1911* saw fire support as the key to solving the problem, emphasising the importance of covering fire from rifles, machine guns and artillery in allowing forward movement.[74] Strenuous efforts were made to inculcate the importance of fire and movement, although much to the frustration of the School of Musketry, there was no commensurate increase in automatic weaponry.[75] There were also some imaginative efforts to solve the problems of bringing troops to the firing line. Experiments

68   TNA, WO 279/53, Aldershot Command Papers, Comments on the Training Season 1913, pp.7-8.
69   'Solando', 'The Decisive Range', *United Service Magazine* (June 1904), p.296.
70   Joint Services Command and Staff College Library, Report on a Conference of General Staff Officers at the Staff College, 9-12 January 1911, pp.11-13, 28.
71   *Combined Training 1905*, p.101; War Office, *Field Service Regulations 1909* (London, H.M.S.O., 1909), p.138.
72   TNA, WO 163/18, IGF Report for 1912, pp.566-568.
73   Ibid, p.567.
74   War Office, *Infantry Training 1911*, (London, H.M.S.O., 1911), pp.104 – 115.
75   On rearmament, see; C.H.B. Pridham, *Superiority of Fire: A Short History of Rifles and Machine Guns* (London, Hutchinson, 1945), pp.53-60; Dominick Graham. 'The British

at Aldershot in 1913 used specially trained ground scouts to find covered approaches for the supports to reach the firing line.[76] In the same year, there were discussions involving the use of man-portable, steel shields to help the firing line establish itself, while larger, wheeled versions were proposed for use in allowing supporting troops to close up.[77] However, lack of time and the need to avoid causing too much damage to the ground upon which training took place meant that the use of entrenchment as an aid to reforming the line appears to have been seriously neglected.

Conclusions

Nevertheless, despite the long running debate and continuing, unresolved issues with regard to reforming the firing line, it is significant that once war had broken out in Europe, the tactics for crossing ground that had worked in South Africa were cited as good examples for the current conflict. *Notes from the Front,* a handbook of tactical advice printed and issued for the Army after the opening months of hostilities in 1914, reiterated the value of extension, stating a formation with '8 or 10 paces intervals [is thought to be] the least vulnerable.'[78] Additionally, in a September 1914 memorandum, Brigadier General Johnnie Gough called for increased usage of dispersed 'loose and irregular elastic formations' as previously employed in South Africa.[79]

In retrospect, it is clear that the long running debate over the value of extension revealed some of the difficulties associated with extracting colonial lessons for application in modern, European warfare. Although the core principles of extension were largely correct, the unique nature of the war against the Boers made direct replication of South African assault tactics impractical. Although there were those within the Army who felt extended formations were overrated, the official manuals continued to endorse their employment, albeit with the caveat of maintaining flexibility. Thus, despite the controversy over extension and its relative value, by the eve of the First World War, British infantry formations were realistic and appropriate for crossing the fire swept zone. Problems persisted, especially with regard to the difficult task of thickening the line at the decisive moment, but the necessity for dispersion, cover, and concealment remained valuable and enduring lessons. The need for revised infantry formations was one of the most striking lessons of the Anglo-Boer War; fortunately, for the British, it remained a key component of infantry tactics.

Expeditionary Force in 1914 and the Machine Gun', *Military Affairs,* 46 (4) (1982), pp.190–93.
76   TNA, WO 279/53, Aldershot Command Papers, Comments on the Training Season 1913, p.7.
77   Major G.H.J. Rooke, 'Shielded Infantry and the Decisive Frontal Attack', *Journal of the Royal United Services Institution,* 58 (1914), pp.771–84.
78   War Office, *Notes from the Front Part II* (London, H.M.S.O, 1915), p.13.
79   TNA, WO 95/588, Gough Memorandum 27 September 1914.

6

Learning to Manage the Army
Edward Ward, Halford Mackinder and the Army Administration Course at the London School of Economics, 1907-1914

Peter Grant

In his recent article on the Army Administration Course at the London School of Economics (LSE), Sloan rightly hails the course as 'a radical experiment in British military education.'[1] Sloan's article is in many ways comprehensive and is especially good on the role played in the course by the LSE's Director, Halford Mackinder. However, Sloan gives insufficient coverage to two respects. First is the highly significant contribution to the development of the course that was made by the Permanent Secretary at the War Office, Sir Edward Ward, second, is the far-reaching influence the course had on later thinking beyond the confines of the British Army. Sloan incorrectly describes Ward as the Under-Secretary of State for War, an error a number of other sources also make. Ward had assumed the permanent secretary role in 1901. Seen as a stage towards the establishment of separate business schools within British universities, this revolutionary course in educating military personnel in business and administrative topics at higher degree level also acted as a precursor for later business related university education alongside similar LSE-inspired courses for those in banking and the railways.

Often cited as the greatest of Britain's peacetime holders of the post of Secretary of State for War, Richard Burton Haldane's modernisation of the War Office was 'little short of revolutionary.'[2] During the reforms of 1905 to 1912, Haldane relied on the assistance of a number of military experts and their contribution, most notably

---

1   Geoff Sloan, 'Haldane's Mackindergarten: A Radical Experiment in British Military Education', *War in History*, 19 (3) (2012), p.351.
2   Simon Higgens, 'How was Richard Haldane able to reform the British Army? An historical assessment using a contemporary change management model', (MPhil Thesis, University of Birmingham, 2010), p.68; K.W. Mitchinson, *Defending Albion: Britain's Home Army 1908-1919* (Basingstoke, Palgrave Macmillan, 2005), p.3. See also R. Blake,

Major-General Douglas Haig.[3] One figure whose contribution to the Haldane Reforms has been underplayed (even totally forgotten) was the Permanent Secretary at the War Office during that period, Sir Edward Ward. Ward was a former army supply officer, it was his ingenuity that ensured the survival of the garrison and civilians of Ladysmith during the siege, and organiser of the Royal Military Tournament who, after retirement, went on to become Director General of Voluntary Organisations during the Great War.[4] During the war Ward also headed the Camps Library that supplied books to the troops, was an extremely active Chairman of the Council of the RSPCA, Honorary Treasurer and member of the General Purposes Committee of the West Indian Contingent Committee (which looked after the welfare of West Indian and Bermudan troops), Assistant Inspector of Shells for the Ministry of Munitions and Commandant-in-Chief of the Metropolitan Special Constabulary.

The Role of Sir Edward Ward

Haldane had great faith in Ward and gave him significant additional responsibilities. Ward was a key figure in many critical improvements to the War Office as he brought his organisational and managerial skills to bear. Haldane often relied on advice from key specialists and, in this case, his chosen specialist advisor was Ward who had first made proposals along similar lines in 1903-04 during the attempted reforms of Haldane's predecessor, H.O. Arnold-Foster, which envisaged the creation of an entirely new class of reserve officer.[5] Teargarden suggests that Haldane's 'greatest asset as Secretary of State was his profound ignorance on military matters. He was therefore able to form an independent judgement.'[6] However, Higgins debunks the idea of Haldane's complete ignorance on military matters suggesting this was a deliberate 'cover' in order to woo the top Generals to his way of thinking.[7] From May 1906, Ward chaired the weekly Directors meetings with important operational issues discussed and actions decided. Like several other key Army officers, including Haig, Ward shared Haldane's views on the need for significant reform and reorganisation to turn the Army into a modern fighting force. Ward threw himself enthusiastically into these tasks, which included officer recruitment, plans for mobilisation and the

'Great Britain: The Crimean War to the First World War' in Michael Howard (ed.) *Soldiers and Governments* (London, Eyre and Spottiswode, 1957), p.34.

3   Most recently in Gary Sheffield's *The Chief: Douglas Haig and the British Army* (London, Aurum Press, 2011), pp.58-60.

4   For a full examination of Ward's innovative military and managerial career, see: Peter Grant, *Philanthropy and Voluntary Action in the First World War* (London: Routledge, 2014).

5   The National Archives (TNA), WO 32/6384, Report of Ward Committee on Organisation and Establishment of Civil Departments 1903.

6   Ernest Teagarden, *Haldane at the War Office: A Study in Organization and Management* (New York, Gordon Press, 1976), p.26.

7   Higgins, 'Richard Haldane', pp.52-56, 71-72.

re-organisation of the Army Medical Department and that of the War Office itself. Between 1907 and 1909, Ward created the framework of the Imperial General Staff that came into existence in November 1909 and was Chairman of the Committee on Civil Employment of Ex-Soldiers and Sailors, a cause close to his heart and demonstrating his keen humanitarian concern.[8] Another of Ward's achievements was the creation of the Officers Training Corps (OTC) that Haldane recognised as Ward's brainchild by making him the chair of the committee in August 1906.[9] Ward was responsible for the compilation of the original 'War Book', which set out, in detail, the actions required on mobilization. Though it was later revised, it was on Ward's basic plan that subsequent versions were based and the fact that mobilization went so smoothly in 1914 was partly a testimony to Ward's organisational skills. In 1908-09, he worked with Haig, now Director of Staff Duties, on the production of 'a codified set of manuals dealing with administration and training' that became *Field Service Regulations Parts 1 and 2*. Williams noted that, 'It was very largely his [Ward's] hand which guided Mr Haldane in his efforts to create the Expeditionary Force and the Territorial Force between 1906 and 1908.' Though written in the 1960s, Williams, unlike many others, is not a Haig critic and so it is unlikely he deliberately overplayed Ward's contribution.[10] In 1908, Ward authored the *Territorial Force Regulations* and became Honorary Colonel of the 2nd London Territorial Division. He was also Chairman of the County of London Territorial Force Association.

Between them, the Haldane reforms transformed the War Office into 'a form so effective that it remained substantially unchanged for seventy years...The new organisation was reminiscent of the board of directors in a modern service company.'[11] In other words, Haldane, Ward and their collaborators were bringing to bear innovative business techniques to the field of military management. This was in a period when modern management theory was in its infancy. The ideas of American Frederick Winslow Taylor were beginning to be known, and were included in the LSE Course. However, Ward's ideas in particular were closer to those of the French pioneer of modern management theory, Henri Fayol. Tadman suggests that:

8   Colonel G. Williams, *Citizen Soldiers of the Royal Engineers Transportation and Movements and the Army Service Corps 1859-1965* (Ashford, Royal Corps of Transport, 1965), p.33.
9   Peter Simkins, *Kitchener's Army: The Raising of the New Armies, 1914-1916* (Manchester, Manchester University Press, 1988), p 12; Ian Worthington, 'Socialization, Militarization and Officer Recruiting: The Development of the Officers Training Corps', *Military Affairs*, 43 (2) (April 1979), pp.90-96.
10   Williams, *Citizen Soldiers of the Royal Engineers*, p.26, 33.
11   Michael Tadman, 'The War Office: A Study of its Development as an Organisational System, 1870-1904', (PhD Thesis, King's College London, 1992), pp.240-256.

…these advances in their appreciation of management principles paralleled the work of the great theorists [notably Taylor and Fayol] quite closely, except for this vital difference – that they anticipated the published works by several decades.[12]

Fayol's ideas rather than Taylor's have stood the test of time. Wren concludes that:

…much of the present-day management literature has been built on Fayol's ideas and terminology that it is difficult to see the uniqueness of his insights. For his time and in the context of the paucity of management literature, his ideas were fresh, illuminating, and milestones on the path of the evolving discipline of management.[13]

Tadman directly links the thinking that characterised the reforms overseen by Lord Esher, Haldane and Ward as directly comparable to Fayol's principles of good management. Most of all Ward had the conviction, like Fayol, that future senior managers should receive specialist managerial education and training.[14] Higgens too recognises the mechanisms of Haldane's reforms as mirroring modern management techniques by demonstrating that what was at work was a classic 'change management process' predicated upon Haldane's deep interest in Hegelian philosophy. Higgens concludes that Haldane 'understood the intellectual complexities of institutional change', it is clear that in his many, and varied roles Ward shared the same understanding.[15]

In all of the above tasks, Ward utilised his previous administrative experience from service in the field in Ashanti and South Africa as well as his organisation of the Royal Military Tournament, putting forward practical managerial solutions to issues that had eluded others. Hailed, as the 'Saviour of Ladysmith' for his organisation of supplies during the siege, Ward, as head of the Tournament, was responsible for the tripling of profits. Ward's belief in sound management and business training was prominent in many of the areas under his auspices. However, in one scheme in particular these principles were taken a stage further, again anticipating much of the later work of management theorists; this was the creation of the Army Administration Course at LSE.

12   Tadman 'The War Office', p.261.
13   Daniel Wren, *The History of Management Thought*, Second Edition (New York: John Wiley, 2005), p.218.
14   For further close similarities between Ward's and Fayol's ideas, see: Ward, *Supply and Transport on Active Service* (Dublin, Sibley and Co, 1893), p.11. Also see papers by two of his protégés from the LSE course: Oscar Striedinger, 'Army Organisation', *Army Service Corps Quarterly*, 3 (1909), pp.365-369, and, especially, Major E.E. Carter, 'The Science and Art of Army Administration', *Army Service Corps Quarterly*, 3 (1909), pp.370-379.
15   Higgens. 'Richard Haldane', abstract.

The Creation of the Army Administration Course

As part of Haldane's extensive reforms, one of the main aims was the creation of an administrative staff for the War Office and Army separate from the General Staff but with the same 'real and far-reaching' strategic control as the General Staff.[16] The subsequent LSE course is, like the creation of the OTC, credited to Haldane, especially as he was a founder of the LSE.[17] This is only partially correct; Ward was as much the initiator as Haldane. Ward had been an administrative officer himself for almost 30 years, so this was his specialist subject; Ward had espoused many of the principles behind the course as early as 1893 and he put forward the idea for the scheme in a memorandum entitled 'The need for a trained administrative staff' in February 1906.[18] Clearly though, both men were of the same view on the topic and in the paper, 'Ward propounded the then revolutionary idea that modern soldiers needed training in modern administrative techniques.'[19] Ward enclosed a draft for a three-year staff training course, of which six months were to be spent on accountancy, commercial methods, public administration and finance, production and trade, railway administration and transport and commercial and international law. The final scheme combined Haldane's aim with Ward's belief that management principles needed to be inculcated throughout the administration of both the War Office and the army. Ward was one of the first to apply business methods in Whitehall, some nine years before Lloyd-George utilised similar principles in his wartime coalition, and the first to introduce management training for civil servants and the armed forces.

Ward and Haldane's conviction that business methods were needed place them within the broader movement for national efficiency that gained credibility after the Boer War. This movement had been vindicated by the failures of the army in South Africa and the enquiries after it, which concluded that major changes were needed. During the Boer War itself, *The Times* correspondent, Leopold Amery demanded, 'nothing less than a revolution' in army organisation and administration. Britain needed an expert army, one in which:

16 Edward M Spiers *Haldane: An Army Reformer* (Edinburgh, Edinburgh University Press, 1980), p.151.
17 *Ibid.*
18 Ward, *Supply and Transport,* pp.18 and 25-26; TNA, WO 163/746, Minutes of proceedings of the Permanent Executive Committee of the War Office (5 January to 4 March 1904) and Important Treasury and War Office Decisions 1904-1906.
19 D.C. Watt, 'The London University Class for Military Administrators 1906-31: A Study of the British Approach to Civil-Military Relations', *LSE Quarterly,* 2 (2) (Summer 1988), pp.157-158.

...the whole caste system the whole idea of the Army as a sort of puppet show where smartness, guilt braid... must vanish and give place to something real, something business like.[20]

Amery's comments gained official support in the recommendations of the Committee on the Reorganisation of the War Office in 1901, chaired by Clinton Dawkins, a partner in the American banking firm of J.P. Morgan.[21] Guided mainly by their public experience the committee concluded that:

A general, if not a precise analogy, can be established between the conduct of large business undertakings and that of the War Office. There are certain well-defined principles of management in all well-conducted business corporations, and the more closely the War Office can be brought into conformity with such principles, the more successful will be its administration.[22]

Among the ideas, the Committee considered transferable were the division of work into well-defined sections; adequate delegation and decentralisation of powers; effective systems that avoided excessive form filling and providing adequate, co-ordination between departments; all principles that remain pertinent in modern management practice.

The movement for national efficiency was led by the former Liberal Prime Minister Lord Rosebery, who had been advocating the need for Britain to be put on a business footing since the 1880s. Other prominent Liberals and left-of-centre figures including Haldane, Halford Mackinder, the polymath Director of LSE, closely associated with the development of geopolitical theory, and the Fabians Sidney and Beatrice Webb, who along with Haldane had helped establish the LSE, supported it. Drawing on a wider political consensus was the dining club the 'Co-Efficients' formed by Leopold Amery and Beatrice Webb in November 1902 to air strategies that could be used to promote national efficiency. While it lasted, it disbanded in 1908 over disagreements around tariff reform; the grouping included those previously mentioned plus Sir Edward Grey, Clinton Dawkins, Bertrand Russell, H.G. Wells and George Bernard Shaw.[23]

20   J. Barnes and D. Nicholson, (eds.), *The Leo Amery Diaries, 1896-1929*, (London, Hutchinson, 1980), p.33.
21   1901 [Cmd. 580 and 581] *Report of the Committee on War Office Organisation appointed by the Secretary of State for War*, 1901, p.xl.
22   [Cmd. 580] *Committee on War Office Organisation*, pp.2-3.
23   W. Funnell, 'National Efficiency, Military Accounting and the Business of War', *Critical Perspectives on Accounting*, 17 (6) (2006), pp.732-733.

Halford Mackinder and the Committee

Halford Mackinder had already introduced programmes at the LSE to serve the executives of the railway, banking and insurance industries as well as the Indian Civil Service. Ward had clearly already discussed the idea of a course with Mackinder and Sidney Webb because on the day he drafted his memo he lunched with Mackinder who then wrote to Webb saying 'it is practically certain that the scheme we blocked out together will go through.'[24] This is a further indication that Ward was at least as involved in the scheme's genesis as was Haldane. In support of the principle of a course, an article had appeared in the *Journal of the Royal United Service Institution* the year before written by Captain H.A. Young of the Indian Ordnance Department. Young compared the army to, 'a vast business organisation' and said that what was needed were people who were, 'businessmen first, and officers last.'[25] The elements of the Geography syllabus for such a course had also been developed by the then Colonel H.S.G. Miles and A.J. Herbotson in the latter's article in the *Geographical Journal* and in a letter Sidney Webb described Ward's contribution to the course as 'indispensable'.[26]

The scheme received the official go-ahead six months later and immediately thereafter, an advisory board was established under Ward's chairmanship. Its senior military member was Director of Staff Duties, Lieutenant-General H.D. Hutchinson who was replaced a year later by Douglas Haig when he took up that post. The other military members were Director of Supplies, Brigadier-General Frederick Clayton (later Inspector-General of Communications in France during the war); Director of Recruiting and Organization, Major-General H.S.G. Miles; Director of Fortifications and Works, Brigadier-General R.M. Ruck and Commandant of the Ordnance College at Woolwich, Colonel G.R. Townsend. Civilian members in addition to Mackinder and Webb were the General Manager of the London and North Western Railway, Sir Frederick Harrison, Sir Hugh Bell, a steel manufacturer from Middlesbrough, and the Governor of the Union of London and Smith's Bank Sir Felix Schuster. Others who later served on the committee included several who featured in prominent roles during the war including Generals Henry Wilson, in his

24 B.W. Blouet, *Halford Mackinder: A Biography* (College Station Texas, A&M University Press, 1987), p.131. Watt 'The London University Class', p.158. Kreis points out that railway workshop were one place where scientific management had made considerable progress in Britain before 1914. Steven Kreis, 'The Diffusion of an Idea: A History of Scientific Management in Britain, 1890-1945', (PhD Thesis, University of Missouri-Columbia, 1990).

25 Captain H. Young, 'Practical Economy in the Army', *Journal of the Royal United Service Institution*, Vol. 50 (July to December 1906), pp.1281-1285.

26 A.J. Herbotson 'The Geographical Training of Army Officers in the Universities', *Geographical Journal*, 21 (1903), pp.465-6; Bodleian Library, *Papers of Percy Noble*, MSS Autogr, C. 17, No. 495, Letter from Webb to Ward, 23 December, 1910.

capacity as Commandant of the Staff College, Launcelot Kiggell, later Haig's Chief of Staff, and William Robertson, Chief of the Imperial General Staff for the majority of the war. Wilson was about the only senior officer to criticise the course because it would 'do an infinity of harm' to the Staff College and 'a complete separation of the Administrative and General Staff.'[27] Bell, Mackinder, Shuster and Webb served throughout the eight years of the course, Mackinder remaining on the Committee after his resignation from the Directorship of the LSE. Mackinder was persuaded to resign and take up politics full time by Leo Amery and Lord Milner. He subsequently became Unionist MP for Glasgow Camlachie from 1910 to 1922.[28] The committee members appear to have got on well and often dined together, Haig being a frequent, and perhaps unlikely, guest of the Webb's.[29]

The Army Administration Course

Though Ward would have liked to have a period of business training that lasted a full three years it was unrealistic for officers to remove themselves from the prospects of promotion for this length of time and so the final agreement was for a six-month course.[30] The military correspondent of *The Times*, Charles à Court Repington, who also thought the course should be extended to selected General Staff officers, supported Ward.[31] The first course ran from January to July 1907, with the second following from October 1907 to March 1908. Six further courses ran annually from October to March and in total 245 officers, mainly of the rank of Captain and Major, attended the course from all branches of the army with the exception of the cavalry. The absence of cavalry officers is not explained in any of the sources but may be connected with the structure of careers in that arm. Additionally, a small number of officers from the reserve list who attended at their own expense. This explains a proportion of the 'Other' listed in Table 1 opposite.

Addressing the opening day of the initial course Mackinder expressed the view that:

> The Army is the greatest single business in this country… It is true, of course, that it is necessarily conducted on a different principle from ordinary city business. The Army is not conducted for profit, but to produce power. This power is used during peace time in order to maintain peace, and in war time to achieve victory.[32]

---

27   Sloan 'Haldane's Mackindergarten', p.331.
28   Blouet, *Halford Mackinder*, p.138.
29   Spiers, *Haldane*, p.151.
30   Watt, 'The London University Class', pp.162-163.
31   'Military Notes, *The Times*, 30 October 1906, p.15.
32   1907 [Cmd. 3696] *Report of the Advisory Board, London School of Economics, on the First Course at the London School of Economics, January to July, 1907, for the Training of Officers*

Table 1 Percentage of Participants in the LSE Army Administrative Course 1907-1914

Branch	Course 1	Course 2	Course 3	Course 4	Course 5	Course 6	Course 7	Course 8
ASC	39	43	47	37	32	26	23	31
Infantry	26	23	23	37	29	35	37	28
Artillery	16	13	17	13	10	9	10	6
Ordnance	10	10	10	10	19	19	13	10
Indian	3	3	3	–	6	9	10	9
RE	6	3	–	–	–	–	–	–
Other	–	3	–	–	3	–	7	6
Total numbers on each course	31	30	30	30	31	31	30	32

Mackinder noted that it was only recently that those in business had recognised the importance of professional training but that:

> What the railways, and what the city, among its more enlightened representatives, is beginning to feel is that administration requires a training similar to the professional trainings, and that experience, in the face of German and other foreign competition, is showing that the old typically British way of blundering into the position of a responsible administrator will no longer do.[33]

So there was recognition both of the novelty of this approach, professional training in management being in its infancy in business let alone in the army, and of the 'threat' that German efficiency posed with its highly trained specialist administrators.

Lectures were given on 14 subjects covering six broader areas: accounting and business methods, commercial law, statistics, transport, banking and economics. They were supplemented by numerous 'observation visits' to such enterprises as the offices of *The Times*, the Great Western Railway Works, the London Docks, the London Omnibus Works, the Railway Clearing House, the Houses of Parliament and Lloyds. Eminent experts in their fields who were drawn from business, the universities and government instructed students. Haldane was a frequent lecturer and several others were politically from the radical wing including Webb, who lectured on the organisation of trade unions, Hastings Lees-Smith, later a Labour Cabinet Minister (on economics) and the Fabian Socialist Graham Wallas, one of the seminal figures in the development of social science (on public administration).[34] Enjoyed by the students,

for the Higher Appointments on the Administrative Staff of the Army and for the charge of Departmental Services, p.11.
33   [Cmd. 3696] *Advisory Board Report 1907*, p 12.
34   Funnell, 'National Efficiency ', p.736.

as one of them wrote 'as a phrase-maker…[Wallas' lectures in particular]…ranks with Bishop Wilberforce.'[35] The course therefore had a radically different content to both that of the staff officer course at the Army Staff College Camberley and the War Course at the Royal Naval War College, both of which focused on military strategy and tactics.[36]

At the outset Mackinder told students that the 'syllabuses are tentative, and not yet complete.'[37] As would be expected in a new course, the balance of topics adjusted as time went on. There was initially rather too much theory, too much history and insufficient reference to military problems and so the second course included some significant changes with increased time given to statistics, public administration and marine transportation at the expense of accounting and economic geography.[38] By the time of the third course a good balance appears to have been struck and the only, significant change to the curriculum thereafter was that Business Organisation, how to structure and organise enterprises for maximum efficiency, became increasingly important. This module included the recognition that 'business organization is organization of the social organism.'[39] It emphasised the importance of process and the elimination of waste and, from 1912, included study of Frederick Taylor's ideas, which had been published in his book *The Principles of Scientific Management* only the previous year. This introduced students to theories of management that were at the forefront of contemporary thinking. Examination questions covered a range of topics that became highly relevant in the future careers of the participants. Examples include comparing the financial resources of Britain, France and Germany in view of an outbreak of war (1907), the impact of conscription in wartime (1908), the pros and cons of local recruiting for the Army (1910) and the impact on the London market and unemployment in the event of a major war (1912 and 1913). As one graduate of the course wrote, it taught the importance of structure and process in business methods, 'to consider ourselves as tiny cogs and parts of a vast plant of machinery, each mutually dependent, mutually working in a great common cause.'[40] This *esprit d'armee*, Airey, suggested, should supplement the already existing regimental spirit. The modular content of the course mirrors in several respects the content and structure of modern Business School syllabi, notably their Executive MBAs.

---

35   R.B. Airey, 'The London School of Economics and the Army', *Army Review*, IV (1913), p.472.
36   Sloan, 'Haldane's Mackindergarten' p.327; Andrew Lambert, 'The Naval War Course: Some Principals of Maritime Strategy and the Origins of "The British Way in Warfare"' in Keith Neilson and Greg Kennedy (eds.) *The British Way in Warfare: Power and the International System, 1856-1956* (Farnham: Ashgate, 2010), pp.219-56.
37   *Advisory Board Report 1907* (Cd. 3696), p.12.
38   Watt, 'The London University Class', pp.164-165.
39   1912-13 [Cmd. 6285] *Report of Sixth Course, 5th October 1911 to 27th March 1912*, p.5.
40   Airey, 'The London School of Economics', p.468.

The course became affectionately known as 'Haldane's Mackindergarden' and its immediate impact was to assist the LSE's finances, allowing them to open a refectory serving all staff and students.[41] It also had the significant result of widening the students' perspective on the world, including the fact that women too could be intellectuals. 'The atmosphere at Clare Market is valuable' Major Airey confirmed. It provided 'social intercourse with men, women and research students ... who are all so different from the average soldier.'[42] Lawrence Dicksee, the course's main accountancy lecturer, was in no doubt that, the course significantly improved military efficiency and that it was responsible for the 'wonderful success of transport and supply' in the early part of the war.[43] Dicksee became the first Professor of Accounting at any British university, holding the post at the University of Birmingham. Those who went through the course became senior administrative officers during the war and had a profound influence upon the supply and management of the army. Examples include:

- G.M. Heath - Chief Engineer for 2nd Corps then 1st Army 1915-16. Engineer in Chief GHQ from November 1917.
- C.W. Gwynn - Director of Military Artillery with the Australian Army during the war. Commandant of the Staff College, Camberley 1926-31. Long has described him as 'One of the outstanding staff officers of the Army, and in peace a notable trainer of future senior commanders.'[44]
- W.A.C. Denny - the first Director General of Military Intelligence of Canada. This appointment may also have been connected with Ward who had a strong link with the Canadian forces. He had been an Honorary Colonel of the Canadian Army Service Corps since 1904. He was a friend of Sam Hughes the Canadian Minister for Militia and Defence during the war and even helped organise Sidney and Beatrice Webb's holiday to that country.[45]
- E.E. Carter - Director of Supplies at GHQ from 1915 until the end of the war. The history of the Royal Army Service Corps (RASC) notes that, 'it was largely due to General Carter that the Army was better fed than any other' during the First World War.[46]

---

41   The nickname came from the student magazine 'The Clare Market Review'. Blouet, *Halford Mackinder*, p.132.
42   Airey, 'The London School of Economics', p.473.
43   L.R. Dicksee, *Business Methods and the War. (Four lectures.)*, (Cambridge, University Press. 1915), pp.71-2.
44   Gavin Long, 'Gwynn, Sir Charles William (1870–1963)', *Australian Dictionary of Biography, National Centre of Biography*, Australian National University, http://adb.anu. edu.au/biography/gwynn-sir-charles-william-6511/text11175, accessed 30 October 2010.
45   M. Young, *Army Service Corps* (Barnsley, Leo Cooper, 2000), p.23; *Percy Noble Papers*, Nos. 145, 147 and 494.
46   Anon, *The Short History of the Royal Army Service Corps* (Aldershot, Gale and Polden, 1939), p.59.

- W.K. Tarver - Deputy Director at the War Office from March 1916. Inspector of the RASC from 1925-9 when he became Colonel Commandant of the RASC.
- C.D.R. Watts - Assisted in instruction on the LSE course in 1908-9. Director of Ordnance Services 1928-31. Colonel Commandant of the Royal Army Ordnance Corps from 1932.
- F.F. Ready - Adjutant-General in Mesopotamia. General Officer Commanding Northern Ireland District in 1926, before becoming GOC of the 1st Division at Aldershot Command in 1929 and then Quartermaster-General to the Forces in 1931.

One aspect of the war that gets unanimous praise is its logistical administration and part of the groundwork for this success was laid in the eight courses of 1907-14. When, after the war, the LSE tried to have it resurrected they commented that 'its value has been testified to be very satisfactory in the War just ended', and this was a major influence in the course's revival in 1924 under William Beveridge, the then Director of the LSE.[47] However, the course was finally discontinued in 1932 in the wake of economies during the Great Depression. Funnell has described the course as 'amongst the most innovative strategies to raise the commercial awareness and accounting expertise of army administrators' and demonstrates how it had a significant impact upon the efficient operation of the Ministry of Munitions.[48]

Conclusion

In his inaugural speech in 1907 Mackinder had stated that what the devisors of the course had in mind was 'to do something more than merely teach and learn; we have to evolve a tradition.'[49] This view was clearly supported at the highest levels of the army as Funnell has commented:

> the creation of an Advisory Board...on which sat some of the most senior officers of the various army departments, was a clear indication of the importance with which the army, the War Office and the government regarded the new Army Class.[50]

The course demonstrates that many of the senior administrative officers and several of the senior commanders of the First World War, not least Douglas Haig, were well-versed in modern business management principles, including the latest thinking from the United States on scientific management. It ensured that Britain had a core group

---

47   Funnell, 'National Efficiency ', p.738.
48   Funnell, 'National Efficiency ', pp.719-720 and p.736.
49   *Report of the Advisory Board 1907* (Cd 3696), p.14.
50   Funnell, 'National Efficiency ', p.736.

of middle-ranking officers with sound administrative training during and after the First World War.

Sloan agrees with this assessment and suggests that the course may have influenced the thinking of Lloyd-George's government in appointing top civil executives like Sir Eric Geddes to key wartime posts.[51] Stoddart has summarised the courses as providing 'a precedent for the later university training of Army and Air Force cadets in wartime... It was the beginning of the thinking soldiers' army' and Funnell has suggested that it was a 'revolutionary innovation in the education of British army officers and in the approach of the War Office to army administration.'[52] There is a good case to be made that the LSE Army Class attempted, and was partially successful, in initiating a management revolution within the administration of the Army.

51   Sloan, 'Haldane's Mackindergarten', p.350.
52   D.R. Stoddart, 'Geography and War: The "New Geography" and the "New Army" in England, 1889-1914', *Political Geography*, Vol. 11, No. 1, (1992), pp.95-97. Funnell, 'National Efficiency', p.736.

7

'Oil Fuel Will Absolutely Revolutionize Naval Strategy'
The Royal Navy's Adoption of Oil before the First World War

Martin Gibson

HMS *Dreadnought* is famous for being both the world's first all big gun battleship and the first battleship to be powered by turbine engines. It is less well known that her engines were fuelled by a mixture of coal and oil, making her the first battleship to be designed to burn oil, although others had been converted to do so.[1] The first warships to be designed to use both oil and coal were the Italian cruisers *Vettor Pisani* and *Carlo Alberto*, launched in 1895-96. The Italians did not follow up with oil fuelled battleships because they lacked secure supplies.[2] Admiral Sir Frederic Dreyer later wrote that HMS *Dreadnought* used both fuels only because supplies were not secure enough to switch fully to oil.[3] The Royal Navy (RN) led the world in the adoption of oil instead of coal to fuel warships, but little has been published on this innovation.[4] The literature concentrates on the involvement of Winston Churchill towards the end of the process and on relations between the Admiralty and oil companies; it does not analyse the manner in which the RN used a technological innovation to transform itself via a process of observation and experiment.[5]

---

1   See: Robert Blyth, Andrew Lambert and Jan Rüger, (eds), *The Dreadnought and the Edwardian Era* (Farnham: Ashgate, 2011) for all aspects of the construction of HMS *Dreadnought*.
2   Brian Sullivan, 'Italian Warship Construction and Maritime Strategy, 1873-1915' in Phillips O'Brien (ed.) *Technology and Naval Combat in the Twentieth Century and Beyond* (London: Frank Cass, 2001), pp.7-8.
3   Frederick Dreyer, *The Sea Heritage. A Study of Maritime Warfare.* (London: Museum Press, 1955), p.38.
4   See: Warwick Brown, 'The Royal Navy's Fuel Supplies, 1898-1939; the Transition from Coal to Oil', (PhD Thesis, University of London, 2003); David Snyder, 'Petroleum and Power: Naval Fuel Technology and the Anglo-American Struggle for Core Hegemony, 1889-1922', (PhD Thesis, Texas A&M University, 2001).
5   Erik Dahl, 'Naval Innovation: From Coal to Oil', *Joint Forces Quarterly*, 27 (2002), pp.50-56; Marian Jack, 'The Purchase of the British Government's Shares in the British

Early Experiments

The driving force behind the construction of HMS *Dreadnought* was Admiral Sir John 'Jackie' Fisher, who was appointed First Sea Lord, professional head of the RN, in 1904. He had been known as the 'Oil Maniac' within naval and political circles since 1886.[6] He was then Director of Naval Ordnance and wrote a memorandum advocating that the RN should switch from coal to oil. In January 1901, whilst commanding the RN's Mediterranean Fleet, he told the naval journalist Arnold White that 'oil fuel will absolutely revolutionize naval strategy.'[7] Fisher was the leading enthusiast for oil in the RN, but the process of adoption was one of carefully experimenting and observing before introducing innovations. It continued even when he was not in a position to affect it directly.

The RN showed interest in the use of oil in warships as early as 1864. By 1867 experiments under the auspices of Admiral Selwyn at Woolwich Dockyard had produced a system of steam spraying. This was considered to be acceptable for the day, but significant progress was not made until the development of pressure spraying in 1902.[8] The Admiralty did no more than study developments elsewhere and experiment until then. It was aware that liquid fuel had some advantages over coal, but until the early twentieth century considered these to be outweighed by the disadvantages. Oil was more expensive, supplies were restricted and technical problems meant that the rate of evaporation of water was poorer in oil fired boilers than in coal fired ones.[9]

In 1896, the Admiralty told T. G. B. Giovanni, an Italian, that it had no need of his system for the use of liquid fuel in ships.[10] Later that year the British Consul in Wilhelmshaven reported to the Admiralty that the German Navy was carrying out experiments based on inventions for heating ship's boilers with liquid fuel that were already in use in Russia and Italy. These had been successful and this method of firing

---

Petroleum Company, 1912-1914', *Past & Present*, 39 (1968), pp.139-68; Geoffrey Jones, 'Admirals and Oilmen: The Relationship between the Royal Navy and the Oil Companies, 1900-1924' in Sarah Palmer and Glyndwr Williams (eds), *Charted and Uncharted Waters: Proceedings of a Conference on the Study of British Maritime History* (London: National Maritime Museum, 1982), pp.107-24; S. Reguer, 'Persian Oil and the First Lord: A Chapter in the Career of Winston Churchill', *Military Affairs*, 46 (3) (1982), pp.134-38.

6   Churchill College, Cambridge (CC), Esher Papers, ESHR 17/5, Some Notes by Sir John Fisher for His Friends, p.39.

7   Arthur Marder (ed.), *Fear God and Dread Nought: The Correspondence of Admiral of the Fleet Lord Fisher of Kilverstone*, (London: Jonathan Cape, 1952-59), Vol. I, p.185, letter dated 28 January 1901.

8   The National Archives (TNA), ADM 265/45, History of Oil Fuel in the Royal Navy, 1922-31, Development of the use of oil fuel in H.M. Navy 4 October 1921.

9   TNA, ADM 265/28, History of Development of Oil Fuel Burning in H.M. Service, 1912, p.1.

10   TNA, ADM 1/10071, Use of Petroleum as Liquid Fuel in Ships, S.18261 1895 4 January 1896.

the boilers was being fitted to new vessels.[11] Despite this early start, the German Navy would by 1914 be well behind the RN in the use of oil. The first British warship to be used for trials with liquid fuel was the destroyer HMS *Surly*. In the late nineteenth century she was used for experiments with the burners developed by the Rusden and Eeles company of Newcastle. In 1894 these had enabled the *Baku Standard* to become the first ship to cross the Atlantic powered by exclusively liquid fuel.[12] *Surly* was also used to trial the Holden burners used by the Great Eastern Railway, but neither type proved satisfactory for use in a warship. Excessive quantities of black smoke were produced and the amount of water evaporated per pound of oil was less than that of coal.[13]

The development of pressure spraying in 1902 made the use of oil more technically feasible. That year James Melrose reported to the Controller of the Admiralty that steamers on the Caspian Sea and railway locomotives in that region of Russia had been powered almost exclusively by oil since around 1880. Hardly any ocean going steamers had used oil as fuel in 1895, although there were then 140 tankers transporting petroleum in bulk. The number of oil burning merchant steamers had subsequently continued to increase.[14] Melrose, who had been Chief Inspector of Machinery in the Mediterranean Fleet under Fisher, was employed by the Admiralty to carry out trials into oil fuel.[15] Reports were made to the Admiralty on oil experiments by the Russian, Italian and Dutch Navies. It was concluded that Britain could at least replicate and probably better their efforts.[16] Experiments continued on *Surly*, with boilers on shore and with a number of other warships, including battleships, cruisers and destroyers.

Oil is Introduced as an Auxiliary to Coal

It was decided in 1904 to use the pressure system of oil spraying. Melrose took out secret patents on the necessary technology on behalf of the Admiralty. The destroyers of the 1905 programme burnt only oil, while all new battleships and cruisers burnt it as an auxiliary to coal. From September 1904 to January 1905 comparative trials

11 *Ibid.*, S.19803 1896 13 July 1896.
12 *Ibid.*, Letter from Rusden and Eeles 27 February 1897, S.4665 1897 6 April 1897, S.7791 1897 12 April 1897.
13 TNA, ADM 265/28, p.1.
14 TNA, ADM 265/26, Experiments in Ships Using Liquid Fuel, 1898-1904, S.13313 1902 23 February 1902, Chief Inspector of Machinery J. Melrose to Controller.
15 Marder (ed.), *FGDN*, Vol. I, Letter from Fisher to Selborne 20 November 1901, p.213 and note 64, p.356.
16 TNA, ADM 1/7676, Controller. N.S Coal 1969 1903 Request 16 October 1902 by Naval Intelligence Department to Captain Dudley de Chair RN, British Legation at The Hague; ADM 265/27, 'Discussion on Oil Fuel between Prince Louis of Battenburg and H.I.H. Grand Duke Alexander of Russia'. 16 May 1902; ADM 265/26, Report on visit to Royal Italian Navy, 4 November, no year given.

between HMS *Surly* burning oil and the otherwise similar HMS *Peterel* burning coal showed the superiority of oil for destroyers.[17] Despite this, the 16 destroyers of the *Beagle* class, ordered in 1908, were fitted to burn only coal because of fears about the supply of oil in wartime. They produced more smoke at high power than did the oil burners and improvements in technology meant that oil burners now had a better evaporative performance than coal ones. This was the last class of British destroyers to be coal fired; the oil supply issue was dealt with by increased storage.[18]

Oil had a number of advantages over coal, which outweighed the disadvantages. It produced more power from the same boiler space. The radius of action from the same weight of fuel was much greater. Oil could be taken to the furnaces and loaded on board more conveniently, the crew had better working conditions and less effort was required to keep the ship clean. It was easier to obtain and maintain full power and to change speed with oil. An oil fired ship was smaller and cheaper to build than a coal burning one of the same performance and required a smaller crew. A oil ship would be superior to a coal one of the same size and cost. Coal did have advantages: coal bunkers provided protection; coal could be temporarily stored in small bags; coal could be obtained from more ports than oil; oil fuel was probably lost if the storage compartment was flooded; and using oil increased the danger of fire. The balance of advantages and disadvantages favoured oil. The use of a combination of coal and oil in destroyers was felt to make sense only if a scarcity in the supply of oil meant that its use had to be restricted.[19]

HMS *Bulldog* of the coal fuelled *Beagle* class of destroyers, launched in 1909, displaced 949 tons and achieved a maximum speed of 27.08 knots on her trials. HMS *Acorn*, an oil burner launched the next year, displaced 736 tons but made 27.3 knots. The 858 ton oil fired HMS *Acasta*, launched in 1912, achieved 32.57 knots.[20] All carried two 21 inch torpedo tubes, but *Bulldog* had the weakest gun armament and the largest crew; one 4 inch, three 12 pounders and 96 men versus *Acorn's* two 4 inch, two 12 pounders and 72 men and *Acasta's* three 4 inch and 73 men.[21] *Bulldog's* sister HMS *Beagle* cost £106,000 versus £86,000 for HMS *Defender*, similar to *Acorn*.[22] The first ships to be fitted to burn oil had produced excessive quantities of smoke, but technological advances had corrected this fault. By 1903 objections to the use of oil came mainly on the grounds of security of supply, a point made by both the Commander-in-Chief of the Channel Fleet, Lord Charles Beresford, and the Engineer in Chief.[23] In

17   TNA, ADM 265/28, pp.4-5.
18   *Ibid.*, pp.8-9.
19   *Ibid.*, pp.12-15.
20   Glasgow University Archives, John Brown shipbuilders, UCS 1/93/19, Particulars of Warships.
21   Randal Gray, *Conway's All the World's Fighting Ships, 1906-1921* (London: Conway Maritime Press, 1985), pp.73-75.
22   TNA, ADM 265/28, p.13.
23   TNA, ADM 1/7676, N.S. Coal 1840 1903, pp.1-2.

1914 Beresford argued in his memoirs that 'nothing is better than oil on one condition - that you have got it.'[24]

It was not then intended that oil should completely replace coal in the RN. It had a global network of coaling stations and would need to set up a costly logistical network if it switched entirely to oil. As well as concerns over the security of foreign supplies of oil, there were fears, expressed by the First Lord of the Admiralty Lord Selborne in 1904, that there was not enough oil in the world for it to replace coal.[25] In 1905, global production of oil was just under 30 million tons, over 60 per cent of it from the United States and little from the British Empire.[26] Globally, in 1905, 930 million tons of coal were mined; the USA led with over 350 million tons, but most was used in North America. Britain was second with 240 million tons and dominated the export market, sending nearly 40 per cent of its 1913 output overseas.[27]

British oil supplies would mostly have to be purchased from abroad; a war or the threat of one would cause an increase in demand for oil, forcing its price up. Storage facilities were required so that oil could be stockpiled in order to counter both potential wartime shortages and price rises. It was believed that sufficient supplies could be obtained, provided that requirements were known three months in advance.[28] The rising use of oil by the RN meant that the Committee of Imperial Defence (CID) considered Burma, one part of the British Empire where oil had been found, to be of vast importance. In 1905 it asked the Indian Government to ensure that the Burmah Company should remain entirely British.[29] Ernest Pretyman, Parliamentary and Financial Secretary to the Admiralty and Chairman of the Admiralty Oil Committee, wanted to keep the major companies such as Standard Oil of the USA and Royal Dutch out of the few oilfields in the British Empire. However, these companies did receive contracts to supply the RN with oil.[30] Another possible source of oil for the RN was in Persia, where William D'Arcy, a British financier, was granted an oil exploration concession in 1901. Within two years he had run short of funds. Sir Boverton Redwood, an oil expert who was an adviser to both D'Arcy and Burmah and a member of the Admiralty Oil Committee, suggested to D'Arcy that he approach the Admiralty for a loan. The Admiralty and the Foreign Office were keen, but the Treasury would not sanction the loan. The Admiralty and the Foreign Office feared

---

24   Charles Beresford, *The Memoirs of Admiral Lord Charles Beresford* (London: Methuen & Co., 1914), Vol. II, p.483.

25   Jones, 'Admirals,' p.111.

26   Daniel Yergin, *The Prize: The Epic Quest for Oil, Money and Power* (New York, NY: Simon & Schuster, 1991), pp.830, note 24. Converted from barrels per day in original at rate of one barrel per day equals 49.8 tons per annum.

27   James Ronaldson, *Coal* (London: John Murray, 1920), pp.5-6, Tables I and II.

28   TNA, ADM 1/7676, S.25546/02.

29   TNA, ADM 116/3807, Burmah Oil Co Ltd: Contract for Supply of Fuel Oil, Letter 10 August 1905 signed by G.T. Clarke.

30   Geoffrey Jones, *The State and the Emergence of the British Oil Industry* (London: Macmillan, 1981), pp.23-26.

that D'Arcy might look overseas for investment. [31] Pretyman introduced him to Burmah, which was concerned that cheap Persian oil might damage its Indian market and was negotiating an oil contract with the Admiralty. In 1905, Burmah took a stake in D'Arcy's company and provided it with the necessary capital. [32]

Fisher's period as First Sea Lord saw growth in the RN's use of oil, but no radical increase in the rate of change. This was an evolutionary process, widely accepted in the RN. While battleships and cruisers, including the new battlecruisers, continued to use oil as an auxiliary to coal, all destroyers built since 1905, apart from the *Beagle* class, were fuelled solely by oil. Fisher retired in January 1911; later that year, the RN had 34 battleships, including all its dreadnoughts, 20 armoured and battlecruisers and 21 smaller cruisers fitted to burn both oil and coal. There were 61 destroyers and 36 coastal destroyers burning only oil and all new destroyers used solely oil. In all cases, the results using oil had been 'satisfactory'. [33] Oil now produced less smoke and had a better evaporative performance than coal. [34]

The Move to an All Oil Fleet

Ironically, the pace of adoption of oil in the RN accelerated after Fisher's retirement, but he was still to be closely involved. There had been no formal Admiralty body dealing with oil since 1906, when the incoming Liberal government had abolished the Admiralty Oil Committee. The increasing importance of oil fuel to the RN meant that a Committee on Oil Fuel, chaired by Captain William Pakenham, the Fourth Sea Lord, was set up to look at the issue. On 19 January 1912 Pakenham's committee reported its interim conclusions. As Britain imported 93 per cent of its fuel oil, reserves of a year's wartime consumption should be built up. This was estimated to be 1,500,000 tons, but by the end of the 1913-14 fiscal year storage for only 471,000 tons would be available. Construction of another 1,000,000 tons of storage must begin immediately and forward contracts for the purchase of the oil should be signed so that the oil would be available to fill the extra storage as it was completed. As storage was insufficient for existing ships, no change towards more oil should be made in ships of the 1911-12 programme. Trials should take place to see if oil of a lower standard than currently used by the RN would be suitable: the high quality required restricted choice and increased price. [35]

Despite these recommendations, the RN was about to increase its use of oil even further. Winston Churchill replaced Reginald McKenna as First Lord of the

31   Yergin, *Prize*, pp.134-42.
32   Ronald Ferrier, *The History of the British Petroleum Company*, (Cambridge: Cambridge University Press, 1982), Vol. I, pp.67-72.
33   TNA, ADM 265/28, p.11.
34   *Ibid.*, p.12.
35   TNA, ADM 265/29, Admiralty Committee on Use of Oil Fuel in Navy: Volume 1, Interim Report, 1912. 19 January 1912, p.149.

Admiralty in October 1911. Fisher, although retired, had become a close adviser to Churchill. The RN's demand for oil was rising because the importance of torpedo armed flotilla craft within the fleet was increasing and most destroyers and all submarines were entirely fuelled by oil. Relatively few light cruisers were built for a number of years as Fisher believed that destroyers could carry out their scouting role. Eventually, it was realized that this was not the case and construction of light cruisers resumed from 1909. Initially, these were fuelled by a mixture of coal and oil, but the *Arethusa* class of 1912 and most subsequent British cruisers were fuelled exclusively by oil. Coal fired cruisers were too slow to work with the newest destroyers and more speed was also required for scouting duties.[36] Additionally, the RN was about to construct its first entirely oil fuelled battleships, the *Queen Elizabeth* class.

British dreadnoughts were generally armed with larger guns than German ones and Churchill wanted to extend the British advantage. Fisher enthusiastically backed his idea of moving from 13.5 inch to 15 inch guns for the next programme of battleships; German dreadnoughts then carried only 12 inch guns. Eight 15 inch guns would fire a more powerful broadside than ten 13.5 inch guns. The possibility thus arose of fitting bigger engines and boilers to the 15 inch armed vessels by sacrificing one gun turret, producing a ship with battleship armour and firepower but battlecruiser speed. Only an oil fired ship could achieve this. In an action between two fleets of otherwise equal speed, if one possessed a division of faster battleships, then these could pull ahead of the enemy and cut across the head of his line, known as crossing the T. The decisive defeat of the Russians at Tsushima in 1905, the most recent naval battle, occurred when the faster Japanese fleet carried out such a manoeuvre. Battlecruisers had the speed to do this, but they lacked the armour to fight enemy battleships and might end up in a separate action with the enemy battlecruisers. A fast division would therefore confer considerable tactical advantages, but its battleships would have to be fuelled exclusively by oil. The *Queen Elizabeth* class of fast battleships would require secure supplies of oil. According to Churchill the quantities of oil used by the RN did not until now make its oil supplies a significant issue, although Pakenham's committee had indicated that storage and reserves were key questions. Now the increased number of oil burning ships made oil supply a vital issue. The best steam coal in the world was mined in south Wales, but oil would have to come largely from overseas. The oil had to be found, stored and bought regularly as inexpensively as possible. There had to be complete security of supply in wartime.

A Royal Commission on Fuel and Engines, chaired by Fisher, was established in 1912 to solve these problems.[37] The Commission produced an Interim Report on 27

---

36   Winston Churchill, *The World Crisis, 1911-1918* (London: Odhams Press, 1939), Vol. I, pp.107-11.

37   *Ibid.*, pp.94-103.

November 1912 and a Second Report on 27 February 1913.[38] The latter reiterated the points already made regarding the superiority of oil over coal as the fuel of warships. Oil was superior to coal whether it was burnt in boilers to power steam turbines or used to power internal combustion engines. Problems with the manufacture of the latter as they increased in size meant a delay in their introduction into major warships. The Second Report emphasized the importance of storage of reserves and of supply. It believed that ample supplies of oil for the RN could be obtained for the next 15 to 20 years. However, these could not be relied upon if the Admiralty continued with its system of ad-hoc purchases, which was forced on it by the lack of sufficient storage facilities for reserves. Unlike coal, oil did not deteriorate, so could be stored for longer. Without reserves naval supremacy would be lost if oil supplies were interrupted in wartime. The oilfields or the refineries might be attacked by the enemy. Refineries then tended to be located near the oilfields rather than the end markets.

It was therefore vital to have reserves. These could be built up at times of depressed prices; the supply of oil was subject to unpredictable periods of both glut and famine, which severely impacted prices. Supplies could not always be relied upon unless long term forward contracts were signed; the price in wartime might be very high, even if enough oil was available on the open market. There were concerns that Royal Dutch Shell (RDS) was taking control of a large proportion of the world's oil supply. Royal Dutch had merged its operations with Shell, a British company, in 1907 on a ratio of 60 per cent Royal Dutch and 40 per cent Shell. Some British companies such as the Anglo-Persian Oil Company (APOC) were short of capital and the government should consider giving them financial assistance.

It would be expensive to build up the necessary stocks but this expenditure would be spread over a number of years. Reserves were vital even if forward contracts were signed. There was a risk of being too dependent on one geographic area as the output of a particular field could be very unpredictable. The country in which the oil was located might come under the control of the enemy or itself become hostile. A geographical diversification of sources and substantial reserves were required; four years' peace consumption was recommended. Large storage capacity also allowed the opportunity to take advantage of short term price weakness and hedged against the risk of the delivery of poor quality oil under contract. The actual quantity to be stored would depend on the extent to which oil was adopted and whether there was a move towards internal combustion engines. Three tons of oil was equivalent to four tons of coal when powering steam turbines, but would substitute for 10 tons of coal if internal combustion engines were adopted. Requirements were rising, as there would be over 100 entirely oil fired destroyers in a year, with up to 20 more being built each year.

---

38   TNA, ADM 265/32, Royal Commission on Fuel and Engines: Volume 1, 1913; ADM 265/33, Royal Commission on Fuel and Engines: Volume 2, 1913. Copies of these documents are also filed at ADM 116/1208 and ADM 116/1209 respectively.

The all oil battleships and light cruisers would increase demand even more over the next three years.

At this stage, it was envisaged that the oil would be used to power steam turbines rather than internal combustion engines. The latter were more economical but meant a reversion from turbines to reciprocating engines. Turbines were more reliable, simpler, could be pushed to run at over theoretical capacity and could be placed below the waterline of armoured ships. It became harder to build internal combustion engines as their size increased, which was not the case with steam turbines. Larger turbines had a lower fuel consumption than smaller ones, although internal combustion engines were always more economical. The latter also had the advantage that they could be started from cold. Fisher's enthusiasm for the internal combustion engine meant that the Royal Commission interviewed a large number of witnesses about its merits. However, it concluded that, although internal combustion engines would eventually become the means of locomotion for warships, the technology was not yet ready. Fisher had written to Viscount Esher in August 1912 claiming that he had infected his colleagues with 'internal combustion rabies.'[39] Despite that it was recommended that, for now, warships should be fitted with internal combustion engines only as auxiliaries. Oil was preferable to coal but should be burnt in boilers in order to drive steam turbines.[40]

Few large warships were ever powered by internal combustion engines. Fisher had argued that warships with engines would not need funnels so could have a low silhouette, but this proved not to be the case, removing one of their potential advantages.[41] Additionally, the 1922 Washington Treaty restricted the displacement of warships, defined as the standard displacement, which omitted fuel: diesel engines were heavier than steam turbines, but required less fuel, so were penalized by the use of this measure.[42]

One member of the Royal Commission, George Lambert, the Civil Lord of the Admiralty, did not entirely agree with his colleagues. He accepted the merits of oil, but argued that more entirely oil burning warships should not be built until sufficient stocks of oil had been built up. A combination of coal and oil should be used until then.[43] However, Redwood, Honorary Adviser to the Admiralty on Petroleum and a member of the Royal Commission, wrote to Fisher on 25 February 1914 stressing that the Commission's recommendations must be accepted so that the RN could be certain of obtaining adequate supplies of oil at a reasonable price. The USA was taking measures to ensure that the United States Navy (USN) had ample supplies and reserves; Redwood argued that the situation was more urgent for the RN.[44]

---

39   Marder (ed.), *FGDN*, Vol. II, p.476, Letter to Lord Esher 7 August 1912.
40   TNA, ADM 265/33, pp.8-17.
41   Marder (ed.), *FGDN*, Vol. II, pp.477-78, Letter to Lord Esher 12 September 1912.
42   Brown, 'Royal Navy', pp.244-45.
43   TNA, ADM 265/33, p.17.
44   TNA, CAB 1/33/2, 'Oil Fuel', 1912, 1914, Copy of letter from Sir Boverton Redwood to Lord Fisher 25 February 1914.

HMS *Queen Elizabeth*, the world's first entirely oil fuelled battleship, was laid down on 21 October 1912, 10 days before her sister ship HMS *Warspite* and a fortnight ahead of the first all oil American battleship, the USS *Nevada*. The United States dominated the global oil industry so security of supply was less of a problem for the USN than for the RN.[45] Four *Queen Elizabeth* class dreadnoughts had originally been planned; a fifth, paid for and named after Malaya, was then added. There were hopes, which were not realized, that Canada would finance the building of three more. It was then intended that future battleships would to revert to a mixture of coal and oil, but the construction of the *Queen Elizabeth* and *Arethusa* classes meant a substantial increase in the RN's oil requirements. This made it necessary to find secure and cheap oil supplies and to build up reserves.

The Admiralty Invests in the Anglo-Persian Oil Company

One potential source was Persia, where D'Arcy's prospectors, led by George Reynolds, had found oil at Majid-i-Suleiman in 1908. Persia was an independent country, but was dominated by Britain and Russia, which in 1907 had divided it into their respective spheres of influence and a neutral zone. Little of the oil was in the British zone in the south, but Britain did have forces close enough to protect these fields and could transport the oil home, either through the Mediterranean or, if that proved to be impossible in wartime, round the Cape of Good Hope.[46]

Formed to develop the discovery of oil in Persia, APOC lacked the capital required to do so. Burmah, which owned most of the shares, was reluctant to invest more; D'Arcy had exchanged his interest for cash and Burmah shares. The prospect of it paying dividends was too distant for it to be able to raise funds from private shareholders. This left it with the options of raising the capital from either another oil company, which had a better understanding than private investors of the risks and rewards involved, or from the government. In early 1913, APOC attempted to persuade the Admiralty to support it financially. The Admiralty was keen to act jointly with the Indian railways, which could halve their fuel requirements by converting their locomotives from coal to oil. Without government support APOC claimed it would have to accept a takeover offer from another oil company, probably RDS. However, the Indian railways had barely begun to experiment with oil, so the Indian government did not think that it could justify an investment in Persian oil.[47]

Thus, there was a risk that RDS would acquire APOC unless the Admiralty made the investment itself. Concern over this issue depended to a large extent on one's view

---

45   For the USN's adoption of oil, see J. A. Denovo, 'Petroleum and the United States Navy before World War I', *Mississippi Valley Historical Review*, 41 (4) (1955) pp.641-56.

46   Yergin, *Prize*, pp.142-49.

47   TNA, CAB 37/115/39, Oil Fuel Supply for H.M. Navy, 1913. Appendix 2, Admiralty Memorandum in Regard to the Anglo-Persian Oil Company's Proposals for a Contract to Supply Fuel Oil, pp.13-24.

of RDS. Many regarded it as a foreign company and feared that the Netherlands might come under major German influence. However, Shell had a British registration and domicile and most of its directors were British.[48] Sir Marcus Samuel, the founder of Shell and a former Lord Mayor of London, was very concerned by the negative views of his company's Dutch links. In May 1914 he wrote to Sir Francis Hopwood, the Additional Civil Lord of the Admiralty, stressing that Shell was a British company.[49] Views were not clear cut even regarding the Dutch side of the company. Fisher was a great admirer of Henri Deterding, the head of Royal Dutch, and was impressed by Deterding's evidence to the Royal Commission on Fuel and Engines.[50] On 31 July 1914 Fisher wrote to Churchill informing him that Deterding had just promised him that the British would not be short of either oil or tankers in the event of war.[51] RDS would supply large quantities of oil to the Allies during the First World War, leading to Deterding receiving an honorary KBE in 1920 and Samuel rising to the peerage as Baron Bearsted in 1921.

In October 1913, an Admiralty Commission was despatched to investigate the Persian oil industry. It was chaired by Admiral Sir Edmond Slade, a former Director of Naval Intelligence; he and another of its members, John Cadman, Professor of Mining at Birmingham University and Petroleum Adviser to the Colonial Office, would become major figures in British oil policy. The final report concluded that APOC's concession would be capable of supplying a substantial proportion of the RN's oil needs for a long time. It was vital to keep the concession and the company in British hands. There needed to be at least one large British controlled oil company that would be financially and contractually obligated to the government. APOC lacked the capital required to develop its potentially very lucrative oilfields. The RN's needs could be met from the existing fields in northern Persia, and further discoveries in the south were possible. The Commission believed that the Admiralty should invest in APOC in order for it to develop the fields whilst remaining independent. Oil could then be supplied to the RN on advantageous terms whilst still allowing the company a reasonable return.[52]

The Commission's recommendations were accepted. The government would provide £2,200,000 in shares and debentures in return for 51 per cent of the ordinary shares and the right to appoint two directors. A contract to buy at least 6,000,000 tons of

48   Jack, 'Purchase', pp.142-50.
49   TNA, CAB 37/120/68, Oil Supply: Two Letters from Sir Marcus Samuel Bart., to the Admiralty, 9 June 1914. Letters both dated 29 May 1914.
50   TNA, ADM 265/34, Royal Commission on Fuel and Engines: Volume 3', 1913. 'Memorandum on Oil and its Fighting Attributes', pp.48-49.
51   Randolph Churchill, Martin Gilbert, (eds), *Winston S. Churchill, Companion Documents* (London: Heinemann, 1967-75), Vol. II, part 3 p.1965.
52   1914 [Cmd. 7419] *Agreement with the Anglo-Persian Oil Company, Limited, with an Explanatory Memorandum, and the Report of the Commission of Experts on Their Local Investigations*, pp.3-7.

oil from APOC between 1914 and 1933, with an option to purchase up to 2,400,000 tons more was signed. The price would be 35 shillings a ton for the first half of the oil and 25 shillings a ton for the rest. It would be transported in Admiralty vessels. The Admiralty had been buying oil on one year contracts until then, but the price at the loading port had risen from 22 shillings a ton in 1912 to 39 shillings in 1913 because demand, from private users as well as navies, was rising. Some contracts for supply in 1914 were at 50 shillings.[53] Subsequent increases in prices meant that the transaction was clearly financially advantageous for the taxpayer.[54] Persia later became a leading producer, but its infant oil industry could not increase output quickly enough to supply the rapidly growing demands of Britain and its allies during the First World War. In 1918, nearly 80 per cent of Britain's oil came from the USA and only 8 per cent from Persia.[55]

The RN's oil fuel supply was debated in the House of Commons when the Naval Estimates were considered on 17 July 1913. A former Conservative Civil Lord of the Admiralty, Arthur Lee, argued that the abolition of the Admiralty Oil Fuel Committee by the Liberals in 1906 had led to a lack of attention being paid to oil storage and transport capacity until it had now become urgent. He criticized Churchill's argument that only one division of fast battleships was required and that the RN would revert to coal for future battleships. What if other navies built and continued to build battleships as fast as the *Queen Elizabeths*?[56] Beresford, now retired from the RN and Conservative MP for Portsmouth, accepted the advantages of oil for warships but said that the oil fired ships should not have been built until the oil supplies and storage for them had been established. The price of oil had risen sharply because contracts had not been signed before the ships were laid down. He was concerned that the oil fired ships would be useless if Britain's oil supply was cut off in wartime and there was insufficient storage at home and overseas ports. He also believed that, in order to obtain the required quantities of oil, the Admiralty must have accepted a substantial reduction in the quality of the oil.[57]

Pretyman reiterated the comments of Lee and Beresford. He suggested that the reason for the reversion to coal was supply, not the tactical one claimed by Churchill. Churchill insisted that the later ships did not require the speed of the oil fired ones, but admitted that the price of oil was a factor. Churchill laid down the principles on which the Admiralty's oil supply policy was based; supplies should be widely spread geographically, sources should be kept open and independent competition maintained.

53   TNA, CAB 37/115/39, pp.3-4, 23.
54   TNA, CAB 27/180, Oil Companies Amalgamation, 1922. Estimate of Return Obtained by His Majesty's Government on their Original Investment of £2,200,000 in the Anglo-Persian Oil Company Ltd.
55   TNA, POWE 33/8, Inter-Allied Petroleum Conference: Minutes of Meetings, 1918. Fourth Informal Meeting, 27 February 1918, Appendix 4.
56   *Parliamentary Debates, Fifth Series, House of Commons*, Vol. LV, pp.1490-92.
57   *Ibid.*, pp.1515-23.

Where possible sources should be under British control with secure transport. Pretyman agreed with these, which he said had been established 11 years previously by the Conservative government, but he did not see how they could be maintained if the Admiralty relied on a single large oilfield. The best that would happen was that maintaining the strength of the RN would cost much more than if oil supply contracts had been signed earlier. The worst was that the strength would not be maintained.[58]

A further debate took place on 17 June 1914 on the specific subject of the Admiralty's intention to invest in APOC. Churchill argued that whilst the RN controlled the seas Britain would be able to import oil even if the enemy declared it to be contraband. The riskiest period would be early in a war; storage of reserves was being provided against shortages of supply in this period. Beresford reiterated his view oil had huge advantages if it could be obtained but that Britain did not have it and could not get it. He felt, however, that he had to vote for a motion to provide oil that the First Lord said the RN required. Other members were concerned over the lack of security of the Persian oilfields. Little of the oil was in the British zone in the south, which had been set as the greatest area that Lord Kitchener said was defendable with the available forces. The Foreign Secretary, Sir Edward Grey, countered that the pipeline could be defended by local forces and that risks were no lower anywhere in the world where oil concessions could be obtained. The debate also included allegations of price fixing by financiers, calls for the money to be spent at home on the shale oil industry and on developing means of extracting oil from coal and concerns over the impact on the Welsh coal industry of a switch by navies around the world to coal. Despite the strength of some opinions expressed, the motion was carried by 254 votes to 18. As well as Liberal and Labour Members, some Conservatives such as Pretyman put aside their qualms about aspects of the government's policy and supported it because they accepted the need to provide the RN with oil.[59]

Conclusion

The RN's adoption of oil was an example of it employing a process of observation and experiment before transforming itself via a technical innovation. Fisher was the British admiral most closely associated with oil, but the process continued even when he was not directly involved. Once oil had been shown to be clearly superior it was adopted despite supply difficulties. The policy was to use the best technology available, and then to solve the supply problems. This focus on technology did mean that supply and storage problems were not always given enough attention. The extra oil required by the *Queen Elizabeth* and *Arethusa* classes could have been bought more cheaply if contracts had been signed when the ships were ordered. Oil was used as an auxiliary to coal until the case for it became overwhelming, whereupon the RN switched entirely

58   *Ibid.*, pp.1568-73.
59   *Parliamentary Debates, Fifth Series, House of Commons*, Vol. LXIII, pp.1131-1251.

to oil. Initially the use of only oil in the *Queen Elizabeths* was supposed to be a one off, with the following *Revenge* class reverting to a mix of oil and coal. When Fisher returned as First Sea Lord in 1914 he had the *Revenges* converted to burn only oil; all future British battleships and most cruisers used only oil. The RN was just ahead of the USN, which did not have the same supply problems, in the adoption of oil. These two were well ahead of all others by 1914; Germany did not build any all oil battleships or cruisers before or during the First World War.

8

Oil and Water
A Comparison of Military and Naval Aviation Doctrine in Britain, 1912-1914

James Pugh

At the birth of organised air power in Britain, the sheer act of leaving the Earth in a heavier-than-air-craft was the challenge that both military and naval aviators faced on a daily basis. For example, during the First World War, 8,000 military pilots died during training accidents alone, more than during combat operations.[1] Nothing was routine about their profession, and the development of aviation concepts, technologies, and practices underwent rapid evolution between 1911 and 1918.[2] For example, squadrons of the Military Wing (MW) of the Royal Flying Corps (RFC) spent much of their time prior to the outbreak of the First World War undertaking routine cross-country flights, specialised experimentation (such as aerial weapons testing by No.3 Squadron), and preparation for manoeuvres with the Army.[3] As Raleigh observed with reference to the pre-1914 period, 'the pilots were new to their work, and the triumph was to get into the air at all.'[4] By 1918, specific squadrons existed to undertake a range of complex tasks including aerial combat, artillery reconnaissance, and, in the case of No.8 Squadron, the highly specialised role of aircraft-tank cooperation.[5]

1   Denis Winter, *The First of the Few: Fighter Pilots of the First World War* (London: Allen Lane, 1982), pp.36-37.
2   In general, see: Richard Hallion, *Taking Flight: Inventing the Aerial Age from Antiquity to the First World War* (Oxford: Oxford University Press, 2003).
3   Walter Raleigh, *The War in the Air: Volume I*, (Oxford: Clarendon Press, 1922), p.214 and p.231; The National Archives, Kew (TNA), Air Ministry Files (AIR) 1/758/204/4/122, H. Musgrave, Report on RFC, MW Experiments, 30 April 1914.
4   Raleigh, *The War in the Air: Vol. I*, p.192.
5   Ross Mahoney, 'The Forgotten Career of Major Trafford Leigh-Mallory, 1914-1918', Paper presented at War Studies Postgraduate Research Symposium, University of Birmingham, 8 May 2010.

A brief examination of the historiography of British air power during the pre-First World War period suggests a significant divide in attitudes toward innovation between military and naval aviators. Historians such as Goulter highlight the progressive attitude of naval aviators toward the process of technological innovation, and to the conceptualisation of advanced and sophisticated roles for air power.[6] Juxtaposed against the efforts of Britain's military aviators, such interpretations characterise the latter as possessing an unimaginative approach to the conceptualisation of air power roles and a lethargic and rudimentary attitude to technological experimentation.[7] Recent research supports such conclusions, and Parton suggests that naval aviators were 'far closer to being "fit for service"' than their colleagues in the military.[8] By examining early British air power doctrine, and by placing such doctrine in its organisational context and constraints, this chapter seeks to explore such contentions.[9]

By adopting a progressive attitude to the production of doctrine, the MW successfully managed the process of integrating air power into the organisational and operational framework of the British Expeditionary Force (BEF). The ability of the MW to articulate a coherent and concise vision for the application of air power, couched in a reassuringly familiar taxonomy, aided the relatively smooth assimilation of air power assets into the British Army of the period. In contrast, naval aviators faced a very different challenge reflecting the diverse and varied roles of air power in a naval context. The Naval Wing (NW) of the RFC deserves its reputation for technological innovation, but naval aviators did not approach doctrine in the same manner as their military colleagues. The result saw naval aviators focussing on the technological aspects of air power at the expense of developing doctrine in a truly progressive fashion. This lack of doctrine had a detrimental effect upon the manner in which air power was integrated into, and accepted as a legitimate part of, the wider Royal Navy (RN).

This chapter begins by establishing a working definition of doctrine, before exploring the Army and RN's attitude and approach to doctrine during this period. The chapter then moves to examine the birth and development of organised air power in Britain, before analysing the specific doctrine produced by the separate Wings of the RFC. This analysis highlights diverse attitudes and approaches to the production of doctrine that, in turn, reflects the wider organisational context in which military and naval aviators approached their profession. As Kier argues, this organisational context can be explored effectively by acknowledging the 'cultural characteristics' of

6   Christina Goulter, *A Forgotten Offensive: Royal Air Force Coastal Command's Anti-Shipping Campaign, 1940-1945* (London: Frank Cass, 1995), p.9 and chapter one more generally.

7   Goulter, *Forgotten Offensive*, pp.7-8; Michael Paris, *Winged Warfare: The Literature and Theory of Aerial Warfare in Britain, 1859-1917* (Manchester: Manchester University Press, 1992), p.188.

8   Neville Parton, 'The Evolution and Impact of Royal Air Force Doctrine, 1919-1939', (PhD Thesis, University of Cambridge, 2009), p.27.

9   Parton, 'Royal Air Force Doctrine', chapter two.

an organisation that serve to influence doctrinal choices and decisions.[10] As such, air power doctrine was not created in a contextual or cultural vacuum during this period, and military and naval aviators came to be influenced by the attitudes toward doctrine held by their respective parent services. For example, the Army possessed an attitude toward doctrine that focussed on infusing its personnel with the correct spirit in which to conduct operations. Moreover, the Army was keen to provide its personnel with such guidance in a written, if non-prescriptive, format, and invested significant intellectual capital in producing doctrinal manuals.

Sheffield suggests that:

> ...doctrine should establish a framework of understanding and action, which should inform the decision making process. Doctrine at the higher levels should permeate the language and thinking of those in high command, and their subordinates should be able to gauge their thoughts, and indeed, anticipate them because of a common background and training.[11]

Parton argues that doctrine can:

> ...also represent something deeper than simply the results of analysis; it can point to the most heartfelt beliefs of an organisation, and consequently to some extent reveals the culture of the organisation at the time that it was produced.[12]

There are three important aspects to Sheffield and Parton's definitions: first, they suggest that doctrine provides organisations with a framework of understanding; second, this framework builds on a shared language; and third, doctrine reflects the cultural ideals of an organisation. In many respects, the explanatory definitions of Sheffield and Parton accord with the thoughts of the naval theorist, Julian Corbett, who noted that '... words must have the same meaning for all.'[13] It is this aspect of doctrine, the provision of a shared framework of understanding built upon a recognisable taxonomy, which provides the basis for this chapter.

10   Elizabeth Kier, 'Culture and Military Doctrine: France between the Wars', *International Security*, 19 (4) (1995), pp.66-67.
11   Gary Sheffield, 'Doctrine and Command in the British Army: An Historical Overview' in *Army Doctrine Publication: Operations* (London: Ministry of Defence (MoD), 2010), p.E-3.
12   Parton, 'Royal Air Force Doctrine', pp.6-8.
13   Julian Corbett, *Some Principles of Maritime Strategy* (London: Longmans, 1911), p.3. For this interpretation, see Peter Gray, *The Leadership, Direction and Legitimacy of the RAF Bomber Offensive from Inception to 1945* (London: Continuum, 2012), p.19.

Doctrine in the British Army

Military aviators possessed an inherent understanding of the importance of language and the need to articulate a vision for air power that would appeal to the Army. This approach was shaped by the organisational context of the Army; the context in which military aviators came to produce doctrine. For example, Bowman and Connelly highlight the historiographical debates that exist in relation to the Army's attitude toward doctrine in the pre-1914 period.[14] Such debates are well illustrated by a focus on the nature of the 'Operations' volume of the Army's *Field Service Regulations* (*FSR*), a manual produced in 1909 and reissued with amendments in 1912 and in 1914.[15]

Travers and Holden Reid both suggest that the Army of this period lacked doctrine that was either 'coherent' or 'official', a position supported by Brown and by Jones.[16] In contrast, Luvaas argues that *FSR* provided the Army with a 'uniform doctrine', and, more recently, Badsey has concluded that manuals such as *FSR* did constitute doctrine and came to play an increasingly important role in shaping the vision and principles of the Army in the period leading up to the First World War.[17] Whilst rejecting the notion that *FSR* was formal doctrine, Palazzo makes use of the concept of 'ethos' to explain how the Army was able to develop a successful approach to warfare during the First World War.[18] As Palazzo suggests, the 'ethos' of the Army was 'more dramatic and all-encompassing than doctrine ... [providing] ... the continuity of thought that welded the army into a whole.' For Sheffield, the Army did evolve and apply a 'doctrine, albeit a semi-informal one, based on the pre-war *Field Service Regulations*.'[19]

14   Timothy Bowman and Mark Connelly, *The Edwardian Army: Recruiting, Training, and Deploying the British Army, 1902-1914* (Oxford: Oxford University Press, 2012), pp.76-78.

15   For example, see: General Staff, War Office, *Field Service Regulations, Part One: Operations*. Reprinted with amendments, 1912 (London: HMSO, 1912).

16   Tim Travers, *The Killing Ground: The British Army, the Western Front and the Emergence of Modern War, 1900-1918* (Barnsley: Pen & Sword, 2003 [1987]), p.54, pp.66-67; Brian Holden Reid, 'A Doctrinal Perspective, 1988-98' in *Strategic and Combat Studies Institute Occasional Paper No.33* (Camberley: SCSI, May 1998), p.12; Ian Malcolm Brown, *British Logistics on the Western Front, 1914-1919* (Westport, CT: Praeger, 1998), pp.31-32; Spencer Jones, 'The Influence of the Boer War (1899-1902) on the Tactical Development of the Regular British Army, 1902-1914', (PhD Thesis, University of Wolverhampton, 2009), p.44, 46.

17   Jay Luvaas, *The Education of an Army: British Military Thought, 1815-1940* (London: Cassell, 1965), p.309; Stephen Badsey, *Doctrine and Reform in the British Cavalry, 1880-1918* (Aldershot: Ashgate, 2008), pp.3-4.

18   Albert Palazzo, *Seeking Victory on the Western Front: The British Army and Chemical Warfare in World War I* (Nebraska: University of Nebraska Press, 2000), pp.8-9, and pp.4-24 more generally.

19   Gary Sheffield, 'Review of *Seeking Victory on the Western Front: The British Army and Chemical Warfare in World War I* by A. Palazzo', *Journal of the Australian War Memorial*, No.35 (Dec 2001), accessed, 16 February 2011. http://www.awm.gov.au/journal/j35/palazzoreview.asp

As it continued to evolve, *FSR* provided the Army with 'broad principles for action', capturing contemporary attitudes to flexibility in command.[20] Simpson also adopts such an interpretation, arguing that *FSR* was a framework upon which sat 'a set of general principles for application by trained and experienced officers.'[21] For Bryson, *FSR* could be considered coherent doctrine, and he asserts that 'pre-war doctrine – both informal and formal – played a significant role in informing debate and development.'[22] Bryson's interpretation is of particular relevance because, in line with the work of Sheffield, of Parton, and of Corbett, it acknowledges the important role played by doctrine in providing a 'framework of understanding.'

In this vein, *FSR* provided the Army with a vehicle to articulate its vision of warfare to both internal and external audiences. Rather than focussing on stifling tactical and operational detail, *FSR* attempted to infuse the Army with the correct spirit in which to conduct operations. Recognising the significance of framing such ideas within a shared taxonomy, *FSR* highlighted several key themes, including the importance of establishing moral superiority over the enemy by launching '*a vigorous offensive*', and the cultivation of an aggressive spirit through emphasising '*a firmer determination in all ranks to conquer at any cost* [emphasis in original].'[23] Such doctrine would come to have a significant influence over the creation and development of military air power doctrine during this period. Moreover, the fact that the Army took time to articulate a coherent vision for warfare reflects that the organisation possessed a progressive and sophisticated understanding of the nature of doctrine.

Doctrine in the Royal Navy

An examination of the RN's attitude and approach to doctrine offers a noticeable contrast. Grove, in examining RN doctrine of this period, argues that the organisation, particularly the Grand Fleet under Admiral Sir John Jellicoe, had 'too much doctrine in Grand Fleet Battle Orders [GFBOs].'[24] Even a cursory glance through GFBOs indicates that these vast documents cannot be considered the RN's equivalent of *FSR*.[25] If GFBOs can be characterised as doctrine, then their prescriptive focus suggests they are more akin to tactical level doctrine or standard operating procedures.

---

20   Sheffield, 'Doctrine and Command', pp.E9-E10.
21   Andy Simpson, 'British Corps Command on the Western Front, 1914-1918', in Gary Sheffield and Dan Todman (eds.), *Command and Control on the Western Front: The British Army's Experience*, 1914-1918 (Staplehurst: Spellmount, 2004), p.99.
22   R. Bryson, 'The Once and Future Army', in B. Bond (ed.), *Eyes to your Front: Studies in the First World War* (Staplehurst: Spellmount, 1999), p.51
23   *FSR* (1912 amendments), p.126.
24   Eric Grove, 'The Discovery of Doctrine: British Naval Thinking at the Close of the Twentieth Century', in Geoffrey Till (ed.), *The Development of British Naval Thinking: Essays in Memory of Bryan Ranft* (London: Routledge, 2006), p.182.
25   For GFBOs, see: TNA, Admiralty File (ADM) 186/595, Grand Fleet Battle Orders, Aug 1914 to May 1916.

In fact, the current doctrinal publication of the RN, *BR 1806*, supports this contention, noting that the Service only started to produce non-tactical doctrine during the latter half of the twentieth century.[26] Tritten's conclusions lend further weight to this interpretation, and he notes that:

> ...the Royal Navy...has primarily devoted its attention to the development of service-unique doctrine at the tactical level of war...The Royal Navy did not have a coherent doctrine at all levels of warfare.[27]

Gordon's *Rules of the Game* argues that the RN had little need for formal written doctrine because, as an organisation, it valued experience rather than theory. In practice, this saw senior naval officers operating in the Nelsonian tradition, a 'band of brothers', commanding with initiative based on a wealth of practical experience.[28] However, contemporary naval officers could see value in the production of doctrine that was more in keeping with the Army's approach to *FSR*. As an officer of the Royal Marines noted in 1913:

> ...the Army have ... complete guidance for their officers in the field service regulations [sic], it is greatly to be wished that some authoritative pronouncement of the same nature might be issued in some form to the Navy.[29]

Thus, Grove's suggestion that the RN was a doctrine-heavy organisation during this period must be contextualised, and, whilst the RN could be considered an organisation that possessed doctrine at the tactical level, it did not produce doctrine that is in keeping with the definitions highlighted in the opening section of the chapter.

The RN spent its intellectual energy in a different direction, and, as Hunt records, it was 'a service whose recent history and whose current sense of urgency were geared to a material ethic.'[30] This ethic stemmed from a period in which technological evolution moved at a rapid pace.[31] As Schurman suggests, the result was a RN preoccupied with 'means rather than ends', manifesting itself in 'a vigorous drive for mechanical

26   MoD, *British Maritime Doctrine, BR 1806, Third Edition* (London, MoD, 2004), pp.1 – 2.
27   J.J. Tritten, 'Doctrine and Fleet Tactics in the Royal Navy', in J.J. Tritten and L. Donolo, (eds.), *A Doctrine Reader: The Navies of the United States, Great Britain, France, Italy, and Spain*, Newport Paper No. 9 (Newport, RI: Naval War College, 1995), pp.18-28, 30-31.
28   Andrew Gordon, *The Rules of the Game: Jutland and British Naval Command* (London: John Murray, 1996), p.156.
29   L.S.T. Halliday, 'Orders and Instructions', *The Naval Review*, 1 (3) (1913), p.172.
30   Barry Hunt, *Sailor-Scholar: Admiral Sir Herbert Richmond, 1871-1946* (Ontario: Wilfrid Laurier University Press, 1982), p.3.
31   Bryan Ranft (ed.), *Technical Change and British Naval Policy, 1860-1939* (London: Hodder and Stoughton, 1977), p.ix.

excellence.'[32] As was the case with the Army, the RN stressed its wider service philosophy to its personnel via the education of its officers, particularly as young officer recruits. Thus, the RN's educational system was oriented toward the technical and the material. Both Lambert and Dickinson reflect upon the syllabus of education for officer cadets, noting its scientific and mathematical focus.[33]

An examination of the educational records of two of the NW's most important officers, C.R. Samson (the NW's first operational commander) and Murray Sueter (the first Director of the Admiralty's Air Department), confirms the technical nature of the syllabus upon which cadets were examined, a syllabus that continued to influence subsequent promotions examinations.[34] The RN's wider educational processes also emphasised a technologically based ethic, and, as Lambert records, 'the work of the Royal Naval College before 1914 was limited, dominated by technical issues and made little contribution to the development of naval thought.'[35] Such educational experiences, which reinforced the RN's material ethic, did much to shape naval attitudes to doctrine. It was within these wider organisational and doctrinal contexts that organised air power and air power doctrine came to be created in Britain.

Up to late 1911, both the Army and Navy had shown some interest in aviation. For the RN, the first tentative steps were to train a small cadre of pilots, whilst, for the Army, a small Air Battalion was created as part of the Royal Engineers.[36] In attempting to give further shape and direction to these efforts, a Sub-Committee of the Committee for Imperial Defence (CID) tasked a small Technical Sub-Committee to take steps to establish a 'National Corps of Aviators.'[37] The Technical Sub-Committee gathered evidence during the winter of 1911 / 1912, before producing its report in February 1912.[38] The report recommended the creation of a joint Army and Navy Flying Corps,

---

32   D.M. Schurman, *The Education of a Navy: The Development of British Naval Strategic Thought, 1867-1914* (London: Cassell, 1965), p.4; Gordon, *Rules of the Game*, p.346.

33   Andrew Lambert, 'The Development of Education in the Royal Navy: 1854-1914' in Till (ed.), *The Development of British Naval Thinking*, p.41; H.W. Dickinson, *Educating the Royal Navy: Eighteenth- and Nineteenth Century Education for Officers* (London: Routledge, 2007), pp.162 – 163.

34   For Sueter's examination records as a cadet, see TNA, ADM 6/470, H.M.S. *Britannia* at Dartmouth; final and term examination mark book. For Samson's records, see TNA, ADM 6/471. For Sueter's promotional records, see TNA, ADM 13/226. See also Imperial War Museum, London (IWM), Papers of Air Commodore C. R. Samson (SP), DS/MISC/100, Examinations and promotion to Lieutenant, May 1902.

35   Andrew Lambert, '"History is the Sole Foundation for the Construction of a Sound and Living Common Doctrine": The Royal Naval College, Greenwich, and Doctrine Development down to BR1806' in Andrew Dorman, M.L. Smith & Matthew Uttley (eds.), *The Changing Face of Maritime Power* (London: Macmillan Press, 1999), p.47.

36   Arthur Longmore, *From Sea to Sky, 1910-1945* (London, Geoffrey Bles, 1946), pp.10-20; Air Ministry, *AP125: A Short History of the Royal Air Force* (London, HMSO, 1936), p.9.

37   TNA, Cabinet Files (CAB) 16/16, Report of Committee of Imperial Defence Sub-Committee on Aerial Navigation, 29 February 1912.

38   *Ibid.*

comprising a Military Wing, a Naval Wing, and a combined Central Flying School (CFS), where the pilots of the Corps could be trained.[39] The Admiralty's enthusiasm for the combined RFC concept quickly waned, and the NW was subsumed into the wider organisation of the RN in mid-1914.[40] However, between 1912 and 1914 the Military and Naval Wings cooperated on a number of issues, or at least planned to do so. As Parton highlights, this included cooperation regarding the production of doctrinal manuals.[41]

An exchange of letters took place during the winter of 1912/1913 regarding the production of a *Training Manual* for the RFC.[42] Whilst the relevant correspondence contained a degree of ambiguity, senior officers within both the Military and Naval Wings agreed on a shared *Training Manual* concept. The first part of the *Manual* was to be jointly produced by both Wings, and was to be utilised in training RFC personnel in the technical aspects of their professions, including flying in the air and the care and maintenance of aircraft.[43] The *Manual* was to be written by Godfrey Paine, the naval officer who commanded the CFS, and Frederick Sykes, who commanded the MW.[44] Meeting the original training/technical functions for the volume, the RFC's *Training Manual, Part I* appeared in print during 1914.[45] In addition, both Wings were to produce separate volumes that provided specialist material on the application of air power in specific military or naval contexts. These volumes appeared in June (MW) and November 1914 (NW) and constituted the second part of the *Training Manual* concept.[46] As the analysis below indicates, the contrast between their content was conspicuous, and the nature of these volumes illuminates the differing attitudes to doctrine held by military and naval aviators, itself a product of the approaches and attitudes to doctrine held by the Army and RN respectively.

39   *Ibid.*
40   S.W. Roskill (ed.), *Documents Relating the Naval Air Service, Volume I, 1908-1918* (London: Navy Records Society, 1969), pp.156-162. Extracts from Admiralty Circular, 'Royal Naval Air Service – Organisation', 1 July 1914.
41   Parton, 'Royal Air Force Doctrine', p.34 and fn. 83.
42   TNA, AIR 1/762/204/4/175, Proofs for correction and amendment of the RFC Training Manual Part I.
43   Parton, 'Royal Air Force Doctrine', p.34 and fn. 83.
44   TNA, AIR 1/762/204/4/175, Proofs, Training Manual, Part I. See various letters between Paine and Sykes, January to June 1913.
45   TNA, AIR 10/179, General Staff, AP143, *Training Manual, Royal Flying Corps, Part I* (Provisional, 1914).
46   See General Staff, AP144, *Training Manual, RFC (Military Wing), Part II* (Jun 1914). See also TNA, AIR 1/824/204/5/71, Admiralty Air Department, *Training Manual, RFC (Naval Wing), Part II* (1914).

The Military Wing and the *Training Manual*

As the correspondence surrounding the production of the MW's *Training Manual, Part II* indicates, Sykes and his staff officers frequently referred to the volume as a 'War manual.'[47] In being a 'War manual', it is clear that Sykes and his team foresaw the purpose of the *Training Manual, Part II* as giving some indication regarding the war fighting functions of the MW. For example, during September 1913, an uncorrected proof copy of the *Manual* was provided to Major-General Charles Monro, commanding the 2nd (London) Division. The aim was to provide Monro with 'an idea of the lines on which the aircraft will be working during the Army Exercise.'[48] Sitting beneath *FSR* in the doctrinal hierarchy of the Army, the general tone of the *Manual* adhered to the linguistic style and philosophical underpinnings of *FSR*. The focus of the content of the MW *Manual* was not on prescription but rather on infusing the Wing with the correct spirit.[49]

Of course, it was difficult to be overly prescriptive at this stage, given that the practical application of military air power was still in its infancy. This was particularly profound in relation to the task of aerial fighting, and the sections in the *Manual* that addressed this subject were understandably limited in both scope and length.[50] More generally, the MW's *Manual* addressed a range of subjects, including reconnaissance (the longest section), offensive action against ground troops, and 'miscellaneous duties', which included artillery reconnaissance; a task that would attain central importance during the First World War.[51] However, tactical and technical prescription was not the overriding purpose of the *Manual*. Stressing that 'opposing aircraft…must be relentlessly pursued and destroyed' was not included to aid pilots in the tactical execution of their duties; it was included to ensure that operations were conducted in the correct spirit, framing the work of the Wing in moral terms.[52] There was also a traditional purpose to the *Manual*, and, as Sykes noted in various letters to the War Office, it was to be used in aiding the instruction and training of MW personnel.[53] As such, the *Manual* was similar, at least in part, to other Army manuals

47   TNA, AIR 1/785/204/4/558, Training Manuals for RFC (Part II), Suggestions redrawing up of Letter, Brooke-Popham to MW, HQ, 6 September 1913.
48   TNA, AIR 1/785/204/4/558, Training Manuals for RFC (Part II). Letter, Sykes to GSO, 'White Force', HQ 2nd London Division, 9 September 1913.
49   F.H. Sykes, *Aviation in Peace and War* (London: Edward Arnold & Co., 1922), p.39.
50   General Staff, *MW Training Manual, Part II*, pp.46-49.
51   General Staff, *MW Training Manual, Part II*, pp.29-46, 49-51. Also, see Parton, 'Royal Air Force Doctrine', chapter two; James Pugh, 'The Conceptual Origins of the Control of the Air: British Military and Naval Aviation, 1911-1918', (PhD Thesis, University of Birmingham, 2012), pp.97-109.
52   General Staff, *MW Training Manual, Part II*, p.49.
53   For example, see TNA, AIR 1/785/204/4/558, Training Manuals for RFC (Part II). Letter, Sykes to Directorate of Military Aeronautics (DMA), War Office, 11 October 1913.

of the period. Whilst *FSR* set the tone for the nature of Army operations, doctrinal manuals such as the *Training Manual* and *Cavalry Training* provided more in the way of practical detail.[54]

The concerted effort to make copies of the *Manual* available for the Wing's training regime during the summer of 1914 reflected this reality.[55] However, Sykes's desire to ensure the widespread dissemination of the *Manual* extended beyond the more traditional training aspects of doctrine. Copies of the *Manual* were made available across the ranks within the Wing, whilst a strenuous administrative effort was made to ensure the volume was available for an important General Staff conference of January 1914.[56] The goal was to provide a coherent vision for the application of military air power, and the *Training Manual, Part II* was to be the vehicle to articulate this vision to all personnel; from junior Non-Commissioned Officers within the Wing to the most senior commanders within the Army.[57] It is also instructive to record that the *Manual* was subject to a period of scrutiny and testing, and senior officers within the Wing were asked to provide feedback on its content.[58] Great care was taken to ensure that the message contained with the volume was coherent and in keeping with the wider doctrinal philosophy of the Army. The senior command team of the MW possessed a clear understanding of this philosophy and the wider organisational goals of their parent service. This is explained in part by the high concentration of Staff College graduates within this group.

The influence and importance of the Staff College education to the Army of this period has been highlighted by Bond, and continues to provoke debate.[59] As Bond concludes, after an inauspicious start, Camberley came to fill an increasingly important role prior to the First World War.[60] A future Chief of the Imperial General Staff, Sir William Robertson, who was the commandant at Camberley from 1910 to 1913, reflected upon the importance of the College, suggesting that:

54 For example, see: General Staff, War Office, *Cavalry Training* (London: HMSO, 1912).
55 TNA, AIR 1/785/204/4/558, Training Manuals for RFC (Part II). Letter, Sykes to DMA, 9 May 1914.
56 TNA, AIR 1/785/204/4/558, Training Manuals for RFC (Part II). Letter, Sykes to DMA, 29 April 1914. See also letter, DMA to Sykes, 13 October 1913.
57 TNA, AIR 1/785/204/4/558, Training Manuals for RFC (Part II). Letter, Sykes to DMA, 29 April 1914.
58 For example, see TNA, AIR 1/785/204/4/558, Training Manuals for RFC (Part II). Letter, Sykes to various senior officers, 5 September 1913.
59 Brian Bond, *The Victorian Army and the Staff College, 1854-1914* (Norfolk: Eyre Methuen, 1972), *passim*; Bowman & Connelly, *Edwardian Army*, p.34 and pp.40-41; Travers, *Killing Ground*, pp.86-88; Simon Robbins, *British Generalship on the Western Front, 1914-1918: Defeat into Victory* (London: Frank Cass, 2005), p.10; Gary Sheffield, *The Chief: Douglas Haig, The British Army and the First World War* (London: Aurum, 2011), pp.25-28; David French, *Military Identities: The Regimental System, the British Army, and the British People, c.1870-2000* (Oxford: Oxford University Press, 2005), pp.160-161.
60 Bond, *Staff College*, p.328.

…there is no position in the army where greater influence can be exerted over the rising generation of officers than that of Commandant of the Staff College… [T]he name [Staff College] is rather a misnomer, and I have always thought that "War School" would be more appropriate.[61]

Bond subscribes to such an interpretation, noting that Staff College came to provide a 'school of thought' to the Army. The aim of such an approach was to 'create a sense of uniformity and harmony in the Army as a whole.'[62] For the MW, Staff College graduates in its senior command team included David Henderson (Director General of Military Aeronautics), Sefton Brancker (Henderson's deputy), Frederick Sykes, Robert Brooke-Popham (senior squadron commander and staff officer), and Herbert Musgrave (officer in charge of technical experimentation).[63] For example, during Sykes's Staff College experience, the most significant lessons driven home included the importance of moral superiority and the need for aggressive, offensive action.[64] In addition, Sykes gained familiarity with the language of the Army, and could frame his ideas using Staff College approved taxonomy and concepts. As a result, when Sykes and his team came to create MW doctrine between 1912 and 1914, words *did* have the same meaning for all, and the *Training Manual, Part II* contained a clear and concise vision for the application of military air power. The well-developed deployment plans for the Wing, the result of extensive staff work between 1913 and 1914, built upon the coherence of this vision.[65]

Gray cautions against overemphasising the influence of official publications, yet Ash suggests that the 'size of the manual and the areas covered by it are less important than its influence. It was the air power bible the RFC carried into battle.'[66] It is telling that Sir John French, who would command the BEF in France from August 1914 to December 1915, was amongst the MW's most prominent supporters. French took an early interest in the development of the MW, chairing a meeting of the Royal Aeronautical Society in early 1913.[67] On the outbreak of war, French took time

61   William Robertson, *From Private to Field Marshal* (London: Constable & Company, 1921), pp.169-170.
62   Bond, *Staff College*, pp.258-259.
63   Examples were selected from the *Army List*. See War Office, *The Quarterly Army List for the Quarter Ending 31 March 1914* (London: HMSO, April 1914).
64   Frederick Sykes, *From Many Angles: An Autobiography* (London: Harrap & Co, 1942), pp.70-73.
65   For example, see TNA, AIR 1/118/15/40/56, Military Wing Mobilisation Plan, 29 July 1914.
66   Gray, *Leadership, Direction and Legitimacy*, p.41; Eric Ash, *Sir Frederick Sykes and the Air Revolution, 1912-1918* (London, Frank Cass, 1999), p.40.
67   F.H. Sykes, 'Military Aviation', *The Aeronautical Journal*, 17 (67) (1913), pp.127-139. 'On French and air power, see J. Pugh, 'David Henderson and Command of the Royal Flying Corps' in S. Jones (ed), *Stemming the Tide: Officers and Leadership in the British Expeditionary Force 1914* (Solihull: Helion & Company, 2013), pp.270-272, 274-276.

from his busy schedule to visit the squadrons of the MW as they landed in France.[68] French commented in his diary that he was 'much impressed with the general efficiency of the aircraft force. I saw the Squadron Commanders and told them so.'[69] His despatches from the opening campaigns of the conflict contained significant praise for the support that Henderson, Sykes, and his units were able to provide to the BEF.[70] French was perhaps even more impressed with the spirit and enthusiasm of the MW and its personnel, and supported the expansion of military air power assets during the winter of 1914. Such efforts continued on an even greater scale by his successor, Sir Douglas Haig.[71]

The Naval Wing and the *Training Manual*

The NW's version of the *Training Manual, Part II* appeared in November 1914, and, as Parton reflects, 'it was very different to the RFC [MW] equivalent ... [containing] ... no reference to the organisation or utilisation of the RNAS [NW].'[72] The volume focussed on the technological and scientific aspects of flight, and initial sections addressed such subjects as the 'theoretical principles of flight' and the 'construction of aircraft.' The volume also contained an entire chapter devoted to tables and formulae.[73] As Parton records, the providence of the document is unclear, although senior officers within the NW were aware of the need to articulate the functions of the Wing to interested parties.[74] For example, the guidelines issued to Sueter as Director of the Admiralty's Air Department (DAD) included instructions to achieve such an aim.[75] Moreover, in discussions surrounding the production of the *Training Manual, Part I*, both Sueter and Paine indicated their interest in producing material that was more in keeping with the MW's approach to the second part of the *Training Manual*.[76]

68   Maurice Baring, *R.F.C. H.Q.* (London: Bell & Sons, 1920), p.17.
69   G. French, (ed.), *Some War Diaries, Addresses and Correspondence of Field Marshal the Right Honourable, Earl of Ypres* (London: Herbert Jenkins, 1937), pp.144-145. Extract from War Diary, 14 August 1914.
70   J. French, *The Despatches of Sir John French, Volume I* (London: Chapman & Hall, 1914), p.16, 58, pp.60-61, 158-159.
71   S.F. Wise, *Canadian Airmen in the First World War: The Official History of the Royal Canadian Air Force, Volume I* (Toronto, CA: University of Toronto Press, 1980), pp.342-343; David Jordan & G.D. Sheffield, 'Douglas Haig and Air Power' in Peter Gray and Sebastian Cox, (eds.), *Air Power Leadership: Theory and Practice*, (London: HMSO, 2002), pp.264-282.
72   Parton, 'Royal Air Force Doctrine', p.37.
73   TNA, AIR 1/824/204/5/71, Admiralty Air Department, *NW Training Manual, Part II*, chapters one, two, and eleven.
74   Parton, 'Royal Air Force Doctrine', pp.37-38.
75   Roskill, *Documents*, pp.60-61. Instructions for the Director of the Air Department, September 1912.
76   TNA, AIR 1/762/204/4/175, Proofs, Training Manual, Part I. Letter, Paine to Sueter, 10 January 1913.

It appears that portions of the content of the NW's *Part II* derived, at least in part, from a lecture produced for delivery to the personnel of the RN. The lecture, published in 1913, addressed various aspects of the use of 'Aircraft for Naval Purposes.'[77] The focus was also extensively technical in nature, and this probably explains why it was not included as part of Parton's survey of air power doctrine of this period.[78] However, it could be suggested that this lecture provides the first example of NW doctrine. There were some sections of the text that considered the organisational and operational context of the NW.[79] It is instructive that these sections were found at the rear of the text. They accompanied qualifying statements stating that the value of air power was still unclear and that, in more general terms, its application would not revolutionise naval warfare.[80] When the NW's edition of the *Training Manual, Part II* appeared in November 1914, these sections had not been included, and preference was given to technical and scientific considerations. Thus, the NW did not produce a second part to the *Training Manual* that was in keeping with the wider objectives expressed for the volume during early 1913.[81] This left the Wing without a document that detailed its war fighting functions and without a clear vision for the application of air power in a naval context, concerns highlighted in Admiralty papers of the period.[82]

Of course, the challenges facing naval aviators were profound, in both a technological and conceptual sense.[83] As Goulter argues, the NW's focus on experimentation and diversification was entirely appropriate, as policy and doctrine would serve only to constrain innovative approaches to the conceptualisation of air power roles and practices.[84] Moreover, the necessity of using aircraft in extremely trying operational conditions, particularly over water, meant that a focus on technology was appropriate.[85] Furthermore, Abbatiello suggests that the

> ...absence of a coherent British maritime air doctrine ... at the start of the First World War comes as no surprise. Theory and history combine to form doctrine, yet at the start of the war, the RNAS [NW] possessed no combat experience to provide a guide for operating their tiny force of aircraft against the Germans.[86]

77   TNA, AIR 1/626/17/47, 'Lecture on Aircraft for Naval Purposes', 1913.
78   *Ibid*, pp.3-16.
79   *Ibid*, pp.26-28.
80   *Ibid*, p.28.
81   TNA, AIR 1/762/204/4/175, Proofs, Training Manual, Part I.
82   For example, see National Maritime Museum (NMM), Papers of Arthur Longmore (LP), MS 51/012 – ADL/2/1/5 – 8: Minutes of Air Department Conference, 8 Jan 1914.
83   H.A. Jones, *The War in the Air, Vol. II* (Oxford, Clarendon Press, 1928), pp.335-337.
84   Goulter, *A Forgotten Offensive*, pp.8-9.
85   Jones, *War in the Air, Vol. II*, pp.335-337.
86   J.J. Abbatiello, 'British Naval Aviation and the Anti-Submarine Campaign, 1917-18', (PhD Thesis, King's College London, 2004), p.98.

However, as the preceding discussion of the RN's attitude to doctrine indicates, the minds of naval officers were attuned to technical and material considerations. Thus, when discussions took place within the NW regarding the production of the *Training Manual*, it was such considerations that, largely, helped shape its content. As current naval doctrine records:

> …doctrine…serves to inform the wider defence community and those with an interest in understanding the role and functions of maritime [read air] power.[87]

When Sueter observed in his autobiography that the Sea Lords 'found themselves quite at sea over air matters', it in fact reflected his own failure to meet the objectives of the post of DAD.[88] Without establishing, recording, and disseminating a doctrine for the application of naval air power, words *did not* mean the same for all. The result was a difficult relationship between the RN and its aerial component.[89]

The service's most senior operational commanders were enthusiastic about the use of air power, and Admirals Jellicoe and Sir David Beatty pressed the Admiralty continuously during the First World War with regard to improving the aerial resources available to the RN.[90] Beatty was especially concerned at the lack of coherence in naval aviation policy during the conflict, and the result was the former's support for the creation of an independent air service.[91] For Beatty, naval aviators were not an integrated element of the RN, and they did not provide adequate support to the fleet.[92] As Gordon argues, the RN of the Fisher era was weighed down by a prescriptive tactical doctrine that stifled initiative, resulting in missed opportunities at the Battle of Jutland.[93] However, whilst the wider RN may have needed less of the 'book', aviation within a naval context would have benefitted significantly from adopting an approach to doctrine that was in keeping with the material produced by military aviators; an approach individuals such as Sueter and Paine had accepted as important.

Conclusion

In examining the RFC's *Training Manuals*, this chapter has explored the differing approaches of military and naval aviators toward the production of doctrine. These approaches were influenced by wider organisational and contextual considerations.

87   MoD, *BR1806*, pp.4-5.
88   M.F. Sueter, *Airmen or Noahs: Fair Play for our Airmen, The Great "Neon" Myth Exposed* (London: Pitman & Sons, 1928), pp.16-17.
89   Pugh, 'Conceptual Origins', chapter six.
90   For a typical example, see A. Temple Patterson, (ed.), *The Jellicoe Papers, Vol. I* (London, Navy Records Society, 1966), pp.173-174. Letter, Jellicoe to Admiralty, 29 July 1915.
91   Roskill, *Documents*, p.497. Letter, Beatty to Geddes, 12 August 1917.
92   Roskill, *Documents*, pp.520-522. Letter, Beatty to Geddes, 22 August 1917.
93   Gordon, *Rules of the Game, passim*.

Producing their *Manual* within a service that possessed a progressive attitude to doctrine, military aviators understood the importance of articulating and disseminating doctrinal material. The process of producing the MW's *Training Manual, Part II* demonstrated a sophisticated understanding of this reality. The message contained within the *Manual* helped to ensure the relatively smooth integration of air power into the Army, based upon the strong support for military aviation offered by senior figures within the BEF. Of course, the ability of the MW to create such coherent doctrine also reflected that the objectives and operational challenges facing military aviators were more straightforward and obvious than their colleagues in the NW.

In contrast, naval aviators, operating within the cultural and contextual constraints of the RN, were attuned to material and technical considerations. The NW continued to innovate, but, without a guiding vision to help shape these efforts, the process of integrating air power into a naval context was slow and painful. The difficulties encountered may have been managed more successfully had the NW adopted a progressive approach to the production of doctrine, spreading a coherent vision for the application of naval air power. The challenges that confronted the NW, particularly the diffuse operational requirements of the RN, and complex technological obstacles, must be acknowledged as factors that limited the ability of the organisation to produce coherent naval air power doctrine. Moreover, in keeping with Gordon's analysis of naval doctrine during this period, which highlights the focus on experience rather than theory, RN personnel lacked experience of producing doctrine in the vein of *FSR*. Nonetheless, had individuals such as Sueter and Paine followed through with their suggestion to produce a manual that provided details of the 'Strategical uses of Aircraft' in a naval context then the wider RN would have been better informed about the functions and roles to be undertaken by their colleagues in the NW.[94] Thus, the development of naval air power doctrine, however simple, could have helped smooth the process of integrating aviation into a naval context. The importance of military aviation doctrine was not in its detail, but came via its deployment of language that helped the Army understand the functions, limitations, and potential of air power. As such, the MW's doctrinal model was worthy of emulation by the NW.

94   TNA, AIR 1/762/204/4/175, Proofs, Training Manual, Part I. Letter, Paine to Sueter, 10 January 1913.

9

"Hopeless Inefficiency"?
The Transformation and Operational Performance of Brigade Staff, 1916-1918

Aimée Fox-Godden

In his wartime memoir, Captain Gerald Burgoyne declared that the red tabs of the staff were 'the insignia of hopeless inefficiency'.[1] The historiography of the First World War has censured the performance and conduct of the staff with commentators citing their ignorance of front line conditions as a key criticism. One of the enduring myths surrounding the staff can be found in Lieutenant-General Sir Launcelot Kiggell's breakdown at Passchendaele. Kiggell, Field Marshal Sir Douglas Haig's Chief of Staff from 1915-1917, supposedly burst into tears at Passchendaele when he saw the appalling conditions, exclaiming 'Good God, did we really send men to fight in this!' Bond has proven beyond doubt that the statement is apocryphal, but it is still used to illustrate the cloistered nature of the staff in the First World War.[2] In contrast to this myth, W.N. Nicholson (GSO I, 51st (Highland) Division) declared that 'it is a fallacy to think that the officer with red tabs has a 'Cushy' job'.[3]

The brigade was the smallest formation to have a formal staff structure.[4] Brigade headquarters formally constituted the brigade commander, a Brigade Major (BM)

1   G.A. Burgoyne, *The Burgoyne Diaries*, edited by C. Davidson (London: Thomas Harmsworth, 1985), p.281.
2   F. Davies and G. Maddocks, *Bloody Red Tabs – General Officer Casualties of the Great War, 1914-1918* (London: Leo Cooper, 1995), pp.16-21.
3   W.N. Nicholson, *Behind the Lines: An Account of Administrative Staff work in the British Army 1914-1918*, New Edition (Stevenage: Strong Oak, 1990), p.116.
4   P. Simkins, "Building Blocks': Aspects of Command and Control at Brigade level in the BEF's Offensive Operations, 1916-1918', in G. Sheffield and D. Todman, (eds.), *Command and Control on the Western Front: The British Army's Experience 1914-18* (Stroud: History Press, 2007), pp.141-172; R. Lee, 'The Australian Staff: The Forgotten Men of the First AIF', in P. Dennis and J. Grey, (eds.), *1918 Defining Victory* (Canberra, ACT: Army History Unit, 1999).

and a Staff Captain.[5] The appointment was far from 'cushy'. The BM fulfilled the 'G' function of staff work, notably planning the brigade's operations, interpreting commands from higher headquarters, and transforming them into precise instructions and specific actions. As Simkins notes, the BM was expected to keep his commander abreast of all matters concerning the efficiency or strength of the brigade, to advise the brigade commander as to which local objectives could and should be reached, and to coordinate actions by smaller units to secure those objectives. This involved liaison with neighbouring formations and the coordination of artillery and trench mortar support on the brigade front. It was at the BM's level that 'the minor tactical planning for the battle was undertaken'. His ability was 'a crucial factor in shaping a brigade's battle performance'.[6] The Staff Captain was responsible for the 'A' and 'Q' function of brigade staff work, ensuring that the brigade was equipped, administered, supplied and, as far as possible, up to strength. He was also expected to supervise the brigade's transport, salvage and dump officers; courts martial; leave; promotions; and spiritual welfare. The 'one Staff' ideal was actively encouraged at brigade level and, despite fulfilling two very distinct roles, it was expected that the BM and Staff Captain would be capable of undertaking the other's duties in case of death, absence or promotion.[7] Although the official roles and responsibilities of brigade staff officers were geared towards administration, these officers were not office-bound. As the war progressed, they often went over and above expectations by directly intervening in front-line operations where appropriate.

Limited scholarship on the various tiers of staff has meant that they are often viewed as a single, homogeneous entity with very little attempt to differentiate their respective roles. Although recent historiography has led to the beginnings of rehabilitation, notably at divisional level and above, scholarship on low-level staff work and military administration has been poorly served despite an increase in doctoral studies at the tactical level of command.[8] This chapter will examine how brigade staff

5   There were officers in addition to the BM and Staff Captain on the brigade staff. These positions included an Orderly Officer (often a staff learner); Veterinary Officer; Intelligence Officer; Bombing Officer; Gas Officer; Musketry Officer; and Trench Mortar Officer.

6   Simkins, 'Building Blocks', p.147.

7   In a conference with his brigadiers in 3rd Australian Division, John Monash reminded his commanders that there were to be 'no watertight compartments' on the brigade staff. Staff Captains were expected to 'know [the] tactical situation' and not act as 'glorified Q.Ms and clerks'. See: Australian War Memorial (AWM), Papers of General Sir John Monash, 3DRL 2316 3/50, Note on conference with brigadiers, 9 August 1917.

8   For an exception to the rule, see, P. Harris, 'The Men who Planned the War: a Study of the Staff of the British Army 1914-1918', (PhD Thesis, University of London, 2014); Lieutenant-Colonel Cuthbert Headlam, *The Military Papers of Lieutenant-Colonel Cuthbert Headlam 1910-1942*, edited by J. Beach (Stroud: History Press, 2010); D. Todman, 'The Grand Lamasery revisited: General Headquarters on the Western Front, 1914-1918', in Sheffield and Todman (eds.), *Command and Control on the Western Front*, pp.39-70; S.

coped and, ultimately, transformed in the face of modern warfare between 1916 and 1918. It will identify the vagaries that brought about this transformation and attempt a preliminary analysis of how the roles, responsibilities, and training of these officers evolved to meet these new challenges through a consideration of formal doctrinal changes and operational examples. In line with current scholarship on bottom up innovation and military adaptation, this chapter will further understanding of how the British Army's low-level administration evolved to meet the challenges of war. As a result, it will expand on Cohen and Grissom's belief that the interaction between 'military people, technology and particular *tactical* circumstances' (emphasis added) drives wartime military innovation.[9]

The Role of the Brigade Staff Officer

The staff that went to war in 1914 was markedly different from the staff that ended the war in 1918. This was, in large part, due to the internal and external impacts of the changing character of warfare that included the rapid expansion of the BEF from four to 76 infantry divisions by November 1918. Additional factors included the inadequacy of battlefield communications, hampering command and control at all levels, and the change from trench warfare to semi-mobile operations in the last months of 1918.[10] These three changes affected all who fought in the BEF and served to have a transformative effect, particularly on the staff officers at brigade headquarters.

The *Staff Manual* (1912) encapsulated the roles and responsibilities of the regular staff officer of 1914. Ordered along similar lines and amplifying the guidance found in *Field Service Regulations* (1909), it provided 'general principles for the guidance of staff officers'.[11] The staff officer had a twofold responsibility: first, assisting his commander in the supervision and control of the operations and requirements of the troops; and second, giving the troops every assistance in carrying out the instructions issued to them.[12] With the onset of trench warfare, headquarters at divisional and brigade levels were positioned much further behind the line giving rise to the belief that staff officers were mentally, as well as physically, remote from the regimental officers in the trenches. On this point, Gerald Burgoyne was particularly scathing.

Robbins, *British Generalship on the Western Front 1914-18: Defeat into Victory* (London: Routledge, 2004).

9   E.A. Cohen, 'Change and Transformation in Military Affairs', *Journal of Strategic Studies*, 27 (3) (2004), pp.395-407; A. Grissom, 'The Future of Military Innovation Studies', *Journal of Strategic Studies*, 29 (5) (2006), pp.905-34.

10   War Office, *Statistics of the Military Effort of the British Empire during the Great War, 1914-1920* (London: HMSO, 1922), p.109.

11   The National Archives (TNA), WO 279/862, *Staff Manual*, 1912, p.7.

12   War Office, *Field Service Regulations: Part II Organization and Administration* (reprint, London: HMSO, 1913), p.35.

The whole time I was out there [on the Western Front] I only on one occasion saw one of our Brigade Staff come round our trenches... The consequence was that the Staff were never in touch with the regimental officer... nothing now irritates the Regimental Officer more than the sight of the Red Tabs.[13]

As early as 1915, Field Marshal Sir John French recognised this divide noting that:

...the great majority of the present Staff Officers are men who have taken their turn in actual fighting at the front as regimental officers.

French further added that:

...the well trained Staff Officer is a valuable asset who cannot be readily replaced, and it is not his duty to expose himself unnecessarily.[14]

The winter of 1914-1915 saw a period of 'great experimentation and improvisation' within British staffs at the same time as the BEF expanded beyond its original two corps structure.[15] This rapid expansion, and the heavy casualties sustained by the staff between 1914 and 1915, led to a severe shortage of trained staff officers at all levels.[16] The resulting dilution of experience and expertise resulted in rapid promotion, particularly amongst lower level staff officers. Unlike the 'Passed Staff College' (*psc*) staff officers who carried out procedures instinctively, newly promoted staff simply did not have the necessary experience or detailed knowledge that had been taken for granted in the past.[17] General Sir Ivor Maxse complained in 1915 that 'the Brigade Majors are inexperienced in staff work' and about one in particular 'who cannot write any sort of operation order and apparently cannot learn any routine work'.[18] This, invariably, led to greater centralisation as commanders often 'thought it less trouble' to do the work themselves.[19]

---

13   G.A. Burgoyne, *The Burgoyne Diaries*, p.218.
14   Imperial War Museum (IWM), Private Papers of Field Marshal Sir John French, 75/46/4 7/2 (1), Note on Staff casualties, c. 31 October 1915. See also N. Barr, 'Command in the Transition From Mobile to Static Warfare, August 1914 to March 1915', in Sheffield and Todman (eds.), *Command and Control on the Western Front*, p.28.
15   N. Barr, 'From Mobile to Static Warfare', p.14.
16   See: J. Hussey, 'The Deaths of Qualified Staff Officers in the Great War: 'A Generation Missing'?', *Journal of the Society for Army Historical Research*, 75, (1997), pp.246-259; N. Evans, 'The Deaths of Qualified Staff Officers 1914-18', *Journal of the Society for Army Historical Research*, 78, (2000), pp.29-37.
17   B. Bond, 'The Staff College, the General Staff and the Test of War, 1914-1915', *Journal of the Royal United Services Institute*, 116, (1971), p.39.
18   Quoted in S. Robbins, 'British Generalship on the Western Front, 1914-1918', (PhD Thesis, University of London, 2001), p.126.
19   TNA, WO 32/5153, Report of Committee under General Sir W Braithwaite on Staff Organisation, 6 March 1919, Clause 59, p.10.

Brigade Staff Training

Instances of sub-standard staff work can be partly attributed to the over promotion of unqualified officers who had to learn on the job, but also due to a lack of formalised training. The closure of the Staff Colleges at Camberley and Quetta on the outbreak of war merely exacerbated the problem of an already limited pool of *psc* staff officers. Prior to hostilities, the Staff College at Camberley was producing approximately fifty graduates per year.[20] The closure of the Staff Colleges denied the Army a formal solution to the growing requirement for staff officers to administer a rapidly expanded army. The shortage of trained officers against the sheer scale of the war was 'a situation for which no precedent existed'.[21] Of the 105 infantry brigades on the Western Front in November 1915, only twenty-seven BMs (26%) were *psc* officers, falling to seven (4%) in the 163 infantry brigades by July 1916.[22]

The lack of formalised training ushered in a period of *ad hoc*-ism, particularly in late 1915 and early 1916. Major Agar Adamson, second in command of Princess Patricia's Canadian Light Infantry, summed this up in a letter to his wife in January 1916:

> I think both the division and brigade staffs are doing their best but they have no experience and are in a shocking muddle… We are in a constant state of change and jump, and so are they, nothing runs smoothly and none of the staff are sure of themselves. Very unlike the brigade they took us from where every officer had been a staff officer for years.[23]

The Army's lack of formalised training contributes to the wider debate over the Army as an 'amateur' or a 'professional' body. Historians such as Jones have argued that the Army's *ad hoc*-ism allowed it to adapt more easily during the first few months of the war.[24] Conversely, Bowman and Connelly have attributed the Army's reluctance to adopt a specific direction partly because of its conflicted strategic policy.[25] The pre-war Army was torn between its imperial commitments and a potential war on the continent. Because of this dual commitment, the Army was required to be flexible in its

20   J. Hussey, 'A Generation Missing', p.247.
21   *Ibid.*, p.254.
22   General Staff, *SS 407 Composition of the Headquarters of the Forces in the Field*, November 1915 (London: Harrison, 1915); General Staff, *SS 407 Composition of the Headquarters of the Forces in the Field*, July 1916 (London: Harrison, 1916).
23   Lieutenant-Colonel Agar Adamson, *Letters of Agar Adamson, 1914-1919*, edited by N. Christie (Ottawa: CEF Books, 1997), p.124; I. McCulloch, '"Batty Mac" Portrait of a Brigade Commander of the Great War, 1915-1917', *Canadian Military History*, 7 (4) (1998), p.14.
24   S. Jones, *From Boer War to World War: Tactical Reform of the British Army, 1902-1914* (Norman, OK: University of Oklahoma Press, 2012), pp.213-4.
25   T. Bowman and M. Connelly, *The Edwardian Army: Recruiting, Training and Deploying the British Army 1902-1914* (Oxford: Oxford University Press, 2012), pp.65-6.

approach. Indeed, it entered the First World War as an institution that prided itself on adaptation and devolved decision-making. This decentralisation encouraged a highly individualised, rather than a 'one size fits all' approach. The initial lack of formalised training represented an extension of its pre-war ethos. The eventual establishment of formal training schools revealed an Army attempting to assimilate and disseminate its experience. However, the fact that the army set its own standards within these schools suggests an organisation that had not fully professionalised.

The lack of experience and the atmosphere of uncertainty often meant that staffs were too busy training themselves. With no formalised system for staff training, some enterprising formations took it upon themselves to devise their own courses for 'instruction in staff duties'. One such formation was 1st Division. The course for junior officers, devised by the 'enlightened divisional commander', Major-General Sir Richard Haking, took place in mid-1915 lasting four weeks with approximately fifteen attendees, representing almost every unit in the division. Captain T.C. Owtram, an officer in 1/5th King's Own, recalled the course instructor, 'a captain on the Division Staff' who 'spoke with refreshing disrespectfulness of the misdeeds of the Higher Command'.[26] The first week of the course provided the 'necessary foundation' of staff organisation from GHQ downwards, while the second week dealt with problems of a practical nature, such as moving a brigade from one part of the front to another without blocking supply lines. The second fortnight offered a series of attachments to a brigade headquarters, a battery of the divisional artillery, and to divisional head-quarters itself. Although this informal method for training was welcome, it did little to provide uniformity among staff trainees within the BEF. These *ad hoc* courses owed their existence to the foresight and vision of the divisional commander and, by exten-sion, the ability and capacity of his own staff to run them.

In April 1916, the War Office attempted to introduce uniformity to staff training through the establishment of Staff Schools in Britain. However, the length of the qual-ification – a month's attachment to the staff and a six-week training course – proved too long to satisfy the urgent demand for staff officers in France in 1916. As such, only home appointments were obliged to undertake the attachment.[27] The lessons of the Somme campaign painfully underscored the inadequacies in staff training, empha-sised by the uncertainty and inexperience displayed by the Territorial and New Army formations. Published in May 1916, prior to the Somme campaign, *SS 109* detailed:

> Officers and troops generally do not now possess that military knowledge... which enables them to act promptly on sound lines in unexpected situations.

26   IWM, Private Papers of Captain T.C. Owtram, 83/17/1, Ts memoir, undated, p.14.
27   TNA, WO 293/4, Army Council Instruction (ACI) 786, 11 April 1916, pp.49-50; TNA, WO 293/5, ACI 1506, 2 August 1916, p.4; B. Bond, 'The Staff College', p.39.

They have become accustomed to deliberate action based on precise and detailed orders.[28]

To compensate for the lack of experience, brigade staff tended to produce extremely detailed operation and administrative orders. Captain H. Ramsbotham (Staff Captain, 53 Brigade, 18th (Eastern) Division) produced orders running to nine pages in length for his brigade's attack on Thiepval Ridge.[29] This tendency to account for every eventuality often inhibited initiative and self-reliance on the battlefield. As Lieutenant R.P. Choate recalled of the fighting in 1916, 'staff work (Divisional, Brigade and Battalion) in the earlier stages of the battle was poor. The most competent officers were working on a scale and in conditions of which they had no experience and they had to learn their job'.[30]

It was not until late 1916 that low-level staff training was formalised with the establishment of the Junior Staff School at Hesdin under Lieutenant-Colonel R.A.M. Currie.[31] The first course commenced on 1 November 1916 and ran for six weeks, concentrating on second grade appointments, such as GSO 2, BM, Deputy Assistant Adjutant and Quartermaster General, and Deputy Assistant Quartermaster General. However, in keeping with the Army's 'amateur tradition' and tendency towards pragmatism, divisions were given latitude to offer 'certain instruction by attachment to formations' alongside GHQ's formal training schools.[32] These attachments were particularly common among Staff Captains, who, at this stage of the war, required no formal training for their role. Usually, the officer in question had been a staff learner or orderly officer on a brigade or divisional staff.[33] For example, Major H.W. House spent two months as a staff learner at 56 Brigade before completing a period of seven months as a learner in 19th Division. House was then appointed Staff Captain to 58 Brigade before eventually becoming BM of 57 Brigade in early 1918.[34]

28 General Staff, *SS 109 Training of Divisions for Offensive Action* (GHQ, 1916), p.3.
29 TNA, WO 95/2034, 53 Infantry Brigade Administrative Orders, 24 September 1916. Gary Sheffield also notes 18th (Eastern) Division's 'careful preparation and training'. See: G. Sheffield, *The Somme* (London: Cassell, 2004), p.130.
30 TNA, CAB 45/132, Letter from Lieutenant R.P. Choate to Brigadier-General Sir James Edmonds, 6 April 1936.
31 TNA, WO 256/15, Summary of Schools of Training for the British Expeditionary Force during Winter 1916-1917, undated, p.1.
32 TNA, WO 256/14, Report of Army Commanders' Conference at Rollencourt, 9 December 1916, p.2. For discussion of the British Army's 'amateur tradition', see D. French, *Military Identities: The Regimental System, the British Army, and the British People c. 1870-2000* (Oxford: Oxford University Press, 2008); I.F.W. Beckett, *The Amateur Military Tradition 1558-1945* (Manchester: Manchester University Press, 1991).
33 Commanders seeking to replace their staff casualties had used the 'learner' system from as early as 1915. See: B. Bond, 'The Staff College', p.39.
34 IWM, Private Papers of Major H.W. House, 88/56/1, Ts Memoir, undated, pp.19-36.

The Junior Staff School was shut down during the spring and summer operations of 1917, reopening at Cambridge University on 1 October 1917 to train staff officers during the autumn and winter.[35] It had a similar setup to its 1916 predecessor, running for six weeks and concentrating on second grade appointments.[36] The mornings at the Staff School were largely theoretical with lectures and outdoor activities. In the afternoon, groups of candidates had to prepare an appreciation of the morning's work, including the preparation of maps, drawing up a march table, and the writing of orders.[37] This work was based on actual operation orders from Armies or Corps, thus placing learning in an operational context rather than an invented theoretical scenario. Generally, once officers had completed their staff training, they undertook attachment positions as assistants or learners. After completing the Staff Course in May 1917, Lieutenant Philip Ledward spent a month attached to 186 Brigade before spending four weeks attached to 62nd (2nd West Riding) Division headquarters. In September 1917, he was appointed Staff Captain to 23 Brigade (8th Division) where he remained until mid-1918.[38]

In conjunction with GHQ's systematic review of Staff Duties in April 1918, the preliminary training of staff officers was reviewed in the July.[39] Staff training devolved from GHQ down to Army level and was based on principles rather than prescription.[40] The guidance recommended that staff officers should be aged between 21 and 35 and should not be above the rank of captain.[41] All potential staff officers were required to undertake a Probationary Course with each Army determining the direction and format of the course. However, the Probationary Course was to include at least three weeks mandatory attachment to the staff of an infantry brigade. If officers were deemed suitable for further training, they were permitted to attend the Staff

35   General Staff, *SS 152 Instructions for the Training of the British Armies in France (Provisional)* (GHQ, 1917); S. Robbins, 'British Generalship', p.128.

36   Third grade appointments (Staff Captain and GSO 3) still adhered to the guidance of late 1916 with the staff learner system and the newly established 'learners' course'. See: TNA, WO 95/365, Outline of System for the Training of Staff Officers during Autumn and Winter 1917 (O.B./1329), 26 July 1917, p.1; TNA, WO 293/7, ACI 1379, 7 September 1917, pp.14-15.

37   IWM, Private Papers of Brigadier T.S. Louch, 12281 P271, Part III – 1917-18 Staff Duties, undated, pp.9-10.

38   IWM, Private Papers of Lieutenant P.A. Ledward, 76/120/1, Personal Ms Diary, undated.

39   IWM, Private Papers of Major-General G.P. Dawnay, 69/21/2, Instructions for the Preliminary Training of Staff Officers in France (O.B./1329), 6 July 1918, p.1.

40   This 'principle' approach to staff training went against the Army's gradual shift away from 'principle' manuals towards more prescriptive ones. As Mitchell has remarked, 'the tendency to prescribe the context and application of principles became more marked and noticeable', see: S.B.T. Mitchell, 'The Training and Preparation of Three Battalions 1914-1918', (MA Dissertation, University of London, 2008), and A. Simpson, *Directing Operations: British Corps Command on the Western Front, 1914-18* (Stroud: Spellmount, 2006).

41   In 1916, the age range was 23-35 years. See: TNA, WO 293/5, ACI 1506, 2 August 1916, p.4.

Course. The content of this course was also to be directed by Army, but had to include six weeks attachment to a staff in all three branches – General, Adjutant and Quartermaster – and a further two weeks in another arm, such as the artillery or cavalry. The decision to ensure that potential staff officers had experience in the different branches and within different service arms suggests a response to concerns that the staff was working in 'watertight compartments'.[42]

Officers who passed the Staff Course and were recommended for staff employment were eligible for appointment as GSO 3 or Staff Captain. It was now no longer enough to learn 'on the job'. The training review aligned with the Army's attempts at professionalism and directly responded to concerns that the supply of trained staff officers was dwindling. The guidance paid particular attention to the shortage of staff officers in its call for the creation of a reserve of qualified staff officers for appointment as BMs.

Brigade Staff in Operations

The transformation of staff training during the war has parallels with the changing role of the brigade staff in operations. The inadequacy of battlefield communications and the transition from static to semi-mobile operations required greater flexibility on the part of the brigade staff. As Brigadier-General H.R. Rees noted, the Somme campaign in particular 'was one of the occasions where any defects in the capacity of the B[riga]de staff would make the completion of [the] arrangements nearly impossible'.[43] Rees detailed the 'multitudinous matters of detail settling' that occupied his staff in October 1916, including:

> H.Q. for Bn. Comdrs, extra ammunition, bombs, water, rations, telephonic communication, allotment of assembly trenches, time table for moving into the trenches, boundaries, spheres of command, liaising with neighbouring troops, prisoners, reserves etc. Add to this reports of the situation and fighting activity of two battalions holding the front line, who have to be relieved by the assaulting battalions.[44]

Unsurprisingly, the planning of operations often resulted in exhaustion. The staff of 3 Australian Infantry Brigade worked 'continuously for six days and five nights' at Pozières in July 1916;[45] while Eric Gore-Browne, then a staff learner in 140 Brigade,

42 This concern was also reflected in the Braithwaite Report. See: TNA, WO 32/5153, Report of Committee under General Sir W. Braithwaite, 6 March 1919, Clauses 4-7, pp.1-2.
43 IWM, Private Papers of Brigadier-General H.C. Rees, 77/179/1, 'A Personal Record of the War 1915 – 1916 – 1917', p.113.
44 *Ibid.*
45 C.E.W. Bean, *The Official History of Australia in the War of 1914-1918* (12 volumes, Sydney, NSW: Angus and Robertson, 1929-1942), III, pp.597-8.

47th (2nd London) Division, declared that '12 hours in the day is not always enough' to carry out the everyday work of a Staff Captain.[46]

In addition to pre-operation details, brigade staff played a key role in organising training and liaising with divisions and battalions. Captain R.A. Chell, an officer in 10th Essex, detailed how, early on 23 September 1916, Captain C.H. Hoare (BM, 53 Brigade, 18th (Eastern) Division), 'was to be seen in the fields between Forceville and Lealvillers marking out a representation of the trenches we were to attack'.[47] Upon its arrival in II Corps' area, the 18th (Eastern) Division requested that all brigade, battalion and company commanders were to be given tours around the area of attack to ensure they were 'thoroughly acquainted with the routes to these areas and the terrain'.[48] For brigade staff, this was of particular use as, during operations:

> it was not too easy to discover the true positions [of the troops] as the trenches shown so clearly on the maps were often blown entirely out of recognition.[49]

Liaison with neighbouring formations was another vital responsibility, particularly for the Staff Captain. Conferences were held between the Staff Captain, Quartermasters and Transport Officers of battalions, while Staff Captains were often in daily correspondence with division.[50] The objectives of the 18th (Eastern) Division's assault on Thiepval required a good deal of forward planning regarding the location of consolidation material and dumps. For 54 Brigade, the direction of the attack necessitated two separate dumps: one if the attack reached the first or second objective, and a second if the final objective was reached.[51] This forward preparation revealed an intimate knowledge of the area, but it also highlighted the thoroughness of staff work and an acknowledgment of potential operational limitations.

Unsurprisingly, the brigade staff's responsibilities during operations were just as demanding as they attempted to cope with poor communications and a centralised approach to command. One former BM recalled 'the extraordinary difficulty of obtaining information and finding out what was really happening' during the fighting in August 1916.[52] For 54 Brigade's initial assault at Thiepval on 26 September, the ability to understand the forward situation was hampered as all the wires to the front from brigade headquarters had been cut by shellfire, necessitating a reliance on runners

46 IWM, Private Papers of Colonel Sir Eric Gore-Browne, 88/52/1, Letter, 4 May 1916.
47 T.M. Banks and R.A. Chell, *With the 10th Essex in France* (London: Gay and Hancock, 1924), p.128.
48 TNA, WO 95/2015, The 18th Division in the Battle of the Ancre, 14 January 1917, p.3.
49 TNA, CAB 45/132, Letter from Lieutenant-General Sir D.F. Anderson to Brigadier-General Sir James Edmonds, 6 April 1934.
50 TNA, WO 95/2046, 55 Infantry Brigade War Diary, 19 October 1916.
51 TNA, WO 95/2041, 54 Brigade Report on Operations, 9 October 1916, p.3.
52 TNA, CAB 45/132, Lieutenant-General Sir D.F. Anderson to Brigadier-General Sir James Edmonds, 6 April 1934.

and pigeons to communicate.[53] The subsequent attack on the Schwaben Redoubt on 28 September required brigade staff to go forward to ensure that battalions were in a position to attack within a short space of time. After a visit from Brigadier-General H.W. Higginson (GOC 53 Brigade), Lieutenant-Colonel M. Kemp Welch (OC 7th Queens) sent a telegram to brigade headquarters, declaring the situation on his front 'unsatisfactory' and thought 'success unlikely'.[54] Captain Hoare, the BM, was sent up to the line and 'issued the orders necessary to put matters straight'.[55] This incident suggests that Hoare was empowered and trusted by Higginson to remedy the situation using his own initiative. In his reconnaissance report, Hoare noted how he 'found the men rather jumpy', but before he left 'everyone was hard at work digging and realised the situation was really very comfortable'.[56] This revealed not only the on-going liaison between brigade staff and battalions, but also the 'hands on' nature of brigade staff work.

Although brigade staff in 18th (Eastern) Division went forward to ascertain the situation and directly assist their battalions, this was not a universal response. When staff did go forward, casualties were inevitable. A former BM in 86 Brigade (29th Division) wrote how his brigade 'lost 150% of its staff during a single operation with the BM and Staff Captain injured whilst attempting to reorganise the advance'.[57] Major W. LaT. Congreve (BM, 76 Brigade, 3rd Division) was awarded a posthumous VC for his efforts in similar circumstances. Congreve's citation reveals how he:

> …carried out personal reconnaissances of the enemy lines [and] established himself in an exposed forward position from whence he successfully observed the enemy, and gave orders necessary to drive them from their position.[58]

During and after the Somme campaign, there was an intense analysis of performance. Lessons learned were circulated through memoranda and notes before codification in formal training manuals such as *SS 135*.[59] This provided the means of addressing the problem of command and control in battle, placing greater emphasis on the role of staff officers within the forward areas to ensure that information flowed in both

53   TNA, WO 95/2041, 54 Infantry Brigade Report on Operations, 9 October 1916, p.7.
54   TNA, WO 95/2034, 53 Infantry Brigade War Diary, 29 September 1916.
55   TNA, WO 95/2034, 53 Infantry Brigade Report on Operations, undated, pp.17-18.
56   TNA, WO 95/2034, 53 Infantry Brigade Report of Reconnaissance (Captain C.H. Hoare), 29 September 1916.
57   TNA, CAB 45/132, Letter from Lieutenant Colonel H.H. Cripps to Brigadier-General Sir James Edmonds, 27 November 1929.
58   *London Gazette* (Supplement), no. 29802, 26 October 1916, p.10393.
59   J. Lee, 'Some Lessons of the Somme: the British Infantry in 1917', in B. Bond *et al.*, *'Look to your front' Studies in the First World War by The British Commission for Military History* (Staplehurst: Spellmount, 1999), p.80.

directions.[60] Problems around communications had been identified with a significant proportion of the pamphlet dedicated to signal communication and situation reports. Realistic measures were put in place in an attempt to mitigate the ill effects of poor communications. These included the active encouragement of personal reconnaissance by staff officers and the positioning of a brigade staff officer at the Advanced Report Centre (ARC) where 'he can get in touch with wounded officers and men... and find out the situation from them'.[61] The message contained within *SS 135* should be viewed as a useful addition to, rather than a replacement of, the guidance found in the original *Staff Manual*. It provided clarity to the original principle that the staff 'must be unsparing in their endeavours to help the troops' and that they should 'avail themselves of all legitimate means of facilitating and expediting their work'.[62] The fact that 'all officers of the Staff' were available for this work highlights the premium placed on accurate knowledge of the battlefront highlighted by the Somme campaign.[63] It also revealed a shift in policy regarding the responsibilities of staff during operations: a more prominent role in the forward area was clearly expected of them.

The core responsibilities of staff in 1917 varied little from those in previous years, although there are far more documented instances of brigade staff acting on their own initiative as they adapted to the conditions of modern war and earned the trust of their commanders. Brigadier-General T.S. Louch, a former BM to 12 and 13 Australian Infantry Brigades (4th Australian Division), offers a good example of this in November 1917. Unfortunately, his resourcefulness was not entirely welcome owing to the micro-management of his commander, Sir John Gellibrand:

> At the 13th B[riga]de General [William] Glasgow left all except the most important paperwork to his staff; but I soon discovered that this did not suit [Brigadier General Sir John] Gellibrand, who liked to do his own staff work... Having prepared what I regarded as a routine order for a move, I sent it out, and put a copy in his basket to read at his leisure. He told me never to issue another order unless he had seen and approved it first.[64]

The significant increase in operations during 1917 gave the staff considerable opportunities for 'on the job' learning. However, they were still hampered by communication problems that had not vastly improved since the Somme. Attempts were made

---

60   J. Lee, 'Command and Control in Battle: British Divisions on the Menin Ridge Road, 20 September 1917', in Sheffield and Todman, (eds.), *Command and Control on the Western Front*, pp.122-3.

61   General Staff, *SS 135 Instructions for the Training of Divisions for Offensive Action* (GHQ, 1916), pp.40-1.

62   TNA, WO 279/862, *Staff Manual*, pp.7-8.

63   General Staff, *SS 135*, p.39.

64   IWM, Louch Papers, 12281 P271, Part III – 1917-18 Staff Duties, pp.9-10.

to improve forward communications with the publication of *SS 148*.[65] However, as Brigadier-General H.R. Cumming recalled, communications broke down during the battle of Bullecourt despite painstaking preparations, leaving his 91 Brigade in 'a state of ignorance as to what was happening'.[66] This resulted in Cumming sending 'one of his staff to the left Battalion Headquarters to obtain news of the situation' as every runner had been 'killed or badly wounded'.[67] Similarly, Major The Hon. W.E. Guinness (BM, 74 Brigade, 25th Division) was sent up to his brigade's ARC to keep in touch with the situation during the capture of Westhoek in August 1917. Through his personal reconnaissance and initiative, Guinness staved off at least one German counter-attack. He was awarded the DSO for his endeavours.[68]

The operations of 1917 revealed a growing confidence at the tactical level with commanders and staff demonstrating outstanding leadership and initiative. The Guards Division's counter-attacks at Gouzeaucourt, Gonnelieu and Gauche Wood highlights the premium placed on these qualities. The 1 Guards Brigade's attack on Gouzeaucourt on 30 November 1917 was initiated by the actions of its GOC, Brigadier-General Sir C.R. Champion de Crespigny.[69] Upon receiving orders to occupy the high ground east of Gouzeaucourt, Champion de Crespigny and his battalion commanders rode forward to reconnoitre. Seeing that the enemy was already in possession of Gouzeaucourt, Champion de Crespigny 'at once made up his mind to launch a counter-attack without any loss of time'.[70] This attack was to be carried out without artillery support. The brigade staff was instrumental in issuing verbal orders to battalion commanders, evidencing the 'on the hoof' nature of command and

65   General Staff, *SS 148 Forward Intercommunication in Battle* (GHQ, 1917). For further discussion on the development of communications in wartime, see B.N. Hall, 'The British Army and Wireless Communication, 1896-1918', *War in History*, 19 (3) (2012), pp.290-321.

66   H.R. Cumming, *A Brigadier in France* (reprint, Uckfield: Naval and Military Press, 2001), pp.75-8.

67   H.R. Cumming, *A Brigadier in France*, pp.78-9.

68   Lord Moyne, *Staff Officer: The Diaries of Walter Guinness 1914-1918*, edited by R. Bond and S. Robbins, (London: Leo Cooper, 1987), pp.166-72.

69   As an 'elite' formation, the Guards Division's experience is not necessarily representative of the British Army as a whole. However, despite an increase in doctoral studies at divisional level, very few of these studies have considered the impact and evolution of brigade staff work. It is clear that much more work is required in order to assess the impact of brigade staff work on combat effectiveness and operational performance at divisional level. An exception to the rule can be found in Simon Peaple's thesis on 46th (North Midland) Division, which details the role of Major R.N. Abadie (BM, 139 Brigade, 46th (North Midland) Division) on 1 July 1916. See: S.P. Peaple, 'The 46th (North Midland) Division T.F. on the Western Front, 1915-1918', (PhD Thesis, University of Birmingham, 2004), pp.131-8.

70   C. Headlam, *History of the Guards Division in the Great War 1915-1918* (2 vols. London: J. Murray, 1924), II, pp.4-5.

administration during this engagement.[71] The attack on Gouzeaucourt commenced at 12.30pm. The whole objective had been taken by 1.30pm. This was no mean feat given the limited time between initial orders and the capture of Gouzeaucourt – a mere three and a half hours.

The 3 Guards Brigade faced a similar situation in its attack on Gonnelieu and Gauche Wood on the following day. The fast-paced tempo of operations placed stress upon the command and staff arrangements. Brigadier-General Lord H. Seymour (GOC 3 Guards Brigade), much like his 1 Guards Brigade counterpart, was actively involved in the conduct of the counter-attack. On the night of 1 December, Seymour could be found in a 'sort of shelter' that had been 'rigged up for him by means of a wagon tarpaulin... with a candle stuck on an old tin'.[72] His staff was away from headquarters, linking in with battalions in an attempt to compensate for the minimal preparation time.

The attacks between 30 November and 2 December 1917 along the whole of Third Army's front revealed numerous instances of brigade staff playing a vital role in operations, over and above expectations. Captain Robert Gee (Staff Captain, 86 Brigade, 29th Division) won the VC for establishing a defensive flank and taking out a German machine gun crew. In the opinion of both his brigade and divisional commanders, Gee's action 'saved the brigade and possibly the division'.[73] Simkins also draws attention to the 'spirited counter-attack' of 88 Brigade (29th Division) in which platoons and companies from several battalions became mixed, but continued 'without any orders', applying fire and manoeuvre tactics. The BM, Captain J.K. McConnell, rode bareback on a transport horse up and down the line.[74]

The reversion to semi-mobile warfare from March 1918 onwards necessitated a review of staff responsibilities. In April 1918, GHQ issued *Notes on Recent Fighting – No. 4* dealing specifically with Staff Duties.[75] This series of pamphlets incorporated lessons learned through the return to a more fluid battlefield. At the core of this pamphlet was the need for frequent, personal reconnaissance by staff. In essence, it was a more defined version of the principles outlined within *SS 135*. The pamphlet declared that:

> In warfare of movement it is neither possible nor desirable for Command and Staffs, especially those of Divisions and Brigades, to carry out their functions with the facilities and the deliberation which have come to be looked on as normal in trench warfare... Staff officers cannot satisfactorily retain touch with units belonging to their own formations or with other units on their flanks if they allow

---

71   TNA, WO 95/1214, 1 Guards Brigade Narrative of Operations 30 November – 1 December 1917, undated, p.2.

72   C.H. Dudley-Ward, *History of the Welsh Guards* (London: John Murray, 1920), p.181.

73   S. Gillion, *The Story of the 29th Division* (London: Thomas Nelson, 1925), p.163.

74   P. Simkins, 'Building Blocks', p.163; S. Gillion, *29th Division*, pp.161-67.

75   TNA, WO 158/70, *Notes on Recent Fighting – No. 4: Staff Duties*, 13 April 1918.

themselves to be bounded by their offices… It is the duty of Staff officers to use every means at their disposal to ascertain the truth by immediate investigation.[76]

This is not to suggest that personal reconnaissance did not take place prior to 1918, rather it was GHQ's attempt at imposing a standardised method in light of the new type of warfare. The high tempo operations of 1918 offered a return to pre-war principles with the devolution of command to the lowest, appropriate level. Fighting was 'controlled and carried out chiefly by the junior officers of the battalions' without waiting for definitive orders.[77] This meant that the brigade staff had to be far more proactive in their awareness of the forward situation. Brigade headquarters was expected to be leaner and able to work 'as far as possible with a message book only'.[78] The simultaneous updating and overhauling of training and responsibilities during this time was a clear attempt to shake off trench bound habits. Communications were, once again, highlighted as a problem.[79] Brigades were required to explore alternative forms of communication, such as visual and wireless, as communication by wire in front of brigade headquarters was increasingly rare.

The decisive emphasis on flexibility and going forward led to a greater number of casualties and a high level of exhaustion among staff and combat troops. Brigadier-General Frank Crozier (GOC 119 Brigade, 40th Division) recalled an incident where his Staff Captain 'entirely lost the use of his legs for two days' owing to fatigue during March 1918.[80] Oliver Lyttelton declared that the return to semi-mobile operations was 'a wonderful sensation', but warned of the danger to staff that 'had to continually move about in the open, under fire, in order to keep in touch with the troops and with the rapidly developing battle'.[81] The case of Captain G.J. Bruce (BM, 109 Brigade, 36th (Ulster) Division) painfully illustrates Lyttelton's warning. Bruce was killed during a German barrage and counter-attack on 2 October 1918:

> It was during this attack that Captain G. J. Bruce D.S.O., M.C. … making his way forward through the barrage to ascertain the position, was killed. His quickness and cleverness, and his wonderful eye for country… made him a very fine example of the 'civilian' staff officer. His personal bravery was quite proverbial among all ranks of the Division. He was one of those rare and fortunate men

76   *Ibid.*
77   H.R. Cumming, *A Brigadier in France*, p.147.
78   TNA, WO 158/70, *Notes on Recent Fighting – No. 4.*
79   TNA, WO 158/70, *Notes on Recent Fighting – No. 8: Signal Communications*, 28 April 1918.
80   F. P. Crozier, *A Brass Hat in No Man's Land* (reprint, Norwich: Gliddon Books, 1989), p.214.
81   O. Lyttelton, *The Memoirs of Lord Chandos* (London: The Bodley Head, 1962), pp.103-4.

who do not seem to require a mental effort… to face great danger. He walked into it as naturally and as unconcernedly as he walked into his office.[82]

It was often the case that brigade commanders and their staff became casualties together whether through reconnoitring positions, visiting battalions, or during the operation itself. Major F. Gunner (BM, 118 Brigade, 39th Division) was taken prisoner along with his brigade commander, while attempting to supervise the right flank and rear guard of his brigade on 28 March 1918.[83] Similarly, Captain F.H. Witts (BM, 150 Brigade, 50th (Northumbrian) Division) was severely wounded, along with the Staff Captain and Intelligence Officer, following the withdrawal from the Aisne in May 1918. His brigade commander, Brigadier-General H.C. Rees, was taken prisoner.[84]

The higher tempo of operations coupled with the increasing experience of the BEF led to the compression of standard battle procedure and the use of verbal orders, rather than the pages of operation orders associated with earlier campaigns. By 1918, operation and relief orders were little more than a page in length indicating the rapidity of operations, but also the proficiency of the staff and troops alike. Pedersen's analysis of 5th Australian Division's battle procedure during the battle of Mont St Quentin highlights the value of experience, training and anticipation to its success.[85] The experience of 15 Australian Infantry Brigade and its role in the battle offers a good example of this. A divisional conference on the evening of 29 August 1918 detailed that 5th Australian Division was to 'side slip' north and take over the sector of 2nd Australian Division.[86] The 15 Australian Infantry Brigade, commanded by Brigadier-General H.E. 'Pompey' Elliott, was expected to move off at 6.00am on 30 August to push along the line of advance. Elliott did not receive this information until 1.30am on 30 August. Concerned that runners would get lost in the dark and inclement weather, his BM, Captain H.R. Gollan, personally sought out the battalion commanders and delivered verbal instructions, thus ensuring that battle procedure, although compressed, remained intact.[87] It is testament to the efforts and preparedness of the staff that the brigade moved off by 6.00am.

82   Cyril Falls, *The History of the 36th (Ulster) Division* (London: McCaw, Stevenson and Orr Ltd, 1922), p.271.
83   F. Davies and G. Maddocks, *Bloody Red Tabs*, pp.112-3.
84   IWM, Rees Papers, 77/179/1, Letter to Mrs Rees from Frank Witts, 5 June 1918.
85   P. Pedersen, 'Maintaining the advance: Monash, battle procedure and the Australian Corps', in A. Ekins, (ed.), *1918 Year of Victory: The end of the Great War and the shaping of history* (Wollombi, NSW: Exisle Publishing, 2010), pp.142-3.
86   A.D. Ellis, *The Story of the Fifth Australian Division* (London: Hodder and Stoughton, 1920), p.344.
87   AWM, AWM4 23/15/30, 15 Australian Infantry Brigade War Diary, 29 August 1918, p.31.

The subsequent attack on Péronne on 1 September was demanding for both 14 and 15 Australian Infantry Brigades. Although there was regular communication from battalions to brigade, the situation was frequently unclear, while contact with neighbouring brigades was often very difficult. For 15 Australian Infantry Brigade, which was required to cross the River Somme, the difficulty was partially mitigated by the close liaison between the Staff Captain, Captain C.W. Lay, and Major H. Greenaway (OC 15th Field Company, RE). As part of this close working, Lay was instrumental in ensuring that 'bridging material to cross the SOMME canal and river [be] got forward'.[88] The location of both men at brigade headquarters allowed for greater co-ordination of RE work with the actual needs of the infantry. With Brigadier-General Elliott's personal reconnaissances to the front, the running of brigade head-quarters was entrusted to the BM, Captain Gollan, who was recommended for the DSO following the storming of the Hindenburg Line on 29 September 1918.[89]

Conclusion

It would be erroneous to suggest that the transformation of the brigade staff was a smooth process. Much like the wider learning process of the Army, the development and performance of the brigade staff was, at times, erratic. However, there is a line of progression. In response to the increased tempo of operations and the ever-present communication problems, the role of the brigade staff expanded. They were still expected to carry out their administrative duties, while involving themselves both in and beyond the front line. As operations transitioned from static to semi-mobile, command decisions had to be taken locally with responsibility devolved to the man on the spot. Invariably, this led to the dramatic compression of battle procedure necessitating verbal orders or very concise operation orders. Brigade staff officers were expected to act on their own initiative. This meant going forward to ascertain the situation in the front line and involving themselves in operations where necessary. This new role was dangerous, but it was no longer appropriate for staff to be 'bounded by their offices'. To see and to be seen was of vital importance in the effective conduct of their duties.

The transformation of staff responsibilities cannot be isolated from the transformation of staff training, which was in direct response to the rapid expansion of the BEF and the changing character of warfare. Without the formalised instruction provided by the two Staff Colleges, training was *ad hoc* and varied in quality. The watershed of the Somme campaign brought about a renaissance in staff training between 1916-1917 and a healthy relationship between formal GHQ schools and division-run

---

88   AWM, AWM4 23/15/31, 15 Australian Infantry Brigade Recommendation for Honours and Rewards, 25 September 1918.
89   AWM, AWM4 23/15/35, 15 Australian Infantry Brigade Recommendation for Honours and Rewards, 31 January 1919.

'learner' programmes. However, the formalisation of staff training during this period was too late to fully address the significant shortage of qualified staff officers. The eventual devolution of staff training to Army in 1918 and divisions' selection of potential officers to undertake this training often saw young, non-regular officers in brigade staff appointments. These 'talented amateurs', men such as Oliver Lyttelton, Anthony Eden and Walter Guinness, formed part of a new breed of staff officer that emerged during the latter stages of the war. They were young, battle tested, and many were decorated for gallantry in both their regimental and staff roles. Out of 184 infantry brigades serving on the Western Front at the end of the war, 130 BMs (71%) and 110 Staff Captains (60%) held the Military Cross.[90]

Although it is debatable whether the Army professionalised during this period, it is clear that the 'civilianization' of brigade staff during the First World War represented a meritocratic approach to promotion. This approach also served to highlight the narrowing skill differential between military and civilian spheres.[91] By 1918, the trade unionism of Regular army officers did not universally apply to the brigade level of command. The staffs, particularly at brigade, were more than just the mouthpiece of the general they served. They were integral to the fighting capability and morale of the formation. Although their work was 'exceedingly arduous and absolutely unceasing', they filled a 'comparatively inglorious role'; yet, as Lieutenant-Colonel Sir Cuthbert Headlam noted, on the efficiency of the staff depends 'the smooth running and efficient action of the whole military machine'.[92]

90   General Staff, *SS 407 Composition of the Headquarters of the Forces in the Field*, November 1918 (London: Harrison, 1918).
91   This meritocratic approach to promotion did not last beyond the First World War. During the inter-war period, promotion reverted back to seniority.
92   C. Headlam, 'Editorial', *Army Quarterly*, 1 (1) (1920), p.10; Headlam, *Cuthbert Headlam*, p.89.

10

Vanishing Battalions

The Nature, Impact and Implications of British Infantry Reorganization prior to the German Spring Offensives of 1918

Simon M. Justice

By the beginning of 1918, the British government had long been engaged in a dispute with Sir Douglas Haig and the General Staff over the solution to chronic manpower shortages. Deciding the issue Lloyd George's executive finally forced a reduction in the number of infantry battalions after rejecting a final plea against such a course by the Army Council. Lord Derby had delivered a petition to the War Cabinet on 9 January 1918 on their behalf, contending that:

> ...the organization of British Divisions has well stood the test of the present war and that it is very undesirable to change it.[1]

Haig had originally warned the Army Council to this effect in February 1917. Then, on reductions in line with the continental system being first raised, Haig also pointed out that reorganization within the French and German armies had:

> ...[enabled] them to escape from the somewhat vicious arrangement of having brigades organized in two regiments, and divisions in two brigades.

---

1   The National Archives of the UK (TNA), CAB 24/38/GT3265, Army Council *Memorandum by the Military Members of the Army Council on the draft Report of the War Cabinet Committee on MAN-POWER (with an introductory note by Lord Derby, 9 January 1918)* (7 January 1918).

Whereas for the British part:

> Our organization of divisions in three brigades and of brigades in four battalions was based on sounder principles. Should the shortage of men necessitate a reduction in the fighting units, I consider that it would be preferable to break up a certain number of divisions rather than to reduce the fighting strength of each division.[2]

Whether or not British infantry organization was founded on 'sounder principles', Haig, as Director of Military Training 1906-07, certainly had a hand in the Haldane reforms, prior to which a British infantry division comprised *two* infantry brigades, each of four battalions.[3] Following the adoption of the new structure, Haig served as Director of Staff Duties to rebuild the principles of formation tactics and training around the model that evolved into *Field Service Regulations, 1909*.[4] Notwithstanding seven years pre-war development of formation deployment and tactics, defensively the principles were enshrined, from the onset of position warfare at the end of 1914 in the two-brigade front. From then it became the norm for each brigade to field two battalions in the front line, with one in support and one in brigade reserve. This system allowed for an adequate garrison, sensible reliefs within the brigade, and a reserve brigade with 'some chance of rest and training while out of the line, and the supply of *extra* working parties' without undue strain.[5] These were the principles, sound or not, which had 'stood the test of the present war'; the principles which Haig, in the end, was unable to protect. The following evidence includes, for the first time, a full quantitative assessment of the reduction process. The intention is to facilitate a more complete comparative analysis of British units and formations concerned in the defensive struggles of March and April 1918 by providing an objective measure of the impact of such establishment change.

Historians and the Reduction in Establishment

For historians, defining the extent to which British divisions transformed due to systematic reductions in infantry establishment prior to 21 March 1918 has proved problematic. This is true both in terms of tactics and performance and, examined here first, simple numerical fact. Issued via the Army Council on 10 January 1918, the War Cabinet's directive on cuts provided guidance on which battalions to disband.

2   TNA, WO 163/22, Army Council *Précis No. 855, 204th Meeting of the Army Council; Sir Douglas Haig on the adequacy of respective drafts* (6 March 1917), p.62.
3   See: J. Gooch, 'Mr. Haldane's Army: Military Organisation and Foreign Policy in England, 1906-7' in *The Prospect of War: Studies in British Defence Policy 1847-1942* (London: Frank Cass, 1981), pp.92-112, fn.60 p.108.
4   E.M. Spiers, *The Army and Society, 1815-1914* (London: Longman, 1980), p.281.
5   A. Hilliard Atteridge, *History of the 17th (Northern) Division* (Glasgow: 1929) p.279.

This came in the form of a list that only stipulated which theatre and line regiments selected.[6] Sensibilities of regimental and army precedence further complicated the order by prohibiting the disbandment of any Regular, 1st-Line Territorial, or Scottish battalions, and laying down priorities to be observed in first reducing 2nd-Line Territorial and New Army units. Scottish battalions avoided cuts indirectly by omitting Scottish regiments from the permitted list. Though Haig was asked to plan for a command-wide application of the reductions, they were never sanctioned and Australian, Canadian and New Zealand divisions were not to undergo this process. British and Australian formations did lose battalions through casualty wastage in the German Spring Offensives and, for the Australians, further disbandments in September 1918 were resisted to the point of mutiny before eventually taking place.[7] The bureaucracy led to a further delay of two weeks while GHQ staff worked out the complex schedule of reductions, amalgamations and transfers required to reach target establishment. The Chief of the General Staff Herbert Lawrence issued explicit directions on how the reorganization was to be effected to formations on 23 January 1918.[8] Thereafter the main body of changes was complete by mid-February 1918, with most reductions accomplished during the first week or so. In considering divisions subject to that order, Sir James Edmonds conclusively stated '115 battalions in France were disbanded, thirty-eight were amalgamated to become nineteen units, and seven were converted into pioneers'.[9] Popular historian Middlebrook repeated Edmonds' numerical claim:

> …115 battalions had completely disappeared, thirty-eight more were amalgamated to make nineteen new battalions, and seven more became pioneers.[10]

Almost thirty years later Terraine somewhat mischievously re-jigged Edmonds' figures to claim that:

6   National Library of Scotland (NLS), Acc.3155/File No.216/d Papers of Field Marshal Sir Douglas Haig, Army Council *121/Drafts/8579 - Direction to Haig on Reduction of Divisions to 9 Battalions including List of Regiments and Number of Battalions in each to be Reduced* (10 January 1918).

7   P. Simkins, '"Building Blocks": Aspects of Command and Control at Brigade Level in the BEF's Offensive Operations 1916-1918' in G.D. Sheffield and Dan Todman (eds.), *Command and Control on the Western Front: The British Army's Experience, 1914-1918*, (Staplehurst, 2004), pp.141-71, particularly pp.142-4.

8   TNA, WO 106/415 Divisions in France (Allotment of New Pioneer Battalions); Reorganization 1918 Jan/Feb, Lieut-Gen. H.A. Lawrence *OB/1851/A* (23 January 1918).

9   J.E. Edmonds, *Military Operations, France and Belgium, 1918 Vol I: The German March Offensive and its Preliminaries* (London: Macmillan, 1935) (BOH 1918 I), p.55.

10   M. Middlebrook, *The Kaiser's Battle: 21 March 1918 - The First Day of the German Spring offensive* (London: Allen Lane, 1978), p.88.

> ...on the eve of the great German offensive, [Haig] was compelled to disband 141 battalions – the equivalent of nearly 12 divisions.[11]

More recently Hart was equally creative in pointing out, with greater accuracy, that '134 infantry battalions disappeared', while Messenger promoted a still different view in asserting:

> A total of 147 battalions were affected. Of these, twenty-two pairs of TF battalions were amalgamated and twenty-one TF battalions disbanded, together with eighty-four Service battalions.[12]

A full analysis of Lawrence's directions, together with detailed examination of contemporary orders of battle, reveals that, in fact 116 battalions were broken up. They disbanded to reinforce their regimental peers; to form general drafts; to create temporary entrenching battalions or to populate corps reinforcement camps.[13] Other adjustments within formations amounted to two battalions being converted and reassigned as Pioneers in their own divisions and thirty-two more redistributed internally to maintain the new three-battalion brigade system. *Inter-division* exchanges comprised twenty-two battalions being moved complete between divisions; nucleus HQ compliments of a further eighteen 1st-Line Territorial units were transferred primarily for amalgamation with their 2nd-Line counterparts and five infantry battalions converted and *transferred* as Pioneers. Matters are further complicated when one considers Edmonds' analysis related only to the forty-seven infantry divisions present on the Western Front in January 1918, whereas forty-eight divisions comprised Haig's command by March and were reduced.[14] Thus, prior to the 1918 German offensives, 119 battalions disbanded, thirty-six amalgamated to become eighteen units and seven converted to pioneers.

All measures (apart from inter-brigade 'balancing') were controlled from GHQ – by type and by division – but only seventy-one battalions were named specifically in its original order. Fates of the remaining 110 were left to divisional commanders in

11   J. Terraine, 'Lloyd George's Expedients, Part Two', *History Today*, 13 (5) (1963), pp.321-30, p.326.

12   P. Hart, *1918: A Very British Victory* (London: Weidenfeld & Nicolson, 2008), p.29; C. Messenger, *Call to Arms: The British Army 1914-18* (London: Cassell Military, 2006) p.275.

13   *Order of Battle of Divisions*, ed. Major A.F. Becke, Four vols. (London: HMSO, 1935-1945); also TNA, WO 95/5467-9, GHQ General Staff *Order of Battle of the British Armies in France, including Lines of Communication Units (and of the Portuguese Expeditionary Force from March 1917)* (1914-18). These sources, including various formation and unit diaries contained in TNA, WO 95, when used in this manner may hereafter collectively referred to as 'Author Dislocation Analysis'.

14   See also P. Simkins, 'The Four Armies 1914-1918' in David Chandler and I.F.W. Beckett (eds.), *The Oxford Illustrated History of the British Army* (Oxford: Oxford University Press, 1994), p.262.

choosing either a 'battalion' or 'battalion of a certain regiment'. Finally, also entirely at their discretion was internal shuffling of the thirty-two battalions required to maintain brigade equilibrium, but when finalised the tortuous procedures had achieved desired results within the Regular, Territorial and New Army constraints laid down. In sum 144 *infantry* battalions were lost to the British Armies in France and a total of 216 fundamental steps had proved necessary to complete the reduction. One hundred and nineteen battalions disbanded, thirty-six amalgamated, seven converted to Pioneers, twenty-two transferred to other divisions and thirty-two shuffled between brigades. Unsurprisingly many historians refer to a reduction of division establishment from twelve battalions to nine and move on.[15]

Turning to the effect of such an upheaval, for his thesis on technological primacy and command failure Travers completely ignores infantry reductions in his treatment of the 1918 manpower shortage and 'manpower versus firepower' debates.[16] Travers, however, does briefly acknowledge the existence of other factors such as morale, weather and systems of defence, views promoted by Middlebrook and Bourne.[17] Whilst not quantifying its effect, Bourne, in particular, acknowledges a link between the arbitrary reorganization of infantry and dislocation when he noted that:

> ...[Haig] was compelled to reorganize the army – except for Dominion troops – into divisions of 9 instead of 12 infantry battalions. This caused considerable dislocation.[18]

Samuels' evaluation of German defensive evolution and of the British effort immediately prior to March 1918, in particular, has become widely quoted. Samuels belongs to a school of North American historians whose work exhibits close attention to the strategy, tactics and sources relating to the Germany's First World War army. They

---

15   For example, see: J.P. Harris and N. Barr, *Amiens to the Armistice: The BEF in the Hundred Days' Campaign, 8 August-11, November 1918* (London: Brassey's, 1998) p.32; G.D. Sheffield, *Forgotten Victory: The First World War - Myths and Realities* (London: Headline, 2001), p.224; W.J. Philpott, *Bloody Victory: The Sacrifice on the Somme and the Making of the Twentieth Century* (London: Little, Brown, 2009), p.499; C. Baker, *The Battle for Flanders: German Defeat on the Lys, 1918* (Barnsley: Pen & Sword Military, 2011), p.12.

16   For the 'manpower versus firepower' debate (attempts to balance manpower shortages with increased use of mechanical methods) see: T. Travers, *How The War Was Won: Command and Technology in the British Army on the Western Front, 1917-1918* (London: Routledge, 1992), pp.32-49; for the British in defence *ibid*, pp.50-109; there is likewise no mention of the reductions in the earlier T. Travers, *The Killing Ground : The British Army, the Western Front and the Emergence of Modern Warfare, 1900-1918* (London: Allen and Unwin, 1987).

17   Travers, *How the War Was Won*, p.50; Middlebrook, *The Kaiser's Battle*; J.M. Bourne, *Britain and the Great War 1914-1918* (London: Edward Arnold, 1989).

18   Bourne, *Britain and the Great War*, p.90.

represent, in some measure, a counter to British revisionists.[19] Samuels explored the nature of the reductions; from an example of the British 36th (Ulster) and 30th Divisions, he argued:

> A comparison of the order of battle of the two divisions before and after the recent reorganisation of divisions from 12 to 9 battalions shows the extent of the upheaval.[20]

Unfortunately, undermined by the fact that assertions on how the order of battle altered are inaccurate, Samuels' comparison is flawed. In the case of the 30th Division, three battalions were disbanded but none were transferred (he claimed three).[21] For the 36th (Ulster) Division, six battalions were disbanded (not eight) and three regular battalions brought in to maintain balance (not five), while two battalions were swapped between brigades in an effort to attain regimental homogeneity (not noted).[22] Notwithstanding flawed data, Samuels' comparison does draw attention to the variety of significant changes and highlights potential disruption.

The implications of establishment change and factors underpinning the British defensive performance in 1918 as a whole, which Edmonds originally suggested in relation to March that year, remained consistent. For example, Baker's recent work on the defence against Germany's Lys 'Georgette' offensive in April 1918 concludes that the nature of fighting on:

> The Lys gives little opportunity to assess the genuine operational and tactical impact of these changes. [23]

Edmonds advanced reasons for British problems throughout his volume on the opening spring offensive. In his preface Edmonds contrasts German preparations – a

---

19 For the genre see: T.T. Lupfer, *The Dynamics of Doctrine: The Changes in German Tactical Doctrine during the First World War, Leavenworth Papers: No.4* (Fort Leavenworth, KS: Combat Studies Institute, 1981); For an examination of offensive capability, see: B.I. Gudmundsson, *Stormtroop Tactics: Innovation in the German Army, 1914-1918* (West Port, CT: Praeger, 1995). For reassessments of German strategy and performance in battle, see: T. Zuber, *Inventing the Schlieffen Plan: German War Planning, 1871-1914* (Oxford University Press, 2002).; T. Zuber, *German War Planning, 1891-1914: Sources and Interpretations* (Woodbridge; Rochester, N.Y.: Boydell Press, 2004); T. Zuber, *The Mons Myth: A Reassessment of the Battle* (Stroud: History, 2010) .

20 M. Samuels, *Command or Control? : Command, Training and Tactics in the British and German Armies, 1888-1918* (London: Frank Cass, 1995), p.249.

21 A.F. Becke, *Order of Battle of Divisions Part 3b - New Army Divisions (30-41) and 63rd (R.N.) Division, Order of Battle of Divisions* (London: HMSO, 1940), pp.4-5 and Notes 38, 39 and 42 p.6.

22 *Ibid*, p.65 and Notes 28-30, 32-4, 42-6 p.66.

23 Baker, *The Battle for Flanders*, p.187.

winter focused solely on training and arrangements for offensive operations – with the British predicament, where the:

> …line which, having recently been taken over from the French, had the weakest defences and for strategic reasons was most thinly held.[24]

Here, the troops were untrained to meet the coming assault, the fog was worse than at any other point along the line and:

> …[as] a further handicap, the first weeks of 1918 were nearly wholly taken up with carrying out the reorganization…[25]

This point comes immediately before Edmonds states that:

> Sir Douglas Haig was moved to say that the unfortunate troops and their commander were at the mercy of an 'Organizer of Defeat'.[26]

Later he amplified this point. Edmonds drew attention to the clear risks inherent in disrupting work on defences to reorganize, and repeated a hope (presumably held by GHQ):

> …that the Germans would defer attack until there had been time for the troops to settle down to the new order of things and for commanders and staffs to accustom themselves to the modifications in orders and tactical methods which the changes involved.[27]

Finally, in a detailed and lengthy 'post-mortem' on the British performance of 21 March 1918, Edmonds remarks indicate that establishment change (among other factors) was subsidiary to the main reason for failure – over-extension of the British line and the inevitable thinning of defences – but notable in that there had been little opportunity for formations to 'shake down into the new organization.'[28]

Terraine, who was particularly adept in analysis and synthesis of Edmonds' reasoning, drew a starker and more vivid conclusion. He perceived an army:

---

24   Edmonds, *BOH 1918 I* preface vii, in reference to the Fifth Army sector between St. Quentin in the centre, and Barisis, just south of the River Oise. The protection of the northern sector was a greater priority containing, as it did, the major ports and ready access to the Channel and England.
25   *Ibid.*
26   *Ibid.*
27   *Ibid*, p.54.
28   *Ibid*, p.254.

...facing the most formidable offensive of the war, actually disbanding units and thrown into confusion by the ensuing arrangements.[29]

Specifically:

...such reorganization meant disorganization to a fearful degree. This entire astonishing and demoralizing exercise took time – time during which the roads of France were filled with British units seeking new homes in strange divisions, and during which an esprit de corps built up over years of common experience was thrown away, while all existing tactical principles and schemes had to be scrapped.[30]

Terraine, like Edmonds and Samuels, may have been inaccurate in his numerical calculations concerning establishment change, but he was most fervent and direct of the three in assessing their negative effects on the BEF's battlefield potential in spring 1918. He misapplied Edmonds' original figures, whilst Samuels, in an over-reliance on secondary sources, compared unofficial orders of battle from 1916 and 1918 without checking the credibility of his claims. Samuels did not consult primary sources, preferring simply to use tables used by Middlebrook, sourced from Edmonds, in his books on the Somme in 1916 and the *Kaiserschlacht* in 1918. Indeed, in using 1916 orders of battle, Samuels' picks up movements during 1917 not related to the reductions in question.[31] In Samuels' defence, it is difficult to validate such a sample without reproducing the entire procedure.

A Measure of Dislocation

Having noted the explicit nature of the GHQ/Lawrence order of 23 January 1918 one might expect the compilation of consequent adjustments to be a simple task. Unfortunately this is not so for two reasons. First, what was ordered cannot be taken as read in terms of compliance and, second, whilst 'explicit' the nature of the order itself allowed some divisional commanders considerable influence over which battalions were broken-up, amalgamated, transferred or converted (see Tables 1 and 2). In the case of the 36th (Ulster) Division, half of its twelve battalions were designated for breaking up; four from the Royal Irish Rifles and two from the Royal Inniskilling Fusiliers. The specific (New Army) battalions affected were to be finally determined

---

29   J. Terraine, *To Win a War: 1918, The Year of Victory* (London: Sidgwick and Jackson, 1978), p.49.
30   *Ibid.*
31   M. Middlebrook, *The First Day on the Somme, 1 July 1916* (Harmondsworth: Penguin, 1984), Appendix I, Order of Battle of British Infantry Units, 1 July 1916, pp.320-2; Middlebrook, *The Kaiser's Battle* Appendix 3, Order of Battle of British Infantry and Cavalry Divisions, 21 March 1918 pp.390-1.

by the GOC Division Major-General Oliver Nugent and the division then brought up to establishment by incoming Regular battalions. The Territorial Forces (TF) Act of 1907 excluded Ireland and no TF units or formations were raised. Consequently, the 36th was entirely a 'New Army' division formed with battalions raised largely from men of the Ulster Volunteer Force (UVF) shortly after the outbreak of war.[32]

Table 1 Reduction of battalions within the 36th (Ulster) and 12th Divisions

Army Corps	Division	No. of Battalions (and regiment) to be (a) broken up; (b) amalgamated	Battalions to be transferred		
				To lose	To receive
XVIII	36th	R. Irish Rif. (a)		3	1st R. I. Rif.
		R. Irish Rif. (a)			from 8th Div.
		R. Irish Rif. (a)			1st R. Innis. Fus
		R. Irish Rif. (a)			from 29th Div.
		R. Innis. Fus. (a)			2nd R. Innis. Fus
		R. Innis. Fus. (a)			from 32nd Div.
XV	12th	R. Fus. (a)			
		11th Middl'x. (a)			
		7th E. Surrey			

(Source: Examples from TNA, WO 106/415 Divisions in France (Allotment of New Pioneer Battalions); Re-organization 1918 Jan/Feb, Lieut-Gen. H.A. Lawrence *OB/1851/A* (23 January 1918), Appendix I)

Conversely, in 12th Division, GHQ designated that 11th Middlesex disbanded along with one battalion of the Royal Fusiliers. The fact that the 7th East Surrey battalion was not designated (a) or (b) is one possible explanation for Edmonds' incorrect figures. The battalion disbanded on 5 February 1918.[33]

Table 2 covers the other general possibilities: The 2nd-Line Territorial 66th (2nd East Lancashire) Division was to disband three battalions, one from the Lancashire Fusiliers and two from the Manchester regiment. In a secondary allocation the division would receive 1st-Line Territorial battalions from its 1st-Line sister division, the 42nd (East Lancashire). The incoming senior battalions were then to subsume their

32   Becke, *Order of Battle, Part 3b* p.67. See an account of Nugent's deliberations explained to the Lord Mayor of Belfast in T. Bowman, *The Irish regiments in the Great War : Discipline and Morale* (Manchester: Manchester University Press, 2003), p.145. See also, N. Perry, "Nationality in the Irish Infantry Regiments in the First World War", *War and Society*, 12 (1) (1994), pp.65-95.
33   See: A.F. Becke, *Part 3a - New Army Divisions (9-26), Order of Battle of Divisions* (London: HMSO, 1938) p.31 and p.32 Note 24. See also Table 3 in this essay.

2nd-Line counterparts by amalgamation, and any surplus men drafted.[34] In the 15th (Scottish) Division no battalions disbanded but the target establishment was to be reached by transferring one battalion of choice to each of the 40th and 35th Divisions, and converting a third into Pioneers.

Table 2 Reductions in the 15th (Scottish) and 66th (2nd East Lancashire) Divisions

Army Corps	Division	No. of Battalions (and regiment) to be (a) broken up; (b) amalgamated		Battalions to be transferred		
				To lose		To receive
XXII	66th	6	Lancs. Fus. (a)		3	Lancs. Fus.
			Lancs. Fus (b)			E. Lancs.
			E. Lancs. (b)			Manchester
			Manchester (a)			from 42nd Div.
			Manchester (a)			*
			Manchester (b)			
XVII	15th	0		3	1 to 40th Div.	
					1 to 35th Div.	
					1 to be converted	
					into Pioneers.	
			* For amalgamation with 2nd line units.			

(Source: TNA, WO 106/415, Appendix I, Third Army and Fourth Army)

Detailed instructions concerning such Pioneer conversions were issued later under a separate order (see Tables 3 and 4). A comparison of conversions ordered against changes that actually occurred illustrates both the complexity and interconnected nature of adjustments to divisional establishment.

Conversions within the 50th (Northumbrian) Division the dispatch of three new Pioneer battalions to fresh homes took place as ordered. Conversion and transfer of the 6/7th Royal Scots Fusiliers from the 15th (Scottish) Division was completed in similar fashion.

---

34   Detailed instructions on this procedure may be found in TNA, *WO 95/415, OB/1851/A*, Para. 4a. and Appendix V of that document.

Table 3 Allotment of new Pioneer battalions

	To be transferred			
	From		To	
Battalion Selected	Division	Army	Division	Army
10th A. & S. Highrs.	9	Fifth	58	Fifth
6/7th R. Scots. Fus.	15	Third	59	Third
1/4th Suffolk Regt.	33	Fourth	32	Fourth
1/5th Border Regt.	50	Fourth	66	Fourth
1/7th North'd Fus.	50	Fourth	42	First
1/9th Durham L.I.	50	Fourth	62	First
2/4th S. Lancs. Regt.	57	First	57	First

(Source: TNA, WO 106/415 Divisions in France (Allotment of New Pioneer Battalions); Re-organization 1918 Jan/Feb, Butler, R., MGGS, GHQ, *OB/1851/A, Allotment of new Pioneer Battalions*, 6 February 1918)

Table 4 Actual conversion and movement of Pioneer battalions

	To be transferred			
	From		To	
Battalion Selected	Division	Army	Division	Army
10th A. & S. Highrs.	9	Fifth	32	Fourth
6/7th R. Scots. Fus.	15	Third	59	Third
16th Highland L.I.	32	Fourth	32	Fourth
1/4th Suffolk Regt.	33	Fourth	58	Fifth
1/5th Border Regt.	50	Fourth	66	Fourth
1/7th North'd Fus.	50	Fourth	42	First
1/9th Durham L.I.	50	Fourth	62	First
2/4th S. Lancs. Regt.	57	First	No Change	No Change
2/5th L.N. Lancs. Regt.	57	First	57	First

(Source: Author Dislocation Analysis with variances from Table 3 highlighted)

Organizing the other three Pioneer battalions proved much harder to achieve. In the end, both the 10th Argyll and Sutherland Highlanders and 2/4th South Lancashire battalion remained as infantry, with the latter staying where it was. The former transferred to 32nd Division, replacing the 16th Highland Light Infantry that converted within the formation. The Argylls' intended spot as Pioneers for the 58th (2/1st London) Division was then filled by the 1/4th Suffolk battalion from the 33rd Division. Conversion of the 2/5th Loyal North Lancashire battalion – which, in common with 16th HLI, had not been detailed as Pioneers in the original order – concluded the transformation on its repurpose within the 57th (2nd West Lancashire)

Division. Mitchinson provides an excellent all-round view of the Pioneers at this time and some of the implications of converting from infantry for these particular battalions.[35] Completing the process illustrated in Table 5 for all forty-seven British infantry divisions on the Western Front in January 1918 provides a benchmark to compare with Edmonds' figures in the official history.[36] When data to account for the return of the 41st Division from Italy in mid-March 1918 (three battalions disbanded 16-18 March) is appended, an accurate order of battle at 21 March 1918 may be reproduced together with a catalogue of all adjustments related to the reduction of divisions.[37]

It is possible to drill down to brigades and battalions in assessing potential dislocation, but division-level data used here to demonstrate the relative level of dislocation within these formations. To achieve this, the main determinants (steps in the reduction process) are each allocated arbitrary scores that represent a level of dislocation and illustrated in Table 6. Excepting the seven instances where divisions received a Pioneer battalion, the steps are scored 5, 7.5 or 10, representing lower to higher dislocation. In the case of incoming Pioneers battalions, recipient divisions previously had no Pioneers on establishment and the incoming units were reinforcements in real terms. All Pioneer battalions were reduced to three companies from four at this time; this change being the reason for a positive (minus dislocation) effect of 2.5 instead of 10 (net 7.5 when balanced with the negative influence of a loss from normal brigade infantry establishment and the move to division troops). In this example, the highest scores are allocated to events involving repurposing as above and the loss of infantry battalions to brigades through disbandment, inter-division transfer or outgoing amalgamation. Inter-brigade transfers are deemed to have a lesser effect and the lowest scores are reserved for cases where incoming HQ nuclei were amalgamated and for incoming battalions transferred complete. Taking the 36th (Ulster) Division as an example, this scoring system produces a dislocation index of 90 (six battalions disbanded; three transferred; two transferred inter-brigade). Conversely the 30th Division scores an index of just 30 (three battalions disbanded).

35   See also, K.W. Mitchinson, *Pioneer Battalions in the Great War: Organized and Intelligent Labour* (London: Leo Cooper, 1997), pp.191-265 which covers the reorganization and period before the spring offensives.
36   Edmonds, *BOH 1918 I*, p.55.
37   Becke, *Order of Battle, Part 3b* p.111 and Notes 33, 35-6 p.112.

Table 5 Actual reductions within 12th, 15th, 36th and 66th Divisions (ref. Tables 1 & 2)

Army Corps	Division	Battalions: (a) broken up; (b) amalgamated	Battalions transferred	
			Lost	Received
XV	12th	8th R. Fus. (a)		
		11th Middl'x. (a)		
		7th E. Surrey (a)		
		3 Amalgamated		
XVII	15th		10/11th High. L.I. to 40th Div.	
			12th High. L.I. to 35th Div.	
			6/7th R. Scots. Fus converted into Pioneers to 59th Div.	
			3 Lost	
XVIII	36th	8/9th R. Ir. Rif. (a)		1st R. Ir. Rif.
		10th R. Ir. Rif. (a)		from 8th Div.
		11/13th R. Ir. Rif. (a)		1st R. Innis. Fus
		14th R. Ir. Rif. (a)		from 29th Div.
		10th R. Innis. Fus. (a)		2nd R. Innis. Fus
		11th R. Innis. Fus. (a)		from 32nd Div.
		6 Amalgamated		6 Received
XXII	66th	3/5th Lancs. Fus. (a)		1/6th Lancs. Fus.
		2/6th Lancs. Fus (b)		1/4th E. Lancs.
		2/4th E. Lancs. (b)		1/9th Manchester
		2/8th Manchester (a)		from 42nd Div.
		2/10th Manchester (a)		*
		2/9th Manchester (b)		
		3 Amalgamated and 3 Broken-Up		3 Received

(Source: Author Dislocation Analysis (* For amalgamation with 2nd line units))

Table 6 Simple dislocation event register and weighting

Event	Abbreviation	Score
Disbanded	DIS	10
Transfer Out	XO	10
Amalgamate Out	AO	10
Pioneer Out (External)	POE	10
Pioneer Out (Internal)	POI	10
Transfer In	XI	5
Amalgamate In	AI	5
Inter-Brigade Transfer	IB	7.5
Pioneer In	PI	−2.5

Some Analysis

Having accurately defined scale and general scope of reductions it is important to recognise the extent to which their organizational impact varied between divisions and brigades. By applying values to each step as outlined above, it is relatively straight-forward to define a simple magnitude of potential dislocation within each formation and grade it from least to most severe. In this sense, the least severe or 'Uniform' change within a division is typified by simplicity, each brigade being reduced to three battalions through a single disbandment or outbound transfer. Conversely, divisions may characterize 'Severe' where many incoming units and multiple inter-brigade adjustments to reach target establishment balanced a high number of disbandment. 'Intermediate' dislocation defines a group that falls naturally between the two. Representative divisions of the latter collection generally exhibited a similar level of disbandment or transfers as the 'Uniform' group, with the addition of single inter-brigade switches. They are also more likely to have received converted Pioneer battalions and incoming units for amalgamation.

Appraisal of the completed dataset reveals the following example results: 'Uniform' divisions are, on the whole, evenly distributed between the Regular, Territorial and New Armies, despite the latter providing more than half of the total divisions reorganized (26/48 = 54%). There are no representatives of the 2nd-Line Territorials in this group. Divisions in the 'Severe' category hail almost exclusively from the New Army (14/17 = 82%). No Regular divisions appear here, whilst two of the other five 2nd-Line Territorial divisions are present. One of these, the 58th (2/1st London) Division, is unique in having the HQ of six of its infantry battalions subordinated by their 1st-Line counterparts. Of perhaps greatest direct relevance is the fact that almost half (7/15) of all divisions in the 'Uniform' group were components of Third Army on 21 March 1918, and three-quarters of all that army's infantry formations are found in the 'Uniform' or 'Intermediate' dislocation categories (12/16, 75%). This is in stark contrast with Fifth Army, where seven of its eleven divisions *in the line* on that day are members of the 'Severe' collection, and almost all of its infantry divisions are present in the 'Severe' and 'Intermediate' dislocation categories (12/14, 86%). The four remaining 2nd-Line Territorial formations, that is the 57th (2nd West Lancashire) [First Army], 59th (2nd Midland) [Third Army], 62nd (2nd West Riding) [First Army] and 66th (2nd East Lancashire) [Fifth Army] Divisions, drop from 'Severe' to 'Intermediate' solely through the receipt of reinforcing Pioneer battalions.

The same criteria can be applied across Haig's command. First and Second Armies faced the renewed ferocity of the German Lys (Georgette) offensives in northern Picardy and Flanders, commencing 9 April 1918. First Army held six British divisions in the line at zero, with the 2nd Portuguese Division dividing them. Of the divisions to the right or south of the Portuguese, three are classed 'Uniform' – including the Portuguese' neighbours the 55th (West Lancashire) Division – and one, the Regular First Division, 'Intermediate'; to the north, the remaining two divisions (40th and 34th) were near the top of the 'Severe' group. In contrast to the rest of First Army, both latter divisions had been heavily engaged in the March Somme battles. When the Lys attacks opened, assaults were directed on the 55th, Portuguese and northern divisions. The Second Army, all in Flanders and not immediately engaged, counted five of its ten divisions among the 'Uniform' group, with one 'Intermediate' and four 'Severe'. The least dislocated were spread throughout, but the formation in touch with the 34th and 40th – the 19th (Western) Division – was likewise in the 'Severe' class. In addition, eight of the ten Second Army divisions had suffered heavy casualties in March.

As a final exercise in formation analysis, in considering the average Dislocation Index per division across the armies, they may be ranked as follows: Third Army 'Intermediate (38.0), Second Army 'Intermediate' (42.8), First Army 'Intermediate' (44.3), Fifth Army 'Severe' (52.7). The First Army ranking makes no allowance for the unfortunate state of the 2nd Portuguese Division.[38] Drilling deeper into the data, further observations may be made, for example, (see Diagram 1) in the case of the 36th (Ulster) Division, six disbandments were balanced by incoming transfers of Irish battalions to produce the nine-battalion infantry complement. Internally, however, the 109th Brigade lost three of its original four battalions and was, to all intents and purposes, an entirely new formation. An inter-brigade switch, to preserve regimental affiliation, had the effect of artificially exacerbating the dislocation in 107th and 108th Brigades. The net result was extreme, causing the loss of eight original battalions from brigade formations; three each from 107th and 109th Brigades and two from the 108th, which was left with mixed regiments. Diagram 2 illustrates the case of the 14th (Light) Division, also scored in the 'Severe' group. It lost four battalions broken up, with a single battalion incoming from the 9th (Scottish) Division to bring it up to establishment. Three of the disbandments occurred in the 43rd Brigade, balanced by the incoming battalion, and an inter-brigade replacement from 41st Brigade. A

38   Baker, *The Battle for Flanders*, pp.26-27.

'Severe' structural pressure was placed on the single 43rd brigade, while its peers underwent 'Uniform' reorganization. Unlike the 36th (Ulster) Division, GHQ had specified all reductions and the GOC, Major-General Victor Couper, did not make the obvious adjustment that would have brought the Rifle Brigade battalions together. Couper was replaced after the opening German offensive.

Conclusion

It has been argued that, five months down the line, infantry reductions did not represent a significant factor in deciding infantry and command performance in the 'Hundred Days'.[39] During preparations for the 1918 defensive campaign(s), however, there are indications that the effects were acute and extreme. The Dislocation Index represents a useful tool for gauging the impact of such establishment change. Further, it serves to underline the fact that dislocation was irregular depending on how various events combined to achieve target establishment. Concomitant difficulties arose in providing working parties for essential construction and maintenance of field fortifications, or finding space in the rotation for rest and training – both central tenets of revised British principles of defence – not from a shortage of men but from the reduced establishment. Most seriously, and in every case, loss of a battalion removed the vital fourth element from deployments long considered a tactical necessity. Introducing such a structural flaw degraded the ability of brigades and subordinate units to deploy in depth, and perform local counter-attacks, precisely at the time when such capability was most crucial and explicitly called for in the defence plan. A comparison of dislocation indices and early events in the Somme and Lys 1918 battles indicates a correlation between dislocation and this degradation. This is significant, as it could not fail to have serious consequences regarding rapid enemy transit of forward areas and a propensity to create or exacerbate 'unforeseen' circumstances. Establishment change within British divisions is not the sole reason for problems in defence in March and April 1918. With due consideration of its potential impact, however, what emerges is a discretely ominous and unfavourable situation for commanders, staff and men. In face of the approaching storm, with the foundations of their 'building blocks' undermined and 'sound principles' cast aside, they got on with it and prepared as best they could.

39   Simkins, "Building Blocks", p.145.

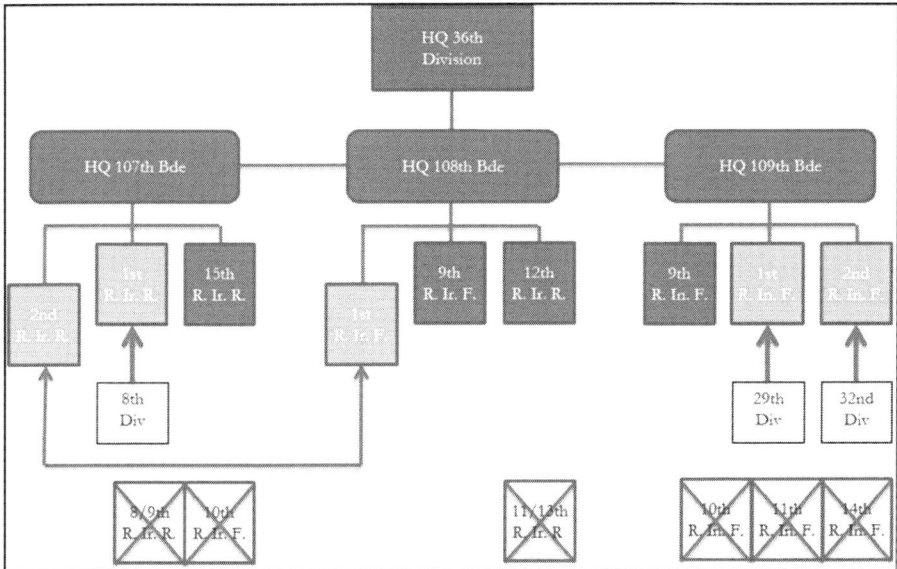

Diagram 1 Brigade reorganization within the 36th (Ulster) Division

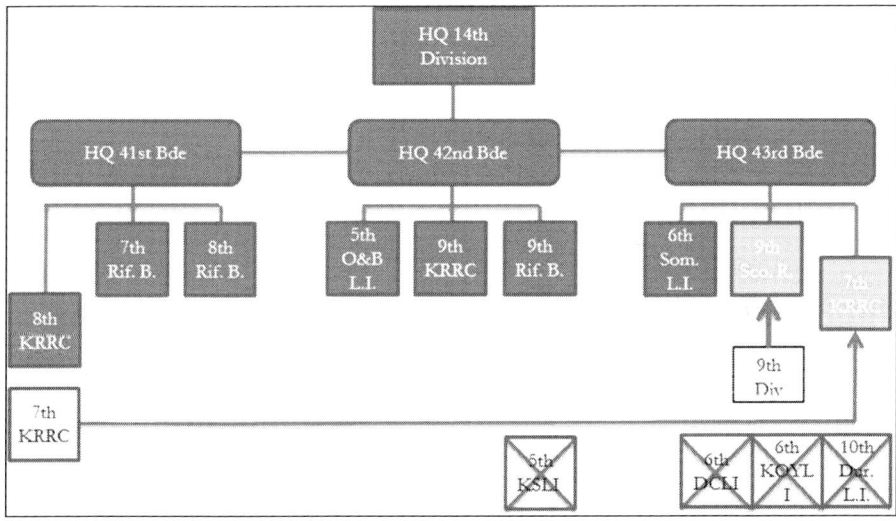

Diagram 2 Brigade reorganization within the 14th (Light) Division[40]

40   The author wishes to acknowledge the work of John Hussey in creating the elegant diagram to accompany text on formation organization which inspired these two charts. See: J. Hussey, 'The British Divisional Reorganisation in February 1918', *Stand To! The Journal of the Western Front Association*, 45 (1996), pp.12-14.

11

Communications in the British Army and the Challenges of Technology, 1914-1940

Sarah McCook

Effective, efficient, and reliable communications are vital to successful warfare, and many operational failures can be traced to a breakdown in the lines of communication. In its evaluation of the lessons of the First World War, the Kirke committee of 1932 established as one of its key findings that communication was 'the crux of the matter.' The committee had been formed in 1932 under the chairmanship of Lieutenant General Sir Walter Kirke who had previously been Deputy Director of Military Operations in the War Office in 1918 and at divisional command in the 1920s. The Committee emerged at the behest of the Chief of the Imperial General Staff, Field Marshal Sir George Milne 'after he read Sir James Edmonds official history of the opening of the Somme' and acted to 'crystallise much of the thinking since 1918' that had emerged within the British Army.[1] It noted, in particular, that:

> Without communication, command cannot function; it can neither receive information, nor get out its orders. The army is then fighting without a brain; or worse still, with a disordered brain which acts regardless of reality.[2]

The report's emphasis on communication can also partially be explained by the context of on-going mechanisation during the 1920s and early 1930s, which brought

---

1   David French, *Raising Churchill's Army: The British Army and War against Germany, 1919-1945* (Oxford: Oxford University Press, 2000), pp.30-31.
2   The National Archives (TNA), WO 32/3116, 'Report on Operations on the Western Front, by Major-General J. Kennedy' in *Report of the Committee on the Lessons of the Great War*, 1932. See: Brian Hall, 'The 'Life-Blood' of command? The British Army, Communications and the Telephone, 1877-1914,' *War & Society*, 27 (2) (2008), p.43.

about the challenges of adapting signals to the changing structure of the Army.[3] Despite the War Office's attestation of the importance of signals in the Kirke report, historians have not offered a discourse concerning the Royal Corps of Signals, which has left the corps and its role in overall victory largely unexplored. By focusing on infantry, air power, and tank tactics, the main body of Second World War history fails to incorporate fully the strategy that evolved from improvisations in logistics.[4] This not only limits the understanding of the ability of the Army to respond to the changing character of warfare, but it also results in a policy-led understanding of change. The British land forces, however, tended to change from the bottom upwards with the forward units improvising to give themselves the advantage. Whether the Army was proactive or reactive in the Second World War remains debateable. By looking at the field accounts in the area of communications and corresponding strategy changes, rather than taking a policy-driven approach, this chapter argues that the debate becomes more complex: that in fact, the proactive changes occurred at the basic, tactical level with operations and strategy inspired by the realities faced by tactical troops.

In re-evaluating communications leading up to the opening years of the 1939-45 war, this chapter will use the position of despatch rider as a vehicle to examine the logistical framework of communications and the ability of the Army to respond to challenges. This chapter begins to redress the lack of analysis of the role of communications by evaluating the change over the course of the war in the approach taken by the signal services. This results in the revelation of a conflation of innovation and implementation, as well as advancement and advantage; this occurs especially since historical studies begin with policy change rather than the events leading to that

---

3   David French, 'Doctrine and Organization in the British Army, 1919-1932,' *The Historical Journal*, 44 (2) (2001), pp.497-515: David French, 'The Mechanization of the British Cavalry between the World Wars', *War in History*, 10 (3) (2003), pp.296-320.

4   The body of academic work investigating the Royal Corps of Signals and British Army communications is slim. The only work to date that solely concerns the Royal Signals during the Second World War is R.F.H Nalder, *The History of British Army Signals in the Second World War: General Survey* (London: Royal Signals Institution, 1953). Simon Godfrey, *Army Communications in the Second World War: Lifting the Fog of Battle* (London: Bloomsbury Academic, 2013), offers the first critical evaluation of communications during the Second World War. For an overview of the Royal Corps Signals history, see: R.F.H. Nalder, *The Royal Corps of Signals: A History of Its Antecedents and Development (Circa 1800-1955)* (London: Royal Signals Institution, 1958); Cliff Lord and Graham Watson, *The Royal Corps of Signals: Unit Histories of the Corps (1920-2001) and its Antecedents* (Solihull: Helion, 2003); and the less analytical Ralph Maxwell Adams, *Through to 1970: Royal Signals Golden Jubilee* (London: Royal Signals Institution, 1970). R.E. Priestley's *Work of the Royal Engineers in the European War, 1914-19: The Signal Service (France)* (London: Chatham, 1921) is one of the few works that solely addresses communications in the British Army on the Western Front of the First World War, and Philip Warner's *The Vital Link: The Story of Royal Signals 1945-1985*(London: Leo Cooper, 1989) addresses Royal Signals post-1945.

change. For example, there is an assumption in the general history that the electronic means of communication, such as radio and telephone, were used widely, an assumption that does not address the challenges faced by the signalmen. Without considering the extent to which doctrinal changes and the resulting standard issue equipment filtered down any true advantage or improvement, the nature of the Army's response cannot be fully appreciated.[5]

General Sir Anthony Farrar-Hockley, recipient of the Military Cross in 1944 and later NATO's Commander in Chief, Northern European Forces, wrote that he knew:

> ...of no military operations which were not dependent to one degree or another on communications; the more difficult the operations the more crucial the dependence.[6]

This dependence resulted in the trial of a multitude of methods of communication in efforts to find the most efficient and effective. The development of electronic means, including telegraphy, telephony, and wireless, offered ostensibly superior options, allowing messages to be sent quickly over long distances. How this technology was developed and adapted to battlefield conditions forms an important part of the history of the Second World War. Nonetheless, the underlying assumption that technological development automatically conferred decisive advantage does a disservice to the fuller understanding of not only the complex management of communications structure but also the more complete picture of how the Army as a whole responded to the varied challenges faced during the Second World War. Sheffield claims that:

> ...the main difference [between the First and Second World Wars was] that in the later war technological advances had provided effective communications and a usable instrument of exploitation.[7]

Whilst the use of 'advanced methods' undoubtedly had great impact, and appears throughout official policy, the widespread use of despatch riders and runners denotes an acknowledgement that policy and technology did not always prove fit for purpose.

---

5   For example, see: Richard Overy, *Why the Allies Won the War* (London: Pimlico, 1996); John Ellis, *Brute Force: Allied Strategy and Tactics in the Second World War* (London: Andre Deutsch Ltd., 1990); Shelford Bidwell and Dominick Graham, *British Army Weapons and Theories of War 1904-1945* (London: George Allen & Unwin, 1982); and, more recently, French, *Raising Churchill's Army* and Jeremy Black, *Rethinking Military History* (London: Routledge, 2004).

6   Cited in Warner, *The Vital Link*, p.3.

7   G.D. Sheffield, 'The Shadow of the Somme: the Influence of the First World War on British Soldiers' Perceptions and Behaviour in the Second World War,' in Angus Calder and Paul Addison (eds.), *Time to Kill: The Soldier's Experience of War in the West 1939-1945* (London: Pimlico, 1997), p.36.

Technology's place in the overall victory has been addressed in works such as Hartcup's *The Challenge of War* and Overy's *Why the Allies Won*, both of which promote the material and technological advantages that Britain enjoyed during the war and tout the conflict as 'a watershed in the progress and organization of science.'[8] The most recent analysis of technology's role is Kennedy's *Engineers of Victory*, which attributes a large portion of the credit to the 'boffins' (lieutenants in particular) of the armed forces.[9] Whilst the development and integration of many scientific advances, including in areas such as improved radio devices and more effective ciphers, was indeed critical to the success of the Allied Powers, the unreserved praise for the merits of technology have left the failures, breakdowns, and improvisations unexplored, and, as a consequence, the notion of technology is rarely addressed critically. By evaluating both the positive and negative aspects of technological advances in communications, the ability of the Army to respond and adapt to challenges can be seen to come from a proactive necessity at a tactical, ground troop level rather than stemming from doctrinal level.

In one of the few exceptions, Lautenschläger addresses the lack of criticism of technology in an article published in the journal *Ethics* in 1985.[10] While focussed on controlling nuclear weapons, Lautenschläger noted that a pervasive assumption of technological determinism exists and is an argument that suggests that technology itself equates to an advantage. Bellamy also notes this assumption and relegates technology to a supporting role in establishing an on-field advantage. Specifically, he notes that readers of military histories 'should be forgiven for thinking that technology is the overwhelmingly dominant factor in war, and that the sophistication of that technology must, of itself, confer a decisive advantage.' This has, he argues, never been the case and is unlikely to be true in future ground conflicts. 'Excessive' focus on technology and its utility (technics) to the detriment of tactics and 'practical soldiering,' he notes, is not a recent problem and has been present since before the First World War. Whilst admitting that technology has greatly affected war, his emphasis is on the limitations of solely focusing upon technology.[11] The argument is similar to that of Black's reiteration of the complexities of qualifying technology. What appears to be a technological superiority is often simply a result of improved technique or change at the tactical level.[12] Bellamy indicates that the issue may be deeper-seated. He asserts that:

8   Guy Hartcup, *Challenge of War: Britain's Scientific and Engineering Contributions to World War Two* (London: David & Charles, 1970), p.17.
9   Paul Kennedy, *Engineers of Victory: The Problem Solvers Who Turned the Tide in the Second World War* (London: Allen Lane, 2013).
10   Karl Lautenschläger, 'Controlling Military Technology', *Ethics*, 95 (3) (1985), pp.692-711.
11   Christopher Bellamy, *The Evolution of Modern Land Warfare: Theory and Practice* (London: Routledge, 1990), p.69.
12   *Ibid.*; Black, *Rethinking Military History*, pp.104-127.

...modern academics are frequently unsympathetic to the problems faced by military men in assimilating new technology as part of a total paradigm change—"new weapons: old mind-sets."[13]

Black has more recently discussed the intricacies of examining technology's impact in the context of warfare; however, the approach has not yet become fully integrated in the general narrative.[14]

This paradigm shift forms the basis of this chapter and is one that indicates the conscious rejection of 'technology' in favour of something 'old-fashioned' but of proven reliability. During the Second World War, reliable radio was not available in all circumstances, situations, and operations, making both incomplete and misleading the argument that developments in communications provided a distinct advantage when compared to earlier conflicts. Furthermore, this chapter argues that by focusing on a distinctly policy-led reading of communications history, the true nature of the Army's effectiveness and adaptability cannot be fully appreciated. Instead, an approach from the ground up should be taken to view change in the order that it actually occurred.

The predicaments faced at the tactical level, such as lingering security concerns and equipment problems, show a discrepancy between the technologically advanced strategy of using radio and the reality of implementing this strategy to gain an advantage, particularly in forward units where improvisation featured heavily. One such example early on in the war can be found in the Norwegian Campaign of 1940. During this campaign, the issue of procuring and supplying batteries and replacement parts for radios in the difficult terrain resulted in units moving to methods such as despatch riders, who were able keep communication intact by physically carrying written documents or transmitting verbal messages between units.[15] A similar situation occurred during the retreat to Dunkirk in May 1940, when the rapid movement of the land forces led to a deterioration of established forms of communication, including disintegration of the Belgian telephone system and immovability of the radio trucks due to blocked roads. The necessity of improvisation in this case again led to the deployment of the Army's ranks of despatch riders in order to ensure the columns had adequate communication and direction.[16]

---

13   Bellamy, *Evolution of Modern Land Warfare*, pp. 30-31.
14   Black, *Rethinking Military History*, pp.104-127.
15   Robert Citino, *'Blitzkrieg' to Desert Storm: The Evolution of Operational Warfare* (Lawrence, KS: University Press of Kansas, 2004), p.41; James S. Corum, 'The German Campaign in Norway 1940 as a Joint Operation', *Journal of Strategic Studies*, 21 (4) (1998), pp.50-77.
16   Imperial War Museum (IWM), 07/54/1, Accounts of George Aldridge; Brian Bond, 'The British Field Force in France and Belgium, 1939-40,' in Angus and Calder (eds.), *Time to Kill*, pp.40-49.

Background

Communications, of course, have always been part of the armed forces. Without intercommunication, it would be impossible to begin to undertake training manoeuvres, let alone campaigns. In the British land forces, signalling duties had traditionally been undertaken by regimental signallers through methods that varied from carrying a message to visual signalling (flag semaphore, heliograph, and lamps, for example), by using pigeons or balloons, and, as the nineteenth century progressed, employing telegraphy, telephony, and, eventually, radio. The period of transition from mechanical to electronic means of communication was not one that was smooth or holistic – it took decades to develop suitable equipment, let alone train operators and centralise command. As the Army transformed to reflect developments in electronic communication, the reorganisation of signalling duties slowly led to a more centralised approach despite regimental signallers' concerns about the increasing establishment of whole Army policies, such as those in the Cardwell Reforms. The Royal Engineers Signal Service, for example, utilised Morse code in flag signalling, whereas regimental signallers, particularly the cavalry, used the semaphore alphabet. As the autonomy of regiments diminished, such basic issues as differences in the alphabet used had to be addressed.

In the latter half of the nineteenth-century, the military took several steps to codify and regularise its communications practices. Visual signalling transformed during this period, as both heliograph and flag signalling adopted Morse code, which had been developed in the 1830s. Introduced in 1865, heliograph became one of 'the most successful and widely used visual signalling systems'.[17] The original instrument, designed by Henry Christopher Mance, utilised a mirror mounted upon a tripod with a single mirror linked to a tilting key mechanism that allowed the signaller to create flashes in accordance with the Morse alphabet. The range was, however, only 'light-of-sight' and limited to the naked eye.[18]

The Army did not formalise its change in flag signalling until 1896, when it adopted Morse code as its language in place of the semaphore alphabet, which had been in use since the mid-seventeenth century. Neither flags nor heliographs were ideal, however, as conditions such as bad weather or rugged terrain could render them useless, and they had no security measures in place.[19] The unpredictability of environmental factors such as cloud cover and altitude presaged the complications that would plague communications until the development of secure radio in the mid-1940s.

The first significant move towards centralised communications command focussed around the telegraph and came in 1870 with the establishment of the "C" Telegraph

---

17   Lewis Coe, *The Telegraph: A History of Morse's Invention and Its Predecessors in the United States* (Jefferson, N.C.: McFarland & Company, 1993), p.8.
18   *Ibid.*, p.9.
19   Priestley, *The Signal Service*, p.9; Adams, *Through to 1970*, p.19.

Troop, Royal Engineers. The Troop had the 'duty of providing telegraph communications for the field army' by way of 'visual signalling, mounted orderlies and telegraph, so linking the expeditionary force into the growing worldwide telegraph network.'[20] It saw service in the 1873 Ashanti campaign and the 1879 Zulu Wars, and its success resulted in the continued central administration of telegraph signals while the majority of other signals remained 'an infantry responsibility with ad hoc sections being formed when required.'[21]

Despite the introduction of various alternate methods of communication, the 1880 *Manual of Instruction in Army Signalling* still articulated the fundamental importance of the army's human messengers by stating that the 'most accurate way of transmitting intelligence is by means of an orderly carrying a *written* message.'[22] Wireless was introduced but failed to have much impact during the next two major conflicts: the Second Boer War and the Russo-Japanese War. Additionally, wireless was seen as highly unconventional and volatile in 1912 when the Royal Engineers Signal Service authorised the formation of a new corps to handle written and verbal messages.[23] Nevertheless, in the aftermath of the Boer War there was a gradual recognition that changing battlefield conditions meant a need for a balance of communication systems that incorporated both human and technological element. Commanders often returned to the most secure message transmission method available to them – messengers. At first, these were on foot or horseback, then in automobiles in the late nineteenth-century, with the motorcycle quickly becoming the most practical mode of transportation. The concept of a unit of motorcycle messengers became reality in 1912 when the Signal Service created the Motor Cycle Corps.[24]

Despite the adoption of a new means of transportation, the concept remained simple: a human messenger transporting either written or verbal messages. This physical transport of messages fulfilled the trust reiterated in field manuals, and with the failures of the infantile wireless structure of the Boer War in recent memory, the 'old mind-sets' deemed the Motor Cycle Corps's establishment as a safe and reliable addition to the infrastructure. The motorcycle, in this case, was not the technological jump in communications. Despatch riders remained *active* messengers, like despatch runners, not *passive* messengers as was with the case with telegraph, telephone, and radio operators. The distinction lay simply in the way in which a message was transmitted: in the former, the sender and recipient interacted with the messenger. In the latter, the sender and recipient saw only one end of the transaction and had to trust an 'invisible third party', for example, telegraph lines and radio waves. The primitivism

---

20   Laurette Burton, *The Royal Corps of Signals: A Pictoral History* (Stroud, Tempus Publishing, 2002), p.9; Adams, *Through to 1970*, p.7.

21   Burton, *Royal Corps of Signals*, p.11; Adams, *Through to 1970*, p.19.

22   Cited in Nalder, *Corps of Signals*, 19.

23   *Ibid.*

24   Sarah Gibbs, 'Nerves of the Army': British Despatch Riders during the First and Second World War', (MA Thesis, Georgia College & State University, 2008), p.11.

of the concept is rooted in the requirement of the messengers to engage actively with the process, to be both the means and the method by initiating, executing, and concluding the operation in its entirety. It is best explained in comparison with the electronic methods that require two users with the work done by the electronic means of the telegraph or radio sets. The availability of wireless, which in theory could have reduced signaller casualties, did not, at this stage result in a signals revolution due to the considerable challenges of security and logistics.[25]

The number of personnel recruited to the role of despatch rider reinforced the overarching trust in physical messengers, as did their automatic promotion to corporal due to the prohibition of privates approaching officers unescorted.[26] Encapsulating the social class expectations of the Victorian Army, the Motor Cycle Corps began with the recruitment of the Officer Training Corps from Oxford and Cambridge, believing it would prove beneficial to have highly literate and educated men within its ranks. It was also a requirement that members provide their own motorcycles, restricting recruitment to those who were able to afford vehicles. The corps remained in existence and saw action during the First World War, particularly during 1914 and 1918, with the interim years of the war reduced to the Despatch Rider Letter Service and despatch runners.[27] The corps received commendation for their service during the retreat from Mons with Field-Marshal Sir John French, on 20 November 1914, writing that he was:

> ...anxious to bring to notice the splendid work which has been done throughout the campaign by the motor-cyclists of the Signal Corps.

French noted, specifically, their commitment to carrying messages 'at all hours of the day and night in every kind of weather, and often traversing bad roads blocked with transport' in order to maintain 'an extraordinary degree of efficiency in the service of communications.' French also indicated, however, that casualties had been high within the Corps's first major campaign.[28]

---

25   Nalder, *British Army Signals*; Field Marshal Sir John French, quoted in Adams, *Through to 197*, pp.35-36; Gibbs, 'Nerves of the Army.'

26   Austin Patrick Corcoran, *The Daredevil of the Army: Experience as a 'Buzzer' and Despatch Rider* (New York: Dutton, 1918).

27   For an account of despatch rider service during the First World War, see: Corcoran, *Daredevil of the Army* and W.H.L Watson, *Adventures of a Motorcycle Despatch Rider During the First World War* (London, 1915. Reprint, Liskeard, 2006). For a variety of other signal experiences, see: Charles Purdom (ed.), *Everyman at War: Sixty Personal Narratives of the War* (New York: J.M. Dent, 1930). For a fuller account of despatch rider service during the First World War, see: Gibbs, 'Nerves of the Army'.

28   John French, cited in Adams, *Through to 1917*, pp.35-36. An alternate version of this despatch can be found in Raymond Priestley's account. His recollection differs only in the first sentence of French's message and reads, 'I am anxious in this despatch to bring to your

During the First World War, the Signal Service, like the larger Army, experienced battle conditions not previously encountered, resulting in the need of adaptation and retooling, though both despatch riders and runners repeatedly distinguished themselves during retreats. Though rudimentary wireless telegraphy and telephony were available, they were neither secure nor widely available due to faulty and ineffective equipment. Where it was viable, the wireless in use was most often wireless telegraphy by Morse code rather than the telephony most associated with the notion of 'wireless'. Line telegraphy and telephony provided the majority of signals traffic; however, their drawbacks included the laying and maintenance of lines within trenches.[29] The hazards of the lines became such an accepted part of trench warfare that Robert Graves included a description in *Goodbye to All That*, and they featured heavily in Charles Purdom's collection *Everyman at War*.[30]

In 1915, in response to the conspicuous insecurity of electronic communication, evidenced by the fact that the German armies repeatedly proved well informed of British plans, Captain A.C. Fuller devised the Fullerphone in an attempt to provide a more secure method of transmission. The adoption of the Fullerphone marked the beginning of the task of recognising and responding to electronic signals security issues; however, it came only after the disastrous effects of intercepted signals intelligence became apparent, clearly showing that advanced methods of communication did not automatically result in an advantage. The most well-known example of this is the Battle of Tannenburg of 1914 in which the Germans routed the Russians due to the interception of unsecured radio traffic.

As a result, despatch riders experienced resurgence in deployment during the mobile offensives of 1918, when trench lines of communication became impractical due to their static nature and the sudden change in the pace of tactics. Despatch riders and runners, however, were still considered a firm and reliable alternative to the electronic means and were utilised largely. The war ended after a period of mobility that did not widely use electronic means of communication. The resulting memory of victory, then, that would be used to shape the future planning was one that involved physical messengers.

Interwar Period

The impact of this memory of the dependability of the despatch riders, as well as radio's failure to make an overall decisive contribution, meant that by the end of the war, the

notice the splendid work which has been done throughout the campaign by the cyclists of the Signal Corps.' Priestley, *Signal Service*, p.42.
29   Hall, 'The "Life-Blood" of Command,' pp.43-44.
30   See: Robert Graves, *Goodbye to All That* (New York: J. Cape, 1930), p.122, for Graves's account of having to avoid low hanging and loose communications lines. Purdom, *Everyman at War*.

preferred method of communication had changed very little.[31] The 1921 creation of the Royal Corps of Signals meant that communications strategy and policy would be a centralised under a single corps. Despite this, however, many units lobbied to maintain the tradition of regimental signallers, creating a dichotomy in the level of training. Later on, this resulted in inadequately trained radio operators, as well as creating an adoption lag between Royal Signals's new policies and implementation in regimental signalling. The land forces saw telephony and telegraphy as the way forward with radio as a promising option if the twin issues of security and integrity could be solved.

During the interwar period, the lack of funds for investment in the Army's research and development meant that by the outbreak of war in 1939, the communications ability of the land forces was not substantially different from that at the end of the First World War. The reduced military funding primarily went to the Royal Navy and the newly formed Royal Air Force. This left the Army in a crisis for development during this period. The funding that did come to the Army most often went to the areas of considerable debate and discussion by theorists such as Basil Liddell Hart and J.F.C. Fuller, particularly into mobility in infantry and tank battalions. In working to mechanise and mobilise the Army's fighting forces, the communications structure failed to attract the heavy investment needed to develop, and make available, the equipment necessary to act on the security issues later outlined by the Kirke Commission's report that highlighted the shortcomings of the First World War and specifically pointed to the failure in reliable signals. The adherence to the Ten Year Rule also resulted in a lack of immediacy in logistical evolution and training, leaving Royal Signals in a static position in terms of developing and responding to the challenges of radio.

Meanwhile, however, in response to their growing popularity amongst the public, civilian industry developed better and more efficient motorcycles. Consequently, Royal Signals, and the Army as a whole, did not have to invest large resources in developing these vehicles and were able to take advantage of the private industry's ingenuity. In the 1930s, after the Great Depression began, motorcycle companies began courting government contracts in hopes of securing their financial futures. As Royal Signals and the Territorial Army (TA) continued to deploy despatch riders to colonial posts, as well as to other regimental postings, the Army kept a large number of despatch riders in the ranks. Policy changes that substituted official army for personal provision of vehicles, plus the allowance for privates to approach officers unescorted shifted recruitment to a wider base. The Army increasingly included men who already had motorcycling experience, resulting in less required training for suitable applicants. E.S. Nicholson, for example, was one of many despatch riders recruited in the 1930s, posted to colonial holdings in India, and on active duty when war began in 1939. His account labours the point of security over long distances in India and the prevalence

---

31   See: Hall, 'The "Life-Blood" of Command.'

of despatch riders as trusted messengers over the available Indian signal service's radio operators.[32]

Early Stages of the Second World War

The outbreak of war in 1939 resulted in the formation of the British Expeditionary Force (BEF) that included many despatch riders. In the rest of the Army, the majority of the TA's mechanics and despatch riders transferred to the regular Army and joined to Royal Signals or the Royal Army Service Corps (RASC). George Aldridge, who joined the TA in 1933, was typical in his experiences and was transferred from his role as a mechanic to a new position as a despatch rider in the RASC in 1939. He was then assigned to the BEF sent to France in 1939.[33]

Throughout the war communication policy and tactics evolved to suit the manner of warfare that developed. The policy at the beginning of the war reflected the economic stringency that had faced the Army in that it had not developed much during the twenty-one years since the end of the last war. Radio sets, as Nalder describes in detail, remained inadequate and bulky.[34] This created the problems of usage and mobility; both, it quickly became apparent, needed to be improved quickly for effective deployment of radio communications on the front lines. The lack of improvement in the logistics of communication mobility meant that a variety of communications techniques and tactics had to be utilised in both the BEF's campaign in France and the campaign in Norway, demonstrating the wide range of options tried by Royal Signals and regimental signal companies. By focusing on the advantage offered by radio, however, most accounts of the war leave unexplored the initial failures of wireless and the scramble for communications that led to an abandonment of failed telephone lines, unusable radio sets, and broken telegraph wires. In these circumstances, with the desperate necessity to keep open the lines of communication, the only option was to send despatch riders or runners in the hope that they would survive the overwhelming German superiority during the early stages of the war.

A divergence between the promise of technological advancement and the lack of realistic advantage became apparent at the end of the 'Phoney War' of 1939-1940 and nearly saw a whole scale collapse in the BEF's communication. At first, the BEF remained practically motionless in France for several months, its only movement occasional forays forward, often carried out for reconnaissance purposes. The Despatch Rider Letter Service (DRLS), which had become firmly established during the First World War, was revived at this time for carrying letters and documents

---

32   E.S. Nicholson, *Adventures of a Royal Signals Despatch Rider* (Leicestershire, 2003), p.143; IWM 07/54/1, Accounts of George Aldridge.

33   Nicholson, *Adventures of a Royal Signals Despatch Rider*; IWM, 07/54/1. Aldridge served in the RASC until he was captured after the surrender of Singapore in 1941 and remained a POW at Changi Camp.

34   Nalder, *History of British Army Signals*.

between units, with the Belgian telephone system and radio trucks utilised for verbal messages. Traversing the area between the units, however, soon became increasingly dangerous, as German forces crept ever nearer to British held territory. The accounts of despatch riders held at the Imperial War Museum depict them as some of the most actively engaged soldiers of the BEF during this stage of the war. They encountered the enemy with an increasing frequency as German forward parties, often with snipers, moved closer to the British lines.[35]

Once British retreat to Dunkirk commenced, however, the despatch riders became the method of choice for message transmission between the units and general headquarters (GHQ).[36] The BEF's sudden retrograde movement, in combination with the forward attack by German forces, meant that the telephone system in use for the past six months, heavily reliant on the public Belgian infrastructure, collapsed and rendered the telephone-dominated communications framework useless. The movement also created issues for radio trucks, as the uneven and refugee-clogged roads complicated passage and made it difficult and impractical to move the vehicles and equipment.[37]

The despatch riders, however, were able to manoeuvre through whilst also directing and leading convoys towards the Dunkirk. They were put to use travelling up and down the columns, delivering evacuation instructions and other such missives. The abandonment of the radio, telephone, and telegraph systems in this case shows reliance on humans messengers in the first major action of the war. In the case of the BEF, the 'advanced' methods of radio and telephone were available but despite their potential, they did not articulate any decisive advantage, instead proving detrimental to the retreat efforts. Bond emphasized the importance of the despatch riders by noting that Royal Signals gave orders to evacuate the motorcycles of its members but to leave the radio equipment behind.[38]

The Army's communications policy and strategy failed again in the Norwegian Campaign of 1940 and laid bare many of the consequential supply issues of wide radio usage. Despite the vast climate and environmental differences when compared to France, the strategy remained the same – the initial primary form of communications would be wireless. Whilst this worked on paper, the battlefield conditions negated any advantage and resulted in signallers disregarding the policies through necessity in order to continue the lines of communication. The first problem encountered was the terrain, which was almost impassable, resulting in radio trucks becoming stuck in the snow, often without drivers (due to the practice of recruiting locals who often fled during bombing raids). The geography also made supply lines very difficult, which

35   IWM, 07/54/1, Accounts of George Aldridge; IWM, 06/72/1, Memoir of Dennis Hustler.
36   IWM, 07/54/1, Accounts of George Aldridge.
37   IWM, 08/108/1, Memoirs of Albert W. Chuter; IWM, PP/MCR/426, Diary of Les Barter, Reel no. 1.
38   Brian Bond, 'British Field Force', pp.40-49.

meant radio batteries and crystals could not be easily replaced; the abandoned radio trucks then clogged available supply roads, quickly leading to a materiel shortage. This lack of planning and forethought by the War Office resulted in a great loss of valuable equipment and the need for the troops on the ground to adapt their tactics.[39]

Citino cited one other issue with the Norwegian campaign – the challenge of routine wireless silence.[40] This security measure meant that not only did the Army have the aforementioned difficulty in transporting the equipment for radio to the forward units, but once it arrived, there was no guarantee that it could be employed. The inability to utilise the technology furthered the disillusionment with wireless signals and again resulted in employing despatch riders as a fall back method, as they could pass through the terrain. The Norwegian campaign was, overall, a resounding loss for the British. Further articulating the operational and organisational failures of the Army, the signals problems clearly demonstrated that enacting a radio-led communications strategy proved more difficult than simply enacting it as policy and distributing the equipment. The drawbacks associated with supplies, security, tactics, and training combined to negate any advantage offered by electronic 'advanced' methods of communication.[41]

Despite the emergence of issues such as supply and security, the strategy did not immediately respond to the difficulties faced, and despatch riders remained important parts of their units in both the UK-based forces and those that deployed to North Africa and, later on, North-West Europe. During both the Italian Campaign and Normandy landings, for example, riflemen, mechanics, and signalmen continued to be transferred to despatch duties in both the Army and Royal Marines (RM), in response to the varied conditions and uncertainty to the pace and tactics that would be encountered.[42] After the Battle of Anzio in 1944, Graham Swain, a rifleman and driver in the 56th (London) Division, joined the attached signal platoon and recalled that he was ordered to go forward and establish contact with the forward companies:

> …because the radio communication had broken down…infantry communication by radio was pretty parlous. Sometimes it worked, sometimes it didn't. There was no communication with forward companies at all.[43]

39   Citino, 'Blitzkrieg' to Desert Storm', pp.39-41, 278; Corum, 'The German Campaign'.
40   Citino, 'Blitzkrieg' to Desert Storm, p.41; Nalder, Royal Corps of Signals, p.278.
41   Ibid, pp.39-41, 278.
42   For an account of a Royal Marine transferred to service, see: Raymond Mitchell, Commando Despatch Rider: With 41 Royal Marine Commando in North-West Europe 1944-1945 (Barnsley: Leo Cooper, 2001), and the corresponding archival records at IWM, 93/97/1.
43   IWM, 22352, Interview of Graham William Arthur Swain.

Conclusion

The issues of maintaining communication that arose in the early years of war clearly challenged the signals arm of the land forces with the Army and the RMs struggling to keep their units well informed and institute secure intercommunication. Despite the Royal Signals continuing to train radio operators and linesmen, however, sourcing and maintaining effective equipment in the field remained a constant challenge for the land forces.[44] Most developments resulted from ingenuity and improvisation in the field with soldiers responding to the landscape and unique circumstances faced in each theatre of war. By focussing on the advancement of technology, particularly in a policy-led understanding of the war, the difficulties and realities of the frontline troops are omitted from the wider narrative. By including an account-based evaluation of communications, the process of how policy and strategy were derived comes into question and can be seen to be responding to what the frontline was already undertaking.

The conflation of technological advancement and advantage, as Lautenschläger and Bellamy rightly assert, pervades the history of the Second World War. A simplistic explanation can be seen in the significant advances implemented to cryptography at Bletchley Park. The results of the undertakings here provided a decisive advantage to the war effort; however, the secure and well-resourced compound at Bletchley Park contrasted greatly with the realities of the frontlines and battlefield conditions in Europe and North Africa. The same advancement of radio had two separate uses and results in the different environments; thus, the thesis that technological advancements in communications contributed an overall definitive advantage is too simplistic for a true understanding of the war. Furthermore, to distinguish the extent to which these developments affected the structure and framework of the Army, historical debates should include an account-driven, policy-reactive methodology alongside the more traditional policy-led strategic understandings.

The question of adaptability of the British forces comes to the fore in influential works such as Overy's *Why the Allies Won*, Ellis's *Brute Force*, and French's *Raising Churchill's Army*.[45] The dominant coverage almost entirely neglects communications in its assessment of the war. Most damagingly, Place justifies the omission in his argument concerning lack of experience within the forces by excluding Royal Signals and the other logistics corps, noting that their primary function was 'facilitat[ing] the fighting action of the infantry and armour.'[46] By using the communications framework as a focus, however, it appears debatable whether or not the Army, and the military as a whole, consciously and intentionally adapted to the new style of warfare,

---

44   Coe, *The Telegraph*.
45   Overy, *Why the Allies Won*; Ellis, *Brute Force*; French, *Raising Churchill's Army*.
46   Timothy Harrison Place, *Military Training in the British Army 1940-1944: From Dunkirk to D-Day* (London: Frank Cass, 2000), p.14.

or remained reactive, transforming only through evolution in response to failures. The answer to this question can only be settled when the histories of the war provide an accurate picture of the realities of front-line technology use by identifying the many failures and setbacks faced by the operators and linesmen in the signalling units.

The purpose of this chapter is not to diminish the unquestionable advances in science that were achieved during the Second World War. Rather, it seeks to re-evaluate the place of technology within the history of the war, in this case communications, and reconcile the misconceptions of advancement and advantage. It also attempts to illuminate the area in between innovation and implementation, whilst contributing to a better understanding of the ability of the British land forces to respond to the challenges it faced. Furthermore, at least in the realm of signals, evolutionary change often triumphed where technological revolution failed, usually due to a change in tactics. Warner captured the danger of relying on revolutionary communications when he warned that:

> We may, perhaps, now have reached a point when all military communications will be made electronically and old-fashioned methods be safely forgotten. However, the enduring lesson of military history is that it is unwise to be complacent about anything.[47]

Nevertheless, this 'enduring lesson' can easily be seen in the many failures that surrounded the widespread introduction of electronic means of communications; furthermore, the vitality and nature of communications also meant that failure could have longstanding and far-reaching consequences, leading to hesitancy towards changes in policy. These complications mean that communications during the war cannot be generalised as part of a technological revolution and should be re-evaluated independently. It is only then that the true extent of the impact of technology on the war, and the military as a whole, can be fully and accurately explored.

47   Warner, *Vital Link*, pp.5-6.

12

From 'Jock Column' to Armoured Column
Transformation and change in British and Commonwealth unit tactics, in the Western Desert, January 1941 to August 1942

Neal Dando

In June 1940, British controlled Egypt came under threat of an offensive from Libya by the Italian X Army, following Mussolini's declaration of war on British bases in the Mediterranean. Facing the impending Italian offensive was the modestly sized Western Desert Force, which had to defend a lengthy frontier with Libya, with only a comparatively weak Motor Infantry Brigade. One experienced commander, Lieutenant-Colonel J.C. 'Jock' Campbell, found the answer to a lack of armour, and created the 'Jock Column', to create a more effective offensive unit from his Artillery and Infantry formations. These Columns were perhaps more extensive and more widely used, and had a significant impact upon higher commanders thinking during the period 1941-1942, than has been previously recognized, despite occasional references to them in the historiography. This localized tactic gave Infantry and Armoured Divisional Support Brigades, an opportunity to be more offensive leaving Cruiser Brigades to operate independently and with mixed success in battle. The Jock Column tactic developed a new mind-set of dispersal of units, just as Axis formations proved that concentration and combined arms was the real key to success in the tactical battle. They contributed to British offensive failures up to First Alamein, (30 June-27 July 1942), which led to dramatic changes in command and tactical thinking and a return to the tactics of consolidating objectives and the use of more powerful armoured columns, first used during the Second Battle of Alamein (23 October-4 November 1942). In later operations armoured columns attacked with powerful air and artillery support, such as at the Tebaga Gap (25-27 March 1943), and later during Operation STRIKE (5-13 May 1943). Yet for two years, Jock columns influenced British thinking, despite mixed successes. At the time, they offered an effective method of engaging the enemy, with orders, 'to take offensive against any enemy threat,' and provided opportunity for Infantry units to engage an Axis formation.[1] They caused attrition to Axis supply units and were to deny the enemy the freedom to manoeuvre. Columns were popular for being independent, modestly sized commands, as well as an innovative, combined arms formation. This chapter concentrates on the development of Jock Columns and their increasing separation from armour as a transformational change in doctrine.

Historiography

The historiography of the North African campaign is vast, yet few works seriously consider the impact of Jock Columns to the same degree as other British tactics. Contemporaries believed they were part of a 'buccaneering, marauding, piratical sort of game, to which Englishmen took like ducks to water' while Moorehead saw them as a brilliant alternative to the bungling of massed formations.[2] David Hunt, an Intelligence officer with XIII Corps, said that many officers believed at the time, they were the right tactic.[3] Playfair's official history notes their use, but offered some cautionary comments that repeated General Sir Claude Auchinleck's revised views of April 1942.[4] Serving soldiers, such as Riflemen R.L. Crimp, Victor Gregg and Gunner H.J. Griffin, noted the mixed success of the Columns in which they served, and provided a useful insight into their effectiveness.[5] Some contemporaries expressed their doubts, Major-General Francis Tuker, commanding 4th Indian Division, criticized the lack of military thinking behind them.[6] Michael Carver, a staff officer with 7th Armoured Division, perhaps with some hindsight, believed they were ineffective, whilst New Zealand Brigadier Howard Kippenberger, thought British military thinking had reached one of its lowest ebbs.[7] Buckley's recent study of British armoured doctrine notes that it tried to adapt to changes to combat against better Axis equipment

1   The National Archives (TNA) WO 201/355, Action at Sidi-Rezegh, 1 Kings Royal Rifle Corps, November 1941.

2   Alexander Clifford, *Crusader* (London: George G Harrap, 1942); Alan Moorehead, *African Trilogy* (London: Hamish Hamilton, 1944), p.230.

3   David Hunt, *A Don At War* (London: Frank Cass, 1990).

4   I.S.O. Playfair *et al*, *The Mediterranean and Middle East, Volume 1: The Early Successes Against Italy, to May 1941* (London: HMSO, 1954), p.205.

5   R.L. Crimp, *The Diary of a Desert Rat*, edited by Alex Bowlby (London: Pan, 1974); Victor Gregg, *Rifleman: A Frontline life from Alamein and Dresden to the fall of the Berlin Wall*, edited by Rick Stroud (London: Bloomsbury, 2011); H.J. Griffin, *An Eighth Army Odyssey* (Bishop Auckland: Pentland Press, 1997).

6   G.R. Stevens, *Fourth Indian Division* (Uckfield: Naval & Military Press, 2011 [1947]), p.144.

7   Michael Carver, *Dilemmas of the Desert War* (Staplehurst: Spellmount, 2002), p.100; Howard Kippenberger, *Infantry Brigadier* (London: Oxford University Press, 1949), pp.81-82.

and doctrine.[8] From the Axis perspective, German memoirs including H.W. Schmidt and von Mellenthin were generally very critical of Jock column weaknesses.[9]

Early Developments

By mid-August 1940, Western Desert Force used 7th Armoured Division's Support Group to relieve armoured regiments which were in need of urgent refitting. Brigadier W.H.E. Gott's Support Group, was ordered forward to hold the frontier from Sollum to Maddalena. Support Group contained three Motor battalions of Infantry, two Artillery batteries, each of twelve guns, two Anti-Tank batteries, along with Engineers, Machinegun platoons, one weak Cruiser Regiment and the experienced 11th Hussars for reconnaissance. His Artillery commander, Lieutenant-Colonel J.C. Campbell developed the Jock column, each one based around a battery of guns.[10] Lieutenant-General Richard O'Connor recalled:

> We decided to have a certain number of small columns of all arms, very mobile, whose job it was to harass the enemy at all times and act offensively…This would keep the enemy in its place and…would dominate no man's land.[11]

Early Columns sometimes included Vickers light tanks and had four, or eight 25pdr field guns, protected by a troop of three 40mm Bofors guns, a 2pdr anti-tank troop, one Infantry company, with attached Engineers, HQ with signals and intelligence. 'B' echelon truck columns from field supply depots (FSDs) supplied them.[12] One gunner officer, Major J.M. McSwiney, noted that their, 'effectiveness revolved around the firepower of the 25pdrs, the rest of us were [just] there to protect them.'[13] They were successful in carrying out harassing and delaying tactics against the Italian X Army, and contributed to their decision to halt at Sidi Barrani by late September.

Jock Columns were also a product of an Imperial heritage in tactics and independent command. Mixed punitive columns had been a vital part of military control on the North West Frontier, many officers like O'Connor had served there and he believed was his most formative experience.[14] This pre-war experience for many officers had

8   John Buckley, 'Tackling the Tiger: The Development of British Armoured Doctrine for Normandy 1944', *Journal of Military History*, 74 (4) (2010), p.1165.
9   H.W. Schmidt, *With Rommel in the Desert* (New York: Bantam Books, 1979); F.W. von Mellenthin, *Panzer Battles* (Stroud: Tempus, 2001).
10   Playfair, *OH, Vol. I*, p.205.
11   George Forty, *The First Victory: General O'Connor's Desert Triumph* (London: Guild, 1990), p.76.
12   *Ibid*, p.76.
13   Imperial War Museum (IWM), Papers of Major J.M. McSwiney, 7th Armoured Division, April 1941.
14   Jon Latimer, *Operation Compass: Wavell's Whirlwind Offensive* (Oxford: Osprey, 2000), p.90.

enabled them to develop a more independent style of leadership. McSwiney thought the columns created leaders of independent thinking. Both Gott and Campbell had become experienced in desert operations and were considered extraordinary leaders, 'who [had] fought alongside their men,' and still raised a, 'current of enthusiasm.'[15] Riflemen Gregg said Campbell was 'revered' by the whole Brigade whilst Kippenburger believed they were two great leaders of the early desert campaigns and quite different to later, more 'scientific soldiers' like Montgomery.[16]

Mixed columns had been used extensively during the Boer war, in the First World War and in Palestine, and were an operational method based on extensive military experience. The deployment of Indian divisions to North Africa influenced British thinking on mechanized warfare because of their own 'heritage of mobile warfare' in colonial operations.[17] It was widely accepted that the desert was an ideal arena for mechanized warfare, where Major-General P.C.S. Hobart had trained the Mobile Division (Egypt) to operate before war had broken out. Jock columns were a logical progression that best utilized Hobart's 'Pivot' or Support Group tactics.[18] The Support Group's equipment reflected this, with the Vickers MKVI light tank designed for frontier duties in India, whilst the 25pdr field guns was lightweight for mobile operations.

Jock Columns were therefore part of the transformational process of creating an effective battle group. Commanders needed an all arms force that was offensively minded, flexible and self-contained. Operating conditions limited their overall size while the 'dispersal' of a formation against air attacks, was another key element from Indian army thinking and planning.[19] Auchinleck came from the Indian Army, and understood the nature of frontier policing and supported the increased use of mixed columns. Auchinleck was Commander-in-Chief (C-in-C) Middle East from early July 1941 and had appointed Indian Army Officers, such as Major-General Frank Messervy to command 7th Armoured Division, who caused friction with British regulars like Major-General Herbert Lumsden, who resented non-cavalry officers taking on armoured command.[20] This friction emphasized differences between British and Indian training, which then

15 Moorehead, *African Trilogy*, p.249. Both unfortunately both died later in the campaign in 1942.
16 Gregg, *Rifleman*, p.68; Kippenburger, *Infantry Brigadier*, pp.195-196.
17 W.M. Ryan, 'The Influence of the Imperial Frontier on British Doctrines of Mechanized Warfare', *Albion: A Quarterly Journal Concerned with British Studies*, 15 (2) (1983), pp.140-141.
18 Kenneth Macksey, *Armoured Crusader, The Biography of Major-General Sir Percy 'Hobo' Hobart* (London: Grub Street, 2004), p.165.
19 Churchill Archive Centre, University of Cambridge, Papers of Lieutenant General Thomas Corbett Papers, Lessons from Cyrenaica, Movement, p.41.
20 See: Carver, *Dilemmas of the Desert War*, p.74. Lumsden blamed Messervy for the defeats suffered by 1st Armoured Division in January 1942, and resented his later transfer to command 7th Armoured. Tank driver Jake Wardrop said Messervy was a, 'silly old man from the Indian Army who had never seen a tank,' Jake Wardrop, *Tanks Across the Desert: The War Diary of Jake Wardrop*, edited by George Forty (London: William Kimber, 1981), p.77.

contributed to a lack of cooperation at the tactical level.[21] The Commander-in-Chief, was described as having a mind, 'of exceptional freshness and originality, seizing on new ideas and explore it at once,' to counter the more effective Axis formations. His support for Jock Columns during Operation CRUSADER (18 November-7 December 1941), raised their popularity beyond any real effectiveness they possessed. Newspaper reports also focussed on their success, and argued that Jock Columns were another reason for this hard fought victory. The *Daily Mail's* Alexander Clifford called them, 'a heritage...from four centuries of pioneers,' using a tactic which was, 'true desert warfare...something against which the Germans found it extremely hard to hit back.'[22] Auchinleck's Brigadier General Staff (BGS), and tactical advisor Major-General Eric Dorman-Smith, was another firm believer in Column use, who later attempted to change Eighth Army organisations and doctrine in the midst of the defeat at Gazala.

There were some transformations during the lifespan of the Columns that kept altering their capability. In January 1941, as XIII Corps advanced into Libya, light armoured units assisted them in pursuing retreating Italian formations. McSwiney thought the early Columns provided, 'mobility and firepower, [which was]...in the same category as a heavy cruiser.'[23] However, after BATTLEAXE (15-17 June 1941), losses forced 7th Support Group to reduce artillery strengths to just four guns per column, which obviously weakened their capability.[24] Columns were more effective in supporting Reconnaissance Regiments to provide frontline intelligence. They provided daily reports that gave a good indication of enemy intentions along the static front.[25] This was probably one of the key successes of their role. In theory, they had the strike power to harass any enemy concentrations, but in reality, their firepower would prove to be not nearly enough.

The Columns in Action

In January 1941, 7th Support Group Jock Columns provided blocking positions to cover the Australian assault on Tobruk. They soon refined the role of reconnaissance and harassing the enemy, moving to blockade the inland desert route near Mechili.[26] Whilst holding the front-line in early 1941, potential challenges with this operational

---

21   Raymond Callaghan, 'Were the 'Sepoy Generals' Any Good? A Reappraisal of the British Indian Army's High Command in the World War II' in Kaushik Roy (ed.), *War and Society in Colonial India, 1807-1945* (Oxford: Oxford University Press, 2006), p.312.
22   Clifford, *Crusader,* pp.108-109.
23   IWM, Papers of Major J.M. McSwiney, 7th Armoured Division, April 1941.
24   TNA, WO 169/1185, Support Group, 7th Armoured Division, January 1941 to February 1942, Operational Order 17, 20 June 1941, Appendix A - Composition of Support Group.
25   TNA, WO 169/1185, 7th Armoured Division, Support Group, January to December 1941, February 1942.
26   TNA, WO 169/1185, Support Group Operational Order No. 1, 9 January 1941. Cyrenaica had two effective routes, the coast road, or *via Balbia*, and the inland desert track via Mechili and Msus.

method emerged in a report on the first retreat from El Agheila by 2nd Armoured Division, which clearly flagged up an early warning about their real effectiveness in difficult terrain, which appeared to be ignored by higher commands. It is worth quoting the views of Lieutenant-Colonel Roscoe, commanding 1st Battalion, the Rifle Brigade, who noted that his Jock Columns quickly lost 40% of their vehicles due to impassable going and a lack of petrol:

> The Col[umn]s imposed no delay on the enemy's advance, though some damage was done...to his transport.

He continued:

> Except on the second day when they marched some 60 miles in order to disengage with a view to striking the enemy...[it] had no liberty of manoeuvre, and... was slowly withdrawn...and extricated ignominiously in darkness.[27]

Roscoe realized that the geography terrain and proximity to other columns often prevented optimal conditions for the Jock Column to fulfil its function when he noted that:

> ....bad going and...restrictions of manoeuvre caused by the proximity of other columns. A weak column pushed right forward in unsuitable ground...is useless against anything more than a minor enemy recce.

This experienced Infantry commander had defined their operational limitations and concluded that:

> ...manoeuvre of a number of columns, in close touch with each other, against enemy armoured forces, only provides [the enemy] with a target and denies columns that freedom of manoeuvre which is their only effective reply.[28]

This report reached Divisional level, but no action was taken perhaps because of the haste of the first retreat, and the later surrender of 2nd Armoured Division HQ at Mechili. However, the basic need to patrol a long front-line again, led to renewed use of Columns along the frontier.

During April, 22nd Guards Brigade operated four Columns and had a retreat planned to Mersa Matruh if there was a further Axis advance, which indicated a delaying tactic by the Columns and their use as a reconnaissance force along the frontier.[29] In June,

27   IWM, Papers of Lieutenant General Sir Harold Rawdon Briggs, RB2/5.
28   *Ibid.*
29   TNA, WO 201/511, 22nd Guards Brigade, March to September 1941, Operational Order No. 5, 17 April 1941.

during the second day of Operation BATTLEAXE (16 June), three Jock Columns of 7th Support Group, operated on the left flank of 7th Armoured Brigade. However, they failed to prevent Rommel's powerful flank move the following day, which convinced Wavell to end the operation.[30] In a follow up report, Jock Campbell wrote:

> If the column system is to continue, I would like to press for some form of hitting force as an integral part of all the columns…By this I mean tanks….when there are plenty of tanks…employed in columns you might get the close co-operation which must be essential to any successful operation.[31]

Therefore, by late June, their originator was calling for closer cooperation with armour in a battle group of all arms. The subsequent lack of real integration raises the question of whether it was a product of inertia by higher command or the intractable nature of getting supplies forward to formations with both armour and artillery using a single B echelon support. Major-General E.P. Nares argued that the lack of petrol was the key issue, with just over half the daily requirement reaching the frontline units.[32]

A nother factor, which weakened the effectiveness of the Columns, was the physical problem of holding a lengthy frontier, with few defensible positions. British thinking developed a partial resolution by using columns to cover the distances and maintain the offensive especially during static phases which complemented Auchinleck's ideas on taking the 'fight' to the enemy. The five month build up from the end of BATTLEAXE to the beginning of CRUSADER, was a period of constant column activity along the front line. HQs demanded continuous assessments of enemy activity, and especially about the 'going' over which the forthcoming advance would occur.[33] Seventh Support Group deployed to meet a potential Axis advance in mid-September and Rifle Brigade Column operations included low-level attacks on units.[34] These attacks were irritating to the Axis but had little impact on their defensive positions.

Operation CRUSADER: The High Point of the Column

During CRUSADER, the typical Column experience was that of 2nd Rifle Brigade where Rifleman Crimp noted the battalion was rapidly dispersed by the sudden appearance of Axis armour. The tendency to disperse or to, 'scarper - was accepted

---

30 I.S.O. Playfair *et al*, *The Mediterranean and Middle East, Volume II: The Germans Come to the Help of Their Ally, 1941*, (London: HMSO, 1956), pp.169-171.

31 TNA, WO 169/1185, Support Group, 7th Armoured Division, January 41 to February 42, Report on Action of Support Group, 14 to 17 June 1941, p.6.

32 Moorehead, *Trilogy*, p.246.

33 TNA, WO 169/1185, Support Group, 7th Armoured Division, January 1941 to December 1941, Order No. 13, 24 October 1941.

34 *Ibid*, Support Group Operational Order No. 1, September 1941; Crimp, *Desert Rat*, pp.22-23.

desert technique when there's...no particular bit of ground...getting thrown up against heavily superior enemy forces leaves no option but to clear out.'[35] The battalion reformed ten miles away but was soon dispersed again by another armoured column. The hit and run mentality created by Jock Column doctrine was having an effect on infantry tactics. Near the end of the battle, 7th Support Group harassed the enemy flanks but Riflemen Gregg remembered that, 'we could only swat at them...until one by one our vehicles gave up the ghost. We had shot our bolt.'[36] In contrast, Auchinleck now believed that, General Erwin Rommel's famous dash to the wire had:

> ...petered out under the attack of our 'Jock' columns... [They] are just what we want. They piquet his movements and give him no rest and are giving us command of that enormous no man's land.

He continued that:

> ...they seem to suit our genius for fighting...No Red Tabs! No written orders!! No ruddy principles of war!!! (except hit him and have after him) No Generals!!!!... of course they need close and careful coordination if the best is to be got out of them...I think the Hun find them somewhat unorthodox.[37]

In comparison, 4th Indian Division's commander, Major-General Francis Tuker, was more critical starting that:

> Jockols...had become a panacea for all those soldiers who did not bother to think what they intended to do,[or] how to do it....'Operate Columns' became a substitute for a plan, especially if the adverb 'aggressively' were added.' They, 'had done well in 'Crusader'...but more solid and concentrated methods were needed.[38]

During CRUSADER, 7th Support Group fought a sustained battle at Sidi Rezegh and later operated as Jock Columns along the flanks of the Panzer Divisions. Thereafter Auchinleck fully believed they were the way forward in desert tactics, whilst onlookers including Alexander Clifford believed they had contributed to Rommel's decision to retreat, after twenty days of hard battle.[39]

---

35   Crimp, *Diary of a Desert Rat*, pp.48-49.
36   Gregg, *Rifleman*, pp.70-71.
37   John Rylands Library, Univermsit of Manchester (JRL) Papers of Field Marshal Sir Claude Auchinleck, AUC 520, Auchinleck to Arthur Smith, 5 December 1941; John Connell, *Auchinleck* (London: Cassell, 1959), p.394.
38   Tuker, *Approach to Battle*, p.83.
39   Clifford, *Crusader*, p.109.

The Second Retreat, January-February 1942

By January 1942, the front line had again reached southern Cyrenaica, near Agedabia, but was again weakly held by just a few Jock Columns. The 200th Guards Brigade had only one battalion unit, the 3rd Battalion, Coldstream Guards, deployed in four columns and supported by 1st and 51st Field Regiments RA, which had supplied one battery to each column. The commander, Brigadier J.C.A. Marriott, was ordered to provide a forward screen and a plan for retreat, if the enemy advanced.[40] Marriott's columns were expected to provide a screen defence only, whilst operating on the flank of the armoured brigade. Brigadier Marriott later provided a detailed report for an investigation concerning the retreat that revealed how the brigade Columns had fought. Marriott defended his actions and argued that Lieutenant-General Ritchie at Eighth Army HQ was setting the wrong tactics. Ritchie had visited the front, prior to 21 January, and ordered each Column to have only one Infantry company, whilst a second company, would not contribute, 'to the hitting power of the columns.' Marriott's after-action report showed that the tactic failed against more powerful Axis formations. Of his four Columns, three were forward and one was in reserve, with one covering the left-desert flank. The distance between the remaining two Columns was too wide and the terrain was almost impassable for his trucks, which prevented any mutual support. A strong Axis column of 40 tanks and 400 vehicles cut past his right flank along the coast road and outflanked the brigade. Major H.M. Ingledew's column, covering the road, was not strong enough to hold up this large Axis force, while the advance by the single reserve Jock Column was itself blocked by the advancing armour. The brigade's other battalion, 2nd Battalion, Scots Guards, was left in the rear because it had no anti-tank guns, and was therefore ineffective in the forward area and unable to mine the approaches to Agebadia, which enabled the Axis to capture this vital road junction.[41] It quickly retreated to avoid capture when outflanked near Antelat.[42] Ingledew's column shelled the town heavily, with over 3,000 rounds being fired by his 25pdr battery in a short time period, which was an impressive performance, but Axis forces continued to push forward despite losses.[43]

This failure to hold the front using Columns highlighted their weaknesses. Von Mellenthin, a staff officer at *Panzerarmee* HQ, described British opposition as being easily driven back.[44] There was no coordination between the Guards and the adjacent 2nd Armoured Brigade, which fought separate actions and was badly mauled by 15th Panzer Division. At GHQ, Auchinleck believed Columns were operating:

40   TNA, WO 201/530B, Report of 200th Guards Brigade, Agedabia, January 1942.
41   *Ibid*, Marriott to HQ, 17 February 1942.
42   *Ibid*, Gott to Ritchie, 23 February 1942.
43   *Ibid*, Marriott to HQ, 17 February 1942.
44   F.W. von Mellenthin, *Panzer Battles: A Study of the Employment of Armour in the Second World War* (Stroud: Tempus, 1986 [1955]), p.90.

...with definite objectives and are coordinated by higher commanders...the columns have been in close and continuous touch with the enemy on a wide front.[45]

However, Marriott's trace maps showed that his Columns were deployed to cover the most likely routes of advance, but could not cover the whole front. The errors of an over-extended front line, and a lengthy supply line, were being repeated.

Ritchie was quick to comment on the apparent failures implying that the Guards failed to make a substantial defence and was generally critical of all the frontline Brigades for failing to stop the Axis advance.[46] Ritchie conceded that his own and Godwin-Austen's requests to GHQ, for a general retreat to the line Tmimi-Tobruk had influenced his decisions.[47] The columns again proved to be too small to hold ground individually and were dispersed across too wide an area.[48] Auchinleck reported that Ritchie had deployed light forces and had received substantial casualties from advancing Axis columns, (thought to total 50-90 tanks). The dilemma remained for Eighth Army of trying to hold a wide frontline with formations that were actually too 'light' and not powerful, enough to hold against an enemy thrust.[49] Tuker believed all the brigades had been scattered across Cyrenaica in Columns, and this dispersal was responsible for the retreat.[50]

As the retreat neared Gazala, Ritchie again committed Columns in the Tmimi area just as 4th Indian Division was outflanked and forced to retreat again. He was still convinced they were effective, despite the loss of most of Cyrenaica.[51] The operational doctrine proved to be ineffective to defend a region that had no defensible terrain north of Agedabia. Column commanders believed they had done all they could, but the units were not strong enough. Both the tactical use and the wide-scale dispersal on an operational level were incorrect because any defensive position was outflanked and Axis forces concentrated higher numbers against positions to overcome them.

The battles around Gazala and Matruh represented the final phases of the Jock Column. As Eighth Army halted near Gazala, Ritchie planned that, 'future intentions are to withdraw main bodies and oppose enemy here with [Jock] columns as far north...and west as possible'. Tuker thought this a nonsense and liable to lose whole

45   JRL, Auchinleck Papers, AUC 524, Auchinleck to Arthur Smith, 6 December 1941.
46   TNA, WO 201/401, Operational Telegrams, January to March 1942, Ritchie to C-in-C, 25 January 1942.
47   *Ibid*, Letter from Ritchie to BGS, 24 January 1942.
48   Playfair, *OH Vol. II*, p.25.
49   TNA, WO 201/401, Operational Telegrams, January to March 1942, From Mideast to Toopers, 23 January 1942.
50   Stevens, *Fourth Indian Division*, p.100.
51   TNA, WO 201/401, Operational Telegrams, January to March 1942, Message 1050, Ritchie to Mideast, 2 February 1942.

Brigades in piecemeal attacks.[52] However the CinC was supportive of this dispersed style of warfare, Auchinleck reported on operations, as the retreat settled, that enemy columns, 'of tanks, lorried infantry and artillery...generally withdrew when engaged by our mobile columns,' and that, 'Our columns have obtained control of NO MANS LAND.'[53] Thirteenth Corps instructions reinforced the doctrine to cover the Corps front, 'by armoured car patrols, and for the operation of mobile col[um]ns...to harass and delay the enemy.' Godwen-Austen continued, 'it is the corps Comds' intention to adopt a more offensive attitude and to increase the number of mobile columns employed.'[54] Plans made for a retreat beyond Tobruk would have exacerbated the loss of Cyrenaica, Benghazi and the key northwestern airfields.[55] The high losses in armour during the retreat (some 120 tanks) had again left Eighth Army with artillery based Jock Columns as the only effective offensive arm to fight with.

Royal Air Force Support and the Axis Viewpoint

The failure of the Jock Columns to hold the frontline during the two retreats also affected RAF/Western Desert Air Force (WDAF) operations. In January 1941, a squadron of Hurricanes and one of Blenheim IVs only, supported the front in Cyrenaica. Air superiority quickly passed to the newly arrived Luftwaffe, leaving British units vulnerable to air attack and contributed to the British columns retreating from Agheila. One year later, the WDAF was more able to match the Axis in numbers, and on focussing on ground attacks and targeting supply columns. However, two factors affected to undermine air operations again. Bad weather and heavy rain prevented fighter cover as forward landing grounds became a sea of mud and remained unserviceable.[56] At Benina airfield the aircraft were, '...sinking into the mud', and take off became impossible.[57] Secondly, the inability of 'light forces' to hold the front also undermined the air support designed to back them up.[58] The rapid Axis advance to Benghazi, forced its closure as a supply base, leaving the WDAF without fuel for the landing grounds. Jock column weakness had contributed to undermine effective air support on the frontline.

52   Tuker, *Approach to Battle*, p.84.
53   TNA, WO 201/401, Operational Telegrams, January to March 1942, CS743, Auchinleck to all, 14 February 1942; WO 201/401, Operational Telegrams, January to March 1942, CS776, Auchinleck to Britmilat Ankara, 28 February 1942.
54   TNA, WO 201/524, 13 Corps Future Policy and Operations, 7 February 1942.
55   TNA, WO 201/401, Operational Telegrams, January to March 1942, Message 1050, Ritchie to Mideast, 2 February 1942.
56   TNA, WO 201/401, Operational Telegrams, January to March 1942, CS643, Auchinleck to CIGS, 23 January 1942, p.2.
57   Moorehead, *African Trilogy*, p.245.
58   TNA, WO 201/401, Operational Telegrams, January to March 1942, 869, Ritchie to Auchinleck, 24 January 1942.

Axis commanders quickly rationalized their effectiveness in combat. Heinz W. Schmidt, an anti-tank company commander, commented on their impact during the Second Retreat:

> ...the desert was alive with small mobile columns...which were a nuisance as mosquitoes...they were never really strong enough to do irreparable damage.[59]

Hans Berendt, an Intelligence Officer at Panzerarmee HQ, noted the panicked tone of British wireless messages, when Jock Columns came under pressure from the larger, more powerful Axis forces.[60] They ran out of fuel/ammunition and struggled to be resupplied as the pace of battle became more fluid. Rommel believed that:

> The result of these tactics of dispersal - was that the British formations were... destroyed one after another and disappeared...whilst the battle was still in progress.[61]

Axis forces soon had the measure of the modest sized units and rapidly overran the Jock Columns breaking through the thinly held line.[62]

In London, Churchill was furious that the Infantry Brigades appeared not to be fighting hard enough to hold their ground, whilst Malta suffered under a major aerial offensive. Auchinleck was still positive and pushed Ritchie to, 'follow up hard with numerous mobile columns while still holding Gazala position securely.'[63] When the retreat halted, Auchinleck added:

> Am delighted by the vigorous and enterprising action which your...mobile columns are taking to keep close touch with the enemy and with the apparently excellent information they are furnishing about his dispositions...would like you to express my warm appreciation of this true soldierly instinct which is essential to further success.[64]

However, by April, despite his earlier enthusiasm, Auchinleck revised his views on Jock columns. He feared that they would lead to 'tip and run tactics' which were in danger of becoming a standard doctrine and would leave Infantry formations losing

---

59   H.W. Schmidt, *With Rommel in the Desert* (New York: Bantam Books, 1979), p.129.
60   Hans Otto Berendt, *Rommel's Intelligence in the Desert Campaign* (London: William Kimber & Co Ltd, 1985), p.136.
61   Erwin Rommel, *The Rommel Papers*, edited by B.H. Liddell Hart (London: Hamlyn, 1984), p.184.
62   TNA, WO 201/2692, Operational Reports, Western Desert, May to July 1942, p.24.
63   TNA, WO 201/401. Operational Telegrams, January to March 1942, CS734, C-in-C to Ritchie, 14 February 1942.
64   *Ibid*, CS750, C-in-C to Ritchie, 20 February 1942.

the ability to make formal brigade assaults. This change found its way in to GHQs *Notes from Theatres of War No.6*, distributed in July, in the midst of the confused battles of First Alamein. Training in Egypt remained a regimental function until formal training schools developed after July 1941. Reinforcements were acclimatized in the Delta base camps before being shipped forward to their new regiments. Lieutenant-General Thomas Corbett's papers offered some insight into local instructions sent to 4th Indian Division for operating in the desert.[65] GHQ formalized Corbett's notes into *The Middle East Training Pamphlet* series that prescribed how Eighth Army was expected to operate. Unfortunately, it remained common for units to be rushed forward because of the urgent needs of operations, with little acclimatization to the environment or before completing any form of training. The newly arrived 50th Division had the time to take up the doctrine along the front-line but did question its validity prior to Gazala.[66]

In the May 1942 spring build up, Columns had operated behind enemy lines but remained vulnerable to retaliation. Near the Rotunda Segnali, 90 Light Division's planned assault to destroy a static Column was only halted by Rommel to maintain the secrecy of the Axis build-up.[67] Gazala proved to be the undoing for the whole doctrine as Columns continued to operate behind enemy lines in a failed effort to weaken the Axis supply routes, despite the static Motor and Infantry Brigade Boxes defences being repeatedly overrun. Operating Columns contributed to a weakening of the Brigade Boxes at Bir Hacheim and 150th Brigade at Sidi-Muftah. By mid-June, the Armoured Brigades had been whittled away during month long fighting and Eighth Army retreated across the frontier. Ritchie ordered the Infantry Divisions to be split into Forward Groups of Regimental Jock Columns and a rear group occupying defences.[68] The failed Brigade Box doctrine was transformed into Regimental Boxes, because of the losses suffered. This directive came amidst another period of change Auchinleck relieved Ritchie and took direct command of the Army.

Gazala proved how ineffective Brigade boxes were and the Armoured Brigades were destroyed in their defence, leaving Jock columns as the only remaining option. Brigade Groups carried out combined Infantry and armoured assaults on static Axis positions with inconclusive results throughout July.[69] Second New Zealand Division took part in three major assaults against the Ruweisat ridge, whilst 9th Australian Division made successive attacks on the Miteiriya ridge and near Tel-el-Eissa. The

65   Lodged at the Churchill Archives Centre, Cambridge.
66   E.W. Clay, *The Path of the 50th: The Story of the 50th Northumbrian Division in the Second World War, 1939-1945* (Aldershot: Gale and Polden, 1950), pp.52-53.
67   IWM, Box E127, Translation of 90th Light Division War Diary, 5 May 1942 to 5 July 1942, Report of 18 May 1942.
68   I.S.O. Playfair *et al*, *The Mediterranean and Middle East, Volume III: British Fortunes Reach Their Lowest Ebb* (London: HMSO, 1960), p.254.
69   Tim Moreman, *Desert Rats: British 8th Army in North Africa 1941-43* (Oxford: Osprey, 2007), p.24.

Armoured Brigades were committed in support but issues remained over coordination with the Infantry that contributed to a lack of effective cooperation. Jock Columns were never part of this type of assault.

As an operational technique, Jock Columns clearly became part of the Eighth Army's doctrine both informally and formally. Transformations to the doctrine were considered before Gazala and during First Alamein. The first *Notes From Theatre of War* was published within three months of the actual combat taking place. In *NTW No.6*, Column doctrine was updated and directly quoted Auchinleck's revised proposals from early April.[70] The use of Jock Columns was less common during July although some experienced New Zealand units developed the idea further, by increasing their firepower.[71] One New Zealand Colonel increased his Column formations to include a full Regiment of 25pdrs and four troops of anti-tank guns, trebling its firepower.[72] By August, Montgomery's first thoughts on Army doctrine quickly signalled the end of 'dispersal' and Jock Columns as a tactic.[73] Divisions would fight as Divisions from then on, although Brigade Groups were still used at Second Alamein and throughout the rest of the campaign.[74]

The Use of Armour in Combined Arms - Or the Lack of it

From the first phases of Operation COMPASS, Army Tank formations, equipped with Matildas or Valentines, cooperated with Infantry in leading set-piece assaults against Axis positions. However, too often they were parcelled out with one squadron per battalion. There are numerous examples of how these hard-pressed squadrons were steadily reduced by attrition, to the point where they became no longer effective. The narrative of the development of 'I' Tanks in action has been well documented in the accounts of BATTLEAXE, CRUSADER and the debacles of Operation ABERDEEN (5-6 June 1942), culminating in the infamous charge by 23rd Armoured Brigade on the 22 July 1942. These actions all highlighted the problem that Infantry and Armour needed more time to train with one another. Even by July 1942, experienced units still suffered from the difficulties of combined assaults against

70   The War Office, *The Campaign in North Africa, Part I: 1940-1943*, edited by M. Taylor (Smalldale: MLRS, 2004), pp.3-4 cited from *Notes for the Theatre of War No.6 – Cyrenaica, November 1941 to January 1942.*

71   David French, *Raising Churchill's Army: The British Army and the War against Germany, 1919-1945* (Oxford: Oxford University Press, 2000), p.216.

72   W.E. Murphy, *2nd New Zealand Divisional Artillery* (Wellington: Historical Publications Branch, 1966), pp.335-338 – Accessed at http://nzetc.victoria.ac.nz/tm/scholarly/tei-WH2Arti-c10-1.html on 12 March 2011.

73   'Review of the Situation in Eighth Army from 12 August to 23 October 1942' in Stephen Brooks (ed.), *Montgomery and the Eighth Army*, (London: Army Records Society, 1991), p.23.

74   Corelli Barnett, *The Desert Generals* (Edison: Castle Books, 2004) p.285.

strong enemy positions. At Tel-el-Eissa, 50th Royal Tanks supported 9th Australian Division and noted that:

> The infantry finally consolidated some 1,200 yards short of the objective and quite a big salient had been made in the enemy line. Losses in A Sqn were heavy and it was a battered regiment that leaguered…20 tanks short.[75]

A further attack took place on 27 July, to clear a way for supplying the infantry. Again it was a tale of scrappy action, casualties and half success.'[76] Armour was being parcelled out and suffered attrition too quickly to be effective.

Most Cruiser Armoured Brigades operated separately during the retreats of spring 1941 and 1942. The Armoured Brigades deployed adjacent to their Support Groups that had deployed in Jock Columns because commanders believed they had a different role. The failure of any effective combined operations was seen in a report by 6th Royal Tanks (6 RTR) on the events of April 1941. The regiment was equipped with poor quality Italian M13s and their CO was highly critical of the poor command shown by 3rd Armoured Brigade HQ, 'Nothing was seen of the rest of the Brigade throughout this march… the regiment moved out and continued its role of protection to the south and west.' After dark, 6 RTR was transferred to the Support Group, but, 'no wireless frequency was given, no replenishment of diesel oil was available, leaving the radius of action…was now 35 miles, and…no location of the Support Group was given.'[77] The cooperation between both Brigade HQs was questionable and contributed to the retreat.

By early 1942, the role of armour was under discussion at GHQ, because of the failures experienced during the Second Retreat. Auchinleck perceived a crisis of confidence amongst armoured crews. One paper argued that armour, once engaged, should not move without close artillery support, which meant breaking the Jock Columns and only using the Infantry for close protection. It acknowledged that armour was being out-gunned by MkIII and MkIV Panzers, even before the arrival of the up-gunned Specials and this required artillery firepower to match them. However, XXX Corps HQ argued against the removal of Support Groups, because Jock Columns had been an, 'inestimable value' in recent operations.[78]

The experience of CRUSADER and the retreat led to discussions about the efficacy of combined arms doctrine in the build-up to Gazala. Armour was never to move towards the enemy without adequate artillery support.[79] Artillery was re-defined as a support for armour in theory, but in practice remained as the main strike unit within

---

75   The Tank Museum Archives (BOV), 50th Royal Tank Regiment War Diary, July 1942.
76   *Ibid.*
77   BOV, 6th Royal Tank Regiment War Diary, 3 April 1941.
78   TNA, WO 201/527, Armoured Formations, 27 December 1941 to 21 March 1942, Norrie to Ritchie, 30 December 1941.
79   *Ibid*, The Role of Armoured formations, 27 December 1941 to 21 March 1942.

Jock Columns. Army HQ looked to combine armour with artillery in a combined assault on a fixed enemy position, instead of using infantry.[80] There were disagreements over such minor details as the correct use of smoke tactics.[81] These delays in disseminating new doctrine meant there was less training time was available to armoured regiments. The 25pdr field gun was now viewed as the main tank-killer, from 1200 yards whereas the Cruiser tank's 2pdr gun was only effective from 800 yards or less. One veteran, Alan Salkield from 50 Reconnaissance Regiment, commented that the 2pdr was still considered an excellent gun at 600 yards.[82] These debates created a subtle transformation in the offensive assault, with armour now protecting an artillery battery gun-line, by mid-1942.

The reality was that most units experienced confusion, a separation of arms and poor command decisions being taken. During the Second Retreat, Lieutenant-General Godwin-Austen at XIII Corps, ordered the remnants of 2nd Armoured Brigade, 'hold the left [desert] flank and protect the Infantry Brigades deployed as Jock columns nearer the coast.[83] Unfortunately, the Brigade had already been heavily defeated and reduced to a weakened regiment by 15th Panzer Division. It was sent to Msus, and remained separated from Fourth Indian Brigade Groups holding the coast route to Benghazi. Tuker was heavily critical of this and further delays imposed by Army HQ.[84] First Armoured Division HQ felt they could not defeat the concentration of Axis armour thought to be in the forward area, with only thirty tanks remaining.[85] Army HQ concluded that only one Brigade could be supplied from Msus and became pessimistic over the strength of Axis armour, (Intelligence had reported some 600 tanks in total), so estimated Eighth Army would need 900 plus, tanks to recapture Benghazi and halt the advance. Any future offensive to retake Cyrenaica or to advance into Tripolitania (Operation ACROBAT) would be severely delayed.[86] Auchinleck's later report highlighted the reasons for the failure. He blamed the short range of the 2pdr, the mechanical reliability of the Cruiser tanks and the poor leadership of the formations. He concluded that British armour needed a 2:1 superiority and that Royal Armoured Corps officers were losing confidence in their equipment. He noted that Jock Columns were maintaining this phase of the battle.[87]

---

80 *Ibid.*
81 *Ibid,* Tactical Handling of Artillery in support of Armour, 27 December 1941 to 21 Mar 1942.
82 Personal conversation with Mr Alan Salkield from 50th Reconnaissance Regiment, 25 January 2012.
83 TNA, WO 201/524, 13 Corps Future Policy and Operations, 7 February 1942, p.2.
84 Tuker, *Approach to Battle,* p.74.
85 TNA, WO 201/524, 13 Corps Future Policy and Operations, Conference of 31 January 1942.
86 *Ibid.*
87 TNA, WO 201/401, Operational Telegrams, January to March 1942, CS878, C-in-C to Prime Minister, 30 January 1942.

The attempts to resolve the problem of combined arms was another factor, which led to the continued reliance on Jock Columns up to mid-1942. From CRUSADER onwards Armoured Brigades continued to operate almost entirely separately from the Infantry with few exceptions. During Operation ABERDEEN, 22nd Armoured Brigade was committed alongside the assault by 10th Indian Brigade into the 'Cauldron' depression. The already weakened armour separated and withdrew under a heavy onslaught of anti-tank gunfire that decimated the Regiments.[88] The Infantry battalions and four Regiments of supporting Artillery were isolated, dispersed and overrun, having been ordered to capture too many objectives. Armour and infantry struggled to cooperate throughout First Alamein, but too often misunderstandings occurred which weakened trust between the two arms.[89] Cruiser Regiments began to cooperate with Infantry again during Alam Halfa (30 August -3 September 1942) and would combine more closely with other arms under Montgomery's new doctrines. Buckley's assessment of doctrine shows that British Armour made valiant attempts to adapt to combat better Axis equipment and doctrine, but struggled even during Operation LIGHTFOOT.[90]

Conclusion

Jock Columns were an integral part of the process of change in developing offensive tactics in the desert and were a response to a specific set of terrain conditions. They developed from an Imperial heritage of independent mixed columns that proved effective against less well-motivated Italian units. They were successful at harassment and ground reconnaissance, many who served in them believed in their effectiveness, and they repeatedly maintained the offensive when armour had been decimated. The weaknesses of the columns included a lack of firepower, the unit strength and being severely hampered by difficult terrain and lacking tracked vehicles. These factors were reflected in their greatest failures of the two retreats from southern Cyrenaica in 1941 and 1942. Their weakness undermined the integration of a defensive front with RAF squadrons that was an integral part of operating with light forces. Their contribution to doctrine was to promote a trend of general dispersal by Infantry formations, as Commanders sought ways to patrol such wide areas of desert, and to limit attrition from air attack. There were minor transformations in organisation, which included using light armour, fewer guns, and later additional artillery to boost firepower. Campbell appreciated the need for organisational change calling for armour to be made part of the formation, but it was Ritchie and Auchinleck who perpetuated their

---

88 BOV, 2nd Royal Gloucester Hussars War Diary, 5 June 42, The Brigade was 2 composite regiments.
89 The 32nd Army Tank Brigade during Operation Aberdeen, 5 June, and 23rd Army Tank Brigade at El Mreir, 22 July 1942.
90 Buckley, 'Tackling the Tiger', p.1165.

traditional use. Auchinleck later modified his views, as he believed they were having a negative effect on the offensive capability of the Infantry. Other commanders at the time saw the weaknesses in their firepower and the errors in their deployment, GHQ lost faith in them after at Gazala and Matruh. Jock Columns had offered an Infantry/Artillery based offensive doctrine in an arena designed for armour, which had persisted beyond their usefulness by August 1942.

13

'Lessons Learnt'
The Royal Air Force, Operation JUBILEE, and the Adaptation of Air Power in Support of Combined Operations, 1942-1944

Ross Mahoney

Studies into military change remain a key aspect of military history with Grissom noting that, 'Innovation and stagnation have been important themes since the earliest writings on warfare.'[1] While Posen's 1984 study, *The Sources of Military Doctrine*, triggered a number of key studies into peacetime military innovation this chapter examines the opposite end of the transformation spectrum, namely how do military organisations adapt to the stresses placed on them in wartime.[2] For Farrell military adaptation is a, 'change to tactics, techniques or existing technologies to improve operational performance', and inherent to this process is whether the military is able to act as a learning organisation, which Garvin has defined as being:

> ... skilled at creating, acquiring, interpreting, transferring, and retaining knowledge, and at purposefully modifying its behaviour to reflect new knowledge and insights.[3]

---

1   Adam Grissom, 'The Future of Military Innovation Studies', *Journal of Strategic Studies*, 29 (5) (2006), p.905.

2   Barry R. Posen, *The Sources of Military Doctrine: France, Britain, and Germany between the World Wars* (Ithaca, NY: Cornell University Press 1984), *passim*; Grissom, 'Military Innovation Studies', p.906. From a historical perspective, key examples of the literature includes: Williamson Murray and Allan Millett (eds.), *Military Innovation in the Interwar Period* (Cambridge: Cambridge University Press, 1996); Harold R. Winton and David R. Mets (Eds.), *The Challenge of Change: Military Institutions and New Realities, 1918-1941* (Lincoln, NE: University of Nebraska Press, 2000).

3   Theo Farrell, 'Improving in War: Military Adaptation and the British in Helmand Province, Afghanistan, 2006–2009', *Journal of Strategic Studies*, 33 (4) (2010), p.569; David A. Garvin, *Learning in Action: A Guide to Putting the Learning Organization to Work* (Boston, MA: Harvard Business School Press, 2000), p.11. For a recent example

While this chapter is not the place to critique the literature on military transformation, it is worth recognising that from a leadership and decision-making perspective, these processes involve getting inside what Colonel John Boyd referred to as the OODA loop, which requires the collection of data (observation), its analysis and synthesis (orientate), determining a course of action (decide), and act.[4] Additionally, as this chapter recognises, issues such as personality and organisational culture can abrogate the effectiveness of any change in the learning process. Indeed, the adaptations that the Royal Air Force (RAF) were involved in between 1942 and 1944 in the sphere of combined operations required it to co-operate with key stakeholders such as Combined Operations Headquarters (COHQ), the Royal Navy (RN) and allies who all had an influence on the need for these changes.

Taking these definitions as a starting point this chapter considers whether the RAF acted as a learning organisation that sought to improve its operational performance by changing its tactics, techniques and technologies. It examines this process by considering the impact that Operation JUBILEE, the raid on Dieppe on 19 August 1942, had on the RAF's learning process as it related to the complex interface of air power with combined operations that was a key characteristic of allied operations between 1942 and 1944 in both the Mediterranean and North West Europe.[5] However, understanding the impact JUBILEE had on learning in the British military more generally has been obscured by the then Chief of Combined Operations' (CCO), Admiral Lord Mountbatten, post-facto moralising on lessons learned. Nonetheless, this learning process is, in part, what was sought more broadly by COHQ in JUBILEE's aftermath when Mountbatten tasked Captain John Hughes-Hallett, the naval task force commander, to compile a combined report on Dieppe.[6] Based on individual reports produced by the force commanders and collated in COHQs so-called 'Dieppe Room' with its attendant study group, Smith has described the final Combined Report on JUBILEE as a, 'point by point defence of the organisation's contribution to planning the raid.'[7] Air Officer Commanding (AOC) No. 11 Group, Fighter Command and the air force commander for JUBILEE, Air Vice-Marshal Trafford Leigh-Mallory, produced the RAF's operational report that fed into the Combined Report. While explored further in this chapter, it is worth noting here that in his

of applying this typology to military history, see: Gregory A. Daddis, 'Eating Soup with a Spoon: The U.S. Army as a "Learning Organization" in the Vietnam War', *Journal of Military History*, 77 (1) (2013), pp.229-54.

4   Grant T. Hammond, 'From Air Power to Err Power: John Boyd and the Opponent's Situational Awareness' in Peter Gray and Sebastian Cox (eds.), *Air Power Leadership: Theory and Practice* (London: The Stationary Office, 2002), pp.115-18.

5   On the RAF during JUBILEE see: Ross Mahoney, '"The support afforded by the air force was faultless": The Royal Air Force and the Raid on Dieppe, 19 August 1942', *Canadian Military History*, 21 (4) (2012), pp.17-32.

6   The National Archives (TNA), DEFE 2/551, Combined Report on Dieppe, October 1942.

7   Adrian Smith, *Mountbatten: Apprentice War Lord* (London: I.B. Tauris, 2010), p.236.

covering letter to the Secretary of State for Air, Sir Archibald Sinclair, Leigh-Mallory considered JUBILEE a success for the RAF.[8] In addition to the Combined Report, Hughes-Hallett authored a 'Lessons Learnt' document that was widely distributed and served a two-fold purpose.[9] Firstly, it distilled the key views outlined by the three force commanders in their separate reports and the challenges that they faced during JUBILEE. Second, it began the process of historicising JUBILEE and provided Mountbatten with evidence for his later views concerning Dieppe's utility. Mountbatten's later position has clouded any meaningful evaluation of JUBILEE as part of the British militaries learning process in the operation's aftermath. For example, Mountbatten exclaimed to an audience composed of the Canadian Dieppe Veterans and Prisoners of War Association on 28 September 1973 that:

> A vast number of allied lives, including of course Canadians, were saved in the "Overlord" landings…and in previous landings in the Mediterranean as a result of the lessons we learned at Dieppe.[10]

Perhaps most significantly, Mountbatten defended his reputation by re-drafting the sections of volume four of Winston Churchill's war memoirs, *The Hinge of Fate*, which dealt with JUBILEE. This re-drafting emerged in the aftermath of Churchill's concern regarding the issue of authorisation and Mountbatten's role in this, though, rather than continue to search for answers he accepted 'Mountbatten's self-serving answers' on lessons learnt rather than his own 'soul-searching questions.'[11] Mountbatten's attempt to defend his reputation has distorted historians understanding of JUBILEE's operational importance as the historiography focuses on the issue of authorisation rather than the implications of what lessons were learnt from Dieppe.[12]

8   TNA, AIR 16/871, Covering Letter to Report by the Air Force Commander on Operation "JUBILEE", 5 September 1942.
9   TNA, ADM 239/350, Lessons Learnt from the Raid on Dieppe, November 1942.
10 Earl Mountbatten of Burma, 'Operation Jubilee: The Place of the Dieppe Raid in History', *Journal of the Royal United Services Institute for Defence Studies*, 119 (1) (1974), pp.25-31.
11 David Reynolds, *In Command of History: Churchill, Fighting and Writing the Second World War* (New York: Basic Books, 2007 [2005]), p.347; Brian Loring Villa, *Unauthorized Action: Mountbatten and the Dieppe Raid, 1942* (Oxford: Oxford University Press, 1989), pp.19-49. For the most useful overview of the historical debate concerning JUBILEE and Mountbatten's role, see: Smith, *Mountbatten*, pp.231-56.
12 On the debate surrounding Mountbatten's role in planning the raid and his relationship with the Chiefs of Staff, see: Brian Loring Villa, 'Mountbatten, the British Chiefs of Staff, and Approval of the Dieppe Raid', *Journal of Military History*, 54 (2) (1990), pp.201-26; Peter Henshaw, 'The British Chiefs of Staff Committee and the Preparation of the Dieppe Raid, March-August 1942: Did Mountbatten Really Evade the Committee's Authority?', *War in History*, 1 (2) (1994), pp.197-214.

Despite the historicising of JUBILEE, Hughes-Hallett's 'Lessons Learnt' distillation highlighted problems that the RAF, and COHQ, needed to confront such as the issue of command and control (C_2), the use of smoke, and the use of airborne forces while Leigh-Mallory's own report also focused on C_2. Overall, from an air power perspective, the various reports and operational experience drew three key conclusions that filtered into developments from other sources between 1942 and 1944; namely, the use of combined operations as a means to draw the *Luftwaffe* into battle, C_2, and the need for greater aerial bombardment. Generally, this chapter suggests that in the aftermath of JUBILEE the RAF illustrated the ability to act as a learning organisation when faced with the need to adapt to operational challenges. However, as this chapter makes clear, these adaptations did not always produce operational advantage as in the example of raiding as an intruder strategy.

Raiding as an Intruder Strategy

In the immediate aftermath of JUBILEE, Leigh-Mallory did not miss the opportunity to stress what he perceived as the key success of the operation, namely that it had allowed Fighter Command to engage the *Luftwaffe* in large numbers under favourable conditions. On 22 August 1942, Leigh-Mallory wrote to Mountbatten and stated that, 'I feel we might profitably conduct a future operation on rather different lines' and drew on Dieppe's only other outright success, Operation CAULDRON, No. 4 Commando's attack on the Hess Battery at Varengeville, as an example of how these two forces could be used more effectively.[13] Later published in the *Notes from Theatres of War* collection of doctrinal pamphlets in 1943, No. 4 Commando's attack itself made its way into British Army doctrine that in itself had implications for future commando operations.[14] Used as an alternative for bombers, Leigh-Mallory pre-supposed that commando forces could act as an element of a new form of intruder strategy, which had emerged as a key element of Fighter Command operations from 1940 onwards. In December 1940, Fighter Command launched offensive operations with the view of, 'leaning forward into France.'[15] During the course of 1941 and 1942, Fighter Command launched a variety of offensive operations over North West Europe with the purpose of bringing

---

13   TNA, DEFE 2/67, Letter from AOC No. 11 Group to Chief of Combined Operations, 22 August 1942.

14   TNA, WO 208/3108, *Notes from Theatres of War No. 11: Destruction of a German Battery by No. 4 Commando during the Dieppe Raid* (1943); Will Fowler, *The Commandos at Dieppe: Rehearsal for D-Day* (London: Collins, 2003). On the dissemination of British Army doctrine during the Second World War, see: Timothy Harrison Place, *Military Training in the British Army, 1940-1944: From Dunkirk to D-Day* (London: Frank Cass, 2000), pp.8-17.

15   Denis Richards, *Royal Air Force, Volume I: The Fight at Odds* (London: HMSO, 1953), p.383.

the *Luftwaffe* to battle, which often consisted of using bombers as bait.[16] The importance of these merged during the planning for JUBILEE in that a key aim of air operations was to bring the *Luftwaffe* to battle in order to attrite the latter's strength while providing adequate air cover per the principles established by the RAF in its involvement in the development of the *Manual of Combined Operations* during the inter-war years.[17]

The other half of this equation was the emergence of raiding by commando forces as an element of British strategy that developed after the withdrawal of the British Expeditionary Force from France in 1940. On 4 and 6 June 1940, the Prime Minister, Winston Churchill, called for the, 'joint Chiefs of Staff to propose me measures for a vigorous, enterprising and ceaseless offensive' against German held territory.[18] This led to the appointment of Lieutenant-General Alan Bourne RM as Commander of Raiding Operations on coasts in enemy occupation and Advisor to the Chiefs of Staff on Combined Operations. Bourne was ultimately replaced by Mountbatten as CCO after the latter supplanted the former's successor, Admiral of the Fleet Sir Roger Keyes who headed COHQ from 17 July 1940 to 27 October 1941.[19] Up to 1942, the size and scale of combined operations grew, which saw air power become an increasingly integrated aspect of their conduct and indeed, JUBILEE itself was the culmination in the growth of this form of operation. From an air power perspective, the evolution of combined operations in 1941 led to creation of the position of Assistant Advisor on Combined Operations (Air) within COHQ as well as the formation of No. 1441 Combined Operations Development Flight, which illustrated the increasing importance of the RAF in this area.[20]

It was from this time that combined operations also became an important aspect of Fighter Command operations as their growth dictated greater integration and the need for air cover became paramount. On 1 May 1942, the Deputy Chief of the Air Staff, Air-Vice Marshal Norman Bottomley, directed Air Officer Commanding-in-Chief (AOC-in-C) Fighter Command, Air Marshal Sholto Douglas that the priorities for his forthcoming operations included:

16   Richards, *The Fight at Odds*, p.383; Norman Franks *Royal Air Force Fighter Command Losses of the Second World War: Volume 2 – Operational Losses: Aircraft and Crews, 1942-1943* (Leicester: Midland Publishing Limited, 1998), p.9.

17   On the RAF's involvement in the development of the *Manual of Combined Operations*, see: Ross Mahoney, 'The Royal Air Force, Combined Operations Doctrine and the Raid on Dieppe, 19 August 1942', (MPhil Thesis, University of Birmingham), pp.33-67.

18   Bernard Fergusson, *The Watery Maze: The Story of Combined Operations* (London: Collins, 1961), p.47.

19   Fergusson, *The Watery Maze*, p.47; Robin Neillands, *The Dieppe Raid: The Story of the Disastrous 1942 Expedition* (London: Aurum, 2006), p.25.

20   TNA, AIR 20/5011, Correspondence between the Chief of the Air Staff and the Advisor on Combined Operations, 1-8 November 1941; AIR 20/5011, Memorandum from D. of Plans to DGO, DWO and DTO, 21 December 1941

a) The intensification of the day fighter offensive which calls for reinforcement of 11 Group with Spitfire squadrons.

b) Maintenance of a proper state of readiness of squadrons ear-marked for operation "Region"

c) The training of fighter squadrons in rotation in Combined Operation (emphasis added)[21]

This reinforced Douglas' own directive to Leigh-Mallory on 13 April 1942 that stressed the need to pick suitable targets along the French coast and employ overwhelming numbers to achieve dominance over the *Luftwaffe* in order to support Fighter Command's overall role of forcing attrition upon the enemy.[22] Based on this context, and building upon the perception of success that JUBILLE produced, Leigh-Mallory's letter of 22 August suggested an adapted operational technique that sought to bring together two *modus operandi* that were elements of British operations in this phase of the Second World War.

Leigh-Mallory's idea received Mountbatten's support and on 7 September 1942, CCO convened a meeting that examined the plausibility of combining offensive fighter operations with raiding, which led to the planning of Operation AFLAME. This marked a shift in Fighter Command's operational technique and illustrated its willingness as an organisation to adapt in the face of intelligence reports that cited the arrival of *Luftwaffe* reinforcements in France and Norway, thus, offering the opportunity for further JUBILEE style operations.[23] Leigh-Mallory clearly identified a need and opportunity for change through the acquisition of operational experience, however, this adaptation in Fighter Command's operational technique required the management of relationships between key stakeholders involved in the process such as Mountbatten and COHQ, the Air Staff and the Chiefs of Staff Committee. The latter two were a key challenge for this new operational technique as Mountbatten shared Leigh-Mallory's enthusiasm for the concept. Despite receiving approval for AFLAME, the operation was ultimately cancelled due to shifting weather conditions and changing service priorities related to the use of commando forces, supporting destroyer and cruiser elements and the use of bombers. Indeed, the use of bombers remained a perennial problem for this form of operation due to sensitivities linked to bombing targets in France and the management of relationships across operational interfaces with differing strategic priorities. Indeed, on the issue of target priorities, AOC-in-C Bomber Command, Air Marshal Arthur Harris raised concerns related to his overriding directives from the War Cabinet concerning the selection of targets

---

21   TNA, AIR 20/829, DCAS to AOC-in-C Fighter Command, 1 May 1942, p.1.
22   TNA, AIR 41/49, The Air Defence of Great Britain, Volume V: The Struggle for Air Supremacy, January 1942-May 1945, p.105.
23   TNA, AIR 16/762, COHQ to Leigh-Mallory, 18 September 1942.

in France.[24] While there were appropriate reasons for AFLAME's cancellation it did not end the preference for this style of operation as COHQ sought to re-launch it as Operation COLEMAN in late 1942 with the objective of inducing an air battle on terms favourable to Fighter Command.[25]

COLEMAN highlighted, as had AFLAME, the need to link such operations with broader deception efforts for Operation TORCH, the invasion of French North Africa planned for early November 1942.[26] However, it also reinforced issues related to Mountbatten's own operating methods as a leader and the opposition it generated with other organisations who felt that the CCO was attempting to force through operations for his own gains. While both Leigh-Mallory and Douglas were undoubtedly aware, and supportive, of the attempt to re-launch AFLAME, it was opposition from the Air Staff that led to COLEMAN's cancellation. Opposition from the Air Staff illustrated how different organisational priorities affect adaptation as the operation failed to receive the support of the Assistant Chief of the Air Staff (Policy) (ACAS (P)), Air Vice-Marshal John Slessor, who described COLEMAN as weak.[27] The Director of Fighter Operations, Air Commodore John Whitworth-Jones, and the Director of Bomber Operations (DBOps), Air Commodore John Baker, supported Slessor's view. Whitworth-Jones described the plan as the 'hurried sort of operation' for which Mountbatten was known, while Baker, in veiled terms, claimed that CCO had lied to the Chiefs of Staff concerning his claim to have had discussions with the heads of Fighter and Bomber Command about the operation.[28] While, as noted, Douglas was aware of COLEMAN, it appears that Harris was not. By 23 October, having been ordered by the Chiefs of Staff Committee to re-evaluate the plan, Mountbatten also had to contend with the RN's decision not to provide him with six Hunt class destroyers as well as the decision by the Chief of the Air Staff (CAS), Air Chief Marshal Sir Charles Portal, not allow fighter aircraft for direct support operations to participate.[29] This growing opposition from key stakeholders, who it must be remembered controlled the operational material required for Mountbatten's plans, ended discussions over COLEMAN's viability; however, it did not end the idea that fighter sweeps could operate in conjunction with raids as priorities began to shift towards planning for Operation OVERLORD. At the Casablanca Conference in

---

24   On this issues see the correspondence between Harris, Douglas and Leigh-Mallory in TNA, AIR 16/762 between 25-30 September 1942;
25   TNA, AIR 20/4529, Operation "COLEMAN" – Outline of the Operation, 18 October 1942.
26   TNA, AIR 20/4529, Covering Letter to Outline of Operation "COLEMAN", 18 October 1942
27   TNA, AIR 20/4529, Memorandum by ACAS (P) on Operation "COLEMAN" for the Chiefs of Staff Meeting on 22 October 1942, 20 October 1942, p.1.
28   TNA, AIR 20/4529, DFO to ACAS (P), 19 October 1942, p.1; TNA, AIR 20/4529, DBO to ACAS (P), 19 October 1942.
29   TNA, AIR 20/4529, Extract from the Chiefs of Staff's 239th Meeting, 23rd October.

January 1943, discussions concerning the nature of operations in North West Europe during the forthcoming year concluded that they would consist of raids; operations with the purpose of seizing a bridgehead; and a possible uncontested return to the continent.[30] These conclusions formed the basis of standing orders to the Chief of Staff to the Supreme Allied Commander (designate) (COSSAC), Major-General Frederick Morgan with raids, or 'amphibious feints', directly linked to the idea of provoking a major air battle and inflicting attrition on the enemy.[31]

As such, small raids and deception operations became a key element of Operation COCKADE, which acted as a camouflage and deception plan undertaken by COSSAC in the summer of 1943 to alleviate pressure on other fronts. COCKADE consisted of Operations TINDALL, STARKEY and WADHAM. The latter two were interdependent with STARKEY acting as the feint main assault and WADHAM as a follow-on force landing on the Brittany peninsula.[32] At its core, STARKEY's planning sought to draw the *Luftwaffe* to battle as it was, 'primarily designed to compel the German Air Force over a prolonged period to engage in air battles of attrition.'[33] STARKEY was to take place over a three-week period in September 1943, which would culminate in a demonstration by amphibious forces and significant air operations in the vicinity of Boulogne in an attempt to bring the *Luftwaffe* to battle.[34] The air commander was Leigh-Mallory, now Air Marshal and AOC-in-C of Fighter Command. In addition to significant fighter forces, STARKEY was to make use of bomber forces. Both Air Chief Marshal Harris, and his American counterpart, Major General Ira Eaker, commanding the US Eighth Air Force, were critical of the plan with former noting that the planned level of support was 'just the sort of thing an idol [sic] army dotes on.' Issued to both Eaker and Harris, the former was not willing waiver from the terms of the POINTBLANK Directive while the latter supported him in this view and subsequently their planned sortie rates were significantly scaled back.[35] This episode illustrated the need to manage relationships between organisations that had independent strategic objectives also proved a challenge when discussions

30   TNA, AIR 20/5105, Report by the British Joint Planning Staff to the Combined Chiefs of Staff on Continental Operations in 1943, 22 January 1943, p.1
31   TNA, AIR 20/5105, Report by the British Joint Planning Staff, 22 January 1943, p.1; General Sir Frederick Morgan, *Peace and War: A Soldier's Life* (London: Hodder and Stoughton, 1961), p.156.
32   John P.Campbell, 'Operation STARKEY: 'A piece of harmless playacting'?', *Intelligence and National Security*, 2 (3) (1987), p.93; TNA, AIR 41/49, The Struggle for Air Superiority, 1942-1943, p.274.
33   TNA, AIR 40/312, Report by the Air Force Commander on Operation "STARKEY", 16th August-9th September 1943, 16 September 1943, p.1. The most useful works on STARKEY are, Campbell, 'Operation STARKEY, pp.92-113; Michael Cumming, *The Starkey Sacrifice: The Allied Bombing of Le Portel, 1943* (Stroud: Sutton, 1996).
34   TNA, AIR 41/49, The Struggle for Air Supremacy, p.275; AIR 40/312, Report by the Air Force Commander, pp.1-2; Cumming, *The Starkey Sacrifice*, pp.25-31.
35   Campbell, 'Operation STARKEY', pp.95-96.

emerged over the use of bombers in support of OVERLORD more broadly and the assault of coastal defences more specifically in late 1943 and early 1944. Designed to protect the naval forces involved and lure the *Luftwaffe* up to battle, STARKEY's air operations fell into three phases.[36] Firstly, reinforcement of Fighter Command's No. 11 Group to a strength of seventy-two squadrons occurred between 16 and 24 August while between 25 August and 7 September, air operations consisted of target reconnaissance and increased bombardment of key installations.[37] Finally, the culminating phase saw continued attacks on vital installations, such as coastal batteries in preparation for the demonstration by naval forces off Boulogne. During the period of D-Day, 7/8 September, Fighter Command flew some seventeen hundred air cover sorties. Despite this air effort STRAKEY was not the success envisioned as the Germans did not respond in the manner hoped for with only small forces engaging the attacking bombers and fighters. By this time, the *Luftwaffe* in northern France had standing orders to avoid combat where numbers were un-advantageous and the Air Historical Branch narrative commented that this was probably a lesson learnt from Dieppe.[38] Additionally, the *Luftwaffe* was also responding to the growing scale of Allied strategic bombing against Germany that required the withdrawal of forces. Indeed, by the time of STARKEY, the desire to use combined operations as means of bringing the *Luftwaffe* to battle, despite whatever strategic rhetoric was used to support it, had not taken into account a key factor affecting the effectiveness of any change in operational technique; namely the enemy's counter-response that should have continued to shape the RAF's own operational responses. That it did not was down to the problems generated by Fighter Command's offensive culture and broader organisational changes in 1943 that included the disbandment of Army Co-Operation Command and the transfer of the former's operational functions to the newly formed Tactical Air Force. This clouded any attempt to effectively interpret and modify Fighter Command's operational technique in the face of changing enemy tactics.

The Question of Command and Control in Combined Operations

The inability to develop an effective Headquarters Ship (HQS) was perhaps the most notable failure concerning combined operations in the inter-war period and it affected JUBILEE's conduct. Backed up by HMS *Berkeley* and *Fernie*, the Hunt class destroyer HMS *Calpe* acted as the JUBILEE's primary HQS, which was generally considered to be too cramped for the operation. Despite assurances that it was manageable, prior to JUBILEE, Leigh-Mallory had highlighted concerns over C_2 in the aftermath of Exercise YUKON II, held on 22/23 June in preparation for Operation RUTTER,

---

36   TNA, AIR 40/312, Report by the Air Force Commander, pp.2-3.

37   TNA, AIR 40/312, Appendix 'A' – STARKEY Order of Battle in Report by the Air Force Commander, pp.1-4.

38   TNA, AIR 41/49, The Struggle for Air Supremacy, p.280.

when he expressed apprehension about communications between RAF Uxbridge and deployed naval forces.[39] The question of C_2 in general was not a new problem as illustrated by the 1934 combined operations exercise conducted off the Yorkshire coast. This exercise highlighted the general problem of coordinating C_2 during amphibious operations for all three services.[40] During the 1934 exercise, the battleship HMS *Nelson* was utilised as a HQS and while it had the necessary equipment to operate as a fleet flagship, it did not have the requisite C_2 suite for combined operations. Indeed, in late 1941, one of Mountbatten's first actions as CCO was to convene an Inter-Service Committee on Communication that produced six reports on the question of C_2 thus, illustrating the general concerns held over this question. The importance of these reports linked to the ordering of two dedicated HQS, HMS *Bulolo* and *Largs*, and the development of C_2 processes that were utilised during JUBILEE. Predicated on the unavailability of either *Bulolo* or *Largs*, the decision to utilise *Calpe* was due to the RN's concerns over the use of capital ships in the English Channel, though the provision of a single cruiser may have abrogated against the challenges presented by using smaller ships.[41] The problem of space was most notable for Leigh-Mallory's liaison officer, Air Commodore Adrian Cole, based in *Calpe*, who had to co-ordinate operations with the military and naval task force commanders, Major-General John Roberts and Hughes-Hallett as well as liaise with HQ No. 11 Group. While Cole provided general C_2 of pre-planned air operations in *Calpe*, Squadron Leader James Scott directed low-level squadron's from HMS *Berkeley*.

In this respect, the broad importance of JUBILEE was that it clearly tested the efficacy of the system then in development and while they were an improvement on the pre-war system, limitations was identified. Therefore, in this respect, JUBILEE acted as a key element in a process of acquiring and transferring knowledge concerning C_2 of air power in support of combined operations that fed into technological adaptations that strengthened operational techniques in 1943 and 1944 but importantly also paralleled lessons being learnt in other theatres. For example, in his report on Dieppe's air operations, Leigh-Mallory compared the efficacy of the system utilised to the development of the Army Air Support Control (AASC) units that were being used effectively in the North African campaign.[42] In essence, in comparison with the AASCs, Cole, on *Calpe*, acted as the Forward Air Controller

39 TNA, DEFE 2/546, Minutes of Meeting held on 25 June 1942; AIR 20/832, Inter-Service Committee on Communications in Combined Operations Interim Report No. 2: Support Communications in Combined Operations, 14 January 1942.
40 Richard Harding, 'Amphibious Warfare, 1930-1939' in Richard Harding (ed.), *The Royal Navy, 1930-2000* (London: Frank Cass, 2005), pp.55-7.
41 TNA, AIR 20/9503, *History of the Combined Operations Organisation, 1940 – 1945*, (1956), p.137
42 TNA, AIR 16/871, Report by the Air Force Commander on the Combined Operation against Dieppe – August 19th 1942, 5 September 1942,p.4; Ian Gooderson, *Air Power at the Battlefront: Allied Close Air Support in Europe, 1943-45* (London: Frank Cass, 1998), pp.22-40.

attached to a Forward Air Support Link tentacle in the HQS and requested air support from HQ No. 11 Group that acted as the Rear Air Support Link. No. 11 Group then tasked squadrons for operations over the battlespace. Based on information gained from both human, in the air and on the ground, and signal intelligence in real-time, requests for air support filtered through this system, however, Cole's physical separation from Scott on *Berkeley* created challenges for co-ordinating operations. Specifically, from the RAF's perspective, the most significant outgrowth of this challenging C_2 set-up was the sinking of *Berkeley*. This occurred due problems concerning airspace management and in particular the relationship between RAF fighters and the RN's anti-aircraft gunners on-board supporting destroyers. *Berkeley* was hit by bombs from *Luftwaffe* Dornier DO217s at 12:45 and HMS *Albrighton* subsequently sunk her at 13:08.[43] In essence, due to C_2 issues related to effective identification of friend or foe, standing orders to RAF fighters did not allow them to pursue *Luftwaffe* aircraft below 3,000 feet where they became the RN's responsibility.[44] This failure led to the loss of the *Berkeley*.

Nonetheless, future operations learnt from these challenges as a process of refinement in the techniques and platforms used to provide adequate C_2 for air support emerged during 1943. Indeed, by the time of OVERLORD, the system had evolved to encompass command, control, communication and intelligence (C_3I) in specialised, though improvised, vessels. This process of refinement illustrated how in adapting to operational conditions both the RAF and the other services drew appropriate lessons from a number of sources in order to develop best practise for future operations. Concerning C_2, it was further recognised after TORCH in November 1942 that air power specific functions then undertaken by HQS needed to be separated due to continuing issues related to space that had been the primary concern during JUBILEE.[45] This led to the development of the Fighter Direction Tender (FDT) in which a Landing Ship Tank (LST) mounted ground-control inception (GCI) radar.[46] Other options for FDTs had included escort carriers and converted passenger vessels such as *Bulolo*.[47] FDT's, as a single vessel tasked with C_3I of air support for combined operations, offered greater flexibility to force commanders seeking rapid responses to changing condition in the battlespace. This was enabled because FDTs brought GCI radar together with radio and wireless transmissions and 'Y' signals intelligence.[48]

43   TNA, ADM 267/108, Extracts from Weekly Intelligence Reports: HMS *Berkeley* – Sunk by Bombs – 19.8.1942, 18 December 1942; Neillands, *The Dieppe Raid*, pp.257-58.
44   TNA, DEFE 2/551, Annex 3 – Detailed Air Plan in The Dieppe Report (Combined Report), p.127.
45   TNA, DEFE 2/954, Proposal to fit CGI, RDF in special vessels for Fighter Direction, 24 December 1942.
46   TNA, DEFE 2/954, Fighter Direction Ships in Combined Operations, 28 January 1943.
47   TNA, DEFE 2/954, Proposals by the Director of Plans (RAF), 8 January 1943.
48   TNA, DEFE 2/954, Preliminary Examination of Detailed Requirements of Special Type of Ship for Fighter Direction, 16 January 1943.

This was important because, for example, during JUBILEE, the management of valuable 'Y' intelligence had been poor and led to an overloading of the C_2 system due to its improvised nature in the ships provided.[49] Stressing the importance of operational requirements and the character of information needed prior to an operation, an RAF report produced in JUBILEE's aftermath, and incorporating early views from it, recommended a refinement of the command chain as it related to the utilisation of 'Y' material.[50] By 1943, the development of FDTs allowed the RAF to state clearly both its operational and personnel requirements for a vessel that operated as the first tentacle of a system that fed back to decoding stations such as Cheadle.[51] This ability to refine and state operational requirements sped up the provision of effective air support within the battlespace.

While undertaken at the behest of COHQ, it is clear that the RAF supported and interfaced with the research and development process for FDTs to ensure an understanding of its requirements existed. This allowed for the rationalisation of C_2 functions, which improved the control of air support for future combined operations. Additionally, the Mediterranean theatre also provided valuable operational experience for the FDT concept where three converted LSTs, Nos. 305, 407 and 430 were used to great advantage in supporting Operations HUSKY and AVALANCHE.[52] In September 1943, this led Leigh-Mallory, now Air Commander-in-Chief (designate) of the Allied Expeditionary Air Force (AEAF) to request further vessels for the invasion of Europe.[53] Operational experience in the Mediterranean and Leigh-Mallory's support led to a decision on 13 November 1943 to convert a further three LSTs, Nos. 13, 216 and 217, to FDTs with a full suite of C_3I equipment.[54] Apart from operational experience, which was interpreted to support the development of FDTs, the open question of operating and manning these vessels also illustrated the inherent advantage of the flexible nature of British military culture that supported this key technical adaptation. Essentially, by late 1943, a compromise was reached whereby the RN operated the FDTs themselves but the equipment was crewed by the RAF.

49   Appendix 13 – 'Intelligence Before and During the Dieppe Raid' in F.H. Hinsley *et al*, *British Intelligence in the Second World War, Volume 2: Its Influence on Strategy and Operations* (London: HMSO, 1981), p.703.
50   TNA, AIR 40/2239, Handling of "Y" Material during Combined Operations, 30 August 1942.
51   TNA, DEFE 2/1072, Combined Operations Ships – "Y" Intelligence Requirements, 21 December 1943.
52   TNA, DEFE 2/1071, Minutes of Meeting to Discuss Personnel for Fighter Direction Ships, 20 December 1943; DEFE 2/954, Trials of GCI Equipment fitted in LST 301, Portland, 27th Feb. to 14th Mar. 1943 – Report by Sub. Lt. D. Alford, 17 March 1943; DEFE 2/421, British Headquarters Ships and Fighter Direction Tenders, p.9.
53   TNA, DEFE 2/1070, Leigh-Mallory to Mountbatten, 10 September 1943.
54   TNA, DEFE 2/421, A report on the Role and Operation of British Headquarters Ships and Fighter Direction Tenders in the Assault on the Continent of Europe, June 1944: Operation "NEPTUNE", September 1945, p.10.

This compromise worked effectively as it allowed the RAF to manage its requirements for C_3I through this wartime adaptation, therefore, taking ownership of its success or failure. Specifically, the RAF formed No. 105 Wing as the parent unit for its controllers and they undertook training at HMS *Warren*, the Combined Training Centre at Largs, and the Fighter Direction Centre at Royal Naval Air Station Yeovilton.[55]

By OVERLORD, the key functions between HQS and FDTs was clearly defined with the former concentrating on pre-planned co-ordination of sorties by squadrons with pre-arranged targets sets while the latter reacted to the changing pattern of operations within the battlespace.[56] FDTs were able to co-ordinate the actions of low-cover squadrons and direct them to points of contact by the assimilation of real-time intelligence. Aided by the paucity of *Luftwaffe* action on 6 June 1944, this flexibility nonetheless represented a learning process within the British military that also had longer-term implications. Recognising that FDTs reduced the usefulness of HQS from the perspective of controlling air power, the concept developed into the planned ocean going Fighter Direction Ships that first emerged in 1943 to support future operations in South East Asia and the Far East.[57] Indeed, an AEAF report produced in September 1945 praised the effectiveness of the FDT concept despite the challenges that emerged due to the unorthodox mating of two dissimilar sets of equipment.[58] In this respect the various stakeholders, including the RAF, re-interpreted knowledge and applied it to new theatres where the adaptation had operational implications.

Aerial Bombardment

In *Unauthorized Action*, Villa contended that a lack of 'fire-power proved fatal to the Canadian and British invaders.'[59] Villa further argued that:

> There was a degree of callousness in Portal's allowing the largely Canadian force to go in without the bomber support they needed.[60]

Villa ascribed a degree of responsibility to Portal (CAS) that is unwarranted. The decision to cancel the pre-operation bombing that formed part of the original operation, RUTTER, was the responsibility of the force commanders. Indeed Villa has claimed that Leigh-Mallory produced a post-facto memorandum on the 'Employment of Bombers', however, while it has no date attached it is clear that this was circulated

---

55   TNA, DEFE 2/1072, Director General of Organisation to Leigh-Mallory, 14 December 1943; DEFE 2/1071, Report of Meeting held at COHQ, 13 January 1944.
56   TNA, DEFE 2/421, British Headquarters Ships and Fighter Direction Tenders, p.1.
57   TNA, DEFE 2/1070, Fighter Direction Ships for Combined Operations, 27 September 1943.
58   TNA, DEFE 2/421, British Headquarters Ships and Fighter Direction Tenders, p.27.
59   Villa, *Unauthorized Action*, p.127.
60   *Ibid*, p.162.

to force commanders on 24 July 1942.[61] Additionally, factors such as Roberts' anxiety regarding friendly casualties, operational concerns from Harris at Bomber Command, and the potential political ramifications of using bombers over France led Leigh-Mallory to cancel direct bomber support on 5 June and never reconsidered when JUBILEE re-emerged. While the addition of RN firepower in the form of cruiser support may have improved JUBILEE's prosecution, it is difficult to see how the use of the RAF's heavy bombers would have made much difference to the operation's success given Dieppe's geographical characteristics. Dieppe's geography, located within a v-shaped valley at the mouth of the River Arques, and flanked by headlands, precluded this. While often used for morale reasons, the use of heavy bombers to support ground operations remained contentious and of variable utility.[62] This was particularly noticeable in the battles around Monte Cassino and Caen in 1944. Additionally, Bomber Command's ability to hit precision targets in 1942 was limited and would have been more of hindrance to the assaulting forces.

Nevertheless, the RAF and COHQ did not ignore the possibility of utilising bombers in support of combined operations in the aftermath of JUBILEE. Indeed, the discussion over the use of bombers in support of combined operations highlighted the role of bureaucracy in interpreting lessons as well as the management of relationships across operational interfaces. From an operational perspective, Leigh-Mallory commented on the operations of the light bombers of No. 2 Group during JUBILEE in his after-action report, citing that what limited bombing had occurred was not as useful as their smoke-laying operations.[63] While planning for No. 2 Group's operations had included attacking German troop reinforcements, Leigh-Mallory was disappointed that the lack of activity in this sphere meant that the light bombers went unused. Consideration of greater fire support from both the RAF and RN also appeared in Hughes-Hallett's 'Lessons Learnt' report, however, it took until the summer of 1943 for the analysis of air support to be undertaken seriously. For example, on 15 September 1942, COHQ produced a report that dealt with the issue of fire support during an assault, however, it did not deal with air support as it fell outside of its remit.[64] Correspondingly, the formation of COHQ's so-called Assault Committee failed to fully consider the role air power could play and simply stated in its report of 6 December 1942 that, 'In all stages of the action

61   TNA, AIR 16/746, Operation "Jubilee": Memorandum by the Air Force Commander concerning the Employment of Bombers; Villa, *Unauthorized Action*, note 54, p.289. For evidence that this was circulated pre-JUBILEE, see: TNA, AIR 16/746, Minutes of the 1st Meeting of the Combined Force Commanders at Combined Operations Headquarters, 24 July 1942.
62   On the debate concerning the role of heavy bombers in support of ground operations, see: Gooderson, *Air Power at the Battlefront*, pp.125-64
63   TNA, AIR 16/871, Covering Letter.
64   TNA, DEFE 2/1024, Short History of the Study of Requirements for Producing Fire Support for an assault Against a Defended Coast, 30 August 1943, p.1.

all forms of air support would be an urgent requirement.'[65] The Assault Committee eventually concluded in August 1943 that close fire support for combined operations was, 'fundamentally a joint naval and air problem' and that there was a need for a 'plan in which naval, military and air action must all play their parts.'[66] The Assault Committee had been formed to examine the problems associated with bombardment and produce proposals on new methods and requirements based upon recent operational experiences, however, its conclusions regarding the potential use of air power was clearly poor and moved little beyond basic statements. Formed on 2 December 1942, in response to a memorandum submitted by CCO to the Chiefs of Staff on 16 November, the Chiefs of Staff Technical Sub-Committee simply reinforced these basic statements though it was formed to examine the potential use of air power in conjunction with naval gunfire.[67] However, DBOps, Baker, represented the RAF on this committee, which in itself illustrated a growing recognition that such tactical problems had to be solved by working across organisational boundaries in order to find joint solutions.[68] Thus, it is clear that JUBILEE had some impact on focussing the attention of requisite bodies into examining the problem of fire support; however, these bodies struggled to move past simple bureaucratic assertions concerning the importance of air power.

This changed in 1943 when planning for OVERLORD became more prominent. Held to examine the problems facing OVERLORD's planners, a conference, Exercise RATTLE was convened in June 1943 to begin discussion of pertinent issues related to the planned invasion of Europe. An early issue for discussion was air support. Given his past and future roles, it is significant that Leigh-Mallory co-chaired this exercise and that he dealt with aspects pertaining to air support.[69] Indeed, Fergusson credited Leigh-Mallory with ensuring that the conference took place at all.[70] Included for discussion at RATTLE was a paper on neutralising gun batteries that summarised possible sources of contention surrounding the use of aerial bombardment, for example, the physical impact that bombing may have on ground force's ability to move and the problem of providing adequate cover over all the proposed invasion beaches were mentioned.[71] The paper also explored the question of why bombardment was desired and whether it was being used as a tool for troop morale or for military expediency.[72] Another question raised was what lessons were being learnt from air operations

65   TNA, DEFE 2/1024, Short History, p.2.
66   TNA, DEFE 2/1024, Appendix A-Summary of Findings of COHQ Assault Committee (November/December), 30 August 1943, p.1.
67   TNA, AIR 20/9503, *History*, p.120-121; DEFE 2/1024, Short History, pp.3-4.
68   TNA, AIR 20/9503, *History*, p.120; DEFE 2/1024, Short History, p.3.
69   TNA, AIR 20/5229, Exercise RATTLE Programme, 23 June 1943, p.1.
70   Fergusson, *The Watery Maze*, pp.273-74.
71   TNA, AIR 20/5229, Air Bombardment – The Problem of Neutralising Coast Defences, 24 June 1943, pp.1-2.
72   TNA, AIR 20/5229, Air Bombardment, p.2.

in the Mediterranean, in particular Operation CORKSCREW, the occupation of Pantelleria on 10 June 1943. Based on a proceeding ten-day preliminary bombardment by air and naval forces, CORKSCREW's success allowed for the occupation of Pantelleria with light casualties for the invading forces.[73] Indeed, it is here that we start to see a divergence from Dieppe's lessons in that the former only highlighted the need for some form of support but did not provide practical experience that would be gained from other theatres of operation.

In the aftermath of RATTLE, and personally appointed by Mountbatten, further discussion led to the formation of an inter-service committee under Air Vice-Marshal Ronald Graham to explore the question of fire support for combined operations against heavily defended coasts. At this point Graham was serving as Chief of Staff (Air) at COHQ and had previously been part of the planning staff for OVERLORD in the Air Ministry. The Vice-Chief of the Air Staff (VCAS), Air Marshal Sir Douglas Evill, ensured that Graham's committee considered all forms of fire support including aerial bombardment.[74] VCAS' support is significant as it illustrated that senior RAF officers took the question of supporting combined operations seriously as did Graham's appointment to chair such an important committee. The committee examined the problem of fire support from three perspectives:

i)   Destruction or neutralisation of the coast defences.
ii)   Destruction or neutralisation of beach defences.
iii) Tactical fire support of landings.[75]

Apart from Graham, key members of the committee from the RAF included the Assistant Chief of the Air Staff (Operations) (ACAS (Ops)), Air Vice-Marshal Alec Coryton, and ACAS (Technical Requirements) (T), Air Vice-Marshal John Breakey and Professor Solly Zuckerman who had run the Bombing Survey Unit in the Mediterranean. Indeed, Zuckerman recalled that he was appointed to the committee as some form of 'oracle' due to his recent experience and represented the use of external experts by the RAF to inform both adaptation and operational decision making.[76] Both ACAS (Ops) and (T)

---

73 For details of CORKSCREW see: Fergusson, *The Watery Maze*, pp.237-40; Ian Gooderson, *A Hard Way to Make War: The Allied Campaign in Italy in the Second World War* (London: Conway, 2008) pp.76-8. For critique of CORKSCREW's efficacy, see: Christopher M. Rein, *The North African Air Campaign: U.S. Army Air Forces from El Alamein to Salerno* (Lawrence, KS: University Press of Kansas, 2012), pp.136-43.
74 DEFE 2/1024 'Extract from COS (43) 190th Meeting regarding Fire Support of Seaborne Landings against a heavily Defended Coast'.
75 TNA, DEFE 2/1024, Minutes of the 1st Meeting of the Interservice Committee to Consider Provision of Fire Support on a Heavily Defended Coast, 4 September 1943, p.2.
76 Solly Zuckerman, *From Apes to Warlords, 1904-46: An Autobiography* (London: Hamish Hamilton, 1978), p.206. On the impact of operational research on decision making within Bomber Command, see: Randall T. Wakelam, *The Science of Bombing: Operational Research in RAF Bomber Command* (Toronto: University of Toronto Press, 2009).

were responsible for two preliminary papers that examined the destruction of beach and coastal defences by aerial bombardment respectively. These papers emphasised the advantages and challenges inherent in the application of air power in this sphere. For example, the paper on neutralising coastal defences noted that bombing would be very useful in dealing with open targets but that concrete defences represented a notable challenge.[77] Considered the most economical method for reducing a heavily defended coastal defence system was Bomber Command's Avro Lancasters blind bombing with OBOE, which was deemed twice as effective as blind bombing by the same aircraft equipped with G-H. Nearly seven times more expensive as this method was day visual bombing by Martin B-26 Marauders of the US Ninth Air Force.[78] Despite the Air Staff's defence of the figures produced, the Assistant Chief of the Naval Staff, Rear Admiral Wilfrid Patterson, queried the figures, which led to the formation of a technical sub-committee to consider issues related to the weight of bombardment used by the methods under consideration by all services. This sub-committee's key findings were that in order to have any effect on coastal positions any medium capacity bombs used had to be greater than 500lbs and that issues relating to altitude and prevailing weather conditions degraded that accuracy with such weapons. Additionally, in order to achieve this it suggested four key methods of operations for aircraft:

   i)   Visual day – level, glide or dive bombing.
   ii)   Visual night – by flare illumination.
   iii) Bombing visually on target indicator bombs dropped by radio aids.
   iv)   Blind bombing using radio aids.[79]

   All of this information was fed back into Graham's committee that issued a preliminary report entitled a 'Report by the Inter-Service Committee formed to consider all existing means of providing Fire Support when Landing Forces on a Heavily Defended Coast' on 25 October 1943.[80] Through the preliminary report, Graham sought views from key stakeholders who had the necessary operational experience in the provision of air support for combined operations. While AOC 2nd Tactical Air Force, Air Marshal Sir John D'Albiac, raised concerns over the problem of managing friendly fire, the key criticism came from Harris at Bomber Command, who described

77   TNA, DEFE 2/1024, Fire Support for an Opposed Landing statement by the Air
      Staff on the Destruction or Neutralisation of Coast Defences, 16 September 1943;
      DEFE 2/1024, Fire Support for an Opposed Landing statement by the Air Staff on the
      Destruction or Neutralisation of Beach Defences, 16 September 1943.
78   TNA, DEFE 2/1024, Fire Support for an Opposed Landing statement by the Air Staff
      on the Destruction or Neutralisation of Coast Defences, 16 September 1943
79   TNA, DEFE 2/1025, Appendix II, p.12.
80   DEFE 2/1025 Report by the Inter-Service Committee formed to consider all existing
      means of providing Fire Support when Landing Forces on a Heavily Defended Coast' 25
      October 1943, p.6. Hereafter the Graham Report.

the report as 'exceedingly questionable.'[81] Harris questioned the assumptions under-pinning the report's figures despite the fact that they emerged from studies under-taken by both the Air Staff and Zuckerman. However, Harris' key concern centred on what would happen to his resources if he had to divert Bomber Command to support future combined operations. This presaged his memorandum of 13 January 1944 on the subject of 'The Employment of the Night Bomber Force in Connection with the Invasion of the Continent from the UK' where Harris sought to outline the best possible use of Bomber Command in support of OVERLORD.[82] This did not include direct support of assault forces and Harris claimed that both Leigh-Mallory and General Sir Bernard Montgomery were in agreement with him. This was not the case and Leigh-Mallory, DBOps, Group Captain Sydney Bufton, and ACAS (Ops), Coryton, each produced counter memoranda addressing Harris' points.[83] Merged into one document, the Air Staff drew upon the Graham Report as evidence of the studies undertaken into the potential efficacy of this form of provision on the issue of "Programme Bombing" or support of assault forces, which Harris claimed 'is ruled out altogether as an operation of war'.[84] Often supporting Harris, his American allies, notably Lieutenant General Carl Spaatz, added an extra dimension to the challenge of adaptation in the form of friction between competing strategic priorities. Indeed, this episode represented a key challenge for the implementation of adaptation when competing viewpoints from senior leaders meet and cannot be reconciled.[85] While Harris eventually co-operated effectively when placed under the operational control of the Supreme Allied Commander, General Dwight Eisenhower, at this time he provided a point friction and, as seen above with the debates concerning STARKEY, the former remained convinced of the efficacy of his position; Harris continually remained a difficult personality to manage.[86]

81   TNA, DEFE 2/1026, D'Albiac to Leigh-Mallory, 9 November 1943; DEFE 2/1026, Harris to DCAS, 10 November 1943, p.1.
82   TNA, AIR 20/3223, Covering letter from AOC-in-C Bomber Command to the Chief of the Air Staff to a memorandum on The Employment of the Night Bomber Force in Connection with the Invasion of the Continent from the UK, 13 January 1944.
83   On the relationship between Harris and Bufton, which is best described as strained, over this memorandum, see: Rex Cording, 'The Other Bomber Battle: An Examination of the Problems that arose between the Air Staff and the AOC Bomber Command between 1942 and 1945 and their Effects on the Strategic Bomber Offensive', (PhD Thesis, University of Canterbury, 2006), pp.205-7.
84   TNA, AIR 20/3223, Comments by Air C-in-C AEAF and the Air Staff on AOC-in-C Bomber Command's Memorandum for the Employment of Night Bombers in Connection with "OVERLORD", 26 January 1944, p.3.
85   On the relationship between leadership and learning organisations, see: Raffaella Di Schiena, Geert Letens, Eileen Van Aken and Jennifer Farris, 'Relationship between Leadership and Characteristics of Learning Organizations in Deployed Military Units: An Exploratory Study', *Administrative Sciences*, 3 (3) (2013), pp.143–65.
86   On the leadership challenges presented by the planning for OVERLORD and its interface with the Combined Bomber Offensive, see: Peter Gray, *The Leadership, Direction*

In addition to views presented by operational commanders, the Graham Report drew on information emanating from Zuckerman's Bombing Survey Unit and a report produced by the Director of Air Tactics, Air Commodore Gordon Vasse, on STARKEY that reaffirmed the preference for the use of heavy bombers to neutralise coastal defences.[87] Distributed to relevant planning departments including COSSAC (designate), the final report was then submitted the Chiefs of Staff on 23 December 1943 and issued as a Cabinet Paper on 7 January 1944.[88] With the effort provided by all service ministries and the technical sub-committee, Graham produced an outline report that, with the exception of minor corrections, outlined key factors determining effective fire support for combined operations. The report separated combined operation into four phases, first, the preparatory phase, second, the approach, third, the assault and establishment of a beachhead, finally, the advance inland.[89] It also noted that all action would be 'joint' and that the effort fell into three tasks. First, silencing coastal defences; second, drenching fire during the assault; finally, provision of support during the build-up of the bridgehead.[90] The report agreed that a mixture of fragmentation and medium capacity bombs would produce the best result in drenching attacks on beach defences while concerning the application of air power, a success rate of twelve and half per cent would render coastal defences inoperable. An average bomb density of quarter of a pound per square mile would achieve advantageous results for the assault. For the final task, it was noted that the methods and density would be similar to the period of drenching fire, however, air support in this task would be based upon carefully prepared bomb lines in order to reduced friendly fire incidents.[91] Devolved onto one of the sub-committees of the Joint Technical Warfare Committee, Graham's committee and its responsibilities did not end with the reports submission as the former body widened the scope of information to include material coming out of operations in South East Asia and the Far East.[92]

Conclusion

Widely recognised by the RAF and in combined operations doctrine throughout the inter-war period as a necessary pre-requisite for combined operations, air superiority allowed for the application of other forms of air power in this sphere, most notably the application of air support for assaulting forces. That the *Luftwaffe* failed to combat

    and Legitimacy of the RAF Bomber Offensive from Inception to 1945 (London: Continuum, 2012), pp.215-24.

87   TNA, DEFE 2/1026, Preliminary Summary of Bombing Attacks – Operation Starkey, September 1943, p.5.

88   TNA, AIR 20/9503, *History*, p.123.

89   TNA, DEFE 2/1025, Graham Report, p.1.

90   TNA, DEFE 2/1025, Graham Report, p.1-2.

91   TNA, DEFE 2/1025, Graham Report, pp.1-11.

92   TNA, AIR 20/9503, *History*, p.123.

allied air superiority effectively during subsequent amphibious operations illustrated the significance of this and on 27 March 1944, the 8th *Abteilung* of the *Luftwaffe's* air staff produced a study that outlined what they viewed as the significance of JUBILEE. It stated that:

> As a result of the experience gained during the Dieppe operation as to the necessity of air supremacy, the Allies made certain of such supremacy in all subsequent operations.[93]

This study argued that the correct use of air power by the RAF during JUBILEE to achieve, 'air supremacy, was necessary to equalise the position in view of the numerical inferiority of the ground troops'.[94] Identified as a necessary pre-requisite for the launch of Operation *Seelowe* in 1940, the Germans had already recognised the importance of air superiority.[95] However, the *Luftwaffe's* stretched resources and ineffective leadership at all levels meant that despite recognising air superiority's importance it was unable to develop effective counter-air tactics that would allow it to combat the Allied air forces in subsequent combined operations from 1942 onwards. Whether the RAF achieved air supremacy remains a point of contention within JUBILEE's historiography, however, the achievement air parity provided much needed support during the operation. Indeed, as this chapter illustrates both the RAF and the British military more broadly continued to learn and apply lessons from JUBILEE into 1943 and beyond though not all were successful in their stated aim. In this respect, the RAF illustrated the ability to act as a learning organisation as outlined by Garvin, however, it is worth noting that further examination is required about how effective some of the changes implemented were.

Each of the adaptations examined in this chapter highlights issues facing military organisations as they seek to manage change under wartime conditions. Firstly, the decision to attempt to marry air power with commando operations in order to bring the *Luftwaffe* to battle represented a failure in adaptation as well as the problem of managing relationship between stakeholders. It is clear that both Leigh-Mallory and Mountbatten sought to build on JUBILEE's perceived success, however, despite being a positive attempt to learn, both operational and personality issues abrogated the chance of success, and by 1943 it became a strategic dead-end for both Fighter Command and COHQ in terms of forcing attrition on the *Luftwaffe*. Fought closer to Germany and due to the technical limitations of Fighter Command's equipment, the US Eighth Air Force would primarily fight this battle. Both the improvement in

93   TNA, AIR 20/7701, Extract from 8th *Abteilung* Staff Study on The Dieppe Landings, August 1942, 27 March 1944.
94   *Ibid.*
95   Joint Services Command and Staff College Library, Shrivenham, OKW Directive No. 16 – Preparations for the Invasion of England, 16 July 1940.

C_2 and the discussions over air support reinforce the necessity to manage the bureaucratic framework within which military organisations operate. Formed at the behest of the Chiefs of Staff and with the support of the Air Staff, who fed into its production process, Graham's committee was able to draw on number of key stakeholders for information but still had to manage friction from those who sought to pursue their own strategic objectives. That Graham managed this process, and that his report was subsequently used a key source of planning information, suggests the importance of having support from key stakeholders such as VCAS who can help shape and form agendas where necessary. The importance of C_2 was clearly an important issue for the RAF for if it was to operate effectively within any combined operation then airspace management was paramount. This led the RAF to fully support COHQ's decision to develop FDTs and manage the challenge represented by the need to work with both the latter and the RN in the development and staffing of these vessels. The development and deployment of FDTs represented a key technological adaptation with the concept having implications beyond their ad-hoc nature, which saw the evolution of a more integrated system incorporating communication and intelligence streams.

Historiographically, this chapter suggests that while Mountbatten continued to overplay the significance of JUBILEE in the planning for OVERLORD for self-serving reasons, it is clear that Dieppe fed into a process of organisational learning through adaptation. However, it is also clear that these lessons emerged in parallel with operations in other theatres. While it is easy to criticise the reports produced by both JUBILEE's force commanders and the overall report authored by Hughes-Hallett as being an attempt to cover their collective responsibility for the failure of Dieppe they did highlight and identify appropriate lessons. These lessons then had a cumulative effect upon the collation of information to support future developments that supported OVERLORD. One clear aspect of continuity in these adaptations from an RAF perspective is Leigh-Mallory's role. Leigh-Mallory was clearly supportive of the implementation of further combined operations with the aim of bringing the *Luftwaffe* to battle and was increasingly involved in the other areas discussed in this chapter. While the former was not successful and debate remains over aspects of his career, Leigh-Mallory's involvement in these adaptations, no matter how peripheral that they may have been, illustrate a leader who was able to get inside the OODA loop concerning the identification of adaptations that had implications for his own profession, plans and operations. Furthermore, identified prior to the operation, the problem of C_2 highlights the historical problem of placing JUBILEE upon a pedestal as Mountbatten sought to do. Nonetheless, JUBILEE did act a key nexus in both the RAF's and COHQ learning process concerning combined operations in that it both confirmed and acted as a trigger for further work. In addition, given JUBILEE's scope, it is unsurprising that it remained a key source of information during 1943.[96] However,

---

96   Combined Arms Research Library, US Command and General Staff College, Fort Leavenworth, Conference of Landing Assaults, US Assault Training Center, European

it is clear that JUBILEE was but one source of information for future developments in combined operations. TORCH, HUSKY, AVALANCHE and CORKSCREW all acted as operational examples for the developments that emerged in 1943 with reports regularly feeding into discussions in the United Kingdom.[97] Similarly, operations prior to JUBILEE were just as important, for example, as Benbow noted, the failure and success of Operations MENACE and IRONCLAD in 1940 and 1942 respectively highlighted the importance of both effective planning and C_2.[98] Ultimately, had JUBILEE not been a failure then there would be little need to separate out the actual lessons learnt from the historic dogma that has emerged over this question.

Theater of Operations, 24 May to 23 June 1943.

97   For example, each of these operations produced their own 'Lessons Learnt' reports, see: TNA, AIR 51/4, Operation HUSKY: Lessons learned by Headquarters section Tactical Air Force, September 1943.

98   Tim Benbow, '"Menace" to "Ironclad": The British Operations against Dakar (1940) and Madagascar (1942)', *Journal of Military History*, 75 (3) (2011), pp.769-809.

14

British Aero-Naval Co-operation in the Mediterranean, 1940-45, and the Creation of RAF No. 201 (Naval Co-operation) Group

Richard Hammond

On 3 October 1941, during the escalating war in the Mediterranean and Middle East, the Royal Air Force (RAF) created No. 201 Naval (Co-Operation) Group. Adapted from the original RAF No. 201 (General Reconnaissance) Group that had been in place with RAF Middle East Command (ME) since 1939, it existed as an independent entity until February 1944, when its units were absorbed into the umbrella organization of Air Defence Eastern Mediterranean.[1]

The Group was the product of great inter-service debate, the latest in a long line of disputes over and between the Royal Navy (RN) and the RAF since the latter's creation. The amalgamation in 1918 of the air arms of the Army and the RN into a single unified service placed the fate of British maritime aviation almost entirely in their hands. This, and the subsequent need of the RAF to justify itself in the competition for limited British resources, led to frequently intense rivalry between the two services in the interwar years. The major disputes were over the control of the Fleet Air Arm (FAA), Coastal Command and even at one stage over the very existence of the RAF itself.

Budgetary constraints meant expansion of the RAF was very limited for much of the interwar era, with the majority of RAF squadrons stationed overseas and often engaged in policing actions. In the face of these limited resources, development in the RAF narrowed to focus primarily on strategic bombing, and to a lesser extent on fighter defence of the United Kingdom. It even offered the Air Ministry the opportunity to claim that the more mobile and flexible option of air power offered a cheaper alternative for 'substitution' of the other more expensive services in roles defending overseas positions such as Singapore. The promotion of bombing as an innovative new

---

1   The National Archives (TNA) AIR 23/7511, 'General Notes Re Middle East and Malta in Eastern Mediterranean, June 1940 to Sept 1944', 5 December 1944; TNA AIR 41/76, Air Historical Branch Narrative (AHBN), The RAF in Maritime War, Volume 7, Part 2 (1962), p.12.

method to secure victory, and of air power as a cheap and effective alternative, allowed them to concentrate limited resources and gave them a unique platform and individual identity from which to champion their continued existence as an independent service.[2] Accordingly, maritime aviation gradually slipped down the list of RAF priorities over the interwar years.[3] Only in the FAA did true development occur in this field, focusing on tactical development for attacking enemy fleets in port, reconnaissance, anti-submarine warfare and fighter defence of the fleet.[4] However, manpower issues, lack of resources, national strategic priorities, issues over control of the FAA and increasingly outdated equipment caused the RN to drop from its leading role in the development of aircraft carriers and their operations, to falling behind Japan and the United States.[5] As one scholar has put it, by the outbreak of the Second World War, the British had seen 'the nadir of maritime aviation', with limited numbers of poorly trained crews flying equally limited quantities of outdated and unsuited aircraft.[6]

Shortly before the outbreak of the war, control of the FAA returned to the Admiralty, but the Air Ministry retained Coastal Command. This was to remain a cause of disagreement up until April 1941 when a compromise handed operational control of Coastal Command to the Admiralty, while the Air Ministry retained ownership and all other aspects of its control. The issue of operational control was subject to several caveats however. While the Admiralty could direct the Air Officer Commanding in Chief (AOC-in-C) of Coastal Command, he would then disseminate orders through relevant group commanders, who were not subject to the direct control of naval commanders. Control was thus not completely in naval hands. Nevertheless, the Admiralty had gained the lead in operational control and a much greater say in other issues such as training, the allocation of resources and tactical development.[7] No. 201 Group was to be born of a similar compromise later that year, as the same debates that occurred over Coastal Command took place once again, only this time centred on the Mediterranean. The competing strategic priorities, corporate cultures and identities of the two services thus affected the issues discussed in this chapter.

2   An excellent, brief summary of these issues is available in Geoffrey Till, 'Competing Visions: The Admiralty, the Air Ministry and the Role of Air Power', in Tim Benbow (ed.), *British Naval Aviation: The First 100 Years* (Farnham: Ashgate, 2011), pp.63-67. The exact same issue of 'substitution' was to be suggested by the Air Ministry again in the debate over carrier aviation in the 1960s, see Gjert Lage Dyndal, *Land Based Air Power or Aircraft Carriers: A Case Study of the Debate about British Maritime Air Power in the 1960s* (Farnham: Ashgate, 2012).

3   See: Christina Goulter, *Forgotten Offensive: Royal Air Force Coastal Command's Anti-Shipping Campaign, 1940-1945* (London: Frank Cass, 1995), pp.34-110.

4   See: Phillip Weir, 'The Development of Naval Air Warfare by the Royal Navy and Fleet Air Arm between the two World Wars' (PhD thesis, University of Exeter, 2007); Till, *Airpower and the Royal Navy 1914-1945: A Historical Survey* (London: Jane's, 1979), pp.137-71.

5   Till, *Airpower*, pp.189-90.

6   Goulter, *Forgotten Offensive*, pp.72-110.

7   Till, *Airpower*, p.195; Goulter, *Forgotten Offensive*, pp.126-7.

British maritime aviation between the wars and during the Second World War has seen multiple pieces of high quality academic research, which tend to focus on either Coastal Command or the FAA.[8] Generally, British aero-naval co-operation in the interwar years and the Second World War is a subject that relies heavily on two older but excellent pieces of scholarship, along with a handful of more recent studies, and also receives a good deal of coverage in the various official histories.[9] Much more recently, Michael Simpson has specifically examined the mechanics of British aero-naval co-operation in the Mediterranean during the Second World War.[10] Simpson's work is largely a piece of operational history, focusing on how the British coped during the first half of the war in the Mediterranean; a period of slender resources, and partic-ularly of aircraft in the theatre. While Simpson has made an important contribution to knowledge of British aero-naval co-operation in the Mediterranean, there has been no complete analysis of this for the entirety of the conflict there. Most importantly, the question of where the Mediterranean lay in the evolving face of British aero-naval co-operation has yet to be fully examined.

This chapter examines the background of aero-naval co-operation in the Mediterranean prior to the creation of No. 201 Group, and the events and debates that led to its creation. The role of the Group and the operations it conducted are discussed before concluding as to its place within British military innovation. 'Innovation' here will follow the definition set by Stephen Peter Rosen as:

8   See, Goulter, *Forgotten Offensive*; Andrew Hendrie, *The Cinderella Service: RAF Coastal Command, 1939-1945* (London: Leo Cooper, 2006); John Buckley, *The RAF and Trade Defence, 1919-1945: Constant Endeavour* (Keele: Keele University Press, 1995); Norman Friedman, *British Carrier Aviation: The Evolution of the Ships and their Aircraft* (London: Conway Maritime Press, 1988); Buckley, 'Maritime Air Power and the Second World : Britain, the USA and Japan' in Sebastian Cox and Peter Gray (eds.), *Airpower History: Turning Points from Kitty Hawk to Kosovo* (London: Frank Cass, 2002), pp.125-144; Till, 'Maritime Airpower in the Interwar Period: The Information Dimension', *Journal of Strategic Studies,* 27 (2) (2004), pp.298-323.

9   Till, *Airpower*; S.W. Roskill, *Naval Policy Between the Wars* 2 Volumes (London: Collins, 1968-76). See also Duncan Redford, 'Inter- and Intra-Service Rivalries in the Battle of the Atlantic', *Journal of Strategic Studies*, 32 (6) (2009), pp.899-928, Buckley, 'Atlantic Airpower Co-operation, 1941-1945' in John Gooch (ed.) *Airpower: Theory and Practice* (London: Frank Cass, 1995), pp.175-197. The following official histories contain much useful information on British aero-naval co-operation and rivalry; N.H. Gibbs et al., *Grand Strategy*, 6 Volumes (London: HMSO, 1956-76) contains much on the debates between the service chiefs in Whitehall; Roskill, *War at Sea* 3 Volumes (London: HMSO, 1954-61) presents the naval view; Dean Richards and Hilary St George Saunders, *The Royal Air Force 1939-1945*, 3 Volumes (London: HMSO, 1953-4) provides that of the air force. Finally, I.S.O Playfair et al., *The Mediterranean and Middle East*, 6 Volumes (London: HMSO, 1954-88), provides some useful detail on the subject focused specifically on the Mediterranean theatre.

10   Michael Simpson, 'Wings Over the Sea: The Interaction of Air and Sea Power in the Mediterranean, 1940-1942', in N.A.M Rodger (ed.), *Naval Power in the Twentieth Century* (Basingstoke: Macmillan, 1996), pp.134-150.

> ...a change that forces one of the primary combat arms of a service to change its concepts of operation and its relation to other combat arms, and to abandon or downgrade traditional missions.[11]

By using No. 201 Group as a case study, this chapter highlights the difficulties faced by the British in creating a framework for successful inter service co-operation overseas in a time of conflicting strategies and policies between them, and of greatly overstretched material and human resources. It thus demonstrates how No. 201 Group was only an example of limited British innovation, failing to fully solve the myriad of problems regarding naval aviation and co-operation in the Mediterranean. While perhaps not satisfying the hopes many had placed on it, and failing to provide the first theatre-wide dedicated maritime air command for the Mediterranean, it did however lay a foundation for greater co-operation there, with positive, but similarly limited, repercussions on a much wider scale in the war.

British Aero-Naval Co-operation in the Mediterranean, 1940-41

June 10 1940, the start of the war in the Mediterranean, saw the British with very few aircraft available in the theatre. In the whole of Egypt, there were just six bomber, three fighter, and two flying boat squadrons and one general reconnaissance unit, along with a handful of support units. To this could be added a single flying boat squadron at Gibraltar, with no functioning RAF aircraft present at Malta at that stage.[12] Not only were the numbers of aircraft a concern, but many were of older or even obsolescent types. Only the Bristol Blenheims of the bomber squadrons and the Vickers Wellingtons of the general reconnaissance unit were truly modern aircraft in 1940. The fighter squadrons were particularly outdated, having to rely on Gloucester Gladiator biplanes.[13] The FAA presence in the theatre was limited to around 30 Fairey Swordfish torpedo bombers split between the aircraft carriers *Eagle* and *Argus*, along with a few catapult launched aircraft on other warships.[14]

Although numbers of aircraft in the theatre grew over the course of 1940 and 1941, they did so rather slowly. British industry was heavily taxed with multiple requirements and the priority for aircraft for much of this period was to stay in the home theatre. The threat of invasion meant the requirement for fighters to defend the skies of the United Kingdom, while bombers were retained for the strategic bombing offensive; the only remaining means of striking directly at Germany. In the face of these varied requirements and limited production capacity, maritime aircraft were accorded

11   Stephen Peter Rosen, 'New Ways of War: Understanding Military Innovation', *International Security*, 13 (1) (1988), p.134.
12   Royal Air Force Museum (RAFM), Longmore Papers, DC 74/102/38, Appendix 'B', Location of Units in Middle East Command as at 11 June 1940.
13   *Ibid.*
14   TNA, ADM 187/8, Admiralty Pink List entry for 10 June 1940.

the same low priority they had been given before the war. Further complication arose when actually sending reinforcements to the Mediterranean and Middle East. Although sending units to Gibraltar was relatively simple, reinforcing Malta required either crated aircraft to be sent to the island as part of a major convoy operation, or aircraft to be flown from an aircraft carrier in the western Mediterranean and travel by air. Both were highly dangerous operations involving passing within easy reach of German and Italian air bases and the Italian Navy.[15] Reinforcing RAF ME was a much longer, albeit safer, process. Aircraft sent to the Middle East came through the 'Takoradi Route', a complex passage going by sea from the UK to the West African port of Takoradi followed by flight through various parts of central and North Africa to Egypt. The aerial route alone was 3,697 miles, but the alternative was to stage aircraft through Malta to Alexandria, with all the danger that involved.[16]

Nevertheless, in spite of this paucity in resources, the few RAF and particularly FAA aircraft achieved impressive feats during 1940 and 1941. The most famous success was the FAA strike on the Italian fleet at Taranto in November 1940. It was hailed by Admiral Andrew Cunningham, the naval Commander-in-Chief (C-in-C) Mediterranean, as 'unsurpassed' as an example of economy of force. He also stated that it would not have been possible without the prior reconnaissance efforts of RAF Glenn Martin aircraft.[17] This early example of effective co-operation producing major results was followed up by the naval victory at Cape Matapan in March 1941. RAF reconnaissance aircraft and later FAA spotting made the interception of the Italian fleet possible once again.[18] The sinking of an Italian convoy the following month by destroyers operating from Malta also owed much to the location efforts of the RAF.[19]

These successes achieved through aero-naval co-operation at a time of such scant resources owed much to the atmosphere of friendly co-operation between the theatre commanders of the respective services. The AOC-in-C RAF ME until May 1941 was Air Chief Marshal Arthur Longmore. Longmore was a 'maritime minded' RAF officer, and had served in the Royal Naval Air Service prior to and during the Great War. He went on to be the first C-in-C of the newly renamed RAF Coastal

15   Details of the various 'club runs' to reinforce Malta by flying aircraft off from carriers, can be found in TNA, AIR 20/9598, 'Enemy Shipping Losses in the Mediterranean, 10 June 1940 to 2 May 1945', pp.1-3. The best single source for the Malta convoys is Richard Woodman, *Malta Convoys 1940-1943* (London: John Murray, 2000).
16   Playfair, *The Mediterranean and Middle East, Vol. 1*, pp.196-7.
17   'Fleet Air Arm Operations against Taranto on 11 November 1940', 16 January 1941, in *The Cunningham Papers, Volume 1: The Mediterranean Fleet, 1939-1942*, edited by Michael Simpson (Aldershot: Ashgate, 1999), pp.178-80.
18   Admiral of the Fleet Andrew Browne Cunningham, *A Sailor's Odyssey* (London: Hutchinson, 1951), pp.325-7.
19   'Report of an Action against an Italian Convoy, 15-16 April 1941', 8 June 1941, in *The Cunningham Papers, Volume 1*, p.347. On the achievement of the FAA in the Mediterranean in general, see Ben Jones, 'The Fleet Air Arm and the Struggle for the Mediterranean, 1940-44' in Benbow (ed), *British Naval Aviation*, pp.79-98.

Command in 1936.[20] Right from the start of the war in the Mediterranean, he had made it clear that maritime operations were an important task of RAF ME. In his dispatch on Middle East operations, Longmore stated that among his main objectives was offensive air action against enemy ports and strategic reconnaissance for the RN. He also made it clear that he had the 'fullest support' of Cunningham throughout his tenure as AOC-in-C.[21]

In June 1941, Longmore was succeeded as AOC-in-C RAF ME by Air Marshal Arthur Tedder. Relations between Cunningham and Tedder were less cordial than with his predecessor. The main point of contention between them was over the control of air power and the question of a dedicated maritime air command being set up for the theatre. Despite having a mixed maritime and aerial background, serving in the Royal Flying Corps in 1916-18 but also attending the Royal Naval Staff College in 1923-24, Tedder saw the role of aircraft primarily as one of striking directly at the enemy air and land forces. He was not completely opposed to the use of aircraft for maritime purposes, but his viewpoint was that 'naval air operations cannot properly be considered as a self-contained activity separate from the main land and air operation in the Middle East'.[22] Disputes regarding the control and role of air power were inevitable in the face of such limited resources, and were quick to flare up, as is shown below.

The Formation and Role of RAF No. 201 (Naval Co-operation) Group

No. 201 Group was the product of much debate between the Admiralty and the Air Ministry, between the RN and the RAF. These debates originated over repeated calls from Cunningham for greater numbers of specialized maritime aircraft and greater emphasis on effective aero-naval co-operation in the Mediterranean. This was then followed up by the request to have an overseas equivalent to RAF Coastal Command set up for the Mediterranean. Cunningham wrote to Tedder in August 1941 stating that 'It has become increasingly clear in the past month that the existing organization for the co-ordination of flying operations over the sea is cumbrous (sic) and inadequate'.[23] He called for:

---

20   He oversaw the renaming and reorganisation of the 'Coastal Area' to RAF Coastal Command. See Air Chief Marshal Arthur Longmore, *From Sea to Sky: Memoirs 1910-1945* (London: Geoffrey Bles, 1946).

21   RAFM, Longmore Papers, DC 74/102/14, 'Dispatch on Middle East Air Operations', 1 February 1941, pp.2-3.

22   Arthur Tedder, *With Prejudice: The War Memoirs of Marshal of the Air Force Lord Tedder* (London: Cassell, 1966), p.148. See also Tedder, 'Air, Land and Sea Warfare', *Journal of the Royal United Services Institution*, 91 (1946), pp.59-68.

23   TNA, AIR 23/1376, Cunningham to AOC-in-C RAF ME, letter on 'Air Co-Operation', 14 August 1941, p.1.

...more aircraft diverted to fleet co-operation and personnel that are trained in work over the sea and we shan't get these without...a special organization running them in close touch with us.[24]

The Mediterranean received no theatre-wide organization though. As a compromise, No. 200 (Naval Co-operation) Group at Gibraltar was placed under naval command to act as a form of miniature coastal command for the western Mediterranean. However, the focus of this Group was mostly into the Atlantic, effectively extending the reach of Coastal Command further south, and it consisted of just two small flying boat squadrons in August 1941.[25] The key areas of the Central and Eastern Mediterranean were left uncovered, with Tedder and the Air Ministry unwilling to offer dedicated support for the RN there, only co-operation for specific operations that had their approval.[26] Chief of the Air Staff Charles Portal had already expressed his opposition to the idea of a dedicated command to the Prime Minister in April:

I notice that the C-in-C has once more suggested the formation of a Coastal Command in the Mediterranean as a cure for the present air situation. I cannot see how this would increase the forces available and I think it would certainly result in failure to apply our forces in the most economical way.[27]

Completely dissatisfied, Cunningham and the First Sea Lord Dudley Pound campaigned hard for their Coastal Command equivalent. In October 1941, No. 201 Group was converted from general reconnaissance duties in response to this, allowing Cunningham to initially conclude that they had 'won, to a great extent, our battle for Coastal Command'.[28] Although again a compromise, No. 201 Group would operate out of Egypt and cover the Central and Eastern Mediterranean, with No. 200 Group covering the Western Basin.[29] No. 201 Group remained a constituent of RAF ME and became its maritime arm, with the Western Desert Air Force conducting tactical operations and No. 205 Group for strategic operations.[30]

While the period from June 1940 to June 1941 had highlighted what effective aero-naval co-operation could achieve even with very little resources, the debate over an overseas Coastal Command had highlighted again the differences between the two services and their strategic concepts. It also demonstrated the problems presented by a clash of personalities and even brought the conflicting identities of the two services

24   Simpson, 'Wings Over the Sea', p.144.
25   TNA, ADM 187/14, Admiralty Pink List, August 1941.
26   Simpson, 'Wings Over the Sea', pp.144-5.
27   Christ Church Library, Oxford (CCL), Portal Papers, Folder 2, File 1, Portal to Churchill, 24 April 1941.
28   Cunningham to Willis, 20 November 1941, in *The Cunningham Papers, Volume 1*, p.533.
29   TNA, AIR 23/1376, Cunningham to AOC-in-C RAF ME, 6 July 1941, p.1.
30   Richards and Saunders, *The Royal Air Force 1939-1945, Vol. 2*, p.160.

to the fore, with substantial debate centring on whether the word 'naval' should be included in the Group's name.[31] Nevertheless, in spite of there being no theatre-wide command, the Mediterranean would in theory at least be fully covered by dedicated maritime organizations of the RAF.

Portal defined the newly designated Group's role as 'conduct of operations over the sea, and co-operation with the Mediterranean fleet as required by the Commander in Chief, Mediterranean'.[32] Upon its creation, the Group consisted of just:

a)   2 RAF and 1 Allied general reconnaissance squadrons
b)   1 RAF and 1 Allied fighter-bomber squadrons
c)   2 RAF long range fighter squadrons[33]

Such small numbers meant it was unable to make an immediate significant impact, but two things should be borne in mind. First, the numbers of aircraft in the entire theatre at this stage were small and the duties for them were many and varied. Second, this was before the addition of disembarked FAA units that were soon to make up an important part of the Group and its operations.

While in the home theatre, the Air Ministry had acquiesced to the Admiralty gaining operational control of Coastal Command with certain caveats in place, naval operational control of any equivalent overseas organization would have to be directly in the hands of the naval C-in-C. The Air Staff claimed this would be completely different from the situation in place with Coastal Command, where the Admiralty could take the development of the war as a whole into account and work in conjunction with the Air Ministry, War Office and so forth. They felt that control of the Group by the naval theatre commander would not reflect these wider issues and would harm the flexibility of air power in the theatre.[34] In essence, this reflected the organizational differences between the metropolitan air force with its overall control of different commands for different strategic purposes, and those more self-contained commands overseas, such as REF ME. With the metropolitan air force, the Air Ministry could dictate the strategic direction and allocation of resources to each of its commands quite easily, even in the face of Admiralty operational control of one of them. If the naval C-in-C Mediterranean were to gain operational control of No. 201 Group however, this would likely not be the case. Its position within the more self-contained RAF ME, divorced from the political-military command structure present in the UK, meant that the RAF felt they must retain operational control to maintain control of resource allocation to and within RAF ME. Efforts to further integrate the Middle East with the War Cabinet by establishing an in-theatre position of 'Minister

---

31   Cunningham to Willis, 20 November 1941, in *The Cunningham Papers, Volume 1*, p.533.
32   TNA, AIR 23/1376, '201 Group Charter', p.1.
33   *Ibid.*
34   Butler, *Grand Strategy, Vol. 3, Part 2*, pp.533-4.

of State with special responsibility for the Middle East' (held by Oliver Lyttelton) in June 1941, had not substantially change the Air Ministry's stance on these issues.[35]

As such, operational control of all units within No. 201 Group was held by the AOC-in-C RAF ME. Units within the Group could even be used, on occasion, for purposes outside of direct naval co-operation, but this held the caveat of needing approval from the C-in-C Mediterranean. Thus, there was a form of naval 'veto' in place over the operations conducted by the Group. The AOC-in-C RAF ME also had the right to draft in other units temporarily for maritime operations with the Group when needed, based on the recommendation of AOC No. 201 Group, C-in-C Mediterranean or even the General Officer Commanding in Chief ME. The C-in-C Mediterranean also retained the right to withdraw FAA units from the Group at any time for service afloat. All disembarked FAA units and units of RAF ME whose role was primarily maritime came under the command of No. 201 Group.[36] In this sense, the compromise regarding operational control of No. 201 Group was not exactly the same as the one reached for Coastal Command the previous April, but the RN did retain a major role in the control of the Group.

The Group thus effectively became the 'Coastal Command of the eastern basin'. Portal also decreed that the broad strategic plan for the employment of the Group, along with the standing operational orders, would have to be agreed between C-in-C Mediterranean and AOC-in-C RAF ME.[37] So in fact, the Air Ministry were stepping back after the creation of the Group and not meddling in its affairs from afar, although this was more likely because they did not want to be bogged down in further inter-service disputes over the Group than for any other reason. Meanwhile, the theatre commanders of the respective services were forced to co-operate closely to define the role and day-to-day operations of the Group.

RAF No. 201 Group had to conduct all duties involved with wartime maritime aviation. This involved the training of aircrews for such purposes and the conduct of maritime operations. These operations were as follows:

1. Reconnaissance, although photographic reconnaissance was met from a central Photographic Reconnaissance Unit (PRU)
2. Convoy escort
3. Escort of the Mediterranean fleet
4. Anti-submarine Warfare (ASW)
5. Anti-shipping strikes
6. Attacks on the Italian fleet
7. Minelaying
8. Air-Sea Rescue[38]

35   J.M.A Gwyer, *Grand Strategy, Vol. 3, Part 1*, pp.168-9.
36   TNA, AIR 23/1282, 'Air Tactics and Operational Notes on 201 Naval HQ', p.1.
37   TNA, AIR 23/1376, '201 Group Charter', p.2.
38   TNA AIR 41/19, AHBN, The RAF in Maritime War, Vol. 6 (1948), pp.288-290.

No. 201 Group as an Example of Innovation in the Mediterranean, 1941-43

No. 201 Group certainly contributed to the war in the Mediterranean, and was the catalyst for some innovation. Immediately upon the creation of the Group, a pool of FAA observers were transferred to it to assist in the training programmes with their expertise on maritime aviation. The Operational Training Unit (OTU) at Shallufa, which had previously been focused purely on training Wellington crews for maritime operations, was dedicated to the wider training of all personnel from No. 201 Group.[39] Disembarked FAA squadrons, bringing some strike units with direct experience to operate with the Group as well, later followed this providing the torpedo bombing capability that had been lacking. The Group thus became the first British unit in the Mediterranean to combine both RAF and FAA squadrons within its command. Although previously done in the home theatre with RAF Coastal Command, this can still be seen as an evolution in British aero-naval co-operation overseas and so is an example of limited innovation.

Evidently, this greater level of training and closer co-operation between the RAF and FAA was starting to transform the quality of British maritime air operations and co-operation between the services in the theatre. Just one month after the creation of the Group, Cunningham praised the 'particularly successful' anti-shipping attacks by some of the Group's Blenheims in his war diary.[40] He repeatedly praised the Group, its conduct and original commander Air Vice-Marshal Leonard Slatter and became much more positive about the effectiveness of those involved with naval co-operation in general.[41]

As the war progressed and the theatre received increasing numbers of aircraft, so did No. 201 Group. The RAF did not just take a greater involvement in maritime operations there; it received better and more specialized types of aircraft for the purpose. Greater numbers of Wellington bombers, with crews experienced in ASW were dispatched from Coastal Command.[42] Martin Marylands and Baltimores gave much needed increased reconnaissance capabilities. Bristol Beauforts and Beaufighters flew alongside and later replaced many of the older Blenheims. These were more effective in a convoy escort role and able to conduct torpedo and later rocket strikes against Axis merchant shipping and naval units, rather than the very costly low level bombing previously used.[43] These shipping strikes had previously been

---

39 TNA, AIR 23/1376, '201 Group Charter', p.2; Roy Conyers Nesbit, *The Armed Rovers: Beauforts and Beaufighters over the Mediterranean* (Shrewsbury: Airlife, 1995), p.19.

40 War Diary, November 1941, 'Summary of Events during November', in *The Cunningham Papers, Volume 1, 1939-1942*, p.542.

41 Cunningham to Pound, 4 December 1941; Cunningham to Pound, 10 December 1941; Cunningham to Pound, 28 December 1941 in *Ibid*, pp.545, 547, 559.

42 Cunningham to Pound, 27 November 1941, in *Ibid*, p.533.

43 For details of the Blenheim losses operating both from Egypt and Malta see CCL, Portal Papers, Folder 12, Longmore to Portal, 2 November 1940; Douglas Austin, *Malta and*

almost entirely the domain of the FAA, with the few RAF efforts frequently ending in abject failure. With this influx of better aircraft, the RAF began to take a greater role in the strikes. October 1941 saw the equal greatest monthly number of merchant vessels sunk by aircraft in the theatre since the start of war with Italy, and the RAF were responsible for eight of the 11 sunk.[44]

By the time of Operation HUSKY, the invasion of Sicily in July 1943, RAF No. 201 Group represented a significant balanced force. It consisted of four separate wings containing 13 different squadrons and further detachments. As demonstrated in Figure 1 below, No. 201 Group was a multinational force, which brought together units from the RAF, Royal Australian Air Force (RAAF), South African Air Force (SAAF), the FAA and the Hellenic Air Force.

Figure 1 No. 201 Group Order of Battle, 10 July 1943[45]

No. 235 Wing	No. 238 Wing	No. 245 Wing	No. 247 Wing
No. 13 Squadron (Hellenic), Bristol Blenheim	No. 16 Squadron, SAAF, Bristol Beaufort	No. 15 Squadron SAAF, Bristol Blenheim/Martin Baltimore	No. 38 Squadron RAF, Vickers Wellington
No. 227 Squadron Detachment RAF, Bristol Beaufighter	No. 227 RAF Squadron Detachment, Bristol Beaufighter	No. 38 Squadron Detachment RAF, Vickers Wellington	No. 203 Squadron RAF, Martin Baltimore
No. 454 Squadron RAAF, Martin Baltimore	No. 603 Squadron, RAF, Bristol Beaufighter	No. 1 General Reconnaissance Unit, Vickers Wellington	No. 227 RAF Squadron, Bristol Beaufighter
No. 459 Squadron RAAF, Lockheed Hudson	No. 815 Squadron Detachment FAA, Fairey Swordfish		No. 252 RAF Squadron, Bristol Beaufighter
No. 815 Squadron FAA, Fairey Swordfish		No Wing Assignment: No. 701 Squadron FAA, Supermarine Walrus	

British Strategic Policy, 1925-1943 (London: Frank Cass, 2004) p. 125 and Hugh Lloyd, Briefed to Attack, Malta's part in African Victory (London: Hodder and Stoughton, 1949), pp.71-5.

44   Figures of these sinkings, with numbers and tonnages sunk broken down by month, are available in TNA, AIR 20/9598, Enemy Shipping Losses in the Mediterranean, 10 June 1940 to 2 May 1945.

45   Richards and Saunders, Royal Air Force, Vol. 2, Appendix XII, 'Order of Battle, Mediterranean Air Command, 10 July 1943'.

However, there were many limitations to the innovation directly caused by No. 201 Group itself. In spite of its creation and clear remit, the Group simply did not receive sufficient reinforcements during the crucial period of late 1941 through to mid-1942. Instead, the bulk of the reinforcements went to the Western Desert Air Force in support of the land campaign there, leaving the maritime air war to be dominated by the Axis for the six-month period. Cunningham was to complain in that:

> ...the requirements as represented by the Air Officer Commanding (AOC) No. 201 Group have not been met and, in the naval view, have not been given due weight as balanced against the more obvious and apparently immediate Western Desert requirements.[46]

It was not only naval personnel who were becoming exasperated with this situation; as late as May 1942 Slatter, the AOC No. 201 Group, was having to make requests for just 'a few' reconnaissance aircraft.[47]

The issue of a lack of aircraft was further compounded by a lack of allocated equipment and weaponry. Just before the end of his tenure as C-in-C Mediterranean, the Admiralty informed Cunningham in March 1942 that the allocation of all 18-inch torpedoes for both the RAF and RN in the Eastern Mediterranean could not exceed 50 per month. The Axis maritime air superiority also hampered the delivery of these, and at the time the signal was sent, only eight of the 108 torpedoes allocated from January to March had actually been delivered. The remainder were either en route or awaiting freight.[48]

These problems affected all aspects of maritime air operations during the period. The Malta convoys of Operations HARPOON and VIGOROUS took heavy losses, and in the case of the latter never actually reached the island, due to insufficient air cover against Axis air and surface attack.[49] Although the recipient of much more aerial support, it is certainly arguable that had sufficient long-range maritime aircraft been available, the famous convoy of Operation PEDESTAL might well have suffered less heavily, and Malta might have been quicker to re-open heavy offensive operations from its striking forces.[50] In spite of the heavy traffic from Italy to North Africa, December 1941 to June 1942 saw few sinkings of Axis merchant vessels by aircraft, with no more than four ships sunk in any one of those seven months.[51]

It was not until after this crucial period that No. 201 Group started to have a major effect. In particular, sinkings through aerial shipping strikes started to increase

46 TNA, AIR 23/1376, Control of Air and Sea Operations, p.1.
47 TNA, AIR 23/1376, AOC 201 Group to Admiralty, 25 May 1942.
48 TNA, AIR 23/1376, Admiralty to C-in-C Mediterranean, 26 March 1942.
49 See Jack Greene and Alessandro Massignani, *The Naval War in the Mediterranean, 1940-43* (London: Chatham, 1998), pp.232-40.
50 See: Woodman, *Malta Convoys*; Austin, *Malta and British Strategic Policy*, pp.160-161.
51 TNA, AIR 20/9598, Enemy Shipping Losses in the Mediterranean, table 2.

after August 1942. This was down to a number of factors, including the increasing numbers of dedicated maritime aircraft being sent to the theatre, and the successful resupply of Malta through PEDESTAL. This released aircraft of the Group from the more intensive convoy escort operations to operate against Axis shipping to Benghazi and Tobruk. However, operational research records also point to the attacks themselves becoming more efficient by this stage. Search sorties for targets, aided by greater availability of Air to Surface Vessel radar (ASV), were clearly improving. In late 1941, location of targets leading to a strike varied between 35% and 70% of occasions depending on the availability of ASV, the time of day or night and the aircraft involved. By late 1942, these figures were between 50% and 80%.[52] This indicates that the better training, equipment, tactical developments and greater levels of reconnaissance conducted by the Group were having an effect.

This was then translating into tangible results. In September and October, the Group took the lead in anti-shipping operations for the crucial period leading up to and during the victory at El Alamein. It accounted for the vast majority of the 41,156 tons of shipping sunk by aircraft in those two months and caused significant damage to the vital Axis forward ports of Benghazi and Tobruk. It also conducted increased levels of reconnaissance that played an important role in locating targets for submarine and surface forces that accounted for a further 52,931 tons. The Group thus made a clear contribution to the Axis loss of a third of the supplies they shipped to North Africa over these two months, and the subsequent shortage they suffered during the battle. As the Axis forces withdrew westward after the battle, the Group shifted its focus to convoy escort and ASW operations. Operational research records indicate a marked improvement in location of targets, success rate of attacks and of co-ordination with RN escort forces.[53]

Due to its nature as a compromise between the two services, No. 201 Group itself was only an example of limited innovation in the Mediterranean that delivered some improvement in aero-naval co-operation. It stands as evidence of the British Military's ability to adapt to situations of limited resources and poor organization, but also of its failure to overcome persistent inter service rivalry and innovate more widely.

52   This has been determined by comparing figures from the following records: TNA AIR 20/5306, Operational Research Section (Middle East) Report No. 4, 'An Account of Anti-Shipping Operations Carried out by Aircraft between Oct 1 and Dec 12, 1941' and 'Anti-Shipping in the Eastern Mediterranean, October/December 1942', 20 June 1943.

53   Shipping losses calculated from TNA AIR 20/9598, Enemy Shipping Losses in the Mediterranean, table 2; Details of increased reconnaisance activities from TNA AIR 20/5306, Operational Research Section (Middle East) Report No. R.33, 'An Account of Anti-Shipping Operations in the Eastern Mediterranean, October-December 1942', p.4; Supply losses calculated from Ufficio Storico della Marina Militare, *La Marina Italiana nella Seconda Guerra Mondiale*, Volume 1: Dati Statistici (Rome: USMM), table LIV, pp.124-7; On the improvement in ASW, TNA AIR 20/1057, Operational Research Section (Middle East) Report No. R.37, 'An Account of Anti-Submarine Operations in the Eastern Mediterranean, January-March 1943'.

However, in general, it did have repercussions for innovation in the Mediterranean and elsewhere.

Innovation and the Legacy of No. 201 Group

After the successful Allied invasion of Northwest Africa (known as Operation TORCH), the Allies had to set up a new organization to command the vast air forces sent there. The result was the Northwest African Air Force (NAAF), set up in February 1943. The NAAF was responsible for all allied operations in Northwest Africa and many over the western Mediterranean, and it effectively became the western equivalent of RAF ME. These two organizations, along with the separate commands of Air Headquarters Malta and RAF Gibraltar, were all placed under the theatre-wide Mediterranean Air Command (MAC). The NAAF was built on what became known as the *Tri-Force* model, and consisted of three separate air forces; one strategic (NASAF), one tactical (NATAF) and one coastal (NACAF). In creating the NACAF, the British and American air forces had developed a dedicated and independent maritime air force, albeit not a theatre-wide one. The NACAF was modelled directly on No. 201 Group; it was even commanded by Air Vice-Marshal Hugh Lloyd, who had been the commander of No. 201 Group since July 1942.[54]

The NACAF and No. 201 Group each took responsibility for one-half of the Mediterranean; the NACAF in the west and No. 201 Group in the east. Cunningham praised their role in the invasion of Sicily (HUSKY), stating the invasion convoys were covered by the two forces that co-operated 'most effectively'. In spite of the complexity of the task facing them, no convoy was bombed and fighter cover was 'excellent'.[55] He did however see room for improvement between the naval force commanders and the fighter forces during the assault itself, but noted these problems were overcome for the landings on mainland Italy (Operations BAYTOWN and AVALANCHE), a view supported by the senior US Admiral in the theatre; H.K Hewitt.[56]

After the successful completion of the North African campaign and the invasions of Sicily and Italy, the Allied forces were no longer 'split' between the eastern and western halves of the Mediterranean. As such, a single over-arching air force for the theatre was created to replace the MAC. The Mediterranean Allied Air Force (MAAF) was created in December 1943, and just as with the NAAF, was organized on the *Tri-Force* model. Thus, the theatre-wide Mediterranean Allied Coastal Air Force (MACAF) could trace its roots, via the NACAF, to the limited

---

54   Richards and Saunders, *Royal Air Force, Vol.2*, p.260; Tedder, *With Prejudice*, pp.393-7.
55   'Report on Operation Husky', 1 January 1944, in *The Cunningham Papers, Volume 2: The Triumph of Allied Sea Power*, edited by Michael Simpson (Aldershot: Ashgate, 2006), 1942-1946, p.117.
56   'Report on Operation Husky', 1 January 1944; Cunningham to Ramsay, 20 September 1943; 'Admiral H.K. Hewitt, US Navy: Report on "Avalanche"', 11 January 1945, in Ibid, pp.119, 130, 137-8.

innovation of No. 201 Group. Finally, the Mediterranean had the overseas equivalent of Coastal Command that Cunningham had fought for back in mid-1941. Despite the decline of the Mediterranean in importance, the MACAF still had important roles to play in supporting the landing in southern France (Operation ANVIL/DRAGOON).

The MAAF itself was a great innovation at that time. It was the largest single air command in the world upon its creation and the first unified theatre-wide air command to bring direct Anglo-American co-operation by containing units and senior commanders from the air forces of both countries. It produced 'new refinements in the employment of tactical air forces and in the procedure of joint command', and set down a model for such commands to be implemented elsewhere in the future.[57]

The legacy of No. 201 Group was not limited purely to the Mediterranean theatre though. The *Tri-Force* model clearly influenced the organization of aerial support for the invasion of North-West Europe. Indeed, during a lunch meeting in January 1944, Tedder and General Spaatz (the commander of the United States Strategic Air Forces in Europe) agreed that air operations in North-West Europe would be conducted in the same manner that had been successfully used in the Mediterranean.[58] This was achieved to some extent, but differences in personalities and the question of control of resources proved once again to be an obstacle. While the model developed by the NATAF in co-operating with ground forces greatly influenced the role of tactical air power within the Allied Expeditionary Air Force, strategic air power remained predominantly independent from it.[59] RAF Bomber Command and the US 8th Air Force largely retained their own control for strategic direction, with only some subordination to the Supreme Headquarters Allied Expeditionary Forces.[60] While the AEAF had maritime air components, RAF Coastal Command also retained independence in its operations over the period, continuing its trade protection role in the Atlantic and interdiction in the North Sea.

Tedder, appointed Deputy Supreme Commander during Operation OVERLORD, identified in his autobiography a clear link between the combined operations of different air forces in the Mediterranean and the campaign in North-West Europe.[61] While he was correct in that the positive developments from the Mediterranean and Middle East influenced the organization and implementation of air power in North-West Europe, this was only limited. In a sense, the situation

57   TNA AIR 41/51, AHBN, 'History of the MAAF, 10 December–1 September 1944' (1945), p.10.
58   Wesley Frank Craven and James Lea Cate, *The Army Air Forces in World War II, Volume 3: Europe: Argument to VE Day* (Chicago: University of Chicago Press, 1951), p.80.
59   Even the exportation of the tactical model ran in to numerous problems, see David Ian Hall, 'The Long Gestation and Difficult Birth of the 2nd Tactical Air Force (RAF)', *Air Power Review*, 5 (3) (2002), pp.21-34.
60   L.F. Ellis, *Victory in the West, Vol. 1* (London: IWM, 1962), pp.41-43.
61   Tedder, *With Prejudice*, pp.500-510.

was a repeat of that in the Middle East, as while some positive developments were taken forward from the theatre, the existing limitations over control, identity and personalities were exported as well.

Conclusions

It is clear then, that No. 201 Group was an example of limited innovation by the British in the Mediterranean. Born of a compromise between two services, its creation in October 1941 was demonstrative of the differing perceived purposes and strategic aims of airpower. It highlighted the difficulties caused by opposing identities and corporate cultures, as well as personalities. Like all compromises, it failed to fully satisfy either party, with Tedder and the Air Ministry largely opposed to its creation, and Cunningham and the Admiralty convinced that far more could have been done.

As such, it is hardly surprising that the initial impact of the Group was less than revolutionary. It did improve the general quality of training for RAF maritime aircrew and along with greater numbers of more specialized aircraft, achieved greater results in ASW, anti-shipping operations, aerial minelaying and reconnaisance. The Group fostered greater relations between the RAF and RN in the theatre, in particular the placing of FAA and RAF units under the same command and having them liaise very closely, was very successful. This was a direct influence from the developments with RAF Coastal Command that had caused it to become, as Till states, a model of inter-service relations.[62]

However, the Group was too small and starved of resources to make any major achievements during the crucial period of the war in the Mediterranean from December 1941 to August 1942, when British fortunes there were lowest. The Axis air forces maintained maritime aerial dominance during this period and losses to the major Allied convoys to Malta were great, while correspondingly Allied attacks upon Axis convoys were greatly hampered. From August 1942 onwards the situation in the theatre improved greatly and No. 201 Group thrived, but this had taken almost 11 months.

If No. 201 Group itself was an example of only limited innovation, it did set the foundation for wider-reaching developments. It became the model that the NAAF was based on, paving the way for the first overseas air forces to combine British and American units under the same command and the first to fully utilize the *Tri-Force* system. This in turn paved the way for the first theatre-wide organization to combine such units and utilize the *Tri-Force* structure; the MAAF – the largest single air command in the world. The organization:

---

62   Till, *Airpower*, p.195.

...brought air force efficiency in the Mediterranean to a new high and established a model for harmony and teamwork between allies.[63]

Increasing effectiveness in aero-naval co-operation was an important factor in the success of a series of complex amphibious operations from 1942 to 1944 and the protection of Allied sea lines of communication.

Through these innovations, the nature of aero-naval co-operation and maritime aviation in the Mediterranean had been transformed. Relevant senior commanders took on board experiences in the Mediterranean and these advances were taken beyond the Mediterranean theatre, and their influence could be seen in North-West Europe. However, just as the Group was the product of limited innovation that was hampered by inter-service rivalry, so was its legacy. No. 201 Group stands as an example of adaptation in the face of difficult circumstances, but also as an example of the failure of the British to overcome internal divisions throughout the war. While making important achievements, it failed to completely fulfil Rosen's definition of innovation by forcing a service to completely change its relations to other combat arms. A framework for inter-service co-operation was created, but not a comprehensive one – the innovation behind No. 201 Group was thus limited, and so was its legacy.

63   TNA AIR 41/51, AHBN, 'History of the MAAF, 10 December – 1 September 1944' (1945), p.10.

Epilogue
Learning the Right Lessons
Military Transformation in Crisis and the Future of Britain's Armed Forces
Matthew Ford

In the depths of the UK's Ministry of Defence, there is a vault of documents, war diaries and battlefield reports from recent British campaigns in Afghanistan and Iraq. Managed by a team previously known as the Army Historical Branch, instead of paper files the archive now mainly contains many terabytes of data, reflecting the way that information technology shapes the operations of twenty-first century military organisations. The sheer quantity of documents - one terabyte might hold as many as 143 million pages of Microsoft Word documents - represents a gold mine for future military historians. However, that very quantity of material belies the problems facing both the historian and those members of the armed forces seeking to derive appropriate lessons from previous experience. The challenge lies in discerning the patterns in the millions of pages of documentation to see whether military change has emerged by accidental, coincidental or an intentional result of purposeful human decision-making.

Whilst the scale may well have changed, for historians these challenges are not new.[1] Since antiquity, scholars have studied war in the hope of deducing central tenets or laws for guiding future military conduct.[2] If the secrets of battle could be unlocked then victory might be guaranteed. Traditionally the historian has been relied on to develop the kinds of insights deemed appropriate by the strategist. More recently, however, historians have tended to be supplanted by scientists who in their application of statistical methods and operational research have attempted to develop an objective analysis of the battlefield. The goal has been to pare away subjective interpretation and

---

1   An interesting perspective on the use of military history in a British context can be found in John Gooch, 'Clio and Mars: the Use and Abuse of History' in J. Gooch and A. Perlmutter (eds.), *Strategy and the Social Sciences: Issues in Defence Policy* (London: Frank Cass, 1981), pp.21-36.
2   Beatrice Heuser, *The Evolution of Strategy* (Cambridge: Cambridge University Press, 2010), p.100.

ward against bureaucratic infighting to help policy makers optimise military structures based on a scientific examination of the evidence.

Irrespective of disciplinary boundaries, however, interrogating the historical evidence is not a simple matter. Indeed, as Holmes noted, identifying what is actually happening on the battlefield is a lot harder than it would appear given the way historians typically recount an engagement.[3] For there is a tension between the efforts of the researcher trying to make sense of what has happened and the lived experiences of those who are in the chaos of battle or trying to direct events there.

The very process of sense making of course does begin with the combatants themselves. Following the Falklands War, for example, Holmes interviewed a number of veterans and soon became aware of the, 'way in which a carapace of accepted fact hardened almost before my eyes.'[4] How this process works is open to a number of interpretations.[5] However, in the context of the literature on military innovation, Russell, in his work on US counterinsurgency operations in Anbar and Ninewa Provinces in Iraq, describes one way to think about the process in which shared experience and knowledge shapes the capacity to find sense out of disorder.[6] Making use of a range of theoretical models for exploring the process of innovation in the US military, Russell cites Eden's suggestion that 'organisational frames' orientate the way in which military personnel think about their experience.[7] These knowledge-laden frames: the norms and values of the military organisation: its 'symbology', doctrine, tactics, techniques and procedures, language and dress code, set the context in which service members orientate themselves to the problems they face. In turn, these framing perspectives are reproduced in the solutions that the military construct.

Similar studies engaging with British military culture also highlight the importance of this framework for shaping action and thought.[8] However, of all the studies considering culture, arguably the most influential is the work by retired US Army Lieutenant Colonel, Dr John Nagl.[9] Not only was Nagl a key figure in the 2006 re-write of FM

3   Richard Holmes, *Acts of War: the Behaviour of Men in Battle* (London: Weidenfeld & Nicolson, 2003), pp.1-7.
4   Holmes, *Acts of War*, p.155.
5   An interesting example of the processes adopted to shape soldier perspective is offered in Brian Newsome, *Made, Not Born: Why Some Soldiers are Better Than Others* (Westport, CT: Praeger Security International, 2007).
6   James A. Russell, *Innovation, Transformation and War* (Berkeley: Stanford Universty Press, 2011).
7   Russell, *Innovation*, p.44.
8   One of the most interesting in this respect is Charles Kirke, *Red Coat, Green Machine - Continuity and Change in the British Army 1700 to 2000* (London: Continuum, 2009).
9   John Nagl, *Learning to Eat Soup with a Knife: Counterinsurgency Lessons from Malaya to Vietnam* (Chicago: The University of Chicago Press, 2005). For a commentary on how the COIN debate has emerged see: Matthew Ford and Jeff Michaels, 'Bandwagonistas: Rhetorical Redescription, Strategic Choice and the Politics of Counterinsurgency', *Small Wars & Insurgencies*, 22 (2) (2011), pp.352-384.

3-24, the US Army/Marine Corps counterinsurgency doctrine, but he has also influenced the British Army as it seeks to learn from its failings in Basra and Helmand over the past ten years.[10] Whereas a great deal of thought on military innovation has tended to focus on changes driven by top down direction or inter or intra-service rivalry, Nagl's work closely focuses on bottom-up innovation, i.e. changes that originated with troops in the field.[11] This notion of bottom-up innovation has subsequently been picked up by a number of British academics working in the field of military innovation and now underpins a burgeoning literature that considers how tactical adaptation leads to organisational change.[12] Bearing in mind the regard to which a number of academics working in the field holds Nagl, this brief chapter considers the problems associated with the theory and offers some tentative implications for Britain's armed forces as they seek to reorient for life after Afghanistan.

Learning to Eat Soup with a Spoon

In his assessment of American performance in Vietnam, Nagl writes that the US Army was so wedded to conventional tactics that it failed to make the changes that were necessary to adapt and win an irregular war. Indeed, according to Nagl the US Army had constructed a hammer to which all problems, irrespective of their nature, began to resemble nails.[13] In Vietnam, the result was the application of a finely honed set of conventional war fighting tools to prosecute a campaign that was more suited to counterinsurgency.[14] By way of contrast, Nagl cites the experiences of Britain's armed forces fighting Communists in the Malayan Emergency of 1948-1960. In the case of Malaya Britain's successes could be put down to the readiness of Far East Land Forces Command to identify poor military performance and embrace and disseminate changes through jungle schools and doctrine. Although since challenged by French

---

10   See, *Field Manual 3-24 Counterinsurgency*, HQ Department of the Army, (2006). For Nagl's influence on the British military see: 'Nagl on Counterinsurgency', *Department of War Studies, King's College London March 2011 podcast*, available at http://warstudies. podomatic.com/entry/2011-03-25T02_58_09-07_00, accessed March 29, 2011; Robert Foley, Stuart Griffin and Helen McCartney, 'Transformation in Contact': Learning the Lessons of Modern War', *International Affairs*, 87 (2) (2011), pp.253-270.

11   For a good description of the field of military innovation studies see: Adam Grissom, 'The Future of Military Innovation Studies', *Journal of Strategic Studies*, 29 (5) (2006), pp.905-934.

12   See: Philipp Rotmann, David Tohn and Jaron Wharton, 'Learning Under Fire: Progress and Dissent in the US Military', *Survival*, 51 (4) (2009), pp.31-48; Theo Farrell, 'Improving in War: Military Adaptation and the British in Helmand Province, Afghanistan, 2006-2009', *Journal of Strategic Studies*, 33 (4) (2010), pp.567-94.

13   Nagl, *Learning to Eat Soup with a Knife*, p.203.

14   A small elite group of officers closely aligned to President John F Kennedy created these counterinsurgency tools. See: Andrew J. Birtle, *US Army Counter-Insurgency and Contingency Operations Doctrine, 1942- 1976* (Washington D.C.: Centre for Military History, 2006), pp.223-290.

and Nolan, what differentiated success from failure was not that the US and British Armies had the answers at the beginning of their respective campaigns but that the different organisational cultures might be more or less effective at encouraging learning and therefore hinder or accelerate change more quickly than one's adversary.[15]

Nagl's interpretation of organisational learning is derived from Downie's work, *The US Army as Learning Institution*.[16] Downie defines organisational learning as, 'A process by which an organization uses new knowledge or understanding gained from experience or study to adjust institutional norms, doctrine and procedures in ways designed to minimize previous gaps in performance and maximise future successes'.[17] Nagl elaborates on this idea and develops an Institutional Learning Cycle made up of six cyclical steps (See Figure 1 below). The initial phases of this process involve some kind of data collection from the battlefield and a recognition that something had not worked out as well as it might. After this, the process moves towards the identification of a performance gap, then recognising the need for and agreeing on an alternative solution and then finally through disseminating a solution through doctrine and changed behaviour within the military.

Given the historical evidence, including the research cited by Nagl himself, it is clear that military organisations have the capacity to change so that they can achieve victory in battle. What is not so clear, however, is whether the model that Nagl describes adequately explains the way in which organisations manage change. Indeed, just as much as the evidence can be used to buttress the explanatory power of the model, it is equally possible to produce evidence that undermines the efficacy of the cycle that Nagl develops. In this respect, it is not just the empirical basis of the organisational learning arguments that can be challenged but also the theoretical dimensions of the claims.

Organisational Learning in Theory

Claims about the process of organisational learning are open to considerable theoretical contestation. At one end of the debate there are those who argue that knowledge can be created, made explicit and captured; and then formalised and codified so that it can be circulated within the organisation.[18] At the other end of the spectrum, the emphasis is on knowledge creation as a multi-faceted, dynamic, provisional and

---

15   See: Victoria Nolan, *Military Leadership and Counterinsurgency: The British Army and Small War Strategy Since World War 2* (London: I.B. Tauris, 2012); David French, *The British Way in Counter-Insurgency 1945-1967* (Oxford: Oxford University Press, 2011).

16   Richard Downie, *Learning from Conflict: The US Military in Vietnam, El Salvador and that Drug War* (Westport, CT.: Praeger, 1998).

17   Cited by Nagl in Nagl, *Learning to Eat Soup with a Knife*, p.6.

18   C. O'Dell and C. J. Grayson, 'If only we knew what we know: Identification and Transfer of Internal Best Practices', *California Management Review*, 40 (3) (1998), pp.154-174.

socially situated activity where context and interpretative frames are essential.[19] For the management scholar much effort has been spent trying to reconcile these two positions by suggesting that organisations seek to make tacit knowledge explicit and thus liable for codification and dissemination.[20]

One of the most influential theories that aimed at overcoming this theoretical divide between those who took the codification position and those who advocated knowledge creation as a social process is called the theory of absorptive capacity.[21] Just like the position taken by Nagl, this theory developed the notion that organisations:

> ...ability to evaluate and utilize outside knowledge is largely a function of the level of prior related knowledge... [Which]...confers an ability to recognize the value of new information, assimilate it, and apply it?[22]

Derived from a distinctly behaviourist perspective on social change, the approach recognises how prior knowledge shapes the ability to assimilate new experiences. However, irrespective of the many iterations of the theory, there is a tendency to treat knowledge in essentialist and mechanistic terms in which the right lessons are out there in the world waiting to be discovered by the organisation, as if the goal was to try to establish a scientific fact. The theory has gone through much iteration as it tries to account for a range of exceptions that do not support the model.[23]

Assuming that scientific methodology can be applied to social phenomena is of course deeply contested in the social sciences.[24] Indeed, the possibility those social facts are in some way independent of the observer like the relationship between scientist and chemical compound has been subject to considerable doubt.[25] Instead, researchers interested in creating knowledge about human endeavours tend to recognise that social facts and data are matters of interpretation. In this respect, the emphasis of research

19   Silvia Gherardi, 'Learning as Problem-Driven or Learning in the Face of Mystery?', *Organization Studies*, 20 (1) (1999).

20   Ikujiro Nonaka, 'A Dynamic Theory of Organizational Knowledge Creation', *Organization Science*, 5 (1) (1994), pp.14-37; Ikujiro Nonaka and Hirotaka Takeuchi, *The Knowledge-Creating Company: How Japanese Companies Create the Dynamics of Innovation*, (Oxford: Oxford University Press).

21   Wesley M. Cohen and Daniel A. Levinthal, 'Absorptive Capacity: A New Perspective on Learning and Innovation', *Administrative Science Quarterly*, 35 (1) (1990), pp.128-152.

22   Cohen and Levinthal, 'Absorptive capacity', p.128.

23   For an examination and critique of the theory of absorptive capacity see, Nick Marshall, 'Beyond Knowledge Transfer: A Pragmatist Commentary on the Theory of Absorptive Capacity', paper offered to Sub-theme 18 'Pragmatism, Organizing and Learning' of the 27th European Group for Organization Studies, Gothenburg, Sweden, 7-9 July 2011.

24   The literature on this subject is vast but for a good introductory overview see Mats Alvesson and Kaj Skoldberg, *Reflexive Methodology: New Vistas for Qualitative Research* (London: Sage Publications, 2000).

25   P. Steedman, 'On the Relations between Seeing, Interpreting and Knowing' in F. Steier (ed.), *Research and Reflexivity* (London: Sage, 1991).

moves out a level of enquiry away from the method used to investigate a social fact towards considering the contexts that shape how a certain type of interpretation has been reached.[26] What emerges is then, the recognition that social factors shape the act of interpretation that constitutes a knowledge claim. Nevertheless, the exploration of these social factors depends on the philosophical and methodological preferences of the researcher and allows whole fields of social scientific research including, for example, hermeneutics, critical theory, post-structuralism, linguistic philosophy, discourse analysis, feminist theory, and constructivism.

Like the theory of Absorptive Capacity, how these social factors operate is only partially explored by Nagl. Culture and pre-existing understanding affect the receptivity to new ideas and the willingness of the organisation to embrace change. However, the relationship between social context, knowledge creation and power are hardly explored at all. In its concentration on observing the changed behaviours of the organisation Nagl does not engage with the possibility that what people publicly say about the reality they experience may not be what they subjectively 'really' think about it. Thus, it is possible then that public utterances change in different social contexts. The idea that context shapes meaning, explored by Wittgenstein, is summed up in the aphorism, 'Meaning is Use'. Thus, instead of words referring to an object, the meaning of a word depends on the context in which it is used.[27] This is a problem for those theorists, like Nagl, who are only focused on externally measurable changes for these say nothing about the inner life or indeed the 'learning' of those who have orchestrated that process. Nor does it say anything about the genealogy of relationships that are invested in the knowledge regime of the organisation, its technologies and techniques.[28]

Crucially then, the relationship between knowledge creation and the exercise of power does not feature in Nagl's work. Consequently, a key social factor that shapes the way evidence is presented within and knowledge is produced by an organisation is left out of his analysis. Lukes' in *Power* explores three conceptions of power, the most radical of which analyses the behaviourist focus on observable processes.[29] Instead, the suggestion made is that power can be exercised in ways that influence the thinking of individuals and social groups to exclude certain possibilities. Thus there is, to paraphrase Foucault, a relationship between what constitutes an acceptable truth and the general politics of truth that exist within that social organisation.[30]

26 Alvesson and Skoldberg, *Reflexive Methodology*, pp.4-7.
27 See: Ludwig Wittgenstein, *Philosophical Investigations*, 3rd Edition (Oxford: Blackwell, 1992).
28 Keith Grint and Steve Woolgar, *The Machine at Work: Technology, Work, and Organization*, (Cambridge: Polity Press, 1997).
29 Stephen Lukes, *Power: A Radical View*, 2nd Edition, (Basingstoke: Palgrave Macmillan, 2005).
30 Michel Foucault, *Power/Knowledge: Selected Interviews and Other Writings, 1972-1977*, 1st American Edition (New York: Pantheon Books, 1980), p.131; Michel Foucault, *The Politics*

In terms of organisational learning such considerations are extremely important for they say as much about the way various conceptions of the military organisation emerge as they do about how different social groups within the armed forces use language and other more material processes to shape broader perspectives and manipulate outcomes. By failing to acknowledge the way that theories of knowledge creation are highly contested and instead choosing to take an uncritical perspective on the relationship between power and the politics of truth, Nagl underlines the naïve empiricism that lies at the heart of his existing conception of organisational learning. Such a highly theoretical critique would come to nothing, however, were it not also the case that empirical evidence can also be produced that underlines the aforementioned considerations.

Organisational Learning in Practice

In describing the limits of a theory of organisational learning as conceived in *Learning to Eat Soup with a Knife,* it is useful to try to bring the process of organisational change to life with a case study. The example that follows investigates the performance of the British infantry during the Second World War. It shows how the impetus for change did not come from the frontlines but instead originated with a group of middle ranking officers and engineers who embraced the possibilities outlined by Major Lionel Wigram a Territorial Army officer, former lawyer, and creator of the Battle School movement.[31] Whilst still at war, Field Marshal Sir Bernard Law Montgomery fundamentally rejected these ideas. After the war, however, the Army and subsequently the US Army embraced the central tenets of the Battle School movement and the technologies that underpinned it. The argument found in the next section is not that the Anglo-American organisation failed to understand the learning opportunities afforded by small unit tactics in the Second World War but that other social factors played a part in shaping what might be an organisationally acceptable lesson. This was not simply that the Army was fighting and could not make the changes necessary; it had already implemented significant reforms to its military organisation throughout the war.[32] Rather, something else

---

of *Truth* (New York: Semiotext(e), 2007).

31   Wigram's tactical contributions are explored in considerable detail in Timothy Harrison-Place, 'Lionel Wigram, Battle Drill and the British Army in the Second World War', *War in History*, 7 (4) (2000), pp.442-462; Timothy Harrison-Place, *Military Training in the British Army, 1940-1944: From Dunkirk to D-Day* (London: Frank Cass, 2000). For more detail on the technological changes envisaged by the Director of Infantry and the Weapons Technical Staff see: Matthew Ford, 'Operational Research, Military Judgement and the Politics of Technical Change in the British Infantry, 1943 – 1953', *Journal of Strategic Studies*, 32 (6) (2009), pp.871-897.

32   Some of these changes had been made in the face of battle. See for instance Niall Barr, *Pendulum of War: The Three Battles of El Alamein* (London: Pimlico, 2005).

was going on, something that had more to do with power, politics and preferences than performance improvement *per se*.

Comparisons between the fighting performance of the British and German Infantry during the Second World War have not between particularly flattering. According to Van Creveld German fighting performance, 'man for man and unit for unit' was 20 to 30 per cent more effective than its British or American counterparts were.[33] Hastings and D'Este reinforce this message in their account of the Normandy Campaign but go further and suggest that British performance was even worse than that of the Americans.[34] If these accounts are accurate there was, and had been for several years during the course of the war, a *prima facie* case for undertaking wide-ranging change in the British Infantry.

To suggest that a number of officers within the army had not grasped this possibility, however, would be a gross misrepresentation of the facts. Indeed, a more accurate representation of the challenges faced by the Army can be summed up in the efforts to introduce tactical, technical and bureaucratic changes so that any shortcomings in the fighting performance of the infantry might be more readily addressed. From a tactical training perspective key among the new developments was the creation of Battle Schools and the School of Infantry. With the objective of transforming a conscript army into an effective fighting force, the first Battle Schools started to appear in the summer of 1941. They were attached to 47th Division located in the Home Army's Southern Command. Established by Wigram, the school taught Battle Drill and soon came to the attention of General Sir Bernard Paget, General Officer Commanding Southern Command. Upon his appointment to command all Home Forces in late 1941, General Paget expanded the Battle School programme and formerly created a School of Infantry in 1942.[35]

The creation of a School of Infantry produced the circumstances for further bureaucratic changes at the War Office and in early 1943 led to the establishment of the Director of Infantry (DInf). Charged with 'giving the infantry a voice on a par with the other teeth arms' the DInf set about drawing together the various administrative levers that had been considering tactical and technical matters relating to the infantry and providing them with a focus and direction.[36] Thus in early 1943, the new DInf, Major General T.N.F. Wilson, working alongside colleagues from Military Intelligence, the Ministry of Supply and representatives from the Field Armies, established a Standing Committee on Infantry Weapon Development. Tactical considerations were integral

33   Martin Van Creveld, *Fighting Power: German and US Army Performance, 1939-1945*, (Westport, Conn: Greenwood Press, 1982), p.5.

34   Carlo D'Este, *Decision in Normandy* (London: Penguin, 2001); Max Hastings, *Overlord: D-Day the battle for Normandy 1944* (London: Pan, 1984).

35   See: Ford, 'Operational Research, Military Judgement', pp.871-897; Place, 'Lionel Wigram, Battle Drill', pp.442-462.

36   David French, *Raising Churchill's Army: the British Army and the War Against Germany, 1919-1945*, (Oxford: Oxford University Press, 2000), p.71.

to the objectives of this new Committee that aimed at forecasting, 'our own Infantry tactics in relation to the enemy's in order to assess the battle conditions under which weapons may be required'.[37] The upshot of these changes in training and bureaucracy was a growing determination to ensure that the infantry had the best possible equipment it could have given that infantry 'casualties on the battlefield are higher than those of any other service'.[38]

The creation of Battle Schools and the DInf established the building blocks for what Nagl would describe as the final phases of his theory of organisational learning: the transmission of new thinking around the organisation leading to actual changed tactical behaviour. More than this, however, the new administrative infrastructure also provided the basis upon which a performance gap could not only be identified but a systematic and scientifically founded search for alternatives could be started. To this end, the DInf not only embraced Wigram's ambitions to improve infantry performance through Battle Drill but also took advantage of the Weapons Technical Staff, who were operational researchers attached to the Ministry of Supply that undertook research into weapons usage and effectiveness with a view to developing new technology to support improved tactical schemas.[39]

Concerning Battle Drill, Wigram had developed the approach in response to the needs of his Division following the defeat at Dunkirk and the significant increase in army personnel through conscription. Rapidly rising to the rank of Lieutenant Colonel, it wasn't until Wigram went out to join the army in Sicily in 1943 that he finally got to see first-hand whether soldiers in the field were properly implementing the ideas that were being taught in Battle Schools.[40] The drills taught at these schools involved combining fire and movement to achieve tactical success and were not dissimilar to those being applied by the Army in the final year of the First World War.[41] Thus, for instance, if an infantry section were split down into a Bren Light Machine Gun (LMG) group and a manoeuvre group, the Bren would lay down covering fire to keep the enemy's head down while the rest of the troops worked their way forward to attack at close quarters. Forming the basis for virtually all of the minor tactics being taught at the Infantry Schools the goal was to get the infantryman to think tactically

---

37 MOD Pattern Room Archive, The Royal Armouries Leeds (PRA), 120 Meetings – Conferences (Future Design of Weapons) – Box 2, Meeting of the Standing Committee on Infantry Weapon Development. Memo circulated by DInf on the Objectives of the Standing Committee, 30 May 1943.

38 PRA, 120 Meetings – Conferences (Future Design of Weapons) – Box 2, Meeting of the Standing Committee on Infantry Weapon Development, 1 September 1943.

39 Ford, 'Operational Research, Military Judgement', pp.871–897

40 Wigram's experiences of Italy are described in very interesting detail in Denis Forman, *To Reason Why*, (London: Abacus, 1993).

41 Details of the techniques taught can be found in Lionel Wigram, *(Infantry) Battle School (1941): a Detailed Description of the Evolution of Battle Drill Training in its Early Stages*, (Cambridge: John Bodsworth, 2005); Place, *Military Training in the British Army, 1940-1944*, p.170.

using the drill as a starting point for more creative approaches to battlefield problems when directly in front of the enemy.

At the same time, the DInf through the Standing Committee on Infantry Weapon Development put considerable effort into ensuring that 'all the available infantry weapons [were] brought to bear on the enemy, not only in the initial advance, but also up to the last possible moment so that the infantry [could] literally be shot into close quarters'.[42] The DInf firmly believed that that there needed to be 'a balance between firepower, assault power and manoeuvrability'.[43] If this was the goal then the infantry had to have the right mix of weapons so that they could increase their battle tempo and deliver more fire that is effective and movement in the attack. Since the beginning of the war, the infantry section had been equipped with 9lb No.4 Short Magazine Lee-Enfields and 22lb Bren guns. Whilst the LMG could lay down covering fire its weight, lack of handiness and the requirement for large quantities of ammunition meant moving the weapon forwards after the initial attack had started would be difficult and require significant manpower. In 1944, it was recognised that the main role of the infantry section in the attack had mainly been concerned with carrying the Bren gun ammunition.[44] Unable to fire automatically the No.4 Rifle hampered the manoeuvre group's ability to generate firepower in the final phases of the assault.

According to analysis undertaken by operational researchers attached to the School of Infantry one solution to this problem was to equip the entire infantry section with the Sten machine carbine.[45] The Sten could generate high quantities of fire, could strike targets at similar ranges to the Bren and given the potential volume of rounds that could be fired could compensate for poor marksmanship and increase the likelihood of hitting the enemy.[46] If the operational researchers were to be believed, it would appear that without having to introduce a new weapon the infantry could solve its problem of fire and movement straight away. Changes in infantry section armament would therefore, provide an immediate solution to the limitation imposed by existing equipment. This in turn, would give time for the small arms community in the UK to develop and put into production a weapon that would be specifically built to balance firepower, assault power and manoeuvre. A number of self-loading and automatic rifles were investigated.[47]

42 Thomas Needaham Furnivall Wilson, 'The Role of the Infantry', *Journal of the Royal United Services Institution*, 89 (1944), p.2.

43 Wilson, 'The Role of the Infantry', p.2.

44 TNA, WO 204/1895, Points Raised by Delegates, Infantry Training Conference, 23 April 1944.

45 Laurier Centre for Military, Strategic and Disarmament Studies, Wilfred Laurier University Canada (LCMSDS), Shephard Papers Box 2 - File 00028, Army Operational Research Group (AORG) memoranda, The Fire-Power of the Infantry Section; TNA, WO 291/473, AORG Memo 125, Interim report on performance of bullet weapons.

46 LCMDS, Shephard Papers Box 2 - File 00028, AORG memoranda on Infantry Battle and The Fire-Power of the Infantry Section.

47 Ford, 'Operational Research, Military Judgement', pp.871-897.

Unfortunately, however the Field Armies were not interested in either re-config-uring the infantry section's weapons mix, new infantry weapons or in the tactics that had worked at the end of the First World War and that were now being taught in the Battle Schools. This became abundantly clear when Wigram and operational researchers from the Ministry of Supply went to the Mediterranean during 1943. Surveys of 18th Army Group by the Ministry of Supply, for example, demonstrated that even after two years of campaigning, few in the Field Armies understood how to get the best out of the small arms and equipment that they had been issued. Thus, they reported that, 'the opinions on quite elementary points are frequently conflicting, if not directly contradictory, as between different units and formations' and that, 'it would appear that many Battalion Commanders are not really qualified to comment usefully on their weapons'.[48] Consequently they concluded that the people least suitable to advise on the distribution of existing or the development of future small arms were likely to be the user community them-selves. Brigadier J.A. Barlow, a renowned marksman in the Army and orchestrator of the Ministry of Supply's operational research, believed that the user community were insufficiently educated to be in a position to advise on potential tactics and technology.[49]

This failure to appreciate the qualities of the technology was underscored by the infantry's tactical prowess. What Wigram found when he got to Sicily, in 1943 was that fire and movement was in reality 'Guts and Movement'.[50] Wigram described the infantry battle in some detail outlining how in practice a number of steps unfold that result in three or four 'gutful men under the Platoon Commander' dashing 'straight in to the enemy position without any covering fire and always succeed in taking the position'.[51] Effectively then, the courageous few did most of the dangerous work and consequently were more likely to become casualties. The 12 or so 'sheep' would follow if well led but as many as six might run away.

Wigram had many opportunities to see the effectiveness of the infantry in battle because whilst attached to 36 Brigade during the Sicilian campaign he was afforded the opportunity to command every unit from a section to a battalion and eventually led the 5th Buffs (Royal East Kent Regiment). In Wigram's subsequent report to the Directorate of Military Training, a report he produced in the hope of refining the Battle Drill being taught in the UK, he offered an intimate analysis of the infantry's

48   PRA, 200 Small Arms General Box 1, 'Summary and Consolidated Report by WTSFF on Infantry Questionnaire and Answers from Units in First and Eighth Armies on Conclusion of N. African Campaign May 1943'.
49   PRA, 200 Small Arms General Box 1, Summary and Consolidated Report by WTSFF, May 1943.
50   Report to Brigadier Kenchington, Directorate of Military Training North African Forces (cc Brigadier Cooney Deputy Director Military Training, War Office) from Lieutenant Colonel Wigram, 17 August 1943, found in Forman, *To Reason Why*, p.199.
51   Forman, *To Reason Why*, p.199.

fighting prowess. Unfortunately, however, this document ultimately found its way to Montgomery, at the time still commanding 8th Army, who called Wigram to his HQ in Bari, demoted him to Major and made it clear that he would not command a battalion again.[52] On top of this, the Directorate of Military Training at the War Office prevented the Wigram report from being circulated as part of the *Current Reports from Overseas* pamphlet and as a result, his evidence could not be examined by other commands.[53] Identifying shortfalls in performance was clearly only tolerated if they were identified by the right man following the right process.

Learning the Right Lessons

What are the implications of all this for Nagl's theory of organisational learning? In the light of the case study, it would appear that the most obvious shortcomings in Nagl's model relate to the process of identifying a performance gap and achieving some consensus for change. Missing is the possibility that there might be competing interpretations of how to achieve success; that consensus is not necessary for organisational change; or that powerful officers may have their own agenda which will fundamentally shape the way in which lessons are not only interpreted but also how they might be presented in the first place.

On the one hand, Nagl might argue that Montgomery's reaction was testament to the lack of a learning culture in the Army. However, since taking command of 8th Army, Montgomery had been instituting his own organisational changes associated with the higher level of command in an effort to improve the overall cohesion and effectiveness of Divisional engagements through a stronger command culture. Encapsulated in his December 1942 pamphlet 'Some Brief Notes on the Conduct of Battle for Senior Commanders', Montgomery was virtually at the point where his efforts were coming to fruition.[54] Challenges to his authority or the success of his scheme were not welcome. It did not matter that Wigram's analysis was based on sound principles derived from battlefield experience. The suggestions he made as a junior ranked former Territorial Army officer to a very senior regular army officer were badly timed and unhelpful. The possibility that his views might also have powerful support from the Director of Infantry and operational research that reinforced Wigram's view those tactical engagements needed better orchestration was even less helpful. Montgomery's ambition was to shape the battle at an operational level in an effort to overcome any tactical and material shortcomings that might exist in the

---

52   Forman, *To Reason Why*, p.72.
53   Forman, *To Reason Why*, p.206.
54   The historiography on British command culture is contested but generally poorly researched. However a survey that effectively challenges the received view can be found in Patrick Rose, 'Allies at War: British and US Army Command Culture in the Italian Campaign, 1943-1944', *Journal of Strategic Studies*, 36 (1) (2013), pp.42-75.

Army.[55] Anything that might unpick this goal was acceptable. After all the 8th Army was achieving battlefield success, therefore, it appeared acceptable not to undermine a winning formula.

Nagl's organisational learning theory does not offer a way for dealing with these situations. The changes instituted by Montgomery were in many respects led by the top and middle of the Field Army, and produced war-winning results. The changes suggested by the advocates of Battle Drill were the results of consideration of the evidence far from the battlefield and sometimes by people, like Wigram, who had to wait before they got first-hand experience of fighting. However, the Battle School movement was not founded on a whim or a fad but on the recognition that the tactics being taught were simply guides for action. Soldiers needed to prepare for war by learning simple doctrine, a doctrine that had been successfully tested in the final year of the First World War and that would go on to form the substantive basis for a great deal of post-war small unit tactics. Indeed, all sorts of material factors might be used to explain away the clash between Montgomery and the Battle School movement. At its heart, however, the commander of 8th Army could not allow his position to be undermined irrespective of how valuable Battle Drill was to those new recruits being sent to formations in Italy.

Conclusion

What becomes apparent then, is that Nagl's theory of bottom up organisational learning is overwhelmingly bedevilled by unchallenged assumptions and theoretical shortcomings. In these circumstances, it would seem wise to be extremely careful with the organisational learning theory as offered up in *Learning to Eat Soup with a Knife*. Indeed, for those people responsible for the future of Britain's armed forces it might make better sense to only use Nagl as an introductory guide for thinking about organisational change.

The questions that leap out from the case study indicate how to reframe Nagl in ways that might explain which of the 'lessons identified' (the term used in contemporary Army parlance) become relevant. Thus, it is important to ask who deems a lesson relevant. What is the social context for and how does this context shape which of the lessons identified is relevant? On the face of it, the case study outlined above suggests that consensus is not necessary for change. Depending on their status, authority and the context in which the individual or team is working in, it may be possible simply to impose change without waiting for willing compliance. Equally, informal channels for making suggestions or finding alternative counter-culture adaptations may produce performance that is more effective. Finally, is it necessary and right for academics and researchers to privilege the voice from below when seeking to explain the learning process?

55   Rose, 'Allies at War'. See also French, *Raising Churchill's Army*, pp.212-273.

When it comes to organisational change, it matters whether the person making the suggestion has authority and credibility. In terms of the Army, it matters what regiment someone belongs to, whether they are from the ranks, a regular or reservist.[56] Battlefield experience conveys a certain weight to the voices of those who have fought there. However, the battlefield is more than the tactical engagement and wider considerations have a direct bearing on whether a particular event is either recognised as the first sign of a performance gap or the indicator of war winning practices. In these circumstances, and especially when experiences are contradictory, what helps arbitrate between the differing interpretations of the battle, are the relative power relationships between those officers and men seeking to deliver military success.

Nagl's model purports to explain organisational learning. As this chapter suggests, however, the theory has problems both at a theoretical level and with the unique and specific circumstances that affect decision-making. Consequently, there is a continuing need for scholars and historians to tap into the depths of the archives to try to assess the impacts of the past to educate those who are responsible for the way future decisions will be made. The alternative is that crucial considerations that affect understanding are left unstated and assumptions left unchallenged. In an organisation like the Army, an organisation that prides itself on adapting in the face of the enemy, to duck the challenge posed by the past invites stagnation and potential defeat.

---

56   Professor Anthony King shows that this is as much a concern for the contemporary Army as it is for its historical forbears. See: Anthony King, 'The Special Air Service and the Concentration of Military Power', *Armed Forces and Society*, 35 (4) (2009), pp.646-666.

Index

INDEX OF MILITARY ORGANISATIONS

INDEX OF PEOPLE

INDEX OF PLACES

INDEX OF MISCELLANEOUS TERMS